Software Development: Engineering and Applications

Software Development: Engineering and Applications

Edited by
Jeffrey Penn

WILLFORD PRESS

www.willfordpress.com

Published by Willford Press,
118-35 Queens Blvd., Suite 400,
Forest Hills, NY 11375, USA

ISBN: 978-1-68285-436-5

Cataloging-in-Publication Data

Software development : engineering and applications / edited by Jeffrey Penn.
    p. cm.
Includes bibliographical references and index.
ISBN 978-1-68285-436-5
1. Computer software--Development. 2. Software engineering. I. Penn, Jeffrey.
QA76.76.D47 S64 2018
005.1--dc23

For information on all Willford Press publications
visit our website at www.willfordpress.com

Contents

Chapter 29   **Oil and Gas Pipeline Design Management System: A Case Study for Domain-Specific Modeling**.. 201
                       Japheth Bunakiye Richard, Asagba Oghenekaro Prince

                       Permissions

                       List of Contributors

                       Index

Preface

Software development helps in developing, testing and operating softwares. These softwares are mostly used in the fields of communication, business, military intelligence, etc. Software engineering can be categorized into a number of steps, like, requirement, design of the software, testing, etc. This book outlines the processes and applications of software engineering in detail. It is an essential guide for both academicians and those who wish to pursue this discipline further. Through it, we attempt to further enlighten the readers about the new concepts in this field.

This book is a comprehensive compilation of works of different researchers from varied parts of the world. It includes valuable experiences of the researchers with the sole objective of providing the readers (learners) with a proper knowledge of the concerned field. This book will be beneficial in evoking inspiration and enhancing the knowledge of the interested readers.

In the end, I would like to extend my heartiest thanks to the authors who worked with great determination on their chapters. I also appreciate the publisher's support in the course of the book. I would also like to deeply acknowledge my family who stood by me as a source of inspiration during the project.

Editor

Orlando nursing process based healthcare information management system

Adegboye Adegboyega[1], Akpan Julius Aniefiok[2]

[1]Dept. of Maths & Statistics, Computer & Information System, Achievers University, Owo Nigeria
[2]Federal Ministry of works, Abuja, Nigeria

Email address:
akanbi2090@yahoo.co.uk (A. Adegboyega), juliuswhiz@gmail.com (A. J. Aniefiok)

Abstract: The processes and management of healthcare records are not trivial exercise; there is need for application of ICT to healthcare management system in order to meet globally accepted health care systems. Many healthcare systems have been designed and implemented, but they do not adequately incorporate nursing process. Also, most of them do not consider the needs and aspirations of patients. In this work, a modified framework based on Orlando's nursing process focuses on improvement in the patient's behavior by actions that are based on a patient's needs found through effective interaction with the patient was designed and proto type implemented. The design was implemented using Visual Basic.Net and SQL because of their supports for implementing web-based systems. The system was hosted on a website for a period of two months. Real life data in respect of medical practitioners' and patients were captured, analyzed and evaluated. Users interacted with the hosted system during the evaluation period. The system was evaluated using usability test and structured questionnaire. The result showed 93.10% participation efficiency, while ease of use, operational efficiency and data protection of Healthcare Information system scored more than 80%.This showed that the Healthcare Information Systems (HIS) is an effective life saving system that can influence and enhance health-workers' quality of services, timely precision decision making process and reduced cost of health care significantly through effective healthcare management. It is applicable in any healthcare environment irrespective of their social economic and technology settings. The application of the framework will prevents the spread of deadly diseases like Ebola Virus.

Keywords: Information and Communication Technology (ICT), Healthcare Information System Healthcare Records, Orlando's Nursing Process, Healthcare Management System and Ebola Virus

1. Introduction

The processes and management of healthcare records are not trivial exercise. Healthcare Information Systems will play an important role in providing patient information to physicians, nurses and administrative staff, and can be a significant factor in developing cooperation among physicians with regard to sharing healthcare information [Yang and Li, 2010, Yang et al., 2011]. Medical practitioners' needs accurate and timely information concerns patients in order to save life, and performed their duties professionally. The traditional manual method of recording, administer drug and billing patient can no longer meets today patient's medical attentions and lack transparency, since medical care is a real time information-intensive activity. The application of (ICT) to Hospital Management will enhance service delivery, streamlined operations, enhanced administration and control, superior patient care, strict cost control, improved profitability, data security and meet globally accepted health care systems. Today's Healthcare Information are in high demand in order to handle increasing population needs and also aids the practicing doctors and hospital service and support staff with timely service with precision there is need for application of ICT to healthcare management system,[Premkumar and Kosalram 2014].

In the existing system of health care management system, a great amount of manual work has to be done, which requires more number of employees who often take advantage of manual work. A hospital employee cannot immediately satisfy the customer/patient in case of past information because it takes a lot of time to search the information regarding to that query, thus increasing response time, [Srilakshmi and Jabasheela, 2014].

Nowadays healthcare organizations globally recognize the importance of applying information technologies to improve the quality of their services and reduce costs,[Negin et al., 2014].Therefore, it is imperative to assess problems and challenges facing healthcare system and suggests solutions to the problems and challenges using information and communication technology (ICT) via the internet, which is the basis of this research work.

2. Related Work on Healthcare Management System

In [Negin et al., 2014],they compared the costs of designing, implementing and running hospital information system with the traditional manual paper method and found that it cost excessively more than the traditional method, they recommended that expensive systems are not applicable for smaller hospitals because of their low income rate. Hence in this research work a low cost hospital information system that applicable for small and large hospitals and even clinics because of its affordability is design and implemented.

In [Srilakshmi and Jabasheela, 2014], they reported that in the existing system of health care industry, a great amount of manual work has to be done, which requires more number of employees who often take advantage of manual work and that a hospital employee cannot immediately satisfy the customer/patient in case of past information because it takes a lot of time to search the information regarding to query, thus increasing response time. Hence they proposed a new system of Hospital Management and Information System using SAP ABAP 4, but ABAP Query needs knowledge of Open SQL commands, this has to be done only by someone who has a little bit of ABAP experience. In a complex reports where data selection are bit complex it may not solve one purpose. A prefer programming language that increase productivity, and overcome the limitation found in the ABAP Programming the .NET environment which offers a unified development environment and a standard set of tools common to all languages and developer tasks is employ in this research work.

In [Nawzat and Yasin, 2014], established that Healthcare Information Systems in hospitals have become an influential factor to provide cooperation among healthcare workers in sharing healthcare information. The research work showed that currently, there is still lack of cooperation among health workers in sharing information and skills in the patients' treatment within the hospital environment. Hence in this research work a low cost hospital information system that allowed cooperation among health workers in sharing information and skills in the patients' treatment within the hospital environment is design and implemented.

In [Jayawardena,2014], found that changing minds of the staff from traditional to new computerization system was the biggest challenge due to most of the staff members thought it is easy to use paper records than computers. In this research

work, a user friendly health information system that take into consideration the busy practice of Health workers is design and implemented.

In [Malinga et al., 2014] reported that patient dying each year from preventable medical errors, one-fifth of these errors are linked to the lack of prompt access to patient health information. Therefore, it is important to review the literature to determine the best approach to patient health information management and to recommend a model that would address the problems mentioned above. Research and development projects have shown the need for strengthening hospital management information systems (HMIS), patient management information system inclusive, but this has proven to be a difficult task, especially in developing countries [Nawzat and Yasin, 2014]. Orlando's nursing process theory by Orlando (1972) is a suitable guideline for designing a user friendly patient management information system, [Malinga et al., 2014]. Hence in this research work Orlando's deliberative nursing process theory (1972) is used as a suitable guideline for designing a user friendly low cost Healthcare management information system.

3. Design Methodology

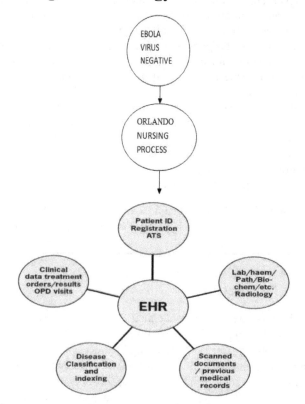

Figure 1. *Framework for Orlando nursing process-Ebola virus based model healthcare information management system*

This study employed Orlando's nursing process theory (1972) as a suitable guideline for designing a user friendly low cost healthcare management information system which is applicable in any healthcare environment irrespective of their social economic and technology settings. The incorporation Ebola check-up into the framework prevent spread of the deadly diseases and it is part of nursing process. It enhances nursing efficiency by standardizing nursing practice and increases care quality through the use of deliberate actions. Healthcare administration requires a large volume of wide-ranging information, and healthcare administrators are limited in their ability to compile and analyze information for healthcare administration. This framework creates methodology for developing a healthcare administration analysis system to aid healthcare administrators in performing outcome analysis, according to the individual needs.

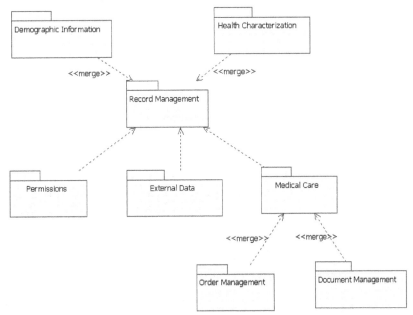

Figure 2. Packages of Patient Information Management System

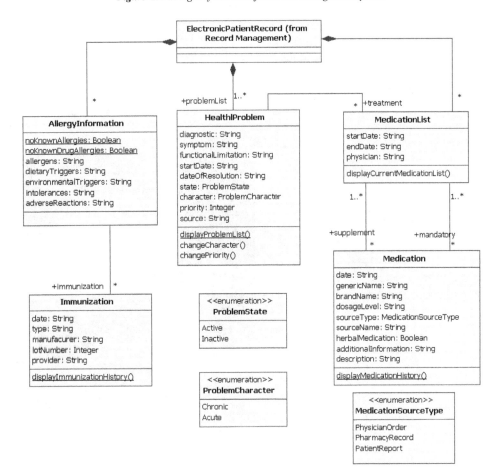

Figure 3. Medical Characterization Package

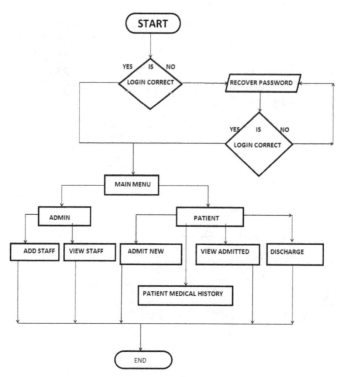

Fig 4. *Flowchart of the healthcare Information Management System*

4. Implementation and Results

VB.net is used as a programming language for the implementation of the design. The programming environment for the database is Microsoft SQL Server 2000 which is connected to VB.net. At the time of admitting the patient, the hospital authorities enter the detailed information of all patients. It includes his/her name, age, sex, and address with phone number etc. It also adds its department, in which the patient is admitted, its bed code, doctor's name, date of admission and the advances taken by hospital. One can get all the information by putting the assigned patient code in the main mouse operated menu bar. During the operational use, the following outputs were obtained according to design modules of Healthcare Management System.

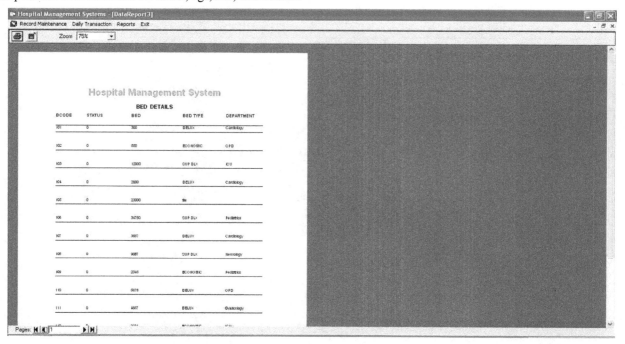

Fig 5. *Patient Details*

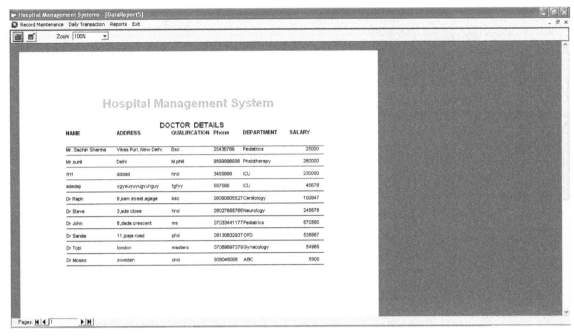

Fig 6. *Doctors Details*

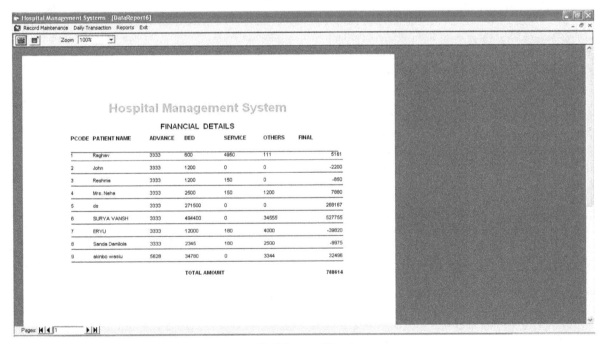

Fig 7. *Financial Details*

5. Evaluation of the Healthcare Management System

5.1. Research Design

The descriptive survey design was adopted which involved the collection of primary and cross sectional data through the use of a structured questionnaire. A preliminary study visit was made to Rabiat Shoaga Triumphant Health Centre Abeokuta Nigeria in April 2014 to find out about the feasibility of the study. The sample frame for this study comprised exhaustive list of the Healthcare Centre units. The purposive sampling method was adopted in selecting the respondents so as to ensure that selected individuals were those that had adequate knowledge of healthcare services.

5.2. Instrument for Data Collection

Data were collected with a structured questionnaire designed in a four point Like scale, comprised four sections: Section A elicited information about units in the Healthcare Centre. Section B asked questions about Health resources available in each Unit. While section C sought to ascertain the stage of Healthcare Global Standard in the Health Centre. Section D, the last section, contained questions that enquired about the challenges encountered by the units in Healthcare information System adoption and implementation processes. The instrument was validated through face and content validity. It was subjected to thorough scrutiny by three experts in Healthcare information System research and two others in the field of information science. Modifications were made on the instrument based on their assessments. Copies of the questionnaire were distributed to the respondents by the researchers who had initially sought the permission of the Director of the Healthcare Centre. A total of 145 copies of the questionnaire were distributed but 135 copies were completed and returned. This constituted 93.10% and was used for data analyses.

5.3. Data Analysis

The Statistical Package for Social Science (SPSS) software was used to carry out the analysis. The variables used to assess the Healthcare Information system using 4-point like scale were re-coded. Strongly Agree and Agree were re-coded as High while Disagree and strongly Disagree were re-coded as Low. Next, a frequency distribution tables was generated for all the variables.

Table 1. Distribution of variables concerns the Healthcare Information System

		Ease of Use		Sustainability		Operational Efficiency		Data Security		Human factors	
		Freq.	%	Freq	%	Freq	%	Freq	%	Freq.	%
Valid	Low	25	18.51	28	20.74	21	15.56	14	10.37	23	17.04
	High	110	81.49	107	79.26	114	84.44	121	89.63	112	82.96
	Total	135	100	135	100	135	100	135	100	135	100

The distribution of variables as relates to the healthcare information system is as presented in table 1.The number of user that interacted with the system and reported that the system is easy to use, its operation is efficient and data are protected and secured are more than 80%.While sustainable of the system is 79.26%, this may due to the fact that user perceive, if required infrastructure is not maintain and upgrade in future this may affect the system. Human or Individual factor is 82.96% this is due to ease of use that make user to easily acquired sufficient knowledge and skills on the use of the system and result to low resistance to change from traditional ways of doing things. A total of 145 copies of the questionnaire were distributed but 135 copies were completed and returned. The system shows 135/145 (93.10%) participation. From the evaluation, we can conclude that (HIS) is highly efficient, effective and satisfactory to the target users (health stakeholders).

6. Discussion and Recommendation

The processes and management of healthcare records are not trivial exercise, healthcare workers practitioners' needs accurate and timely information concerns patients in order to save life, and performed their duties professionally. The framework and healthcare information system presents in this research works will offer a standard approach in developing cooperation among healthcare workers with regard to sharing healthcare information and performed their duties professionally through the application of ICT and Orlando nursing process in the healthcare services. The study offers a demonstration of the application of ICT tools and Orlando's nursing process nursing process to improved healthcare services. The framework and Healthcare Management System are adequate enough to address global demands in health service delivery irrespective of social-economic and technology set-up of the healthcare setup making use of them. It is user friendly and low cost healthcare management information system.

Today's Healthcare Information are in high demand in order to handle increasing population needs and also aids the practicing health workers, health services and support staff with timely service with precision, in design and implementation of this Healthcare Management System the busy practice of Health workers is put into consideration.

The Healthcare Management System was evaluated with usability testing, by allowing users to run through the system with real life data and structured questionnaire. The results show (9.9%). The number of user that interacted with the system and reported that the system is easy to use, its operation is efficient, stored data are protected and secured are more than 80%.While sustainable of the system is 79.26%, this may due to the fact that user perceive, if required infrastructure is not maintain and upgrade in future this may affect the system. Human or Individual factor is 82.96% this is due to ease of use the Healthcare Information System that make user to easily acquired sufficient knowledge and skills on the use of the system and result to low resistance to change from traditional ways of doing things. From the evaluation, we can conclude that (HIS) is highly efficient, effective and satisfactory to the target users (health stakeholders). The application of the framework will prevents the spread of deadly diseases like Ebola Virus.

This system is recommended to any healthcare service provider that wishes to move its service forward by healthcare global standard. The basic infrastructure that will make such a system work should be provided and made affordable by the healthcare provider.

References

[1]   Jayawardena AS (2014) The Electronic Hospital Information System Implemented at the District General Hospital Trincomalee-An Experience of Business Process Re-engineering. J Community Med Health Educ S2: 001. doi:10.4172/2161-0711.S2-001

[2] Igira, F., T., Titlestad, O., H., Lungo, J., H., Makungu, A., Khamis, M., M., Sheikh, Y., Mahundi, M., Ngeni, M., J., Suleiman., & Braa, J.(2009). Designing and Implementing Hospital Management Information Systems in Developing Countries: Case Studies from Tanzania – Zanzibar http://www.sim.hcuge.ch/helina/19.pdfPp 77-83

[3] Malinga Ramadhan B.*, Ssenyonga T., and Novembrieta R. Sumil (2014) Development and implementation of patient management information system of kampala international university teaching hospital(kiu-th), bushenyi district, Uganda. Journal of Poverty, Investment and Development - An Open Access International Journal Vol.4 2014,Pp. 77-83.

[4] Nawzat Sadiq Ahmed and Norizan Mohd Yasin (2014): Factors affecting cooperation among physicians in sharing information within the hospital environment: a study of two hospitals. Journal of Computer Science 10 (5): 794-808, 2014.Pp794-808.

[5] Negin Karimi Hosseini, Md Jan Nordin, Mitra Mahdiani and Samira Sadrzadeh Rafiei (2014): A Low Cost Hospital Information System: A Case Study of the Mehr Hospital in Mashhad City. Research Journal of Applied Sciences, Engineering and Technology 2014.Pp1132-1138.

[6] Premkumar Balaraman and Kalpana Kosalram (2014): E – Hospital Management and Hospital Information Systems – Changing Trends. International journal of Information Engineering and Electronic Business, 2013, 1Pp. 50-58.

[7] SrilakshmiSatyapraba J and L.Jabasheela (2014): Hospital Management and Information System Using SAP,International journal of advanced computer technology a Special Issue of 4th National Conference on Advanced Computing, Applications & Technologies, May 2014.Pp21-26.

[8] Yang, H., K. Liu and W. Li, 2010.Adaptive requirement-driven architecture for integrated healthcare systems. J. Comput., 5:Pp. 186-193.

[9] Yang, T.H., Y.S. Sun and F. Lai, 2011. A scalable healthcare information system based on a service oriented architecture. J. Med. Syst., 35: 391-407.

2

Design and implementation of image search algorithm

Zhengxi Wei, Pan Zhao, Liren Zhang

School of Computer Science, Sichuan University of Science & Engineering, Zigong Sichuan 643000, PR China

Email address:

413789256@qq.com (Zhengxi Wei), zhaopan@suse.edu.cn (Pan Zhao), zhangliren@whu.edu.cn (Liren Zhang)

Abstract: Image search is becoming an urgent problem of the next generation of search engine. We firstly review the developed situation of image search engine in this paper. Then, the main difficulty and key technologies about this engine are analyzed. Next, the design method is elaborated in detail, which mainly includes image recognition, perceptual hash algorithm, system solution, image retrieval procedure as well as software module, and so on. As a result, we develop an image search engine according to above design methods and implement searching image on the Internet. The testing results finally prove the overall performance of our image search engine is excellent and achieves the desired design requirements. By using data filtering technology and perceptual hash algorithm, the search time-consumed is less than 1 second and is of high search efficiency.

Keywords: Image Search Engine, Perceptual Hash Algorithm, Image Recognition, Feature Index, Grey Classification

1. Introduction

With the explosive growth of the Internet, Web Search technology marked by keywords has acquired a great success in the tremendous information retrieval. As the network develops into the Web2.0 era, people no longer satisfy with merely the text-search, also want to be able to find more images from the sample image. In the future, image search engine [1] will become the main tool of the user to retrieve images in the network.

Google, Yahoo and Baidu, as three common search engines for users to search kinds of information, have launched keyword-search-image service, but the application of the image-search-image is still in testing phase. The image content is more abundant and more complexity than the text content and its amount of information is also that the text cannot be compared with. In addition, the text itself is able to express some semantic meaning, but images can only be expressed through their own content features. Therefore, image retrieval to be implemented is much more difficult than text retrieval.

Image search software is being developed towards the trend of the intelligence and the diversification. On the one hand, image-processing technology plays a key role to support image retrieval. On the other hand, people have developed many convenient development toolkits, which are capable of establishing image feature database. That makes it possible that the image search technology becomes more and more

mature. As the same time, the efficiency of retrieving image becomes higher than that of the past and people's workloads are reduced greatly.

2. Image Recognition and Retrieval

Image search is not available without image recognition [2] and retrieval technology. Design and implementation of image search is based on the latter methods.

2.1. Image Recognition

In general, image recognition process can be divided into three main parts: (1) image preprocessing; (2) image segmentation and extraction feature; (3) the judgment or classification. The block diagram is shown in figure 1.

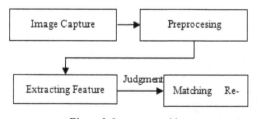

Figure 1. Image recognition.

Any kind of image recognition methods first through a variety of sensors convert a variety of physical variables to values or set of symbols that the computer can receive. Traditionally, the space of this value or symbol is called the pattern space. In order to extract effective identified information from these numbers or symbols, it must be the following processing, eliminating noise, excluding irrelevant signals, calculating feature (such as the shape of the object, perimeter, area, etc.) as well as the necessary transformation (such as Fourier transformation).

Then by feature selection and extraction, the pattern feature-space is established. The subsequent pattern classification or pattern matching is based on the feature space. Finally, the system will output object's the type or a model number that means this object in model database is the most correlative to the object to be searched.

2.2. Image Retrieval

Images can be manually labeled character information based on contents in the text annotations. Web Crawler [3] can collect pictures from the web environment or extract some image marked similar text information in an HTML page, and establish originally keywords. Then it performs a preprocesses to these image, which includes de-nosing, setting standard size etc.. The image is stored to the memory in development board and its feature-index will be further perfected after processing of relevant algorithms. And this index can later be retrieved and compared to the search keywords. In this way, it can determine whether they are the retrieved objects.

The image information will be abstracted to a generic string main through caliphemir algorithm library. Such as color histogram and other information can be extracted through the adjustment of parameters. Open source tools package (Java caliphemir) extracts the features such as color histogram and layout, convert them to the corresponding string from the image. The correspondence between extracted strings and images is established through the inverted algorithm used to file-search, co-exist in the index file. Different picture information can be stored in different fields, together constitute one document for the query. The feature string of image acts as a search keyword, and a picture of the maximum likelihood is found by querying the index file. Finally, a group of image in the picture library is found. Subsequently these pictures are extracted according to their path information.

3. Image Processing Algorithm

The key content of our design is image match algorithm, which is to search the similar images from a sample image according to image feature index. This index is established mainly by image grey value. Grey match can determinate the similarity between two pictures resorting to some measures, for example, correlation function, covariance function, mean square error, etc.. Perceptual hash algorithm [4] is one of the most representative algorithms. The image processing is as follows according to this algorithm.

(1) Formating Image

The resolution of sample image is firstly shrinked to n×n (n≤8), total n^2 pixels. This can exclude the details of pictures, only leaving some basic information such as structure and gray, and get rid of the differences that the contribute of

resolution and brightness gives rise to.

(2) Grey Degree Deduction

Image grey is uniformly decreased to T-class, that is, to make the all pixels be only T kinds of colors, T≤64 class. Such treatments are designed to exclude the differences of the color number in the image and set the gray value of every pixel into a same range.

(3) Calculate Mean Grey Value of Image

Mean grey value u is figured out in an image composed of total n^2 pixels, using (1). In equation, x_i denotes a value of a pixel and p_i denotes the probability value that this pixel appears in the image.

$$u = \sum x_i \cdot p_i \qquad x_i \in [0,T] \qquad (1)$$

(4) Pixel Binary Mapping

According to (2), every pixel is mapped into a binary number. The gray of each pixel is compared with the average value of image, if greater or equal, 1 is recorded; on the contrary, 0 is recorded.

$$f(x_i) = \begin{cases} 1 & x_i > u \\ 0 & x_i \le u \end{cases} \qquad (2)$$

(5) Construct hash value sequences

The comparison result of previous step is combined together, obtaining a sequence of binary integer with n^2 bits, such as {1,0,0,1, ..., 0, 1}. It is exactly the image fingerprint [5] of each picture.

(6) Image Comparison.

Comparison algorithm is to find how many different binary bits between two images with n^2 bits binary integer number, which is equivalent to compute the Hamming distance between images. In general, if the different data bits are not more than five, it shows two pictures are very similar; however, if more than 10, they are two different pictures.

Having carried out the previous five steps of the algorithm, we can calculate image fingerprint from the sample picture, and write the key information including image fingerprint, sample picture location in storage as well as its URL into the database. The next work is to compare the fingerprints of different image and then figures out the similarity degree between the pictures.

4. Software Solution

4.1. Main Function Analysis

Compared with the text search engine, image search engine should complete the following four tasks: collecting images on the Internet, calculating the image similarity, maintaining the image-index library, and responding user's query. So an image search engines need to be provided with the following four basic functions.

(1) Multi-threading Technique

Start multiple threads to surf the Internet and obtain a large of images and their URL. There are two image sources, namely the image directly from HTML pages or indirectly from the image database on the Web.

(2) Image Feature Extraction

Various image properties (such as the color histogram, the shape histogram, multi-resolution texture features, and so on) are calculated in order to obtain the feature vector and index vector.

(3) DBMS Maintenance

The index records in the database needs to be periodically maintained and updated, and keep the databases time validity and data integrity.

(4) Man-machine Interface

User-oriented image-retrieval interface allows the user can use the example query, such as uploading images, and the interface returns the corresponding result set.

4.2. Software Module

Web crawler (also known as web spider, web robot) is a kind of in accordance with certain rules, automatic program or script to crawl the World Wide Web information. Heritrix is a web crawler developed exclusively for downloading the Internet Webpage. The image search engine uses the Heritrix to download the specified website picture, then the downloaded image will be preprocessed to create image index, and finally the index information will be stored in a Berkeley DB database (a high-performance embedded database). When the user upload pictures to query, the search engine opens images index, matches the corresponding index, and extracts the similar images in the database and return them to the user. The whole process is as following.

1) Capture image
2) Preprocess
3) Extract Feature
4) Judgment and Matching

According to the above model, image search engine is mainly composed of three modules: crawler module, create index module and search module.

(1) Crawler module

Web-crawler Heritrix is used to visit some specific websites and download the pictures in WebPages crawler module: Web crawler Heritrix is used to visit some specific websites and download the pictures in the WebPages. Then, these images will be stored in various hierarchical directories of the local file system.

(2) Create index module

The image information will be abstracted into a generic string main through caliphemir algorithm. Such as color histogram and other information can be extracted through the adjustment of parameters. Open source tools package (Java caliphemir) extracts the features such as color histogram and layout, convert them to the corresponding string from the image.

The correspondence between extracted the string and the image is established through the inverted algorithm that is used to file-search, co-exist in the index file. Different picture information can be stored in different fields, together constitute one document for the query.

(3) Search module

Search module receives the pictures uploaded by users and finishes the flow process: firstly preprocessing user picture, analyzing image feature, next extracting features to compare to the images on the server, obtaining the index number of similar pictures, and then further getting more information(such as image path, index text, etc.) from the image library, at last returning the most similar images to the client for the user to view.

According to the different bit number of image fingerprint, image search engine can calculate the matching degree between the sample image and the similar image.

4.3. Improved Technique and Flow Chart

(1) Data filtering

Heritrix [6] embedded extractor cannot crawl links according to a format, but crawl down all the information in WebPages. As a result, it is not able to specify the content crawled down. This will result in the mirror information is too complicated and there are a lot of redundant information. Obviously, that is not what the search engine needs.

In the extension process to the Heritrix extractor, we use the regular expressions to match the link being crawled down. The matched link will be added to the Heritrix processing queue, only to crawl a specific link (such as the Computer Science Department website, http://jkx.suse.edu.cn/ *) This makes the Heritrix to only crawl the specific data format, play the role of data filtering, and also quicken the speed of data acquisition.

(2) Search flow chart

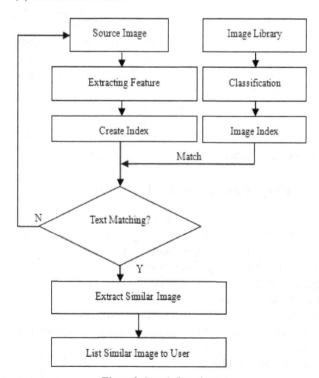

Figure 2. *Search flow chart.*

The search process is shown in Figure 2. The feature string of image acts as a search keyword, and a picture of the maximum likelihood is found by querying the index file. The most similar image in the picture library is obtained from its path information. The contradistinction process among images is according to the index keywords to match, calculates the image match-degree, and returns the high match-degree images to the user.

(3) Heritrix software toolkit

In the case of default, Heritrix software toolkit uses Hostname-Queue-Assignment-Policy to make that the same host name URL will be placed in a queue. In this way, it can cause that a length of the queue is very long when crawling a single website. According to Heritrix rules, a thread always gets a URL link from the head of the queue. Then the queue will be blocked and it will not recover from the blocking state until that link is processed over.

In order to avoid the occurrence of that case, we adopt the perceptual hash algorithm to solve this problem. This algorithm inherits Queue-Assignment-Policy algorithm and extends its function. It allows the crawling process can create multiple threads so that the entire process will not be suspended due to a single thread blocking. On the other hand, this way also improves the speed of crawling data.

5. Experimental Results

The user interface of our image search engine is shown in Figure 3 and the user clicks on the "Browse" button to select images to be searched. If the selected picture is valid and meets the format requirement, the progress bar will show the name and image size of the picture. The "Upload" button becomes available and the search engine automatically works for users to search similar images.

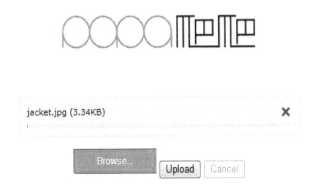

jacket.jpg (3.34KB)   ✕

Browse   Upload   Cancel

Figure 3. Upload image interface.

The image retrieval results are shown in Figure 4. There are some pieces of image and hyperlink addresses in the search result page for users to show URL of the picture. Users are able to visit the relative website as long as they click on these pictures or their URL. Below the URL, we also give the matching degree of the returned images.

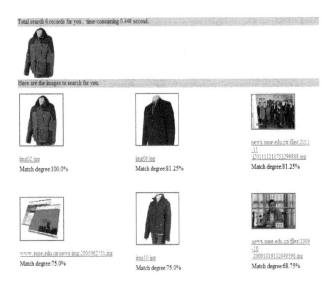

Total search 6 records for you，time-consuming 0.448 second.

Here are the images to search for you.

img02.jpg
Match degree:100.0%

img06.jpg
Match degree:81.25%

news.suse.edu.cn/files/2011
-11
/20111121175]296888.jpg
Match degree:81.25%

www.suse.edu.cn/news-img/2005062751.jpg
Match degree:75.0%

img10.jpg
Match degree:75.0%

news.suse.edu.cn/files/2009
-10
/20091019152049598.jpg
Match degree:68.75%

Figure 4. Search results.

About 50000 pictures in the image library are used for the test. Even if the amount of pictures is up to 50000, the search engine returns the search results in less than 1 second. The tests show that under this query condition the retrieval speed of the image search engine is also very high efficient.

6. Conclusions

Combined with image-recognition technology, the paper presents a design method for image search engine, which mainly includes image recognition, perceptual hash algorithm, system solution, image retrieval procedure as well as software module, and so on. The experimental results show that the software based on image search algorithm works stably and its search velocity is very fast, compared to the other similar soft wares.

The design idea for developing image search engine can be referenced because the perceptual hash algorithm is well fit to image processing and the method of image grey classification is easy to implement. After a few modifications, our search engine can be applied to more equipments, which is used in not only the personal computer or web workstation, but also mobile phones and other portable devices.

Acknowledgements

The research was supported by Artificial Intelligence Key Laboratory of Sichuan Province (No. 2013RYY04) and the Sichuan Provincial Education Department's Key Project (No.14ZA0210).

Our work was also supported by university Key Laboratory of Sichuan Province (No. 2013WYY09) and Fund Project of Sichuan Provincial Academician (Experts) Workstation (No.2014YSGZZ02).

References

[1] Cao Y, Wang H, Wang C, et al. Mindfinder: interactive sketch-based image search on millions of images[C]//Proceedings of the international conference on Multimedia. ACM, 2010: 1605-1608.

[2] Zhu B B, Yan J, Li Q, et al. Attacks and design of image recognition CAPTCHAs[C]//Proceedings of the 17th ACM conference on Computer and communications security. ACM, 2010: 187-200.

[3] De Groc C. Babouk: Focused web crawling for corpus compilation and automatic terminology extraction[C]//Web Intelligence and Intelligent Agent Technology (WI-IAT), 2011 IEEE/WIC/ACM International Conference on. IEEE, 2011, 1: 497-498.

[4] Sarohi H K, Khan F U. Image Retrieval using Perceptual Hashing [J]. IOSR Journal of Computer Engineering (IOSR-JCE) e-ISSN, 2013: 2278-0661.

[5] Ghose T, Erlikhman G, Garrigan P, et al. Perception, Image Processing and Fingerprint-Matching Expertise[C]//PERCEPTION. 207 BRONDESBURY PARK, LONDON NW2 5JN, ENGLAND: PION LTD, 2013, 42: 11-12.

[6] Liu D F, Fan X S. Study and Application of Web Crawler Algorithm Based on Heritrix [J]. Advanced Materials Research, 2011, 219: 1069-1072.

3

Local Feature Extraction Models from Incomplete Data in Face Recognition Based on Nonnegative Matrix Factorization

Yang Hongli[1, *], Hu Yunhong[2]

[1]Science College, Shandong University of Science and Technology, Qingdao, Shandong, P. R. China
[2]Applied Mathematics Department, Yuncheng University, Yuncheng, P. R. China

Email address:
yhlmath@126.com (Yang Hongli)

Abstract: Data missing usually happens in the process of data collection, transmission, processing, preservation and application due to various reasons. In the research of face recognition, the missing of image pixel value will affect feature extraction. How to extract local feature from the incomplete data is an interesting as well as important problem. Nonnegative matrix factorization (NMF) is a low rank factorization method for matrix and has been successfully used in local feature extraction in various disciplines which face recognition is included. This paper mainly deals with this problem. Firstly, we classify the patterns of image pixel value missing, secondly, we provide the local feature extraction models basing on nonnegative matrix factorization under different types of missing data, thirdly, we compare the local feature extraction capabilities of the above given models under different missing ratio of the original data. Recognition rate is investigated under different data missing pattern. Numerical experiments are presented and conclusions are drawn at the end of the paper.

Keywords: Local Feature Extraction, Incomplete Data, Face Recognition, NMF, Model

1. Introduction

Data missing often happens in the process of data collection, transmission, processing, preservation and application due to various reasons. For example, in EEG signal acquisition process, the electrodes will cause some loss of signal data due to the fault or other reasons; satellite images data may also be lost during the transmission; during the process of the image denoising, division and segmentation, image data may be lost. There are many types missing data for an image, of which pixel values data missing is considered in this paper. When the pixel value data is lost, the corresponding pixel value matrix is called incomplete matrix. Incomplete matrix factorization and corresponding feature extraction problem has been raised for decades[14][15],the most commonly used method is principal component analysis [12][13][14][15]. However, principal component analysis method is generally based on the global feature extraction by virtue of the statistical properties of the data. NMF is a low rank matrix approximation for nonnegative matrix based on a nonnegative matrix factorization. It is an effective way to obtain the local feature of the data matrix representation. Nonnegative matrix factorization model has been successfully applied to many fields, but most of these applications is for complete matrix without missing data. For incomplete matrix, research is not so much.

Weighted nonnegative matrix factorization model is pioneered by[7] after NMF model was proposed. It was originally used to extract the characteristics of the environmental data. After the model was proposed, many different algorithms for solving this model have been given. Weighted matrix decomposition model was firstly used for the problem with missing data is[16] but without considering nonnegative constraints; [10] considered the nonnegative constraints and applied it to the missing data model, more applications can be found in [4][11]. [4] is also the first model to combine the EM algorithm and NMF algorithm, the author used model and algorithm to solve the case of testimonials with missing data. Recent research results about weighted nonnegative matrix factorization and its application is the following: [2] gave two new matrix factorization algorithm, [3] presented a semi-supervised classification model based on weighted nonnegative matrix decomposition, [5] studied the weighted tensor decomposition and its application, which gave an weighted tensor decomposition model to extract feature from missing data, but [5] did not consider the nonnegative constraints. Other studies about weighted nonnegative matrix factorization in facial feature extraction and the application are [18][19][20].

This paper studies the local feature extraction problem in face recognition from incomplete matrix by nonnegative matrix factorization. Three NMF models are presented in this paper: direct interpolation model, weighted nonnegative matrix factorization model, the combination of taking the mathematical expectation of the missing data (Expectation) and nonnegative matrix factorization model. The organization of the paper is as follows: inspired by [10], we classified the pattern of the missing data in section 2, presented three local feature extraction models for different types of missing data in section 3, compared the computation cost and the performance of different models are given in this section, in section 4 numerical experiments verified the effectiveness of several algorithms, conclusions and future research directions are given at the end of this paper.

2. Classification of the Missing Data Pattern

The classification of missing data problem was first put up by Little and Rubin[16] in the field of the humanities. He classified the pattern of missing data in the humanities field into three categories. In the experimental science field, Giorgio and Bro[10] also divided the missing data into three categories: random missing values (RMV in brief, which means the position of the missing data is at random); missing at random spectral values (RMS in brief), that is, the entire column or row data is missing randomly, missing system spectral values (SMS in brief). Inspired by their classification as well as the specific application background of the missing data, we divide the missing image pixel values of an image into two categories. 1) Randomly missing values(RMV for brief), in this case, the position of the missing pixel values is random, which often occurs due to the denoising of the image. 2) The missing of image data is not at random, this type of missing is divided into two categories. One is due to the faults of signal collecting equipment, which makes the data in whole rows or columns of the image matrix missed. Since this type of data missing is related to the system, it is called Systematically missing values (SMV for brief). For example, in EEG signal analysis, due to the fault of the electrodes which make the system could not collect the data successfully, so data is missing or wrong. The other is caused by the person's choice, such as image segmentation, it requires all pixel value that below 0 be changed the same value, it is called the systematically missing spectral values (SMS for brief).

3. Model

This paper deals with the problem of local features extraction from incomplete pixel value matrix by virtue of the following nonnegative matrix factorization models.

3.1. Model 1 (Interpolation NMF Model)

If the ratio of the missing data is small (such as less than 5 percent), the usual method to restore the incomplete matrix is to in place of the missing data with some data (such as expectation), then to extract the local feature from the restored matrix. The method is called interpolation. The regular interpolation methods are such as mean imputation, regression imputation, pattern matching [21]. When the ratio of the missing data is large, the interpolation method does not fit in the reason that the error between the restored matrix and the former matrix is large. The feature obtained by the NMF methods is the local feature, the missing data means the missed local feature. If we ignore the effect of missing data and are only interested in the available data, the local feature can be obtained by weighted NMF method (model 2).

3.2. Model 2 (Weighted Nonnegative Matrix Factorization Model(WNMF))

$$\min_{U,V \geq 0} f(U,V) = \frac{1}{2} \sum_{i,j} W_{ij}(A_{ij} - (UV)_{ij})^2 = \min_{U,V \geq 0} \frac{1}{2} \|W \otimes (A - UV)\|_F^2$$

in which W is a $(0,1)$ matrix, $W_{ij} = 1$ if A_{ij} is not missing, otherwise $W_{ij} = 0$, "$\otimes$" is the Hadamard product of the matrix. Model 2 becomes the usual complete NMF model as all the entries of matrix W are 1. When the entries of W is 0, it means the missing of the element at the position of (i,j): The effect for the objective function is 0, so model 2 does not take into account the missing data. For the unconstrained minimization problem, the first order optimality condition is $\nabla f = 0$, We note $\nabla f = [\nabla f]^+ - [\nabla f]^-$, in which $[\nabla f]^+, [\nabla f]^-$ is the positive and negative part respectively with positive elements, then we can reformulate NMF iteration formula as

$$U \leftarrow U \otimes \left(\frac{[\nabla_U f]^-}{[\nabla_U f]^+} \right), V \leftarrow V \otimes \left(\frac{[\nabla_V f]^-}{[\nabla_V f]^+} \right),$$

and

$$\nabla_U f = [\nabla_U f]^+ - [\nabla_U f]^- = [W \otimes (UV)]V^T - [W \otimes A]V^T,$$
$$\nabla_V f = [\nabla_V f]^+ - [\nabla_V f]^- = U^T[W \otimes (UV)] - U^T[W \otimes A].$$

Then the iteration updates can be reformulate as

$$U \leftarrow U \otimes \frac{(W \otimes A)V^T}{(W \otimes (UV))V^T},$$

$$V \leftarrow V \otimes \frac{U^T(W \otimes A)}{U^T(W \otimes (UV))}.$$

The above model has the same form of the iteration update

as the update that in [22], it is called weighted NMF model (WNMF for brief).

Remark: There are some difference between Model 1 and Model 2. Model 1 uses the interpolation method to restore the missing data matrix before iteration updates, all the elements of the matrix are involved in the operation, while in model 2, the missing data does not participate in the operation.

3.3. Model 3 (EM-NMF Model)

Paper[4] presented a local feature extraction model based on a modified NMF algorithm for the matrix with missing data(called EM-NM algorithm). We use the idea and the algorithm for the local feature extraction in face recognition with incomplete data in this paper. In the proposed model, EM algorithm estimates the unknown parameters generally involves two steps: taking expectation (Expectation Step) and solving maximization (Maximum Step). The method utilizes the idea of maximum likelihood estimation. Firstly, it classifies the data of the matrix into not missing data and missing data, takes the missing data as unknown parameters. In the first step, it selects the initial value of unknown parameters, calculates the parameter by taking mathematical expectation of the unknown parameters. The second step is to use the missing data as the predicted value of the maximum likelihood function of the unknown parameters obtained by the new estimate, repeating the above procedure until a solution satisfies the conditions to be obtained. It needs more computational cost in the process expectation maximization. Paper[4] gave an EM-based standard NMF approach, numerical experiments showed that results of EM-NMF method significantly better than results obtained by the WNMF method. The algorithm step is as follows.

E-step

$$Y \leftarrow W \otimes A + (1_{m \times n} - W) \otimes (UV)$$

M-step

$$U \leftarrow U \otimes \frac{YV}{UV^T V},$$

$$V \leftarrow V \otimes \frac{Y^T U}{VU^T U}.$$

in which $1_{m \times n}$ is a $m \times n$ size matrix with all entries are 1. The above model is called expectation maximize nonnegative factorization(EMNMF for brief).

3.4. The Computational Cost of Models

The computational cost of the above three models is different in the reason that the iteration updates of the algorithms is not the same. If the data matrix A is $m \times n$ size, WNMF algorithm will cost more $4mn$ multiplication operation in each iteration than the standard NMF[22]. EMNMF algorithms has an additive computation of taking expectation in each iteration, which will have $2mn$ more multiplication operation than WNMF model, if the iteration times for E-step and M-step is k, l respectively, EMNMF will has more $2lmn$ multiplication operation than WNMF algorithm, and will have $(4k + 2l)mn$ multiplication operation more than that of NMF.

4. Numerical Experiments

Four experiments are given in this paper. The database we used is the Standards ORL face Database for face recognition. The size of the matrix is 644×400. The aim of Experiment 1 to Experiment 3 is to test the performance of three models in local feature extraction aspect. We test these models with three type of data missing(Experiment 1 for RMV, Experiment 2 for SMV, and Experiment 3 for SMS), the criterion of the performance is iteration times, iteration time and the approximation error between matrix A and UV. We also consider the local feature error between the original and the results we obtained, as well as the sparseness of the extracted local feature. The aim of Experiment 4 is to test the recognition rate by virtue of the local feature obtained. In model 1,we use 0 to fill in the missing data, the stopping criterion for the iteration is the error between continuous two iteration is less than $1e - 004$.We use the same initial value for different models in order to avoid the different local optimizer of algorithms.

4.1. Experiment 1

4.1.1. Experimental Results

(a) some of original images from ORL Database

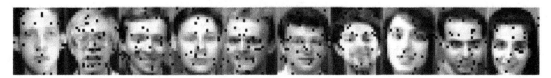

(b) some of images with 5% RMV missing data

(c) some of images with 10% RMV missing data

Figure 1. *(a)some of original images from ORL Database,(b)some of images with 5% RMV missing data,(c)some of images with 10% RMV missing data.*

Table 1. *Experimental results about time, iteration, error with RMV missing data.*

	Original image（data not missing）				5% data missing			
	Time	$\|A-UV\|_F$	Iteration	$\|U-U^*\|_F$	Time	$\|A-UV\|_F$	Iteration	$\|U-U^*\|_F$
Model 1	132.07	51.0778	3120	–	93.11	76.8583	2200	0.1971
Model 2	–	–	–	–	114.77	51.4471	2714	0.1202
Model 3	–	–	–	–	159.51	50.0011	2828	0.0939

	10% data missing				20%data missing			
	Time	$\|A-UV\|_F$	I Iteration	$\|U-U^*\|_F$	Time	$\|A-UV\|_F$	Iteration	$\|U-U^*\|_F$
Model1	74.41	92.7477	1757	0.1791	65.42	113.8371	1543	0.2220
Model 2	185.70	51.2849	4355	0.1585	140.74	51.7154	3326	0.1919
Model 3	148.27	48.6117	2626	0.1675	193.98	46.1209	3427	0.1971

	40% data missing				70 % data missing			
	Time	$\|A-UV\|_F$	Iteration	$\|U-U^*\|_F$	Time	$\|A-UV\|_F$	Iteration	$\|U-U^*\|_F$
Model1	59.54	132.6979	1402	0.2626	59.15	137.9275	1392	0.3012
Model2	89.87	52.1856	2124	0.1559	80.41	53.3961	1899	0.1682
Model3	156.03	41.2126	2746	0.1632	156.90	34.8928	2759	0.1679

Table 2. *Sparseness of base matrix for different algorithms with RMV missing data.*

	0%	5%	10%	20%	40%	70%
Model1	0.4082	0.3982	0.3965	0.3944	0.4026	0.4310
Model2	—	0.4100	0.4125	0.400	0.4040	0.4029
Model3	—	0.4039	0.4150	0.3982	0.4032	0.4045

4.1.2. Analysis of Experiment Results

As illustrated in Table 1 and Table 2, for RMV type missing data, Model 3 has the least approximate error between extraction of local feature and original local feature, while the iterate time is the most. Model 1 has the most approximation and the least iteration time. The error becomes more with the increase of the missing data. When the ratio of missing data is large, the approximate error for Model 2 and Model 3 tends to the same. As shown in Table 2, the sparseness of local feature obtained by Model 3 is the best, and Model 2 follows, Model 1 is the worst.

4.2. Experiment 2

4.2.1. Experimental Results

Figure 2. *Some images with SMV missing data.*

Table 3. *Experimental results with SMV missing data.*

	5%data missing				10% data missing			
	Time	$\|A-UV\|_F$	Iteration	$\|U-U^*\|_F$	Time	$\|A-UV\|_F$	Iteration	$\|U-U^*\|_F$
Model1	128.28	49.529	2661	0.2292	122.52	48.306	2488	0.2218
Model2	105.61	69.085	2156	0.2261	85.72	93.072	1774	0.2166
Model3	153.11	49.528	2664	0.2289	142.24	48.306	2488	0.2208

	25% data missing				40% data missing			
	Time	$\|A-UV\|_F$	Iteration	$\|U-U^*\|_F$	Time	$\|A-UV\|_F$	Iteration	$\|U-U^*\|_F$
Model1	137.46	49.729	2785	0.1674	81.90	37.979	1795	0.3731
Model2	125.62	68.982	2599	0.1665	37.75	199.394	796	0.3646
Model3	158.85	49.729	2784	0.1670	100.97	37.979	1800	0.3620

	70% data missing			
	Time	$\|A-UV\|_F$	Iteration	$\|U-U^*\|_F$
Model 1	92.56	22.8694	1961	0.6225
Model 2	25.22	242.5778	520	0.5703
Model 3	103.07	22.8855	1850	0.5639

Table 4. Sparseness with SMV missing data.

	0%	5%	10%	25%	40%	70%
Model 1	0.4936	0.4163	0.4248	0.4190	0.5798	0.7409
Model 2	—	0.4148	0.4235	0.4186	0.5726	0.7215
Model 3	—	0.4153	0.4228	0.4180	0.5658	0.7102

4.2.2. Analysis of Experiment Result

As illustrated in Table 3 and Table 4, the local feature approximate error between original data and data with missing data becomes more with the increase of the missing ratio, as well as the iteration times, which means the restore ability becomes weaker. An interesting phenomenon for SMV type data missing is that the iterate times and the results of Model 1 and Model 3 is the same, this is because the position of the missing data is the same. For Model 2, the values at these position don't attend the operation, which is the same as that for Model 1, so the M-step does not work in Model 3. For this type of missing data, Model 1 fits well. The sparseness of the local feature becomes more with the increase of the missing data.

4.3 Experiment 3

4.3.1. Experimental Results

Figure 3. Some images with SMS missing data.

Table 5. Experimental results with SMS missing data.

	5% data missing (value<21)				10% data missing (value<36)			
	Time	$\|A-UV\|_F$	Iteration	$\|U-U^*\|_F$	Time	$\|A-UV\|_F$	Iteration	$\|U-U^*\|_F$
Model 1	134.18	51.0781	3127	0.0012	99.75	55.5599	2239	0.1204
Model 2	152.93	52.6064	3567	0.2175	172.21	55.4450	3650	0.2223
Model 3	154.36	45.9197	2711	0.2226	139.96	48.7178	2455	0.2168

	20% data missing (value<60)				40% data missing (value<107)			
	Time	$\|A-UV\|_F$	Iteration	$\|U-U^*\|_F$	Time	$\|A-UV\|_F$	Iteration	$\|U-U^*\|_F$
Model 1	102.51	63.9386	2361	0.1923	179.77	86.8741	2826	0.2217
Model 2	116.42	66.1317	2736	0.2142	96.71	104.9639	2721	0.2357
Model 3	152.75	45.9197	2711	0.2226	152.89	27.6253	2726	0.2327

	70% data missing (value<166)			
	Time	$\|A-UV\|_F$	Iteration	$\|U-U^*\|_F$
Model 1	57.83	103.0335	1185	0.3832
Model 2	93.27	168.9273	2634	0.2567
Model 3	252.44	11.8293	4544	0.2424

Table 6. Sparseness with SMS missing data.

	0%	5%	10%	20%	40%	70%
Model 1	0.4936	0.4082	0.4224	0.4321	0.5028	0.6002
Model 2	—	0.3799	0.3742	0.3505	0.2780	0.2373
Model 3	—	0.3802	0.3743	0.3743	0.2680	0.2205

4.3.2. Analysis of Experiment Results

As illustrated in Table 5 and Table 6, Model 2 costs less iterate time than that of Model 1 and Model 3, the iterate time for Model 1 and Model 3 is almost the same. As for the approximate error, Model 1 and Model 3 is similar. They are better than Model 2. The sparseness for Model 1 becomes bigger with the increase of missing data, which means that the local feature becomes less. The sparseness of Model 2 and Model 3 becomes bigger with the increase of the missing data, which means that the restore ability becomes weaker.

4.4. Experiment 4

4.4.1. Experimental Result

Table 7. Recognition rate for different models when 20% data missing.

	Original data	Model 1	Model 2	Model 3
Not missing	87%	—	—	—
RMV	—	64%	70%	71%
SMV	—	70%	72%	72%
SMS	—	62%	63%	66%

4.4.2. Analysis of Experiment Results

As illustrated in Table 7, the recognition rate of data without missing is more than that of data with missing data. Under the same ratio of the missing data, the restore ability of Model 3 is better than Model 2, and Model 2 is better than Model 1. The type of the missing data affects the recognition rate, the recognition rate for SMV data missing is better because the image with SMV missing data lost less local features.

5. Conclusions

This paper studied three local features extraction models in case of the training set has missing data basing on nonnegative matrix factorization algorithm: interpolation NMF model, weighted NMF model, and expectation-maximization NMF model. Three models are derived based on non-negative matrix factorization iterative formula. This paper compares the computational cost of three models. The second contribution of the paper is the classification of the missing data for image pixel values. We compared the local feature ex-traction ability of three modes by virtue of numerical experiments. Further research problem includes fast convergent algorithms, initial point scheme and different objective function will be considered in the future.

Acknowledgement

This work is supported by National Natural Science Foundation of China (No.11241005) and Yuncheng University Youth Foundation granted YQ-2012020.

References

[1]   Hongli Yang. Nonnegative matrix and tensor factorization and their applications. Ph.D thesis, 2011.

[2]   Y. D. Kim and S. Choi. Weighted nonnegative matrix factorization. ICASSP 2009: 1541-1544.

[3]   H.Lee,J.Yoo and S.Choi. Semi-supervised nonnegative matrix factorization IEEE Signal Processing Letters, 2010, Vol (17) (1): 4-7.

[4]   S. Zhang W. H. Wang, J. Ford and F. Makedon. Learning from incomplete ratings using nonnegative matrix factorization. SIGCOMM 2006: 267-278.

[5]   E. Acar, D. M. Dunlavy, T. G. Kolda, and M. Morup. Scalable tensor factorization with missing data. Proceedings of the 2010 SIAM International Conference on Data Mining, 2010.

[6]   N. Srebro,T. Jaakkola. Weighted low rank approximation. IMCL2003: 720-727.

[7]   P. Paatero. Least squares formulation of robust, nonnegative factor analysis. Chemometrics and Intelligent Laboratory Systems, 1997, Vol (37) (1): 23-35.

[8]   A. M. Buchanan and A. W. Fitzgibbon. Damped Newton algorithms for matrix factorization with missing data CVPR2005, Vol (2): 316-322

[9]   V. D. Blondel, N. D. Ho, and P. V. Dooren. Weighted nonnegative matrix factorization and face feature extraction. Image and Vision Comput-ing, 2008.

[10]   G. Tomasi and R. Bro. Parafac and missing values. Chemometrics and intelligent laboratory systems.2005, Vol (75) (2): 163-180.

[11]   A. P. Dempster, N. M. Laird and D. B. Rubin. Maximum likelihood from incomplete data via the EM algorithm. Journal of Royal Statistical Society, 1977, Vol (39) (1): 1-38.

[12]   E. J. Candes and Y. Plan. Matrix completion with noise.arXiv: 0903.3131v1vl, 2009.

[13]   E. J. Candes and T. Tao. The power of convex relaxation: near-optimal matrix completion.arXiv:0903.1476vl,2009.

[14]   K. R. Gabriel and S. Zamir. Lower rank approximation of matrices by least squares approximation with any choice of weights. Technimetrics, 1979, Vol (21)(4): 489-498.

[15]   A. Ruhe. Numerical computation of principal components when several observations are missing. Technical report, University of Umea, Sweden, 1974.

[16]   R.J.A.Little and D.B.Rubin. The analysis of social science data with missing values. Sociological Methods and Research,1989,Vol(18)(2-3):292-326.

[17]   R. L. Carter. Solutions for missing data in structural equation modeling. Research and Practice in assessment, 2006, Vol (1)(1): 1-6.

[18]   D. Guillamet, J. Vitria and B. Schiele. Introducing a weighted nonnegative matrix factorization for image classification. Pattern Recognition Letters, 2003, Vol (24)(14): 2447-2454.

[19]   X. Li and K. Fukui. Fisher nonnegative factorization with pair wise weighting. MVA 2007, IAPR: 380-383.

[20]   P. J. B. Koeck. Missing data in image and signal processing: the case of binary objects. International journal for light and electron optics, 2004, Vol (115)(10): 459-472.

[21]   R. B. Kline. Principles and practices of structural equation modeling. Third edition, John Wiley &Sons, Inc., New York, 1988.

[22]   D. D. Lee and H. S. Seung. Learning the parts of objects by nonnegative matrix factorization. Nature, 1999, Vol (401)(6755): 788-794.

4

Vehicle Routing Problem Based on Particle Swarm Optimization Algorithm with Gauss Mutation

Ting Xiang, Dazhi Pan, Haijie Pei

College of Mathematic and Information, China West Normal University, Nanchong, China

Email address:

1198715106@qq.com (Ting Xiang), pdzzj@126.com (Dazhi Pan)

Abstract: In order to solve the vehicle routing problem, this paper introduces the Gauss mutation, which is based on the common particle swarm algorithm, to constitute an improved particle swarm algorithm (NPSO). In the process of solving vehicle routing problem, the NPSO is encoded by integer and proposes a new way to adjust the infeasible solutions. The particles are divided into two overlapping subgroups, and join the two-two exchange neighborhood search to iterate. Finally, the simulation experiments show that the proposed algorithm can get the optimal solution faster and better, and it has a certain validity and practicability.

Keywords: Particle Swarm Optimization, Vehicle Routing Problem, Gauss Mutation, Neighborhood Search

1. Introduction

Routing Problem Vehicle (VRP) is a typical NP-hard problem, and proposed first by Dantzig and Ramser in 1959. Recent years, it has been a hot research field in computer science, operations research and combination optimization. Many problems in our daily life can be abstracted as vehicle routing problem, such as logistics distribution, power dispatch, postal delivery, school bus and routing problem, etc. This problem is full of important theoretical significance and engineering value on improving production efficiency and improving economic efficiency. Those years, many scholars have tried to introduce the general heuristic algorithm, genetic algorithm, ant colony algorithm for VRP problems and have achieved some good results [1-3].

Particle swarm optimization (PSO) is a global optimization evolutionary algorithm, which was put forward by Kennedy and Eberhart first in 1995 to solve the optimization problem of continuous domain function [4-5]. PSO is affected by the history optimum and global optimum of the particles, which can quickly converge to the global optimum or the local optimum. Since PSO has the characteristics of easy implementation, simple structure and strong robustness, many scholars have used it to solve the problem of discrete domain in recent years. For example, shop scheduling problems, etc. Based on the quantum particle swarm algorithm, crossover and mutation operation are added in [6] to improve the local

search ability of the algorithm. In [7], a two-way vehicle scheduling problem model is established with the basis of the particle swarm algorithm and the mountain climbing operation is introduced, which effectively solves the problem of logistics distribution; In paper [8], a new particle swarm optimization algorithm is designed, which introduces the local neighbor mechanism and can optimize infeasible solutions. The algorithm obtains comparatively satisfactory results in solving the vehicle routing problem with time window. Paper [9] introduces multigroup parallel way and different initial methods are applied for each subgroup, besides the opposite population poor particle will be replaced by memory particle to solve the vehicle routing problem with time windows.

In this paper, based on the basic particle swarm algorithm, a new algorithm (NPSO) with the Gauss mutation is proposed. In the process of solving the vehicle routing problem, we introduce a series measures including the integer encoding (see [6]), how to deal with the infeasible solution and the neighborhood search so as to improve the ability of the particle to jump out of the unfeasible solution region and the local optimal position.

2. Vehicle Scheduling Problem Description and Mathematical Model

This paper investigates Capacity Vehicle Routing Problem for short vehicle routing problem, which is the most basic problem in all vehicle scheduling problems. Specifically described as follows:

There are a central warehouse with No.0 and k vehicles in total with the capacity $q_i (i = 1,2,\cdots k)$; Moreover, N customer point transportation tasks needs to be completed with No.1 to N with customer demand $g_1, g_2, \cdots g_N$. Each vehicle from the central warehouse deliver to each customer and finally back to the central warehouse; c_{ij} represents the distance between the customer i and customer j. Moreover the mathematical model in [2] is introduced in this paper.

First, define the 0-1 variable:

$$x_{ijk} = \begin{cases} 1 & \text{if vehicle } k \text{ goes throught the i-th customer point to the j-th one} \\ 0 & \text{otherwise} \end{cases}$$

$$y_{ki} = \begin{cases} 1 & \text{if the i-th custom's task is done by the k-th vehicle.} \\ 0 & \text{otherwise} \end{cases}$$

The mathematical model is established as follows:

$$\min Z = \sum_{k=1}^{K}\sum_{i=0}^{N}\sum_{j=0}^{N} c_{ij}x_{ijk}$$

$$s.t \begin{cases} \sum_{i=1}^{N} g_i y_{ki} \le q_i & \forall k \\ \sum_{k=1}^{K} y_{ki} = 1 & \forall i \\ \sum_{i=1}^{N} x_{ijk} = y_{kj} & \forall j,k \\ \sum_{j=1}^{N} x_{ijk} = y_{kj} & \forall i,k \end{cases} \quad (1)$$

The constraints in the model ensure that the carrying capacity of each vehicle is not over the load, and each customer will receive the service until the last service is finished. Therefore, vehicle routing problem is just the minimum path in these conditions.

3. Particle Swarm Optimization Algorithm with Gauss Mutation

The standard particle swarm optimization algorithm is an optimization algorithm based on population, in which the individual is called particle and each particle's trajectory is determined by the Global best position ($Gbest$) and the particles' historical optimal solution ($Pbest$).

Let particle $X_i(t) = (x_{i1}, x_{i2}, \cdots x_{iD})$ for the t generation in a D dimensional space. The velocity is $V_i(t) = (v_{i1}, v_{i2}, \cdots, v_{iD})$, global best position $Gbest = (P_{g1}, P_{g2}, \cdots P_{gD})$, particle's past best position $Pbest_i = (P_{i1}, P_{i2}, \cdots P_{iD})$. In the iterative process, the position $X_i(t)$ is updated by the velocity $V_i(t)$ with the next iteration via the following equation:

$$X_i(t+1) = X_i(t) + V_i(t+1), \quad (2)$$

while velocity $V_i(t)$ can be calculated as below:

$$V_i(t+1) = w \times V_i(t) + c_1 \times rand(0,1)(P_{ibest} - X_i(t)) + c_2 \times rand(0,1)(G_{best} - X_i(t)). \quad (3)$$

The learning constant c_1 and c_2 are popularly equal to 2. The inertia parameter w is an important parameter, which affects the performance of the algorithm. To make the algorithm better convergence to global optimal solution, we generally set $w = 0.9$ initially and gradually decrease to 0.4 in a linear way with the increase of iteration t, furthermore, it follows the equation as blow:

$$w = 0.9 - 0.5 * \frac{t}{T}, \quad (4)$$

where T is the maximum iteration number.

From the particle's position change formula (2) and (3), the update information of each particle is derived from itself and the whole group. The particle can rapidly move to the global optimum and the local optimal in the iterative process. But in the late stage, the group diversity is reduced and particles are easy to fall into local optimum. In order to improve the particle swarm optimization algorithm, this paper, based on the original individual, introduces a Gauss perturbation term. Specific way is: set a mutation probability

P_c and randomly select individuals about $NP \times P_c$ from the population with NP in total. Gauss mutation is applied for each individual in the j-th dimension under the mutation formula:

$$X_{ij} = X_{ij} + L \times N(0,1) \times X_{ij}, \quad (5)$$

where X_{ij} is the j-th dimension of particle X_i, j is a random integer, L is the parameter of Gauss mutation; $N(0,1)$ is a random vector of the Gauss distribution, which is subject to a mean of 0 and 1 of the variance.

There is something that we have to mention here. $L \times N(0,1) \times X_{ij}$ in formula (5) is Gauss random perturbation term, which makes full use of the known information of the current such that it does not increase the diversity of the group and has advantageous to jump out of the local optima to carry on the global search, but also improves the search speed.

4. Improved Algorithm for Vehicle Routing Problem

4.1. Particles of Encoding and Decoding

Using the particle swarm algorithm to solve practical problems, what we need to do first is the particle encoding. In this paper, we use the integer encoding method in [6].

Step1. The central warehouse with No. 0, N customer with No. 1 to N. Each particle is represented by a N dimensional integer vector $X = [a_1, a_2, \cdots a_N]$, where a_i is an integer from 1 to N, corresponding to the a_i-th customer.

Step2. Each particle according to the customer loading is not more than the vehicle capacity principle, and ultimately in accordance with the vehicle arrangement of customers to get the solution vector. if $g_{a1} + g_{a2} + \cdots + g_{a_{b1}} \leq q_1$ and $g_{a1} + g_{a2} + \cdots + g_{a_{b1}} + g_{a_{b1+1}} > q_1$, then 1-th vehicle's customer order is $[a_1, a_2, \cdots a_{b1}]$; similarly if $g_{a_{b1+1}} + g_{a_{b1+2}} + \cdots + g_{a_{b2}} \leq q_2$ and $g_{a_{b1+1}} + g_{a_{b1+2}} + \cdots + g_{a_{b2}} + g_{a_{b2+1}} > q_2$, the 2-th vehicle's customer order is $[a_{b1+1}, a_{b1+2}, \cdots a_{b2}]$. In this way, when vehicle passes all the customer point, the customer order is obtained and corresponding solutions vector is $M = [b1, b2, \cdots bk]$.

For example, there are 2 vehicles in total with the capacity of 8, 8 customer points with demand $[1,2,1,2,1,4,2,2]$. If the position vector of a particle is $X = [1,3,4,5,2,7,6,8]$, according to the above method, the corresponding distribution plan is:

Path 1: $0 \to 1 \to 3 \to 4 \to 5 \to 2 \to 0$; path 2: $0 \to 7 \to 6 \to 8 \to 0$; solutions vector: $M = [5,8]$

4.2. Initialization of Particles

Initial particle generation process is:

Step1. Generates a particle randomly and calculates its solution vector;

Step2. If the final value of the solution vector bk is N, then the particle is a feasible solution. Otherwise adjusts the infeasible solution in accordance with the 4.4 and the particle will be discarded if the result of adjustment is still not feasible.

Step3. Repeat step 1 and step2, generate NP effective particles in total, and construct the initial group.

4.3. Standardized Processing of Particles

The particles are iterated by the formula (2) (3) (5), the component of the particle will appear decimal number and negative number. In order to ensure that every vector of each particle has a corresponding path arrangement, the particle is required to be standardized. Specific method is follows:

Step1. The value at each dimension of particle X can be obtained by the formula (2) if it is limited in a range of $-(k-1)$ to $k-1$, or replace it with boundary value directly.

Step2. By the above step, we can obtain $X = [a_1, a_2, \cdots a_N]$. Now, we replace $a_i (i = 1, 2, \cdots, N)$ with it's ascending ordinal number $c_i (i = 1, 2, \cdots, N)$ to get a new $X = [c_1, c_2, \cdots, c_N]$.

For example, given particles $X = [-2.3, 1, 4, 1.3, 5, 7, 6.4, 8]$, through standardized process, we obtain $X = [1, 2, 4, 3, 5, 7, 6, 8]$.

4.4. Adjustment of Infeasible Solution

Whether in the initial population or the algorithm in the iterative process, particles X may appear a lot of infeasible solution path (if the final value of the solution vector bk is not N). In order to guarantee the validity of the algorithm, this paper proposed a kind of adjustment strategy, which can adjust most of the particles to the feasible solution. Specific methods are divided into three parts:

The first part.

Step1. Calculate the residual load of each vehicle $\Delta q_i (i = 1, 2, \cdots k)$ for the current infeasible solution and rank the sequence with the order from small to large: $\Delta q_{i1}, \Delta q_{i2}, \cdots, \Delta q_{ik}$, where ik is the number of vehicle. The non-scheduled customer point is arranged as $s_1, s_2, \cdots s_m$ with the order of corresponding customer demand $g_{s_k} (k = 1, 2, \cdots, m)$ from large to the small.

Step2. For any customer $s_j (j = 1, 2, \cdots, m)$, find out some vehicle from $\Delta q_{ij} (j = 1, 2, \cdots k)$ with the order of $\Delta q_{i1}, \Delta q_{i2}, \cdots, \Delta q_{ik}$ such that the vehicle can load customer. Take customer s_j for example, if $\Delta q_{i_{l-1}} < g_{s_j} \leq \Delta q_{i_l}$, we put customer s_j into the vehicle i_l. In the i_l-th path to find the adjacent two customer points P and q such that the distance $p \to s_j \to q$ is the shortest and insert s_j between P and q, modifying Δq_{il} at the same time.

Step3. According to the step2, if all of the customers have been arranged, directly into the third part, otherwise enter the second part.

The second part

Step1. Since the conduction in this step are similar to the step 1 at first part, so we omit here.

Step2. If $g_{s_1} \leq \Delta q_{i_1}$, put the customer s_1 into vehicle i_1 directly, otherwise we find out the the minimum customer x of the vehicle i_1 with corresponding customer demand g_x such that $g_x + \Delta q_{i_1} \geq g_{s_1}$. If $g_x < g_{s_1}$, place s_1 at the location of x, consequently x becomes a customer point that is not scheduled and update g_{s_1} with g_x.

Step3. If the adjustment in step2 does not work for customer s_1, then consider whether customer s_1 should be put the into the next vehicle, Of course, s_2 can be applied with the same way.

Step4. Repeat step2 and step3 until that we can not find out a vehicle to arrange s_1 or $g_x = 0$.

Step5. Repeat the step1, 2, 3, 4 for $s_1, s_2, \cdots s_t$ respectively until all the non-scheduled customers are traversed.

The third part

Particle vector and the corresponding solution will be calculated after the above two parts. If the final value of the solution vector is still not N, then particle is judged infeasible and set the objective function as infinite.

4.5. Neighborhood Search

With the iterative process, the group is easy to fall into local optimum, but the global optimal solution is near the local optimum. In this paper, to ensure that the algorithm convergence to the global optimum more quickly, global optimal solution is searched by a two-two exchange neighborhood search per 20 generations.

The specific method is stated as follows.

Set a neighborhood search parameter sd first, which represents neighborhood search times. Then randomly we select the $i-th$ and $j-th$ location of $Gbest$ and exchange their position each time. After the adjustment in 4.4 to get the new particle $\overline{Gbest}$. If $\overline{Gbest}$ is better than the previous $Gbest$, then replace $Gbest$ with $\overline{Gbest}$.

4.6. The Implementation of the Improved Algorithm for VRP

Particle swarm algorithm is applied to continuous space, while the VRP is a discrete integer programming problem, so we need to modify the algorithm for the specific application. The specific process is as follows:

Step1. Particles initialization

(1) Within the initialization method in 4.2, about NP particles in total are randomly generated and divided into two overlapping adjacent subgroups. The number of overlapping particles is cd, and the number of particles in each subgroup is $\dfrac{NP+cd}{2}$.

(2) Calculate the initial value of each particle, the historical optimal solution ($Pbest$) and the global best position ($Gbest$).

Step2. Repeat the following steps until the maximum number of iterations.

(1) In each subgroup, every particle is updated by formula (2) (3), randomly select $floor(\dfrac{NP+cd}{2} \cdot P_c)$ particles to participate in the Gauss mutation by formula (5). Then we employ a standardize process for particle via the method in 4.3, and adjust unfeasible solution according to 4.4, calculate the fitness value.

(2) Replace overlap particles with optimal location in two groups.

(3) If current iteration number is a multiple of 20, then global optimal solution is searched by a two-two exchange neighborhood search with 4.5.

(4) Calculate the Global best position ($Gbest$) and the particles' historical optimal solution ($Pbest$).

Step3. Finally, global best position is taken as the final optimal path, and the corresponding path length is the optimal path length.

5. Experimental Results and Analysis

In the present work, to compare results conveniently, we use Matlab 7.0 to write the program of particle swarm optimization (PSO) and the improved algorithm(NPSO) to solve the vehicle routing problem with the computer operating system 3.3GHz, 8.00GB, Win7.

5.1. Experiment 1

We take the data of paper [9] in our experiment 1. The vehicle routing problem has a central warehouse, 2 vehicles in total with the capacity of 8, and 8 customer points with demand [1,2,1,2,1,4,2,2]. The following table gives the distance and the demand of the customers. Now it is required to arrange a suitable driving route so that the total mileage of the vehicle route is minimized. This paper tells us that the optimal solution path length is 67.5 and the path is arranged as follows: Path   1:   0→4→7→6→0;   path2: 0→1→3→5→8→2→0.

Table 1. The distance between customers (km) and demand.

C_{ij}	0	1	2	3	4	5	6	7	8
0	0	4	6	7.5	9	20	10	16	8
1	4	0	6.5	4	10	5	7.5	11	10
2	6	6.5	0	7.5	10	10	7.5	7.5	7.5
3	7.5	4	7.5	0	10	5	9	9	15
4	9	10	10	10	0	10	7.5	7.5	10
5	20	5	10	5	10	0	7	9	7.5
6	10	7.5	7.5	9	7.5	7	0	7	10
7	16	11	7.5	9	7.5	9	7	0	10
8	8	10	7.5	15	10	7.5	10	10	0
demand		1	2	1	2	1	4	2	2

Parameter setting of PSO: population size $NP=40$, learning constant $c_1=c_2=1.5$, the maximum iteration number $T=50$.

Parameter setting of NPSO: population size $NP=40$, learning constant $c_1=c_2=1.5$, the maximum iteration number $T=50$, overlapping particles' number $cd=2$, the parameter of Gauss mutation $L=1.8$; mutation probability $P_c=0.8$, neighborhood search parameter $sd=2$. PSO, NPSO runs each 20 times and compares with the results of the algorithm proposed by [9]. The test results are showed in table 2.

Table 2. The optimal path length (km) of the three algorithms.

Running times	Algorithm of paper [9]	PSO	NPSO	Running times	Algorithm of paper [9]	PSO	NPSO
1	67.5	67.5	67.5	11	67.5	67.5	67.5
2	67.5	70.5	70.0	12	67.5	70.0	67.5
3	71.0	70.0	67.5	13	69.0	70.0	67.5
4	67.5	70.0	67.5	14	67.5	67.5	69.0
5	67.5	67.5	67.5	15	67.5	70.5	67.5

Running times	Algorithm of paper [9]	PSO	NPSO	Running times	Algorithm of paper [9]	PSO	NPSO
6	72.0	67.5	67.5	16	67.5	67.5	67.5
7	67.5	71.0	67.5	17	69.0	67.5	67.5
8	67.5	70.0	67.5	18	67.5	67.5	67.5
9	71.5	67.5	67.5	19	70.0	70.0	67.5
10	67.5	67.5	67.5	20	67.5	70.0	70.0

From table 2, the algorithm in the paper [9] has 6 times without finding the optimal solution, and PSO has not found the optimal solution about 10 times, while the NPSO has only 3 times that the global optimal solution is not reached.The probability of NPSO finding the optimal solution is 85%.Table 3 gives a more comparison results of the NPSO and PSO, including the achieve times, the not achieve times, average running time, the best value(best), average value(avg), worst value(worst).

Table 3. Comparison of experimental results with NPSO and PSO.

algorithm	Achieve times	not achieve times	Average running time(s)	Best value	Avg value	Worst value
PSO	10	10	0.0833	67.5	68.85	71.0
NPSO	17	3	0.1397	67.5	67.83	70.0

Experimental results shows that the search success probability of the algorithm in paper [9] is 70% and PSO only 50%, however NPSO can reach as high as 85% and the search success probability increased significantly. Because of the existence of subgroup exchanges, neighborhood search, Gauss mutation, not feasible solution, the calculation time becomes relatively longer, but not so much. Consequently, we can get that the improved algorithm NPSO has a higher search efficiency and better stability. It is an ideal method for the VRP problem with fewer number of customers.

5.2. Experiment 2

In order to verify the effectiveness of NPSO in the process of dealing with more customers, this paper uses NPSO and PSO to run 10 times for VRP with different scale (Here we select data fromfrom http://branchandcut.org/). For each instance corresponds to a different parameter, we set as follows, learning constant $c_1 = c_2 = 1.5$; the parameter of Gauss mutation $L = 1.8$; mutation probablity $P_c = 0.8$; population size NP about 5~8 times the number of customers; $cd \in [2,20]$ and increased with the particle number NP ; neighborhood search parameter $sd \in [\frac{N}{3}, \frac{N}{2}]$. The final results are compared in table 4.

Table 4. PSO and NPSO results for each instance.

instance	Theoretical optimal solution	Parameter setting	algorithm	Best value	Average value	Worst value	Running time
P-n16-k8. vrp	450	$NP = 100; cd = 4;$ $sd = 6; T = 1000$	PSO	451.34	451.46	451.95	37.01
			NPSO	451.34	451.34	451.34	38.16
P-n22-k8. vrp	603	$NP = 160; cd = 6; sd = 8;$ $T = 2000$	PSO	627.30	647.36	680.21	175.72
			NPSO	602.72	618.78	639.36	180.09
B-n31-k5. vrp	672	$NP = 160; cd = 6;$ $sd = 10; T = 2000;$	PSO	795.18	834.21	881.82	26.27
			NPSO	724.23	794.17	823.59	31.03
P-n40-k5. vrp	458	$NP = 200; cd = 10;$ $sd = 14; T = 3000;$	PSO	790.87	829.76	914.70	41.90
			NPSO	636.26	735.26	778.36	47.94

With the increase of the number of customers, the search of the optimal solution is more difficult, and the effect of PSO and NPSO will have a certain effect. But from table 4, it can be seen that the results of NPSO have obvious advantages. We have to admit that there are many operations in NPSO and takes much time, but they are always in an acceptable range. Therefore, the experiment proves that the improved algorithm NPSO is effective and feasible to solve the problem of VRP.

6. Conclusion

In this paper, a particle swarm optimization algorithm with Gauss mutation (NPSO) and neighborhood search is designed to solve the vehicle routing problem. In the process of solving vehicle routing problem, NPSO uses the integer encoding divided into two subgroups respectively iteration and enhances the search ability of the group. Finally, the simulation experiments show that the proposed algorithm can get the optimal solution faster and better. However, when solving the VRP with a larger scale, the algorithm in this paper will be more difficult with the customers increasing and the searching ability of the algorithm still needs to be improved.

Acknowledgement

Project supported by the Natural Science Foundation of

Sichuan Education (14ZA0127) and Doctor Foundation of China West Normal University (12B022).

References

[1] Jun Li, Yaohua Guo. Theory and method of logistics distribution vehicle scheduling [M]. Beijing: China material press, 2001.

[2] Laporte G. The vehicle routing problem: an overview of exact and approximation algorithms [J]. European Journal of operational Research, 1992, 5(9): 345 — 358.

[3] Hongchun HU, Yaohua WU, Li LIAO. Optimization and application of logistics distribution vehicle [J]. Journal of Shandong University (Engineering Science), 2007, 37(4): 104-107.

[4] Eberhart R, Kennedy J. A new optimizer using particle swarm theory [A]. Proceedings of the International Symposium on Micro Machine and Human Science [C]. Piscataway, NJ, USA: IEEE, 1995: 39-43.

[5] Kennedy J, Eberhart R. Particle swarm optimization [A]. Proceedings of the IEEE International Conference on Neural Networks [C]. Piscataway, NJ, USA: IEEE, 1995: 1942-1948.

[6] Zhen Huang. Hybrid quantum Particle Swarm Optimization algorithm for vehicle routing problem [J]. Computer Engineering and Applications, 2013. 49(24): 219-223.

[7] Dongqing Ma, Wei Wang. Logistics distribution vehicle scheduling based on improved particle swarm optimization [J]. Computer Engineering and Applications, 2014, 50(11): 246-270.

[8] Yaohua Wu, Nianzhi Zhang. Modified Particle Swarm Optimization algorithm for vehicle routing problem with time windows [J]. Computer Engineering and Applications, 2010, 46(15): 230-234.

[9] Ya Li, Dan Li, Dong Wang. Improved chaos particle swarm optimization algorithm for vehicle routing problem [J]. Application Research of Computers, 2011, 28(11): 4107-4110.

[10] Ning Li, Tong Zou. Particle swarm optimization for vehicle routing problem [J]. Journal of Systems Engineering, 2004, 19(6): 596-600.

[11] Bing Wu. Research and application of particle swarm optimization algorithm for vehicle routing problem [D]. Zhejiang University of Technology, 2008.

[12] Yuanbing Mo, Fuyong Liu. Artificial glowworm swarm optimization algorithm with Gauss mutation [J]. Application Research of Computers, 2013, 30(1): 121-123.

[13] Xing Liu, Guoguang He. Study on tabu search algorithm for stochastic vehicle routing problem [J]. Application Research of Computers, 2007, 43(24): 179: 181.

5

Numerical Analysis of Diversion Flow Stream Around of Bend Canal Wall in Dez River Intake

Ahadiyan J.[1], Haji Ali Gol S.[2]

[1]Hydraulic Structure Water Science Engineering Faculty of Shahid Chamran University (SCU), Ahwaz, Iran

[2]Hydraulic Structure in Sharab Consulting Engineers, Ahwaz, Iran

Email address:
Ja_ahadiyan@yahoo.com (Ahadiyan J.), Hj_sd@yahoo.com (Haji A. G. S.)

Abstract: Investigation of flow pattern through intake structures is one of important issue which should be considered under design procedure. In this study, simulation of flow regime of side way intake structure with T shape-Intake which is feed from Dez River has been done. Because of different problem in Sabili intake of Dez River, the process of utilizing curved cancel is studied scientifically. To achieve the purpose, velocity distribution profile accompany turbulent Energy at inlet of structure have been studied. As a result, energy turbulence has been increased gradually to 60 percent and energy disputing from beginning to end a path of river has increased 31 percent. But maximum velocity at situation (without intake structure) decreased from 61% to 42% subsequently.

Keywords: Curved Canal, T-Shape, Water Intake Structure, Flow Algorithm, Flow – 3D

1. Introduction

Generally, water Intake from river is very complicated operation and usually has been done in two categories, (1) pumping method (2) gravity method. Although some standards, according to the studies, have been achieved, many pump station and turnout structures have faced to side erosion and many of them have sedimentation problem. In other words, inlet path always are attacked with sediment and erosion. It is correct that human tried had to use water from river, but many studied remain and one complete resource didn't gathered carefully, more over shape of specific hydraulic structure is function of many factors such as, project location, directing water from river and many related equations and formula. So, many sciences are used such as soil mechanic, hydrology, hydraulic and etc as base. The pump station of Sabili is located at upstream of Dez diversion dam at Khuzestan province, in order to water conveying to land of Sabili region. This intake designed to convey water from Dez River to pump station. This conveying path (channel) is compound with the side wall slope 2:1 and the length is about 385 meter, designed bed level of convey channel is 126, and bed level of river is about 123 to 124.The studies of flow

regime at beginning of inlet in order to determine hydraulic properties at cross section of turn out channel is aim of this research: Safarzade et al (2002) studied three dimension of concept of turbulent flow at side water intakes, with using two phases model and they concluded that validation had acceptable convergence and bed lead could been studied scientifically. Vahid et al (2010) investigated water profile at new method of water intake with using bottom intake method and concluded that uniformity of flow stream at low discharge is more than profile uniformity at high range of flow Discharge. Moazen and shafaee (2008), attempt to study sediment dredging efficiency through vortex tube and they finally found out, Froud number increasing has great effect on vortex tube and make it decreased enormously. Sajadi and Shafai (2009), tried to evaluate sediment trap basin models and they deducted that imperial model of stilling basin, because of lack of knowledge of flow algorithm here very high rate of mistakes. Keshavarz et al (2009), tried to simulate 3 Dimension of algorithm around vertical and angled spur dike with different boundary condition and according to the results, modeling with free surface and assumption of rigid Doer has been done. Using time (rigid- lid) has great effect on. Calculation and decrease rapid process of program, but unfortunately the results from model is not so logical and has a lot mistakes. Shamloo et al (2010) tried to study effects of Geometrical and hydraulic Dimension on flow separation zone; through side wall water Intakes with using fluent software, they finally found out choosing suitable turbulent model. Suit to flow Condition is more important, therefore, investigation the effect different hydraulic parameter. Such as, Geometric and hydraulic like width of Directed channel through main channel, angle of diversion, Froude number of inlet flow, and Discharge distribution show that, at all condition, when flow rate Increase then dimension of flow separation zone through diverted canal is going to be smaller. In constant distribution discharge using by two gate outlet, the dimension of separation zone is independent of inlet flow condition. In this regards, this case is dependent of bottom width of either canal or deflection angle. Godsion et al (2010) studied effect of canal curve on bed scouring depth and concluded that at almost experiments, position of maximum depth of scouring are related to discharge increase and Froude number and after a while, will be transferred to the downstream of channel. Maximum scouring depth is always created at about 60-90 degree location of curve start point and must of them are located at 80-90 degree location. Pirestasni et al, (2008) investigated flow pattern on lateral intake in the curved channel by using physical model. They showed that the variation of velocity profiles and water surface have a significant influence of diversion discharges. In addition they concluded that increasing longitudinal velocity in inlet of intake the water surface increases and on the base of energy equation the lateral discharges increases. Neishaboori et al, (2004) evaluated of the 3D numerical model on lateral intake and showed that the k- ε model have a good accuracy and the results satisfactory compliance with results of physical models.

2. Methods and Materials

As it is mentioned before the introduction proposes of this study is simulation and investigation of flow algorithm at

bend shape canal of sabili water intake structure. So for achieving this purpose flow-3D has been used. This model is multi-dimensional model for simulation of complicated hydraulic problem. The method of solving the equations is based on finite volume method and it included of continuity and momentum equations and diffusion has numerical solution. The continuity Equation is from derived from moss equilibrium for one fluid cell of below:

$$v_f \frac{\partial p}{\partial t} + \frac{\partial}{\partial x}(P.U.Ax) + R(PleAg) + \frac{\partial}{\partial z}(pv.AZ) + \varepsilon \frac{P.UAX}{x} = R_{DIF} + R_{SOR} \quad (1)$$

In which: Vf is portion of open flow volume at x direction Ax, Ay, AZ are one sections of open flow volume at x,y,z direction. At this equation, R, are operational Coefficients. For Cartesian coordinate system R parameter is equal to 1 and is equal to zero. First term at right side of (2) equation is turbulent diffusion term and calculated of below:

$$R_{DIF} = \frac{\partial}{\partial x}\left(V_P A_x \frac{\partial p}{\partial x}\right) + R\frac{\partial}{\partial Y}\left(V_P A_Y R \frac{\partial p}{\partial Y}\right) + \frac{\partial}{\partial z}\left(V_P A_z \frac{\partial p}{\partial z}\right) + \varepsilon \frac{\rho V_P A_X}{x} \quad (2)$$

Where in this equation v_ρ is equal to $c_\rho \mu / \rho$ and μ is diffusion equation coefficient and c_ρ is coefficient which is related to turbulent Schmitt member. This term is mass distribution and related to validate turbulent combination process and is only usable for non-uniformity practical fluid. the last term, at equation (2) is related to source at under condition of 2 phases fluid has been used. Navier- stockes equation with velocity component (u,v,w), are from other equation of flow

Analysis which these has been showed of below:

$$\frac{\partial U}{\partial t} + \frac{1}{V_f}\left[uA_x \frac{\partial U}{\partial X} + vA_y \frac{\partial U}{\partial Y} + wA_z \frac{\partial U}{\partial z}\right] = -\frac{1}{\rho}\frac{\partial p}{\partial x} + G_x + f_x \quad (3)$$

$$\frac{\partial v}{\partial t} + \frac{1}{V_f}\left[uA_x \frac{\partial v}{\partial X} + vA_y \frac{\partial v}{\partial y} + wA_z \frac{\partial v}{\partial z}\right] = -\frac{1}{\rho}\frac{\partial p}{\partial y} + G_y + f_y \quad (4)$$

$$\frac{\partial w}{\partial t} + \frac{1}{V_f}\left[uA_x \frac{\partial w}{\partial X} + vA_y \frac{\partial w}{\partial y} + wA_z \frac{\partial w}{\partial z}\right] = -\frac{1}{\rho}\frac{\partial p}{\partial z} + G_z + f_z \quad (5)$$

Fig. 1. Schematic picture of Sabili water intake structure.

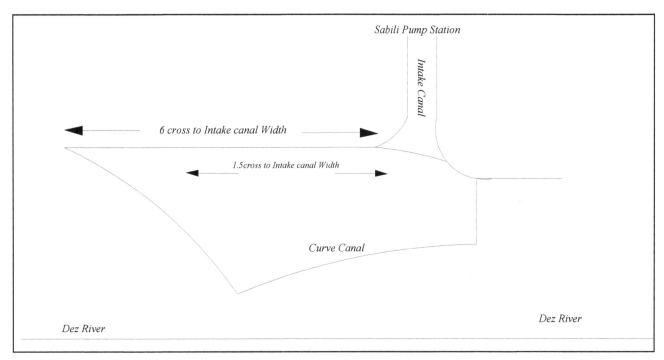

Fig. 2. *Schematic curved canal of Sabili intake.*

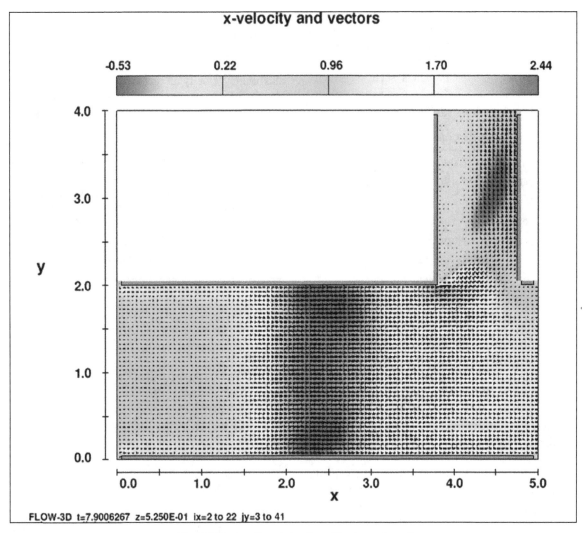

Fig. 3. *Flow algorithm at situation without curved canal.*

At these equations, (G_X, G_Y, and G_Z), mass acceleration And (f_x, f_y, f_y) are viscosity acceleration : so, in this research, water intake structure of sabili had been simulated. Figure 1 shows the pumping station and water intake of sabili.

Accordance of Figure 1 and as mentioned before, Sabili intake has a shape in form of T shape and its water is supplying form Dez River. Now, this structure has too many problems, such as problem of water in taking due to sedimentation, so the rehabilitation is necessary. In the research simulation has been followed at two conditions: first T shape canal has been modeled without bend curve canal and second, simulation has been done with curved canal. Schematic curved canal has been shown as follow:

3. Results and Discussions

In the study, effect of bend canal on flow algorithm at Sabili pump station has been studied. To achieve of these purposes the models was run on 2 cases: one without any curved canal and two with a curved canal. Figure 3 shows the results of without any curved canal

As observed a figure 3, in location of canal intake, some points through in takes have minimum velocity which cause to sediment deposition through connected canal. Thus, to more accurately investigation, velocity depth profiles through path line flow for the more near points to intake has been plotted. The results of this subject were shown at figure besides; average of hydraulic parameters such as velocity, rate of turbulent energy and turbulent dissipating through inlet of intake has been illustrated at table 1.

Table 1. Hydraulic properties of flow in inlet canal (without curved canal).

X	U_{ave}	tke	dtke
3.825	1.961101	0.010738	0.01511
3.925	1.931423	0.011474	0.015676
4.025	1.88628	0.011967	0.015685
4.125	1.805836	0.012202	0.015182
4.225	1.67497	0.012274	0.014411
4.325	1.475544	0.014463	0.015948
4.425	1.168398	0.015949	0.017628
4.525	0.928202	0.017109	0.018251
4.625	0.740048	0.018304	0.017625
4.725	0.606701	0.023044	0.020984
4.825	0.689537	0.025023	0.022173

Where in table 1: x coordinate is longitudinal streamline of river, U_{ave} is average velocity at each of x point (x=3/825 is beginning point in intake canal at river Geometric data of flow-3D).

"tke" is turbulent energy, and "dtke" is average dissipating energy at local position. The turbulent energy consists of turbulent conveying equation at kinematical energy and fluctuated turbulent velocity which is of below:

$$K_T = \frac{1}{2} (\overline{u'^2} + \overline{v'^2} + \overline{w'^2}) \quad (6)$$

At this equation: u', v' and w' are turbulent velocity fluctuations coefficients. A coefficient ½ observed in this equation is closed based on kinematical energy from three directions with Cartesian axis. Moreover, it is necessary explained that energy dissipating was modeled with k-ε model for simulation. Figure 4 shows the velocity profiles at inlet point.

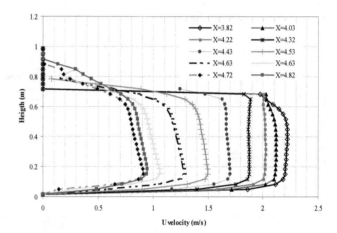

Fig. 4. The variation of velocity profiles at inlet beginning point.

On the base of Fig 4: these have been deducted that maximum velocity at entering point of intakes occurred. However, velocity decreased less than half at end point of canal. These variations of velocity is from 2.2 m/s to 0.85 m/s which may caused vortex velocity at beginning point of inlet. Therefore, energy dissipating has been occurred again. For quantities investigations show that the variation energy turbulence from start point of canal to end point decreased steadily approximately 60%. While the value of turbulence energy dissipation increase in start path of river to end is about 31%. Figure 5 shows velocity profile at start point of inlet. Moreover, table 2 shows average hydraulic parameter at inlet point of T shape intake structure.

Fig. 5. Schematic view of model results at curved canal.

Figure 5 demonstrates model with curved canal which work as baffled at upstream of water intake structure.

Table 2. *Hydraulic characteristic at intake inlet point.*

X	U_{ave}	tke	dtke
3.8250	0.0020	0.0015	0.0194
3.9250	0.0313	0.0535	0.0535
4.0250	0.0419	0.0860	0.5702
4.1250	0.0344	0.0729	0.8784
4.2250	0.0250	0.0496	1.0665
4.3250	0.0194	0.0342	1.0849
4.4250	0.0265	0.0411	0.8152
4.5250	0.0320	0.0464	0.6099
4.6250	0.0331	0.0427	0.3999
4.7250	0.0071	0.0097	0.0915

According to the table 2, turbulence energy is from inlet point at longitudinal profile is almost 85% increase and energy dissipation is increased to 75%. At second situation, curved canal has been simulated. Figure 6 shows the velocity profile at inlet structure in instruct of river.

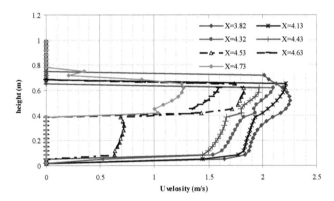

Fig. 6. *The variation of velocity profile in the intake inlet (river).*

As it is mentioned before, due to baffled structure of intake construction, flow velocity has been broken eventually. Generally, from inlet point to end, flow velocity at intakes is decreased from 2.35 m/s to 1/3 m/s. In comparison, using curved canal, velocity gradient gradually decreased, subsequently vertex speed. Which influenced on sedimentation is decreased to as aspect of quantity maximum velocity gradient decreased from 61% to 42% (without using bend channel). According to this using bend channel at modifying flow algorithm is so effective vertex velocity of energy table 3: shows turbulent parameters and turbulent energy and average velocity at beginning point. Table 3 shows the flow characteristics with using bend channel through river at inlet point of intake.

Table 3. *Hydraulic characteristic in the intake canal inlet with bend canal.*

X	tke	dtke	Uave
3.8250	0.0386	0.0527	1.8620
3.9250	0.0430	0.0636	1.8370
4.0250	0.0460	0.0748	1.7647
4.2250	0.0512	0.1120	1.6159
4.2250	0.0436	0.0972	1.6515
4.3250	0.0484	0.1162	1.5802
4.4250	0.0612	0.4741	0.8137
4.5250	0.0612	0.4741	0.8137
4.6250	0.0330	0.1477	0.4538
4.7250	0.0336	0.0833	0.4469
4.7750	0.0506	0.1039	0.4568

According to table 3 maximum velocity at inlet point of river is decreased from 1.86 m/s to 0.45 m/s in addition, variation of turbulent energy (if channel is exist) has been grow to 23% percentage. Although, if bend channel is not exist velocity changing has been increased to 60%, as a result bend channel is so affection. Moreover, turbulent energy dissipating at existence of bend channel is about 50% but for none existing decrease of version flow potential is at condition which bend channel has been used.

4. Conclusion

According to this research the brief results as follow.
- If the bend channel is not used: velocity changing at inlet point to water inlet is fell down from 2.2 m/s to 0.85 m/s and may cause vortex velocity (eddy flow) through entrance bend channel has declined from 61% to 42%.
- Turbulent energy changing: from beginning point to the end give up to 60% forint. But energy dissipating increased only 31%.
- Turbulent energy at enterers point (at longitude direction) grows to 85% as well as turbulent energy dissipating (which is about 78%).
- to sum up is bend channel has been used, maximum velocity is normally decreased from 1.86 to 0.45 m/s, beside turbulent energy of at (bend channel existence) is rocket to 23% and turbulent energy dissipating is changed up to 50%.

References

[1] Vahid, koorosh., "Experimental consideration of water surface profiles formation in new method of intake by palmer intake with permeable conduit", the 8th international conference of civiling Engineering, shiraz., Iran, (2009).

[2] Moazen, Iman., "Sediment efficiencies experimental of vortex pipe sedimentary in beginning of canals", National congress of Irrigation and Drainage networks management"., shahid chamran uni, (2005).

[3] Keshavarz, M. H., "3D numeral simulation of flow pattern around the vertically and transverse coast Epees with various boundary conditions", Iranian sea Engineering association, Sea engineering publication. 4th year. No-8 (2008).

[4] Shamloo, hamid., "Experimental effects of hydraulic and Geometrical parameters on dimensions of Flow separation region with Fluent software"., surveying and caviling engineering publication. Technical college. P487-495, No 4,44 (2010).

[5] Pirestani, M. R, "Flow assimilation over the side intake in arch floodway with physical model", soil water magazine (Agricultural industries and sciences). 22 copies, No2 (2008).

[6] Salehi neyshaboori, Seid Aliakbar, "Numerical Modeling of 3D flow pattern in side intake", 1st national congress of civil engineering, sharif industrial university. (2003).

[7] Barkdoll, B. D., "Sediment Control at Lateral Diversion", PhD dissertation, Civil and Environmental Engineering, University of Iowa, Iowa City, Iowa, 1997.

[8] Shettar, A. S., and Murthy, K. K., "A Numerical Study of Division of Flow in Open Channels", J. Hydr. Res., V. 34, No. 5, 1996, pp. 651-675.

[9] Issa, R, I., and Oliveira, P. J., "Numerical Prediction of Phase Separation in Two-Phase Flow Through T-junctions", Comp. Fluids, V. 23, No. 2, 1994, pp. 347-372.

[10] Neary, V. S., Sotiropoulos, F., and Odgaard, A. J. Three-Dimensional Numerical Model of Lateral-Intake Inflows", J. HYDRAUL. ENG. ASCE, V. 125, No. 2, 1999, pp. 126-140.

[11] Lee, D., and Chiu, J. J. "Computation of Physiological Bifurcation Flows Using a Patched Grid", Comput. Fluids, V. 21, No. 4, 1992, pp. 519-535.

[12] Hsu, Chung-Chieh, Tang. Chii, Jau, Lee, Wen-Jung and Shieh, Mon-Yi. (2002). "Subcritical 90 equal-width open-channel dividing flow." ASCE J. HYDRAUL. ENG.. Vol. 128, No. 7, PP. 716-720.

[13] Song, T., and Graf, W. H. 1998. Velocity and Turbulence Distribution in unsteady Open channel Flows. J. Hr. Eng. Vol. 122, No. 3.

[14] Reid, Ian, Laronne, Jonathan. b., and Powell, Mark.1998. Prediction of Bed-Load Transport by Desert Flash Floods. J. of hyd. Eng. vol., 122, No. 3.

[15] Rankl, j. G. 1987. Analysis of sediment production form two small semiarid basins in Wyoming: U.s. Geological Survey Water Resources Investigation Report 85-4314,27p.

[16] Graf, W. H., and Suszka, L. 1985. Unsteady Flow and its Effect on Sediment Transport. 21st IAHR congress Melbourne.

[17] Duan J. G., He L., Fu X., and Wang Q., (2009). Mean flow and turbulence around experimental spur dike. Advances in Water Resources, Vol. 32, No. 22, pp. 1717-1725.

[18] Vaghefi M., Ghodsian M. and Salehi Neyshabori S. A. A., (2012). Experimental Study on Scour around a T-Shaped Spur Dike in a Channel Bend. Journal of Hydraulic Engineering, Vol. 138.

6

The analysis of GCFS algorithm in medical data processing and mining

Xiao Yu Chen, Bo Liu*, Zhe Feng Zhang, Xin Xia

Department of Information Centre, East Hospital, Tongji University, School of Medicine, Shanghai, China

Email address:

alexander191@sina.com (Xiao Yu Chen), liubonew@126.com (Bo Liu), zhang_zf26@126.com (Zhe Feng Zhang), xinye_000@163.com (Xin Xia)

Abstract: Feature selection plays a significant part in medical data processing and mining, it can reduce the dimensionalities of datasets and enhance the performance of the classifiers, and it is also helpful to clinical decision support to a great extent. At present, the clinical decision support is more performed by physicians subjectively based on clinical knowledge, which may hinder the diagnosis and treatment. This paper mainly outlines the performance of GCFS (Genetic Correlation-based Feature Selection) algorithm in the processing and mining procedure of medical data, and medical UCI datasets are employed as the studied materials for proving the improvement of feature selection in data classification. Compared with the algorithms of CFS and GA (Genetic Algorithm), ensemble learning methods are employed as the testing classifiers, and the results show GCFS algorithm almost improves the performances of the testing classifiers better than CFS and GA.

Keywords: Feature Selection, GCFS, Ensemble learning

1. Introduction

The applications of computer and information technology have made a new highlight research direction with a rapid development in medicine. In clinics, medical diagnosis is considered as a classification problem: a case represents a patient's information, condition features are the patients' data and the category is the diagnosis, so it is essential to build classification model which can predict the uncategorized cases. Medical datasets are inevitable to contain irrelevant and noisy features, the selection of appropriate subset of the available features can produce compact and interpretable results for modeling the data adequately, and it can improve the classification accuracy in medical region [1].

Some research efforts have been devoted to the applications of data mining techniques for discovering useful medical knowledge and rules; such as Wang et al. [2] proposed a DFP-growth (Database Frequent Pattern) feature selection algorithm for the classification of children pneumonia cases; H. M. Yan proposed a real-coded genetic method to select critical features essential to the heart diseases diagnosis, and the critical features and their clinic meanings are in sound agreement with those used by the physicians in making their clinic decisions [3]. R. E.

Abdel-Aal used the group method of data handling (GMDH) to reduce the data dimensionalities for the breast cancer and heart disease, and it also lead to the improvements in the overall classification performance [4].

In this paper, the feature selection algorithm of GCFS is adopted in the mining procedure of medical data, and it is compared with CFS and GA based on the ensemble learning classifiers of Bagging and Boosting methods for demonstrating its suitable application and better performance. This paper is organized as follows. Section 2 describes the studied materials, and the data processing and mining procedure and methods are shown in Section 3. The results and analysis about GCFS are given in Section 4 and 5, and Section 6 summarizes this paper and gives the conclusions.

2. Materials

In this paper, there are four UCI medical datasets employed as the studied materials, they are downloaded at http://archive.ics.uci.edu/ml/datasets.html, including: diabetes, Breast cancer, Hepatitis survival, and CTGs (cardiotocograms).

Table 1 shows the description about the studied datasets. In the datasets, the missing feature values are replaced by mean values of the corresponding features, and missing values of all the features are less than 1%.

Table 1. *Description of the studied medical datasets*

Dataset Name	Categories	Features	Instances	Data type	Category Instruction
Diabetes	2	8	768	Continuous	negative=0, positive−1
Breast cancer	2	9	699	Nominal	benign=2, malignant =4
Hepatitis survival	2	19	155	Mixed	live=1, die=2
CTGs	3	21	2126	Continuous	normal=1, suspect=2, pathologic=3

3. Methods

In this paper, the data processing course includes GCFS algorithm for feature selection, ensemble learning, and C4.5 decision tree for classification, and Figure 1 gives the framework of data process for instruction.

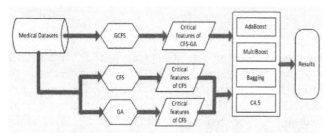

Figure 1. *Framework of data processing and classification*

3.1. GCFS algorithm

GCFS algorithm is the attribute selection part in the data process. CFS (Correlation-based Feature Selection) is a classical filtered algorithm of attribute selection; in this algorithm, the heuristic evaluation for a single feature corresponding to each category label is used to obtain the final feature subset, and the assessment method of CFS is as follows:

$$Ms = \frac{k\overline{r_{cf}}}{\sqrt{k + k(k-1) + \overline{r_{ff}}}} \quad (1)$$

In (1), Ms is the evaluation for an attribute subset S including k attribute items, $\overline{r_{cf}}$ is the mean correlation degree between attributes and the category label, and $\overline{r_{ff}}$ is the mean correlation degree among attributes. And the evaluation of CFS is a method of correlation based on attribute subsets. A bigger $\overline{r_{cf}}$ or smaller $\overline{r_{ff}}$ in acquired subsets by the method produce a higher evaluation value, and in CFS, the correlation degree among attributes is calculated by information gain, and the formula of information gain is shown below. Y is the category attribute, y is any possible value of Y, the entropy of Y is shown in (2), and for an attribute X, entropy of category attribute Y under the condition of X is in (3).

$$H(Y) = -\sum_{y \in Y} p(y) \log_2(p(y)) \quad (2)$$

$$H(Y|X) = -\sum_{x \in X} p(x) \sum_{y \in Y} p(y|x) \log(p(y|x)) \quad (3)$$

The difference of H (Y) − H (Y|X) (i.e. the entropy reduction of attribute Y) can reflect the information amount provided by attribute X to attribute Y, and a bigger difference means a higher correlation degree between X and Y. Information gain is a symmetrical evaluation method; it tends to select the attributes with more values. Therefore, it is necessary to normalize information gain to [0, 1] for keeping equivalent comparison effect among attributes, and (4), below, shows the calculating formula.

$$U_{XY} = 2.0 \times \frac{H(Y) - H(Y|X)}{H(Y) + H(X)} \quad (4)$$

As a filtering algorithm, CFS evaluates the correlation between attributes and category label, and the redundancy degree among attributes [5]. Although the algorithm performs well in dimension reduction, it cannot approach a global optimum result. The Genetic algorithm (GA) is a wrapping algorithm in dimension reduction for its global search capability [6-8]. In this paper, CFS and GA are combined to make the GCFS algorithm, and this algorithm evaluates new individuals of GA through the correlation degree in CFS as the fitness function of GA. The design of GCFS algorithm mainly includes four parts: coding scheme, selection operator, crossover operator and mutation operator.

In the coding scheme, each entity is encoded with classical binary code. The method of roulette wheel is employed for selection operator. For the crossover operator, single- point crossover is used to produce new individuals by swapping the cross point part through the crossover points. And basic bit mutation is used in binary encoding for the mutation operator, from 0 to 1, or from 1 to 0.

In the selection of the crossover rate and mutation rate, for producing more new individuals and avoiding causing too much damage to the better attribute subset, the crossover rate range is from 0.40 to 0.99 and the mutation rate is from 0.0001 to 0.1 commonly. The description of GCFS algorithm is shown in Figure 2.

Input: Encoding records of the dataset with binary code; Selection operator; Crossover rate Pc; Mutation rate Pm; The iteration number of population g ; The initial amount of population P ;

Output: Features selected by GCFS ;

(1) Initialize the population P, and generate P attribute subsets randomly;

(2) Evaluate the population P and calculate the Fitness value of each individual h in the population;

(3) while (the optimal result not approached or less than iteration number)

{ ① According to Fitness value, select the optimal invidual from the parent generation to the next by Selection operator;

② According to Fitness value, select feature subsets by from the parent generation, set the crossover point for each attribute subset, then swap the structures before or after the point for producing two new inviduals by Crossover operator ;

③ Through the mutation rate and mutation operator, crossover subsets are mutated at random bits to produce two new individuals;

④ Add new individuals into the population to form a new one;

⑤ Evaluating individuals of the new population by Fitness value.   }

Figure 2. Description of GCFS algorithm

3.2. Ensemble Methods

Ensemble methods have become a mainstay in the machine learning and data mining literature. They are designed based on "No classifier is perfect" as the guideline, and combined the performance of many weak classifiers to produce a powerful committee. Boosting and bagging are popular choices.

The main idea of Boosting algorithm [9] is the learning enhancement based on the misclassified samples. At first, each sample is endowed with the same weight, then the first basic classifier is employed to classify the samples and test the training dataset based on the weights. For the misclassified samples, their weights will be upgraded, and the second classifier will be trained on the dataset with modified weights by iteration until an optimal classifier can be obtained. Based on the idea, various boosting algorithms are proposed for different problems, such as AdaBoost [10], and MultiBoost [11].

Input: A dataset S with categories contains the training samples $(x_1, y_1),..., (x_m, y_m)$;

Among them, $x_i \in X$, decision feature $y_i \in Y$, L: Number of training datasets.

Output: H classifier (x)

Procedure Bagging:

1.   dataset S into L training sets

2.   for l=1 to L

3. H_l classifier is trained.

4.   end for

5. $H(x) = argmax \sum_{i=1}^{L} h_i(x)$

6.   **end procedure**

Figure 3. Bagging Algorithm

Bagging (Bootstrap Aggregating) is a method based on

resampling technique [12]. In Bagging method, a weak learning algorithm and a training set $((x_1, y_1), ... ,(x_m, y_m))$ are given, the algorithm generates a number of training sets including some samples by random from the initial training set, and the training sets and the initial training sets are nearly in the same size. Samples of the initial training set in a round may appear or not, and the learning algorithm classifier is trained on each training set and obtains a predicted sequence $g_1, g_2, ... ,g_t$, and the final function G can be predicted by voting. And the description of Bagging algorithm is shown in Figure 3.

3.3. C4.5

C4.5 [13] is a suite of algorithms for classification problems in machine learning and data mining. It aims at supervised learning: Given an attribute-valued dataset where instances are described by collections of attributes and belong to one of a set of mutually exclusive classes, and C4.5 learns a mapping from attribute values to classes that can be applied to classify new, unseen instances. The generic description of how C4.5 works is given in Figure 4. All tree induction methods begin with a root node that represents the entire, given dataset and recursively split the data into smaller subsets by testing for a given attribute at each node. The sub trees denote the partitions of the original dataset that satisfy specified attribute value tests. This process typically continues until the subsets are "pure," that is, all instances in the subset fall in the same class, at which time the tree growing is terminated. Considering the characteristics of the datasets, C4.5 decision tree is employed and it is fit for continuous or nominal features in datasets.

Input: a feature-value dataset D

1.   Tree={}

2.   **if** D is "pure" or other stopping criteria met **then**

3.   terminate

4.   **end if**

5.   **for** all feature $a \in D$ **do**

6.   Compute information-theoretic criteria if we split on a

7.   **end for**

8. a_{beast}= Best feature according to above computed criteria

9.   Tree= Create a decision node that tests a_{beast} in the root

10. D_v= Induced sub-datasets from D based on a_{beast}

11.   **for** all D_v **do**

12. $Tree_v$= C4.5(D_v)

13.   Attach $Tree_v$ to the corresponding branch of Tree

14.   **end for**

15.   **return** Tree

Figure 4. Description of C4.5 Algorithm

4. Results

4.1 Feature Selection of GCFS

Feature reduction is an approach for improving the

performances for classifiers, the GCFS algorithm parameters are defaulted as follows: the population size and the number of generations is 20, the probabilities of crossover and mutation are 0.6 and 0.033 respectively. In Table 2, we can see that GCFS can achieve the purpose of feature reduction on the medical datasets through ten-fold cross validation. The feature reduction rate of GCFS is up to 26.31%.

Table 2. *The feature selection rate of GCFS*

Datasets	Full Features	GCFS
Diabetes	8	4
Breast cancer	9	9
Hepatitis survival	19	13
CTGs	21	16
Ave. feature number	14.25	10.5
Feature reduction rate (%)	0	26.31%

4.2. Performances of GCFS on the Testing Classifiers

To evaluate the performances of GCFS on the testing classifiers, two criteria of ACC (classification accuracy) and AUC (area under ROC curve) are used within the framework.

- ACC is calculated as the percentage of the correctly classified testing samples over all the test samples.
- AUC is a relative evaluation standard, and it has been recently proposed as an alternative single-number measure for evaluating the predictive ability of learning algorithms [18].

Through ten-fold cross validation, ACC (%) and AUC of the three types of testing classifiers (Bagging, Boosting and C4.5 decision tree) on the UCI medical datasets filtered from GCFS are listed in Table 3.and Table 4. For meeting the homogeneity of the testing classifiers, C4.5 is also employed as the basic classifiers of testing ensemble learning methods of AdaBoostM1, MultiBoostAB, and Bagging. From Table 3 and Table 4, we can see GCFS performs well in medical data classification of the testing classifiers.

The testing classifiers are running based on the hardware environment of an Intel Core 2 Duo CPU 2.4GHz and a Memory of 2G. Figure 5 shows the time-running status of the testing classifiers on the medical datasets filtered from GCFS, and we can see that the running times of the testing classifiers are in fast speeds and acceptable.

Table 3. *ACC(%)of the testing classifiers on GCFS*

	AdaBoostM1	MultiBoostAB	Bagging	C4.5
Diabetes	72.47	74.76	74.49	71.79
Breast cancer	95.85	95.85	95.42	94.85
Hepatitis survival	83.23	81.29	81.29	80
CTGs	94.78	94.83	94.31	93.09

Table 4. *AUC of the testing classifiers on GCFS*

	AdaBoostM1	MultiBoostAB	Bagging	C4.5
Diabetes	0.761	0.789	0.812	0.745
Breast cancer	0.983	0.990	0.983	0.968
Hepatitis survival	0.780	0.806	0.787	0.661
CTGs	0.982	0.983	0.976	0.924

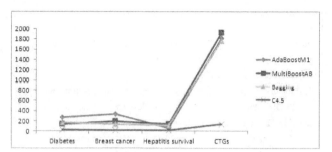

Figure 5. *Running times of the testing classifiers on the datasets from GCFS (ms)*

4.3.Comparisons with CFS and GA

GCFS in feature selection is compared with the algorithms of CFS and GA on through ten-fold cross validation. Table 5 gives a comparison of the feature selection approaches on the UCI medical datasets, the reduction rates of CFS and GA are 42.11% and 7.02% in feature selection, and it shows that the GCFS makes a higher rate of feature reduction than GA, but it is lower than that of CFS.

From Table 6 to Table 9, we can see the classifiers of AdaBoostM1, MultiBoostAB, Bagging and C4.5 generally perform well based on the feature selection methods of CFS and GA. Figure 6 and Figure 7 show the running times of the testing classifiers on CFS and GA, and we can see the classifiers based on CFS consume shorter running times than based on GA.

Table 5. *The comparison of feature selection rates with CFS and GA*

Datasets	GCFS	CFS	GA
Diabetes	4	4	7
Breast cancer	9	9	9
Hepatitis survival	13	12	17
CTGs	16	8	20
Ave. feature number	10.5	8.25	13.25
Feature reduction rate (%)	26.32	42.11	7.02

Table 6. *ACC(%) of the testing classifiers on CFS*

	AdaBoostM1	MultiBoostAB	Bagging	C4.5
Diabetes	72.47	74.76	74.49	71.79
Breast cancer	95.85	95.85	95.42	94.85
Hepatitis survival	83.87	85.81	81.94	80
CTGs	93.79	94.03	93.41	93.04

Table 7. *AUC of the testing classifiers on CFS*

	AdaBoostM1	MultiBoostAB	Bagging	C4.5
Diabetes	0.761	0.789	0.812	0.745
Breast cancer	0.983	0.990	0.983	0.968
Hepatitis survival	0.827	0.817	0.810	0.651
CTGs	0.97	0.973	0.968	0.916

Table 8. *ACC(%) of the testing classifiers on GA*

	AdaBoostM1	MultiBoostAB	Bagging	C4.5
Diabetes	72.20	74.36	74.36	73.14
Breast cancer	95.85	95.85	95.42	94.85
Hepatitis survival	84.52	83.23	82.58	81.94
CTGs	94.40	94.26	93.89	92.89

Table 9. *AUC of the testing classifiers on GA*

	AdaBoostM1	MultiBoostAB	Bagging	C4.5
Diabetes	0.762	0.788	0.813	0.754
Breast cancer	0.983	0.990	0.983	0.968
Hepatitis survival	0.8	0.799	0.799	0.693
CTGs	0.978	0.982	0.975	0.914

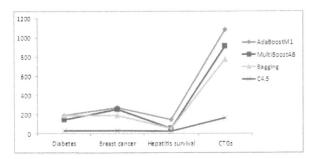

Figure 6. *Running times of the testing classifiers on the datasets from CFS (ms)*

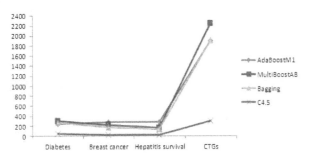

Figure 7. *Running times of the testing classifiers on the datasets from GA (ms)*

5. Discussion

For analyzing the performances of the testing classifiers on the feature selection methods, ACC, AUC and running time of the testing classifiers are employed within the course of data processing, and Figure 8 to Figure 10 give the related results. In Figure 8 and Figure 9, we can see the average ACC values of GCFS are almost the highest on AdaBoostM1 and Bagging, the average ACC values of CFS and GA are higher than those of GCFS on MultiBoostAB and C4.5; and GCFS performs the highest average AUC values on the boosting classifiers except C4.5. Compared with the better performances in classification, GCFS shows a shorter running time than GA, but a longer time than CFS.

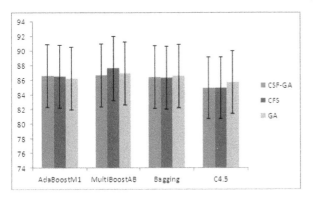

Figure 8. *Ave. ACC(%) of three feature selection methods on the testing classifiers*

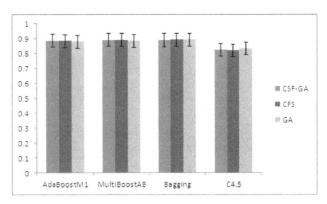

Figure 9. *Ave. AUC of three feature selection methods on the testing classifiers*

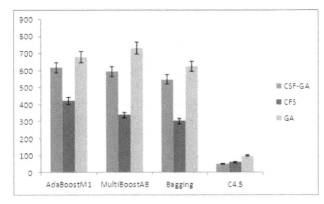

Figure 10. *Ave. running times of three feature selection methods on the testing classifiers*

6. Conclusions

Compared with the algorithms of CFS and GA, GCFS is analyzed based on the ensemble learning methods (AdaBoostM1, MultiBoostAB and Bagging) of C4.5 in medical data classification and running times. Obviously, GCFS performs a medium reduction rate between GA and CFS in feature selection, it performs well in classification, especially a better average ACC (%) than CFS and GA on AdaBoostM1; it almost makes the highest average AUC values on the ensemble learning classifiers.; and GCFS performs a medium running time between CFS and GA on the testing ensemble learning classifiers.

References

[1]   G. Eason, B. Noble, and I. N. Sneddon, "On certain integrals of Lipschitz-Hankel type involving products of Bessel functions," Phil. Trans. Roy. Soc. London, vol. A247, pp. 529–551, April 1955. (references)

[2]   J. Clerk Maxwell, A Treatise on Electricity and Magnetism, 3rd ed., vol. 2. Oxford: Clarendon, 1892, pp.68–73.

[3]   I. S. Jacobs and C. P. Bean, "Fine particles, thin films and exchange anisotropy," in Magnetism, vol. III, G. T. Rado and H. Suhl, Eds. New York: Academic, 1963, pp. 271–350.

[4]   K. Elissa, "Title of paper if known," unpublished.

[5]   R. Nicole, "Title of paper with only first word capitalized," J. Name Stand. Abbrev., in press.

[6]   Y. Yorozu, M. Hirano, K. Oka, and Y. Tagawa, "Electron spectroscopy studies on magneto-optical media and plastic substrate interface," IEEE Transl. J. Magn. Japan, vol. 2, pp. 740–741, August 1987 [Digests 9th Annual Conf. Magnetics Japan, p. 301, 1982].

[7]   M. Young, The Technical Writer's Handbook. Mill Valley, CA: University Science, 198.

[8]   I. Skrypnik, V. Terziyan, S. Puuronen and A. Tsymbal: Proceedings of the 12th IEEE Symposium on Computer-Based Medical Systems. 1999, p. 53–58.

[9]   B. Wang, M. Zhang, B. Zhang and W. Wei: Proceedings of the 7th International Conference on Parallel and Distributed Computing, Applications and Technologies. 2006, p. 128–131.

[10] H. M. Yan, J. Zheng, Y. T. Jiang, C. L. Peng, S. Z. Xiao, "Selecting critical clinical features for heart diseases diagnosis with a real-coded genetic algorithm", Applied soft computing, no.8, (2008), pp. 1105-1111.

[11] R. E. Abdel-Aal, "GMDH-based feature ranking and selection for improved classification of medical data", Journal of Biomedical Informatics, vol. 38, no.6, (2005), pp. 456-468.

[12] M. A. Hall, Correlation based feature selection for machine learning [D]. Hamilton, New Zealand: University of Waikato, 1999: 51-69.

[13] B. Zheng, Y. X. Jin. "The analysis of marine human error causes based on attribute reduction", Journal of Shanghai Marine University, vol. 31, no. 1, pp. 92-93, 2010.

[14] J. T. Ren, J. H. Sun, H. Y. Huang, et al. "A feature selection method based on information gain and genetic algorithm". Computer science, vol. 33, no. 10, pp. 194, 2006.

[15] S. C. Song, H. Pang, X. J. Ding. "The application research of GA-SVM algorithm in text classification". Computer simulation, vol. 28, no. 1, pp. 223-225, 2011.

[16] R. E. Schapire, "The strength of weak learn ability", Machine learning, vol. 5, no.2, (1990), pp. 197-227.

[17] Y. Freund, "Boosting a weak algorithm by majority", Information and computation, vol.121, no.2, (1995), pp. 256-285.

[18] G. I. Webb, "MultiBoosting: A technique for combining boosting and wagging", Machine Learning, vol. 40, no.1, (2000), pp. 159-196.

[19] J. R. Quinlan, C4.5: Programs for machine learning, Morgan Kaufmann Publishers, San Francisco, 1993.

[20] L. Breiman. Bagging predictors. Machine learning. 1996(24): 123-140.

7

Cyber-Physical Systems: A Framework for Prediction of Error in Smart Medical Devices

Sunday Anuoluwa Idowu[1], Olawale Jacob Omotosho[1], Olusegun Ayodeji Ojesanmi[2], Stephen Olusola Maitanmi[1]

[1]Department of Computer Science, Babcock University, Ilisan Remo, Ogun State Nigeria
[2]Department of Computer Science, Federal University of Agriculture, Abeokuta, Ogun State, Nigeria

Email address:
saidowu07@gmail.com (S. A. Idowu), ojomotosho1@yahoo.com (O. J. Omotosho), dejioje@yahoo.com (O. A. Ojesanmi),
maitanmi@yahoo.com (S. O. Maitanmi)

Abstract: The objective of medical care services is designed to bring improvement to the health of patients. This is pursued with great vigor today with the use of modern health care systems which include medical sensors and automatically controlled actuation to deliver smart and proactive health services. The embedded devices control Smart Medical Devices (SMDs) used by physicians, Nurses, and Medical Staff which continuously interact with the human body or patient in one form or another. Cyber-Physical Systems (CPS) are integrations of computation with physical processes which are monitored and controlled by the embedded systems. CPS has positively affected a number of application areas which include communication, consumer energy, infrastructure, healthcare, manufacturing, military, robotics and transportation. The inappropriate use of these SMDs generate errors which are under-emphasized by stakeholders. Most users are only interested on the benefits derived in the use of SMDs and care-less on the danger that these devices can contribute to patients when used inappropriately. The error tendencies, possible factors and way forward is the subject matter of this paper. In order to achieve the stated objective, Input data was provided through a critical incident analysis of online database which provide readings from medical experts. These readings were compared to the standard world benchmarks and best practices. The difference between the readings and the standard benchmark were used to validate the existence of errors. A framework was developed for error prediction to improve safety in the use of SMDs. Due to the complexity of the problem, an algorithm was further developed to obtain an optimal solution of P_1 to P_5 within an acceptable threshold runtime which shows the gravity of these challenges on patients.

Keywords: Cyber Physical Systems, Embedded System, SMDs

1. Introduction

The future of information technology (IT) largely depends on evolving terminologies such as ubiquitous computing, pervasive computing, ambient intelligence, disappearing computer, and post-personal computer (PC) era. Ubiquitous computing reflects the fact that computing and communication will be everywhere. The expectation is that information will be available anytime, anywhere [1]. The intensive involvement of our daily life with computing devices led to the term pervasive computing [2]; [3]. Ambient intelligence refers to some emphasis on communication technology in future homes and smart buildings [4]; [5]. Ubiquitous computing, pervasive computing, and ambient intelligence have diverse application areas. Ubiquitous computing focuses more on the long-term goal of providing information anytime, anywhere, whereas pervasive computing focuses more on practical aspects and the exploitation of already available technology. Disappearing computer refers to the expectation that processors and software will be used in much smaller systems and will, in many cases, even be invisible [1]. While post-PC era denotes the fact that, in the future, standard-PCs will be less dominant hardware platforms. However, disappearing computer entails that processors and software gave rise to embedded systems where processes are highly accelerated not because of the visible components, but by powerful processors. Despite these advancements, almost all the technological devices came with their challenges.

Crucial among many pervasive technological tools are the SMDS used in supporting health related researches and medical processes in providing solutions to health care. The inappropriate use of these SMDs generate errors which are under-emphasized by stakeholders. The error tendencies, possible factors and way forward is the subject matter of this research paper.

Error prediction involves the future expectations that error will occur due to some violated rules or metrics. Embedded software is a piece of software that is hidden in a system or

hardware components written specifically in a coordinated fashion to achieve an objective. Embedded systems are used in many areas ranging from vehicles and mobile phones to washing machines and printers to increase and enhance productivity.

Cyber-Physical Systems (CPS) are integrations of computation with physical processes which are monitored and controlled by the embedded systems usually with feedback loops where physical processes affect computations [6]. A summary of the CPS application domain is found in Table 1.

Table 1. CPS application domains.

Innovative Products or Applications	Cyber-Physical Systems	Impacts
Smart Manufacturing and Production		
• Agile manufacturing • Supply chain connectivity	• Intelligent controls • Process and assembly automation • Robotics working safely with humans	• Enhanced global competitiveness • U.S.-based high -tech manufacturing • Greater efficiency, agility, and reliability
Transportation and Mobility		
• Autonomous or smart vehicles(surface, air, water and space) • Vehicle-to-vehicle and vehicle to infrastructure communication	• Drive by wire vehicle systems • Interactive traffic control systems • Next- generation air transport control	• Accident prevention congestion reduction (zero fatality highway) • Greater safety and convenience of travel
Energy		
• Electricity systems • Renewable energy supply • Oil and gas production	• Smart electric power grid • Plug-in vehicle charging systems • Smart oil and gas distribution grid	• Greater reliability, security, and diversity of energy supply • Increased energy efficiency
Civil Infrastructure		
• Bridges and dams • Municipal water and wastewater treatment	• Active monitoring and control system • Smart grids for water and wastewater • Early warning systems	• More safe, secure, and reliable infrastructure • Assurance of water quality and supply • Accident warning and prevention
Healthcare		
• Wireless body area networks • Assistive healthcare systems • Wearable sensors and implantable devices	• Medical devices • Personal care equipment • Disease diagnosis and prevention	• Improved outcomes and quality of life • Cost-effective healthcare • Timely disease diagnosis and prevention
Buildings and Structures		
• High performance residential and commercial buildings • Net-zero energy buildings • Appliances	• Whole building controls • Smart installed equipment • Building automation systems • Networked appliance systems	• Increased building efficiency, comfort and convenience • Improved occupant health and safety • Control of indoor air quality
Defense		
• Soldier equipment • Weapons and weapons platforms • Supply equipment • Autonomous and smart underwater sensors	• Smart (precision-guided) weapons • Wearable computing/sensing uniforms • Intelligent, unmanned vehicles • Supply chain and logistics systems	• Increased war fighter effectiveness, security, and agility • Decreased exposure for human war fighters and greater capability for remote warfare
Energy Response		
• First responder equipment • Communications equipment • Fire-fighting equipment	• Detection and surveillance systems • Resilient communications networks • Integrated emergency response systems	• Increased emergency responder effectiveness, safety, efficiency, and agility • Rapid ability to respond to natural and other disasters

Source: [7]

This is the era of proliferation of technology where most laborious and herculean works are carried out in a matter of seconds with the help of embedded system. This involves the inbuilt of tiny devices called microprocessors which leads to the increase in smartness and intelligence of automated devices in agriculture, transportation, health sectors and others. Healthcare is one of the areas where advancements in technology remain inestimable through the introduction of embedded systems and CPS. The use of technical equipment such as SMDs is increasing exponentially every year. This extensive use of technology puts large demands on the operators' capabilities to handle the equipment in a proper

way. However, this is not true in most cases. There appears to be a number of research issues militating against its successful implementations as outlined below: lack of patient safety measures make medical care unsafe and produce opportunities for medical errors to occur [8] also justified by [9] who stated that 2,000,000 defective devices were recalled in the last decades due to deficiency in outputs. The process of safety began in 1999 with Harvard Medical Practice study that showed adverse events in 3.7% of hospitalization and errors which could be related to 27.6% of adverse events [10]. In 2001, the Institute of Medicine published a study tagged 'to err is human: building a safer health system' [11]. This study estimated that preventable medical errors are responsible for between 44, 000 and 98, 000 deaths annually in United States.

Subsequently, in 2010, the Office of Inspector General for Health and Human Services in Nigeria admitted that bad hospital care contributed to the deaths of 180,000 patients in Medical care alone in a given year. A more heart touching news from the Journal of Patient Safety reports that the numbers may be much higher which was put between 210,000 and 440,000 annually for patients who visit the hospital [12]. Such patients are likely to suffer some type of preventable harm that contributes to their death [12].

However, it is good to mention that this research paper is aimed at proposing a framework to achieve safety and error free in the use of SMDs, paper layout.

The rest of the paper is organized as follows: apart from the introduction section, the next section deals with literature review, methodology of the research paper, results, discussions and conclusion.

2. Literature Review

2.1. Expert System for Reducing Medical Errors

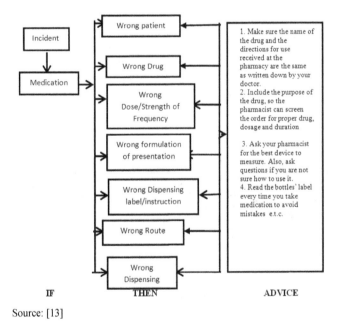

Source: [13]

Figure 1. Expert System for reducing Medical Errors.

The research work carried out by [13] proposed a framework for computer-based medical errors diagnoses of primary systems deficiencies as presented in Fig. 1. Results of this research assisted in developing the hierarchical structure of the medical errors expert system which was written and compiled in CLIPS with numbers of rules. Despite efforts put in place to check users input for consistency within the given limits, it was discovered that error can still be transmitted unknowingly. Medical personnel may lack the knowledge of the right use of the device which are likely to result into error. This is illustrated in Fig. 1

2.2. Safety Requirements of Infusion Pump-An Example of SMD

In an attempt to ensure safety in infusion pump [14] defines infusion pump as medical devices used to deliver drugs to patients at precise rates and in specific amounts. The authors proposed a Generic Infusion Pump (GIP) model project in an effort to enhance security in the use of infusion pumps. The process of building these formal models started with requirements and hazard analysis which contains the informal requirements and hazard analysis used to create a generic pump model. Their work majors on using models and properties to generate tests which can be used for conformance testing of infusion pump implementations. However, it appears that there are limitation with this method because infusion pump safety was not totally solved and this create a gap in knowledge for other research works.

To further strengthens the trust in the use of infusion pumps, [15] discovered that a combination of faults including software errors, mechanical failures and human error can lead to catastrophic situations; causing death or serious harm to the patient. Dependability analysis techniques such as failure mode effect analysis (FMEA) can be used to predict the worst case outcomes of such faults and facilitate the development of remedies against them. The research work of [15] presented the use of model-checking to automate the dependability analysis of programmable, real-time medical devices.

The challenges faced by medical device manufacturers in bringing safe, reliable, low overall life-cycle cost products to market in a timely manner is increasing rapidly as proposed by [16]. The increasing complexity and criticality of medical devices and the increasing number of safety recalls is driving the need for a good design for reliability (DFR) program in the medical industry. However, theoretical knowledge of a good DFR is not enough.

2.3. Error Analysis in Anesthesia

Analysis of error in anesthesia was carried out by [17]. Their outcome stated that human factors constituted the highest degree of anesthesia errors of about 82% which were known to be preventable, such errors include breathing-circuit disconnections, inadvertent changes in gas flow, and drug syringe errors being frequent problems while only 14% were caused by equipment failure which include inadequate experience, insufficient familiarity with equipment, inadequate communication among medical staff, lack of precaution and distraction. The authors employed modified critical-incident analysis technique. Their research output is commendable though this direction differs from the existing research paper.

Furthermore, [18] investigated the causes of surgical errors using secondary data obtained from four hospitals. They discovered that System factors contributed to major errors of about 82% which include inexperience. While technical errors constituted 54%. They concluded that closed claims analysis can help to identify priority areas for intervening to reduce errors.

In addition, the research carried out by [19] discovered that major factors constitute adverse reporting errors in anesthesia.

3. Methodology

A critical incident analysis approach was adopted to look into the use of the SMDs because of the sensitivity of the devices. Secondary input data was retrieved from an online database of Medline, Web of Science, Health Technology Assessments and Health and Science Care Information Center which provides database of readings from medical experts. The SMDs analysed in this research paper include thermometer, sphygmomanometer, infusion pump and insulin pump. These SMDs were chosen because of their relevance in the implementation of CPS as regards technological advancement to health care systems. These readings were further compared with the standard world benchmarks. The readings also served as input to the framework for error prediction. Due to the complexity of the problem, an algorithm was further developed to obtain an optimal solution of P_1 to P_5 within an acceptable threshold runtime which shows the effects of the problem on patients.

3.1. Thermometer for Both Benchmark and Readings

The following represent the analysis of digital thermometer:

Table 2. Temperature readings and standard benchmark (^0C) Source : Appendix A-C.

Symptoms	Benchmark (P)	Time(t)	Readings P(t)	Error(t)
Malaria	37.9	0	37.9	0
	38.5	10	36.0	2.5
	38.7	20	36.1	2.6
	38.9	30	36.2	2.7
	39.5	40	36.3	3.2
	39.6	50	36.3	3.3
URTI	37.7	0	37.7	0
	38.5	10	37.7	0.8
	39.0	20	37.8	1.2
	39.5	30	37.9	1.6
	39.8	40	38.0	1.8
	40.0	50	38.0	2.0
Tonsilitis	36.4	0	36.4	0
	37.8	10	36.5	0.4
	39.2	20	37.0	2.2
	39.9	30	37.6	2.3
	40.0	40	38.0	2.0
	40.5	50	38.5	2.0
Severe Head Injury	39.8	0	39.8	0
	39.9	10	39.8	0.1
	40.5	20	39.9	0.6
	43.5	30	40.0	3.5
	45.5	40	40.0	5.5
	47.5	50	40.1	7.4
Septicaemia	39.9	0	39.9	0
	40.0	10	39.0	1.0
	45.3	20	39.5	5.8
	47.3	30	39.9	7.4
	47.8	40	40.0	7.8
	48.0	50	40.0	8.0

Where URTI= upper respiratory tract infection.

Table 3. Sphygmomanometer readings and standard Benchmark (mmhg) Appendix D.

Systolic	Diastolic				
	BM/RD/error	BM/RD/error	BM/RD/error	BM/RD/error	BM/RD/error
	≤84	85-89	90-99	100-109	110-119
≤129	2 1 1	3 2 1	4 3 1	5 4 1	6 5 1
<130-139	2 2 0	3 2 1	4 3 1	5 4 1	6 5 1
<140-159	3 3 0	3 3 0	4 3 1	5 4 1	6 5 1
<160-179	5 4 1	5 4 1	4 3 1	5 4 1	6 5 1
<180-209	5 5 0	5 5 0	5 4 1	6 5 1	6 5 1
≥210	7 6 1	6 6 0	5 4 1	7 6 1	7 6 1

Where N=161, BM= benchmark and RD= readings

3.2. Infusion Pump for Both Benchmark and Readings

Table 4. Infusion Pump readings and standard Benchmark (msl/hr.) Source: [20].

Benchmark	Readings	Error	Time (Mins)
Adult -100mls/hr	80mls/hr	10	60
500mls/hr	480mls/hr	20	60
500mls/hr	490mls/hr	10	60
4 litres/day	4litres/day	0	1,440
500mls/12rs	480mls/12rs	20	720
500mls/day	495mls/day	5	1,440
Children 300mls/day	280mls/day	20	1,440
10mls/hr	10mls/hr	0	60
1 liter/day	1 litre/day	0	1,440
2 litres/day	2 litres/day	0	1,440

3.3. Insulin Pump for Both Benchmark and Readings

Table 5. Insulin Pump readings and standard Benchmark.

Time	Benchmark Blood Glucose	Amount of Carbohydrates	Benchmark Insulin intake	Readings Insulin intake	Errors
Day 1					
7:30am	5.7	60g	4	8	4
1:30pm	11.2	50g	3.3	6.6	3.3
6:00pm	7.2	72g	5	10	5
10:00pm	8				
Day 2					
7:30am	6.8	60g	4	8	4
1:30pm	12.3	50g	3.3	6.6	3.3
6:00pm	7.1	90g	6	12	6
10:00pm	11.3				

1 unit of insulin for every 15g Carbohydrates taken. Insulin Pump Workbook. Source: [21].

3.4. Algorithm Development

Relationship between Model and Thermometer table

Performance at optimum level is represented in Table 3.1 as the Benchmark of temperature taken when error is not involved (P) which is equivalent to 100%.

Performance with respect to time is represented in Table 3.1 taking note of the time in minutes when temperatures were taken P (t). The recorded time were decimated to reduce the magnitudes of error such as 0.1, 0.2, 0.3 and so on for Malaria. These values are not constant for other ailments.

Error as shown in Table 3.1 gives the difference between benchmark and actual readings which was also decimated to reduce error value thereby realizing (E) of Malaria to be 0.25, 0.26, 0.27, 0.32 and 0.33

P^1 = the change in performance over the change in time of measurement

P1-P5 is the performance level of the SMDs and the model with respect to the introduced error.

P= Performance at optimum level

$P(t)$= Performance with respect to t

$E(t)$= Error introduced at any time t

$$P(t)=P-E(t) \qquad (3.4.1)$$

Equation 3.4.1 gives the difference between the benchmark and the actual reading which is a function of time.

$$P^1(t) \propto E(t)P(t)$$

P^1 (t) is the change in performance which is proportional to the product of performance and the error at any time t

$$P^1(t)=-KE(t)P(t)$$

$$P^1(t)=-E(t)P(t)$$

Substituting $P(t)$ in (3.4.1) gives

$$P^1(t)=-E(t)[P-E(t)] \qquad (3.4.2)$$

$$P_{n+1}=P_n+h(P^1)_n \qquad (3.4.3)$$

(Euler's representation)
Declarations
Step 1: Initialize fractional variables (double) h, t, E

Step 2: Initialize whole numbers (Int) P, n

Step 3: let all values of n be between 0 to 4

Step 4: Let E0=0.25, E1=0.26, E2=0.27, E3=0.32 and E4=1.85

Step 5: Let 0.1 be stored in t as fractional number

Step 6: Let 1 be stored in P as whole number

Step 7: Let 0.1 be stored in h as fractional number

Starting the Euler's iterations

Step 8: making reference to step (4) substituting it in equation (3.4.2) where $(P^1)_0 = -E_0(t)[P-E_0(t)]$ Find $(P^1)_0$ to $(P^1)_4$

Step 9: starting iteration where the values of n= 0 to 4 starting with n=0 to begin

$P_1=P_0+h(P^1)_0$ store the result in P_1

Step 10: Use the value obtained above in step 8 on $(P^1)_1$ to find $P_2=P_1+h(P^1)_1$ and store the result in P_2

Step 11: Use the value obtained above in step 8 on $(P^1)_2$ to find $P_3=P_2+h(P^1)_2$ and store the result in P_3

Step 12: Use the value obtained above in step 8 on $(P^1)_3$ to find $P_4=P_3+h(P^1)_3$ and store the result in P_4

Step 13: Use the value obtained above in step 8 on $(P^1)_4$ to find $P_5=P_4+h(P^1)_4$ and store the value in P_5

Step 14: Display the values of P_1, P_2, P_3, P_4, P_5

4. Results and Discussions

4.1. Algorithm Interpretation

If the figures of E0=0.25, E1=0.26, E2=0.27, E3=0.32 and E4=1.85 are appropriately slotted into the equation as the indicated errors from the algorithm, also if $(P^1)_0$ to $(P^1)_4$ are adequately calculated. Then P1to P5 will be given as 99.8%, 99.5%, 99,2%, 98.9% and 98.6% accuracy in measurements. These values indicated that P1 to p5 refers to percentage analysis of the performance of the predicted error, the higher the error, the lower the performance of the SMDs which will have adverse effects on patients who are meant to have maximum performance without errors.

4.2. Framework

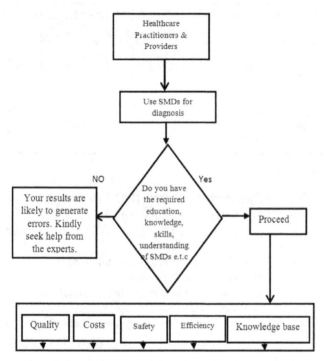

Figure 2. *Proposed Framework for Safety and Verification of SMDs.*

Tables 2-5 has shown clearly that there is the possibility of committing errors when the SMDs are used inappropriately. However, in an attempt to resolve these errors, we developed a framework in Fig. 2 which consists of the usage and administration of SMDs with respect to the embedded systems and CPS. It may also be referred to as a window that predicts the existence of error in the use of SMDs. Such errors and its effects might prevent individual users from committing errors by either having the right educational experience to guide them, read prescription extensively or meet others for more understanding in case of doubt.

The framework consists of healthcare practitioners or providers that are willing and ready to take care of patients with the advancement of healthcare innovations such as embedded systems and CPS. If these innovations were adequately understood with adequate knowledge of SMDs, it will affect the patients positively in diagnosis. This will improve the quality of treatment, reduce the cost of further treatments, increase safety, improve efficiency and provide knowledge base for future diagnosis. However, if the healthcare providers flout these principles, there is likelihood that error may be generated in the result. Therefore, the medical personnels are expected to seek help through sufficient and updated training in the use of the SMDs.

5. Conclusion

Conclusively, it has been discussed that CPS is a growing area of research with an evolving number of application domains in particular health care systems. This research paper has predicted with the aid of algorithm and framework the possibility that error can occur if SMDs are used inappropriately. This effects can prolong the stay of patients in hospital, prolong their healing time or even cause permanent damage.

Acknowledgement

I will like to appreciate Mr. Semiu Ayinde of the department of Basic Sciences, Babcock University, the Head of Department of Radiology, Babcock University Teaching Hospital (BUTH) Dr. Yusuf, Adebola and one of his vibrant staff, Dr. Ajiboye, Bimpe who contributed immensely to the completion of this research paper.

Appendix A: Temperature Measurement

Fever in adults
If you or a family member has a fever, it means your body temperature is above normal.

Around 37°C is normal
A digital thermometer is the best type to use to get an accurate temperature reading.

A fever is usually a normal response of your immune system to a virus or bacterial infection. Most healthy adults can tolerate a fever well.

Fever ranges and symptoms
38–38.9°C – mild fever
With a mild fever you might have flushed cheeks, feel a little lethargic, and be warm to touch. You will generally be able to carry out normal daily activities.

39–39.9°C – high fever
With a high fever you may not feel well enough to go to work, you may have aches and pains, and you'll feel hot to touch.

40°C or higher – very high fever
With a very high fever you will usually want to stay in bed or be inactive – you won't feel well enough to carry out normal activities. You may have lost your appetite. You'll feel hot to touch.

When to see your doctor
Some mild diseases produce very high fevers – and severe illnesses can produce mild fever. Therefore, when considering what medical attention you need, it's important to look at other symptoms and how unwell you feel.

You should see your doctor if you or a family member:
- has a very high fever (over 40°C)
- is still feverish after three days of home treatment, or seems to be getting sicker
- is shivering or shaking uncontrollably, or has chattering teeth
- has a severe headache that doesn't get better after taking painkillers

Appendix A
- is having trouble breathing
- is getting confused or is unusually drowsy

- has recently travelled overseas.

When it's urgent

See your doctor or go to the Emergency Department immediately if you notice the following symptoms (along with a fever):

- Hallucinations
- Vomiting
- A stiff neck (they're unable to put their chin on their chest or have pain when moving their neck forward)
- A skin rash
- A rapid heart rate.

Also get medical help if the person has a seizure (fit), or has signs of a seizure about to happen, such as regular twitching or jerking.

Call Healthline 0800 611 116 if you are unsure what you should do.

Fever in pregnancy

If you're pregnant and have a temperature of 38.5°C – or any fever lasting for three days or more – you must see your lead maternity carer. They'll need to monitor the effects of the fever on your baby.

Self care

Most fevers last only three to four days – and a mild fever may not need any treatment at all.

Try these ideas if your fever is mild and you don't have any other worrying symptoms:

- Drink plenty of fluids – water is best.
- Get plenty of rest.
- Wear light weight clothes and use lighter bedding. Keep the room temperature normal.
- Put cool cloths on your face, arms and neck to help you cool down. Don't use any rapid cooling methods that may make you shiver. (The muscle movement in shivering will actually raise your temperature and can make your fever worse.)

Appendix B: Temperature Measurement

Fever and Night Sweats

Fever is a common sign that on its own is usually little help in making a diagnosis. Persistent high fever needs urgent treatment. Fever over 42.2°C (108°F) producesunconsciousness and leads to permanent brain damage if sustained. Fever can be classified as:

- Low: 37.2-38°C (99°-100.4°F).
- Moderate: 38.1-40°C (100.5°-104°F).
- High: >40°C (104°F).

Fever may also be described as:

- Remitting - the most common type with daily temperatures fluctuating above the normal range.
- Intermittent - daily temperature drops into the normal range and then rises back above normal. If temperature fluctuates widely causing chills and sweating, it is called a hectic fever.
- Sustained - persistent raised temperature with little fluctuation.
- Relapsing - alternating feverish and a febrile periods.

- Undulant - gradual increase in temperature, which stays high for a few days then gradually reduces.

Fever may also be described in terms of its duration; brief (<3 weeks), or prolonged. The term pyrexia of unknown origin (PUO) is used to describe a condition where no underlying cause can be found.[1] Night sweats are common and there is a long list of possible causes, mostly benign but important to diagnose in order to manage effectively. Serious causes of night sweats can usually be excluded by a thorough history, examination and simple investigations if required.[2]

Appendix C: Body Temperature

What is body temperature?

Body temperature is a measure of the body's ability to generate and get rid of heat. The body is very good at keeping its temperature within a narrow, safe range in spite of large variations in temperatures outside the body.

When you are too hot, the blood vessels in your skin expand (dilate) to carry the excess heat to your skin's surface. You may begin to sweat, and as the sweat evaporates, it helps cool your body. When you are too cold, your blood vessels narrow (contract) so that blood flow to your skin is reduced to conserve body heat. You may start shivering, which is an involuntary, rapid contraction of the muscles. This extra muscle activity helps generate more heat. Under normal conditions, this keeps your body temperature within a narrow, safe range.

Where is body temperature measured?

Your body temperature can be measured in many locations on your body. The mouth, ear, armpit, and rectum are the most commonly used places. Temperature can also be measured on your forehead.

What are Fahrenheit and Celsius?

Thermometers are calibrated in either degrees Fahrenheit (°F) or degrees Celsius (°C), depending on the custom of the region. Temperatures in the United States are often measured in degrees Fahrenheit, but the standard in most other countries is degrees Celsius.

What is normal body temperature?

Most people think of a "normal" body temperature as an oral temperature of 98.6°F (37°C). This is an average of normal body temperatures. Your temperature may actually be 1°F (0.6°C) or more above or below 98.6°F (37°C). Also, your normal body temperature changes by as much as 1°F (0.6°C) throughout the day, depending on how active you are and the time of day. Body temperature is very sensitive to hormone levels and may be higher or lower when a woman is ovulating or having her menstrual period.

Appendix D: Blood Pressure Chart

Use the blood pressure chart below to see what your blood pressure means. The blood pressure chart is suitable for adults of any age. (The level for high blood pressure does not change with age.)

Blood pressure readings have two numbers, for example

140/90mmHg. The top number is your systolic blood pressure. (The highest pressure when your heart beats and pushes the blood round your body.) The bottom one is your diastolicblood pressure. (The lowest pressure when your heart relaxes between beats.)

The blood pressure chart below shows ranges of high, low and healthy blood pressure readings.

Blood pressure chart for adults

Using this blood pressure chart: To work out what your blood pressure readings mean, just find your top number (systolic) on the left side of the blood pressure chart and read across, and your bottom number (diastolic) on the bottom of the blood pressure chart. Where the two meet is your blood pressure.

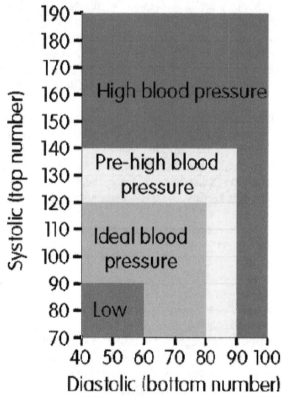

Appendix D Cont'd

What blood pressure readings mean

As you can see from the blood pressure chart,only one of the numbers has to be higher or lower than it should be to count as either high blood pressure or low blood pressure:

- 90 over 60 (90/60) or less: You may have low blood pressure. More on low blood pressure.
- More than 90 over 60 (90/60) and less than 120 over 80 (120/80): Your blood pressure reading is ideal and healthy. Follow a healthy lifestyle to keep it at this level.
- More than 120 over 80 and less than 140 over 90 (120/80-140/90): You have a normal blood pressure reading but it is a little higher than it should be, and you should try to lower it. Make healthy changes to your lifestyle.
- 140 over 90 (140/90) or higher (over a number of weeks): You may have high blood pressure (hypertension).Change your lifestyle - see your doctor

or nurse and take any medicines they may give you. More on high blood pressure

So:

- if your top number is 140 or more - then you may have high blood pressure, regardless of your bottom number.
- if your bottom number is 90 or more - then you may have high blood pressure, regardless your top number.
- if your top number is 90 or less - then you may have low blood pressure, regardless of your bottom number.
- if your bottom number is 60 or less - then you may have low blood pressure, regardless of your top number.

References

[1] M. Weiser, "Ubiquitous computing" http://www.ubiq.com/hypertext/weiser/UbiHome.html., 2003

[2] U. Hansmann, "Design Personal Computer real- time and embedded systems Wireless". Springer- Verlag New York, Inc., New York, 2001.

[3] J. Burkhardt, "Pervasive Computing: Technology and Architecture of Mobile Internet Application" Addison-Wesley Longman Publishing Co., Inc. Boston, MA, USA, 2001.

[4] P. E. N.V. Koninklijke, Ambient intelligence. http://www.research.philips.com/technologies/projects/ambint el.html., 2003

[5] S. Marzano, and E. Aarts, The New Every day. 010 Publishers, 2003.

[6] E. A. Lee. "Cyber physical systems: design challenges" Technical report, EECS Department, University of California, Berkeley, January (CPS Steering Group), 2008.

[7] Workshop Report. Foundations for Innovation in Cyber-Physical Systems. http://events.energetics.com/NIST- CPS Workshop/downloads.html

[8] D.C. Stockwell, & A. D. Slonim. Quality and safety in the Intensive Care Unit. J Intensive Care Med 2006 Jul; 21(4):199-210.

[9] M. Paolo. Formal verification of Medical user interface software in PVS, Queen Mary University of London, 2014.

[10] NAP Committee on Quality of Health Care in America IoM. 'To err is human: building a Safer Health System'. Washington, D.C.: National Academy Press, 2001

[11] M. Soares, J.I.F, Salluh,., F.A. & Bozza, Current definitions of patient safety. In: Chiche, J. D, Moreno R, Putensen C, Rhodes A, editors. Patient Safety and Quality of Care in Intensive Care Medicine. Berlin: Medizinisch Wissenschaftliche Verlagsgesellschaft; p. 9-17. 2009.

[12] T. J., John, A New Evidence-based Estimate of Patient Harms Associated with Hospital Care Journal of Patient Safety Volume 9, Number 3. 2013

[13] R. Mohamed, and A. Khalid "Development of an expert system for Reducing medical errors" International Journal of Software Engineering & Applications (IJSEA), Vol.4, No.6, November 2013 DOI : 0.5121/ijsea.2013.460329

[14] R. J. Arney, J. Paul, L. Insup, R. Arnab, S., Oleg, and Z., Yi, Generic Infusion Pump Hazard Analysis and Safety Requirements Version 1.0, 2009

[15] S. Sriram, H., Hadjar, and L., Clayton. Model- Based Dependability Analysis of Programmable Drug Infusion Pumps University of Colorado, Boulder, CO, 2011.

[16] H. Vaishali, R., Philips, and R. Dev. Design for Reliability in Medical Devices Patient System Safety 978-1-4244-5103-6/10/$26.00 ©2010 IEEE, 2010

[17] B. C. Jeffrey, S. N., Ronald, D.L., Charlene, and M., Bucknam, Preventable anesthesia mishaps: a study of human factors. Qual Saf Health Care 2002;11:277–283 https://www.bu.edu/av/courses/med/05sprgmedanes thesiology/002/cooper%20study.pdf,

[18] O. R. Selwyn, M. K. Gawande, P. Ann Louise, Y. Catherine, A.B. Troyen, and M.C. David, Analysis of surgical errors in closed malpractice claims at 4 liability insurers. Harvard Risk Management Foundation and the Harvard School of Public Health, 2006

[19] C. H. Gaylene, M. H. Fanzca, M.S. Penelope, D.T. and T. Rowan. Barriers to Adverse Event and Error Reporting in Anesthesia. International Anesthesia Research Society, 2012 http://citeseerx.ist.psu.edu/viewdoc/download? doi=10.1.1.380.1686&rep=rep1&type=pdf

[20] FDA. Infusion Pump Improvement Initiative Center for Devices and Radiological Health U.S. Food and Drug Administration 2010.

[21] E. Joan, and L. Helen "Insulin Pump Workbook" (n.d) 5 www.diabetes-education.net/pdf/resources/insulin_pump_workbook.pdf.

8

An Improved Genetic Algorithm-Based Test Coverage Analysis for Graphical User Interface Software

Asade Mojeed Adeniyi, Akinola Solomon Olalekan

Department of Computer Science, University of Ibadan, Ibadan, Nigeria

Email address:

princedeniyiasade@hotmail.com (M. A. Asade), akinola.olalekan@dlc.ui.edu.ng (S. O. Akinola)

Abstract: Quality and reliability of software products can be determined through the amount of testing that is carried out on them. One of the metrics that are often employed in measuring the amount of testing is the coverage analysis or adequacy ratio. In the proposed optimized basic Genetic Algorithm (GA) approach, a concept of adaptive mutation was introduced into the basic GA in order for low-fitness chromosomes to have an increased probability of mutation, thereby enhancing their role in the search to produce more efficient search. The main purpose of this concept is to decrease the chance of disrupting a high-fitness chromosome and to have the best exploitation of the exploratory role of low-fitness chromosome. The study reveals that the optimized basic GA improves significantly the adequacy ratio or coverage analysis value for Graphical User Interface (GUI) software test over the existing non-adaptive mutation basic GA.

Keywords: Software Test Coverage Analysis, Graphical User Interface, Quality Software, Genetic Algorithm

1. Introduction

Graphical User Interface (GUI) is a means of interaction between an end user and a software system. Software systems have gained an unprecedented popularity for so long and the biggest factor behind this success is Graphical user interface. Software developing companies and developers have always shown a desire for fully assured high quality software. In order to ensure this desire is fulfilled, software must go through a comprehensive testing. It seems almost impossible to test GUI application manually because of the involved complexity thereby creating the need for test data automation [1].

The quality of software products is of paramount importance to users. According to Pfleeger [2], quality software is *"Software that satisfies the needs of the users and the programmers involved in it"*. Technological advancements have been responsible for the complex nature of computer and in particular the software that drives it. Based on this, the correctness of the software is of high importance which cannot even be guaranteed by the developer that designs the software.

Chayanika *et al.*, [3] assert that the main purpose of software industry is to ensure that the software delivered to the end users is of high standard. Testing of software therefore cannot be overemphasized as this plays a major role in deciding the quality and reliability of the delivered software as well as ensuring the software meets the users' requirements.

Our everyday life dependence on computer; be it mobile, home appliances or office has rather placed an importance on software testing since we cannot afford to let the system fail us. Glenford [4] views testing as a process, or a series of processes, designed to make sure computer code does what it was designed to do and that it does not do anything unintended. Software should be predictable and consistent, offering no surprises to users. Software testing is more properly viewed as the destructive process of trying to find the errors (whose presence is assumed) in software. Glenford [4] opined further that a successful test case is one that furthers progress in this direction by causing the software to fail.

In reality, planning for software testing should begin with the early stages of the software requirements process, and test plans and procedures should be systematically and continuously developed (which could possibly be refined) as software development proceeds [5]. This is so because the test planning and designing activities serve as a clue to software designers/developers by assisting to highlight likely weaknesses, such as conflicts or oversights /contradictions, or ambiguities in the [5].

Coverage analysis can simply be defined as a measure of test case completeness. It can further be inferred as a means of determining how much test needs to be conducted in order to ascertain the quality of the developed software. Test coverage analysis can be done in order to determine test effectiveness, test suit improvement and software reliability estimation. Coverage is the extent to which a structure has been exercised as a percentage of the items being covered [6]. According to Muhammad *et al.* [6], test coverage is regarded as a key indicator of software quality and a crucial part of software maintenance which assists in carrying out the efficacy of testing through the provision of data on diverse coverage items. Test coverage is an indicator that gives insight to the test generators to focus on creating test cases that cover the areas that have not been tested.

Genetic Algorithms (GAs) have been applied to a broad range of searching, optimization, and machine learning problems. GAs are iterative procedures implemented as a computerized search and optimization procedure that uses principles of natural selection. It performs a multi- directional search by maintaining a population of potential solutions (called individuals) and exchange information between these solutions through simulated evolution and forward relatively "good" information over generations until it finds a near optimal solution for specific problem [7]. More often than not, GA's converge rapidly to quality solutions. Although they do not guarantee convergence to the single best solution to the problem, the processing power associated with GA's makes them efficient search techniques [8].

There have been a number of studies that employ genetic algorithms for software testing. In this study, a concept of adaptive mutation was introduced into the basic genetic algorithm in order for low-fitness chromosomes to have an increased probability of mutation, thereby enhancing their role in the search to produce more efficient search. Section 2 of this paper highlights some related works while Section 3 gives the methodology for the study. In Section 4, results are presented and discussed and conclusion is drawn in Section 5.

2. Related Works

Memon, [9] in his PhD research focused on developing a testing framework for Graphical User interface (GUI) which covers the areas of testing environments, test coverage criteria development, test case generation, test oracles and regression testing. Research at that time on GUI was still at its infancy. So he had to adapt techniques from general software testing for GUI testing. The GUIs are differentiated from the traditional software with some characteristics like user events for input and graphical output and thus require different testing techniques.

Capture /Replay is a popular method that is being used for GUI software testing. One merit offered by this method is that it is able to determine test cases that are usable and unusable in a situation that the states of the GUI is modified, and furthermore determines which of the unusable test cases can be repaired and make it usable for the modified graphical user interface. This attribute made it usable for regression testing [10]. The observed laps with the Capture / Replay method is that it does not provide functionality to evaluate the coverage of a test suite mainly because it does not have a global view of the GUI.

Misurda, *et al.*, [11] described a demand-driven framework for program testing having scalability and flexibility features. It makes use of test paths for the implementation of test coverage. This framework also has a means of ensuring performance and memory overheads are kept low through the use of dynamic instrumentation on the binary code which can be inserted and removed as at when required.

Matteo *et al.*, [12] in their own work proposed a framework called Covertures which is a virtualized execution platform meant for cross-compiled application on the host. This framework has the ability to carry out measurement of structural coverage of both object and source code without application instrumentation.

Sakamoto *et al.*, [13] proposed a framework for consistent and flexible measurement of test coverage. This framework has support for multiple programming languages and also provides guidelines for the support of several test coverage criteria. The flexibility attribute of this framework is that it allows for the inclusion of user defined test coverage and new programming language. This framework is called Open Code Coverage Framework (OCCF).

Even though, models are costly to create and have a limited applicability, approaches based on modeling have been employed often in carrying out testing of software. In view of this fact, model based approaches are not being employed frequently for testing GUI software [14].

A Genetic Algorithm (GA) can be defined as a problem-solving approach that is developed as a programming technique by imitating the theory of natural evolution of species as proposed by Charles Darwin. In solving a specific problem using the genetic algorithm concept, it begins with a set of individuals (solution candidates) that forms a population which is generated in a random way. The genetic algorithm now selects parents from which to generate offspring by using reproductive operators that are analogous to biological processes mainly crossover and mutation [15]. The resulting chromosomes are then evaluated using a fitness function in order to determine how strong they are, the fitness values are then employed in taking a decision on which chromosome to be eliminated or retained [15].

In order to generate a new set of solution candidates (new population), the chromosomes having a high fitness value are retained while those that are not fit are discarded. Afterwards, a check is carried out to determine an individual in the population that connects the same two points as the newly generated individual. If not exist, new individual is added to the population and if yes, the old individual is replaced by the new one if its fit value is higher. These variation and selection steps are repeated until a termination condition is met [16].

A genetic algorithm is especially appropriate to the solution of indefinite problems or non-linear complex problems [17]. Jones et al. [18, 19] proposed a technique to generate test-data for branch coverage using genetic algorithm. The technique revealed good results with number of small programs. Though Control Flow Graph (CFG) was employed in guiding the search; they based the fitness value on branch value and branching condition. In another study by Michael et al. [20], a tool for generating test data was developed using four different algorithms, two of which are genetic algorithm. This tool is called Gadget. With Gadget, they were able to obtain good condition / decision coverage of C/ C++ code.

Pargas et al. [21] also made use of genetic algorithm using the Control Dependence Graph (CDG) to search for test data that will give good coverage. They did a comparison of their system with random testing using six C programs of varying sizes. The outcome of their experiment revealed no difference with the smallest programs but the genetic algorithm based method gave a better performance for the three largest programs.

Shunkun et al, [22] capitalized on the pitfalls in the traditional Ant Colony Optimization algorithm for test cases generation in software testing engineering. Some of the flaws are relative scarcity of early search pheromone, low search efficacy and simplicity of the search model. They came up with three improved Ant colony algorithm which are now integrated to form A Comprehensive Improved Ant Colony Optimization (ACIACO), and they were able to generate higher coverage results.

Abdul Rauf et al., [14] proposed a system for GUI testing and coverage analysis based on traditional genetic algorithm. Their method is subdivided into three major blocks; Test data generation, path coverage analysis and optimization of test paths. The proposed system made use of traditional genetic algorithm for the optimization of test paths.

The present study considers an improvement over the GUI testing coverage analysis by Abdul Rauf et al., [14]. They made use of the basic Genetic Algorithm to optimize the test paths, but here, we modify the basic Genetic Algorithm to optimize the test paths with the hope of achieving a higher coverage analysis than what they obtained.

3. Research Methodology

3.1. Experimental Approach

A GUI is a hierarchical, graphical front-end to a software system that accepts as input user-generated and system-generated events from a fixed set of events and produces deterministic graphical output. A GUI contains graphical objects; each object has a fixed set of properties [14].

To test GUI and analyse the coverage, the proposed methodology was divided into three major blocks listed below as earlier suggested by Abdul Rauf et al., [14].

　i. Test data generation.
　ii. Path Coverage Analysis.
　iii.Optimization of Test Paths.

The test data generation is a set of events that were generated from the application that was used for the experiment. This was generated manually by carrying out several test cases on the application to be used for the GUI test while keeping the event identities (ids) being generated in a text file. These event ids were then arranged to determine the path coverage analysis, which is the second block in the methodology being employed.

This study employed the event flow graph (EFG) technique of the GUI test. A User defined calculator was built in C# programming language. This user defined calculator had an in-built instrumentation code that logs parameters like the event_id (widget id), button_name etc. as the application is being interacted with. Another application used in testing our methodology was a user defined Notepad that was developed with Java programming language. It also had an in-built instrumentation code that logs parameters like the event_id (widget id), button_name etc. as the application is being interacted with. Thereafter, we extended our testing to Microsoft (MS) Notepad application.

3.2. Fitness Function Evaluation

Given an input to a program, the fitness function returns a number that indicates the acceptability of the program. The selection algorithm uses the fitness function to determine which variants survive to the next iteration, and this is employed as a termination criterion for the search. In this work, our fitness function was based on how much test cases were successfully validated in line with Abdul et al., [14].

Fitness function is hereby defined as Test paths covered by chromosome divided by the total number of test paths i.e.

$$\text{Fitness} = \frac{\text{Test paths covered by chromosome}}{\text{Total number of test paths}} \text{ (Abdul et al., [14]).}$$

3.3. The Modified Reproduction Operation

There are basically two reproduction operators in genetic algorithm: Crossover and Mutation. In this work, the reproduction operators were employed in order to increase the coverage efficiency. However, this work is capitalizing on the pitfalls of the basic genetic algorithm in the area of reproduction operator known as Mutation. In the basic genetic algorithm, there is equal application of mutation operator which can as well be referred to as total randomness of mutation irrespective of their fitness. The implication of this action is that a very good chromosome (chromosome of high fitness) is equally likely to be disrupted by mutation as a bad one. Though we know that bad chromosome are less likely to produce good ones through crossover due to their lack of building blocks.

After the crossover operation has been performed we

introduced the evaluation of the mean fitness of the chromosome; thereafter making a comparison of each chromosome to the mean fitness value. The chromosomes having fitness greater than or equal to the mean fitness were made to join the new population without passing through mutation exercise while those with fitness value below the mean fitness value were made to pass through the mutation

exercise so that they can benefit most from the operation. This process continues until the termination criterion is met and the whole process comes to a halt and the result is displayed. Figure 1 shows the design and execution flow of basic GA [8]; while figure 2 shows the proposed modified GA Algorithm for optimization of paths.

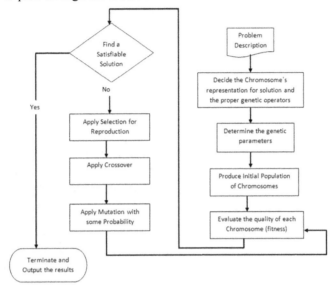

Figure 1. *Basic Genetic Algorithms - Design and Execution Flow (Samarah, 2006).*

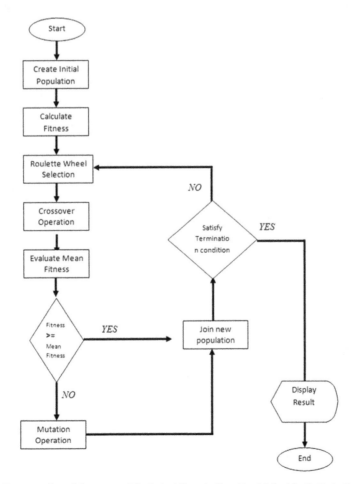

Figure 2. *Execution flow of the proposed Optimized Genetic Algorithm Method for Optimization of Paths.*

Figure 3 represents sample test cases for the calculator that was used to test the project while Figure 4 represents the widgets on the calculator with corresponding labels for each of the widgets. For instance, if we pick (the last entry in Figure 3) 4, 5, 8, 13, 5, 17 it implies 458 divide (13) equals (17).

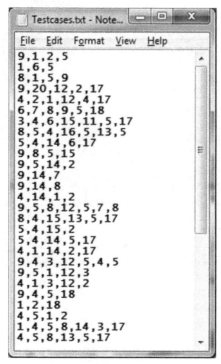

Figure 3. Sample Test Cases for Calculator.

Figure 4. Representations of the Calculator Widgets.

3.4. Formation of Chromosomes

An Actions File was used to denote what each of the paths in the test cases file represents for ease of transformation from numerical value to the widget name. The test case having the longest length determines the length of the chromosomes to be generated. For instance, if the longest test case is having a length 10, then the length of the chromosomes will be 10. From Figure 3, the longest test case is having length 7, if that test case file is used for the experiment, the chromosomes to be formed will be of length 7 i.e. consists of 7 genomes.

3.5. Software Tools

Earlier works in GUI software testing have explored several software packages for the execution of their experiments based on their proposed approaches. Some of the available packages that have been used are GUITAR (Graphical User Interface Testing fRamework) GUI Ripper (This is meant for reverse engineering), PATHS (Planning Assisted Tester for grapHical user interface Systems), C++, Java, C# (C-Sharp) and MATLAB (MATrix LABoratory). Software interfaces to be tested are sometimes written in C++, Java or C-Sharp programming languages. The tool for the optimization of test paths in our proposed approach was developed using the Java Programming Language because of its comprehensive and powerful exploration capabilities.

3.6. Test Data Generation

The use of events to produce data for the testing of GUI software has become a common practice since the software is characterized by states. The technique for the test data generation is based on events. We made use of user-defined calculator, user-defined notepad application and we extended it to an off –the-shelf MS Notepad application. The interface of our Calculator and user defined Notepad is shown in Figures 5 and 6 respectively. As event takes place, the event ids as well as the widget get stored into a notepad from where they will be picked up for further analysis. This approach made the path coverage analysis to be carried out easily.

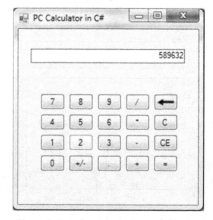

Figure 5. Interface of calculator application.

Figure 7 represents the internal labels that were used to represent each of the calculator widgets within the program for the calculator for ease of logging in order to know the particular calculator button that is pressed.

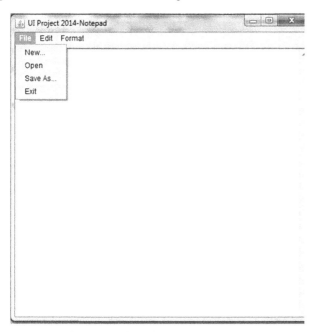

Figure 6. Interface of User Defined Notepad.

+/- button: 3005	**Backspace button:** 1003	**0:**2000	**/:**3004	**1:**2001
CE button: 1000	**2:**2002	**+:**3001	**3:**2003	**-:**3002
*****:**3003	**C button:** 1001	**4:**2004	**=:**3000	**5:**2005
6:2006	**Point button:** 2010	**7:**2007	**8:**2008	**9:**2009

Figure 7. Event ID's of Calculator application.

Path coverage (%) = ((no. of paths Covered) / (total no. of independent paths)) × 100

2009	3004	2003	2009	3003	2003	2005	3001
2008	3002	2003	3000	2007	1001	2005	1000

Figure 8. Sample of Sequence of Generated Events.

Figure 8 is a set of sequence of events generated while using the calculator. The numbers displayed are the internal labels that were used to represent each of the widgets in the calculator. For instance, looking at Figure 7 that displays 2009, 3004, 2003, 2009, it implies the following widgets on the calculator 9, /, 3, 9 were pressed. The formula adopted for calculating the Coverage is as follows:

4. Experimental Results

Table 1 gives a summary of the details of the parameters that were used during experimental run. The initial population was set to 100 while the number of generations ranges between 300 and 500 at a step of 25. The crossover probability was set to 0.88 while the mutation probability was set to 0.03. The termination criteria was used to halt each run of the experiment either when the coverage achieved is 88% or the number of generation reached the set threshold.

Table 1. Parameters Used.

Parameters	Values
Population	100
Number of generations	300-500
Mutation Probability	0.03
Crossover Probability	0.88
Termination criteria	Coverage >88% or Generation = 500

Table 2 shows the results of the coverage achieved for each of the three applications that were used with the Basic Genetic Algorithm as well as the average coverage per generation with generation ranging between 300 and 500 at a step of 25. The highest coverage obtained for Ms-Notepad, User Defined Notepad and User Defined Calculator at 500 generations were 85%, 87.67% and 71.43% respectively which are also in line with what Abdul *et al.*, (2010) obtained using the basic Genetic Algorithm except for calculator that was slightly higher. The average coverage achieved with the basic genetic algorithm after 500 generations was 81.37%.

Table 2. Coverage with respect to number of generations using Basic Genetic Algorithm.

Number of Generations	MS Notepad	User Defined Notepad	Calculator Coverage	Av. Coverage
300	68.00%	73.33%	50.00%	63.78%
325	72.00%	73.33%	57.14%	67.49%
350	76.00%	76.33%	57.14%	69.82%
375	76.00%	76.67%	64.29%	72.32%
400	76.00%	83.33%	64.29%	74.54%
425	76.00%	84.67%	71.43%	77.37%
450	80.00%	86.67%	71.43%	79.37%
475	84.00%	87.67%	71.43%	81.03%
500	85.00%	87.67%	71.43%	81.37%

Table 3. Coverage with respect to number of generations using Optimized Basic Genetic Algorithm.

Number of Generations	MS Notepad	User Defined Notepad	Calculator Coverage	Average Coverage
300	72.00%	80.00%	57.14%	69.71%
325	76.00%	80.00%	57.14%	71.05%
350	84.00%	83.33%	64.29%	77.21%
375	84.00%	86.67%	64.29%	78.32%
400	84.00%	86.67%	64.29%	78.32%
425	84.00%	86.67%	64.29%	78.32%
450	88.00%	88.67%	72.43%	83.03%
475	88.00%	90.00%	72.43%	83.48%
500	92.00%	90.00%	73.43%	85.14%

Table 3 displays the results of the coverage achieved using the Modified Basic Genetic Algorithm on the same data set as the basic genetic algorithm for each of the three applications that were used for the experiment. The same numbers of generations were used and the average coverage achieved was 85.14% at 500 generations starting from 300 at a step of 25. This result shows a significant improvement over that of basic genetic algorithm that gave us an average of 81.37%. However, looking at the obtained coverage for

MS-Notepad application at 500 generations, the obtained coverage of 92% is higher than what the Abdul *et al.*, (2010) obtained with the basic genetic algorithm. This is an indication of better performance with our proposed methodology.

Table 4 highlights a comparison of the average coverage of the basic and the proposed (modified) Gas.

The results obtained for the proposed methodology from our experiment reveals some significant improvements over the results obtained from the benchmarked methodology. The comparisons of both methodologies are shown in Figures 9, 10 and 11 via graphical charts for each application with an average coverage of 81.37% and 85.14% for Basic Genetic Algorithm and Optimized Genetic Algorithm respectively.

Table 4. *Comparison of Basic GA and Optimized GA on Average Test Path Coverage.*

Number of Generations	Basic G. A	Optimized G. A
300	63.78%	69.71%
325	67.49%	71.05%
350	69.82%	77.21%
375	72.32%	78.32%
400	74.54%	78.32%
425	77.37%	78.32%
450	79.37%	83.03%
475	81.03%	83.48%
500	81.37%	85.14%

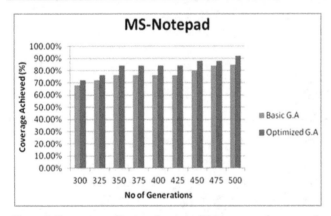

Figure 9. *Comparison of basic and optimized GAs on test path coverage for MS-Notepad.*

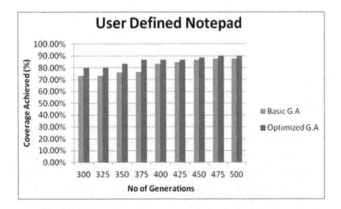

Figure 10. *Comparison of basic and optimized GAs on test path coverage for User-defined Notepad.*

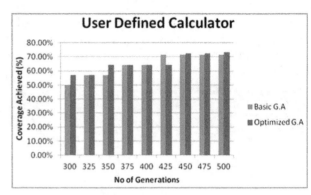

Figure 11. *Comparison of basic and optimized GAs on test path coverage for user-defined Calculator.*

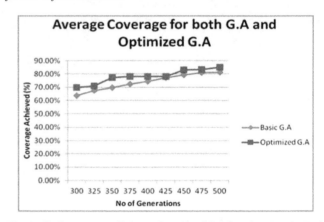

Figure 12. *Comparison of basic and optimized GAs based on Average Path Coverage for all the applications.*

The results reveal that an increase in the number of generations is directly proportional to an increase in percent coverage. The study reveals that the Optimized Basic Genetic Algorithm produces better results than the Basic Genetic Algorithm. The overall average coverage achieved for both methodologies is shown graphically in Figure 12.

The implication of the achieved coverage is that there is still need for more testing to be carried out, which is an indication for the test case generators to focus on the area that have not been tested and generate more test cases from there. By this, we can be rest assured of the quality and reliability of the software to be delivered.

5. Conclusion

From the obtained result in this study, it is hereby concluded that the optimized Genetic Algorithm improves significantly the Adequacy Ratio or Coverage Analysis value for GUI software test over the existing non-adaptive mutation basic Genetic Algorithm.

References

[1] Abdul R., Aleisa E. and Bakhsh I. (2013). GUI Test Coverage Analysis using NSGA II, *The Proceeding Of International Conference on Soft Computing and Software Engineering* [SCSE'13], San Francisco State University, CA, U. S. A., March 2013.

[2] Pfleeger S. L. (2001). Software Engineering Theory and Practice, Prentice Hall.

[3] Chayanika S., Sangeeta S. and Ritu S. (2013). A Survey on Software Testing Techniques using Genetic Algorithm, *International Journal of Computer Science Issues*, Vol. 10, Issue 1, No 1, January 2013.

[4] Glenford J. M. (2004). The Art of software Testing, Second Edition, Revised and Updated by Tom Badgett and Todd M. Thomas with Corey Sandler, John Wiley & Sons, Inc. 2004.

[5] Pierre B. and Richard E. F. (2014). Guide to the Software Engineering Body of Knowledge V3.0, A project of IEEE computer Society 2014.

[6] Muhammad S., Suhaimi I. and Mohd N. M. (2011). A Study on Test Coverage in Software Testing, *International conference on Telecommunication Technology and Applications*, Proc of CSIT Vol. 5 IACSIT Press, Singapore, 2011.

[7] Michalewics Z. (1992). Genetic Algorithm + Data Structures = Evolution Programs, Springer, 1992.

[8] Samarah Amer (2006). Automated Coverage Directed Test Generation Using a Cell-Based Genetic Algorithm (An Unpublished publication).

[9] Memon A. M. (2001). A Comprehensive Framework for Testing Graphical User Interfaces, Ph. D. Thesis, University of Pittsburgh, Pittsburg, PA.

[10] Memon A. M. and Soffa M. (2003). Regression Testing of GUI's, *Proceeding of European Software Engineering Conference* /FSE'03. Sep. 2003.

[11] Misurda J., Clause J. A., *et al.* (2005). Demand-driven structural testing with Dynamic instrumentation, In *Proceedings of 27th International Conference on Software Engineering*, 2005 ICSE 2005, pp. 165-175.

[12] Matteo B, Cyrille C., Tristan G., Jerome G., Thomas Q. and Olivier H. *et al.*, (2009). Covertures: an Innovative Open Framework for code coverage analysis of safety critical applications, Covertures Open Repository at Open-DO.org, http://forge.open-do.org/projects/couverture.

[13] Sakamoto K., Washizaki H., et al. (2010). Open Code Coverage Framework: A Consistent and Flexible Framework for Measuring Test Coverage Supporting Multiple Programming Languages, *10th International Conference on Quality Software, QSIC*, 2010, pp. 262-269.

[14] Abdul R., Arfan, J. and Arshad A. S (2010). Fully Automated GUI test coverage analysis using GA, *Seventh International conference on information technology.* IEEE 2010, pp. 1057-1063.

[15] Wen-Yang L., Wen-Yuan L. and Tzung-Pei H (2003). Adapting Crossover and Mutation in Genetic Algorithms" *Journal of Information Science and Engineering,* 19, 889-903 2003.

[16] Benjamin D., Edda H. and Christian K. (2008). Crossover Can Provably be Useful in Evolutionary Computation.

[17] Wu, Y., Ji P. and Wang T. (2008). An empirical study of a pure genetic algorithm to solve the capacitated vehicle routing problem, *ICIC Express Letters*, Vol. 2, No. 1, pp. 41-45, 2008.

[18] Jones B. F., Sthamer H. H. and D. E. Eyres (1996). Automatic structural testing using Genetic algorithms, *The Software Engineering Journal*, Vol. 11, No. 5, pp. 299-306, 1996.

[19] Jones, B. F., Eyres D. E. and Sthamer H. H., (1998). A Strategy for using genetic algorithms to automate branch and fault-based testing, *The Computer Journal,* Vol. 41, No. 2, pp. 98-107, 1998.

[20] Michael C. C., McGraw G. and Schatz M. A. (2001). Generating software test data by evolution, *IEEE Transactions on Software Engineering*, Vol. 27, No. 12, pp.1 085-1110.

[21] Pargas R., Harrold M. J. and Peck R. (2008). Test-data generation using genetic algorithms, Journal of Software Testing, Verification and reliability, *Science and Software Engineering*, Vol. 9, No. 4.

[22] Shunkun Y., Tianlong M. and Jiaqi X. (2014). Improved Ant Algorithms for Software Testing Cases Generation, the *Scientific World Journal* Vol. 2014, Article ID 392309, 9 pages Hindawi Publishing Corporation.

9

Computer programs - new considerations in teaching and learning mathematics science

Qamil Kllogjeri[1, *], **Pellumb Kllogjeri**[1, 2]

[1]University of Gjovik, MSc Student of Information Security, Gjovik, Norway
[2]University "Aleksander Xhuvani ", Department of Mathematics and Informatics, Elbasan, Albania

Email address:
q.kllogjeri@gmail.com (Qamil Kllogjeri), pkallogjeri@gmail.com (Pellumb Kllogjeri)

Abstract: There are many applications of computer informatics like in computations, plotting graphics to use them in math papers and to study the properties of the functions, in solving and discussing problems of mathematics or physics, in economics, in social topics and so on. This paper presents the topic of how much the computer programs (while we are studying something or making some trials by manipulating) help the teacher in finding answer for different mathematical problems or for the formulation of mathematical statements or facts (in other fields of science, as well). We are presenting here several examples in order that teachers and students have them into consideration while using computer programs to teach and learn. It is important that the teachers and the students try themselves again these examples and others by manipulating with computer programs, making trials and keeping notes in order to find out that there are limitations in the computer programs. The computer program used is Geogebra.

Keywords: GeoGebra, Virtual Tools, Discrete Medium of Computer Programs, Limitations of Computer Programs

1. Introduction

The computers age has fundamentally changed many things in our culture. The ways we learn mathematics and do mathematics and, the kinds of problems we can consider and solve have changed. Our creative visions and our sense of what is possible have been altered. The computers are as discrete machines, capable of dealing only with finite information. Discrete mathematics deals with many real-world applications and it has very close ties with computer science. The range of applications of both discrete mathematics and computer science is growing so rapidly that becomes so difficult to decide what program or what algorithm is better.

Applications of discrete mathematics include project communication networks, systems analysis, management, social decision making, population growth, and finance.

The wide range of the applications oblige the teachers to provide students the knowledge and skills of discrete mathematics to prepare them for life-work by positively responding to these fast changes in sciences and in culture.

In the teaching and learning process, also in applications, are treated and used continuous mathematics and discrete mathematics. Continuous mathematics is the mathematics based on the continuous number line or the real numbers. The simplest meaning is: for given any two numbers we can always find another number between them, furthermore we can find an infinite set of numbers between them. Geometrically, a function is continuous if its geometric representation is a perfectly smooth curve, without any gaps.

Discrete mathematics is the mathematics based on distinct values. Geometrically speaking, given any two numbers (points), there aren't an infinite number of numbers (points) between them. So, in the teaching and learning process the teachers have to take into consideration that the computers are as discrete machines that deal only with finite information. We are not sure that a computer program written to compute an expression S is correct. For instance, let be the expression: $S = (a + b)^n$. There are infinitely many possible input values (that is, values of a, b and n). Who and what can be able to test the correctness of the program for infinitely many cases?!

There is another approach related to the problem of correctness of computer programs. This is the well-known "Halting Problem". This problem asks whether or not a given computer program stops on a given input after a finite amount of time. This problem is known to be unsolvable by computers, as well. No one can write a computer program to answer the above question (John Tabak, 59).

Discrete mathematics is the foundation for the formal approaches. It discusses languages used in mathematical reasoning, basic concepts, and their properties and relationships among them.

GeoGebra is a computer software, it is a dynamic mathematics software that joins geometry, algebra and calculus (Josef Böhm-2008). It is an interactive geometry system with which we can make different constructions using geometry virtual tools offered by this software or, by directly entering into the input field equations, functions and points coordinates that are their algebraic representatives. We can also change them dynamically. Characteristic of GeoGebra are two views of the object in study: the algebraic expression of the geometric object in the algebra window and the object in the geometry window, and the two windows can be seen simultaneously (Markus Hohenwarter, Judith Hohenwarter, 2008). The graphical representation of all objects is displayed in the graphics window (geometry window), while their algebraic representations are shown in algebra window. Any change done in the object is reflected with changes in its algebraic representation and vice versa.

The benefits of using computer programs in solving different problems are well-known. In the following explorations we are drawing the attention of the teachers, including the program users as well, to keep in mind that there are limitations as to the scale the computer programs are used in micro-world or macro-world. The explorations are done using GeoGebra software.

2. Limitations of Computer Programs in Exploring Mathematical Issues

2.1. The Problem of Intersection of Two Circles

The problem of the intersection of two circles regarding the determination of the intersection points can be easily studied by using a computer program, and a very good software is GeoGebra with which we can get geometric and algebraic answer (Lu Yu-Wen Allison, pp.2). Let see some examples in referee to this problem. In the obvious cases the demonstration of the fact that the circles are intersected or not is done in a very easy way. It is understandable by the students and there is no question raised.

For instance, the intersection of the circles with equations
$$x^2 + y^2 = 4 \ and \ (x-1)^2 + y^2 = 4$$
is seen by the geometric construction.

If we take the circles
$$x^2 + y^2 = 4 \ and \ (x - 4 + 10^{-6})^2 + y^2 = 4$$
where the second equation can be written as
$$\left(x - \frac{399,999}{100,000}\right)^2 + y^2 = 4$$

the geometric view shows that they are tangent, but by using the intersection tool of GeoGebra (*Intersect Two Objects*) to find the intersection points of the two circles we get the right answer of two intersection points.

Taking other examples by choosing the circle center close to point (4, 0) and on its left, with the same radius (r = 2), the problem of detecting the intersection points becomes more difficult. Taking the circle
$$c: (x - 4 + 10^{-10})^2 + y^2 = 4$$
it is noticed that it is registered as $(x-4)^2 + y^2 = 4$ in the algebra window.

Using *Intersect Two Objects* tool to find the intersection points of the two circles we get the answer of two intersection points: D (2, 0) and E (2, -0). This is an approximate numerical answer for their coordinates.

GeoGebra offers tools to see more details in the graphical representation of the object.

So, applying the *Zoom in* tool (by which the picture is magnified), as much as the program allows, we detect the two points D and E close to point (2, 0), and there is only one point on the circle: $x^2 + y^2 = 4$. In fact, there are two different points on the two circles.

This fact shows that the program cannot give the right answer about the intersection of the two circles when their central distance is very close to number 4 and less than it.

Take the circle c with equation,
$$(x - 4 + 10^{-15})^2 + y^2 = 4$$
which is again registered in the Algebra window as,
$$(x-4)^2 + y^2 = 4$$

The central distance between the circles
$$(x - 4 + 10^{-15})^2 + y^2 = 4$$
and $x^2 + y^2 = 4$ is much, much closer to number 4 and less than it.

Applying the *Intersect Two Objects* tool, to find the intersection points of the two circles, we get the answer of two intersection points in the Algebra window, appeared as D(2, 0) and E(2, 0). That means: one point!!! Then, applying *Zoom in* tool, as much as the program allows, we see no different intersection points. This is a stronger confirmation that the computer program is limited, it cannot give answer for every problem we present to it for solution. They are of limited use in micro-world.

2.2. The Problem of Intersection and Parallelism

Let see now the problem of parallelism of the lines using GeoGebra software. Entering into the *Input* field the following line equations
$$y = 2 \cdot x - 3 \ and \ y = \frac{1}{2} \cdot x + 1,$$
it is easily demonstrated by the program that they are intersected, that means they are not parallel. We choose other

equations that their angular coefficients differ very little from one another. Let us take the example of the lines with equations:

$$a: y = 10^{-8} \cdot x + 5; \quad b: y = 2 \cdot 10^{-8} \cdot x - 5$$

The way to check if the lines are parallel or not, by using GeoGebra program, is calculating the distance between them. If the lines are intersected the distance between them is zero, and if the lines are parallel the distance between them is a positive number. Using the *Distance* tool in this case we get the right answer: the distance between them is zero (because they intersect one another). We take another example, in which the angular coefficients of the lines differ very, very little from one another. We enter into the *Input* field the equations:

$$c: y = 10^{-9} \cdot x + 5; \quad d: y = 2 \cdot 10^{-9} \cdot x - 5$$

They are simply registered as y = 5 and y = – 5 in Algebra window.

The "*distance*" command shows that the distance between them is 10!!!, meaning they are parallel, contrary to the fact that they are not parallel. Applying *Zoom out* tool (because this command moves much faster the pane to the "Far East" or "Far West" of the coordinative plane), as far as the program allows, and later applying *Zoom in* tool to magnify the area at these extremes in order to see the parts of the lines, they look parallel !!!?.

Entering the equations,

$$f: y = 10^{-10} \cdot x + 5; \quad g: y = 2 \cdot 10^{-10} \cdot x - 5$$

they are also registered as y = 5 and y = – 5, and the distance between them is 10, meaning they are parallel !!! (in fact, the two lines intersect). We can bring many other examples.

The same conclusion can be drawn regarding the parallelism axiom of the lines. From a point A, outside a line d, passes through only one line d' parallel to d. But, this fact cannot be demonstrated by GeoGebra software. We can construct a great number of lines passing through the point A for which their angular coefficients differ from one another and from d' by a very small amount. All they are different, but Geometry window shows that they take the position of the line d'!!!

Here again, we are facing a problem that the computer program cannot demonstrate the property of intersection or parallelism for the lines. GeoGebra does not help us to get right answers in every case of macro-world as well.

2.3. Can the Program Demonstrate that any Two Lines Can be Perpendicular or not?

Consider the lines with equations: y = 2x and y = -0.5 x. Entering these equations in the *Input* field are got the two lines in Geometry window, and measuring the angle between them by using the *angle* tool is shown that it is 90°. This is a true fact because the production of their angular coefficients is -1 as well. We take another equation, y = - 0.4999 x, enter it in the *Input* field and measure the angle between the line of this

equation and the line d (y = 2x). The answer is 90°, meaning that they are perpendicular as well. In fact, they are not because the production of their angular coefficients is not -1. We can take a great number of lines with equations: y = - 0.49999 x, y = - 0.499999 x, …, and so on. Constructing their respective graphs by entering their equations in the *Input* field we notice that all the respective lines take one position: there is no difference between them. Measuring the angle between them (represented by a line alone) and the line d we get the same answer by the program: the measured angle is 90°. Actually, the lines must take different positions. They have only one point in common: the intersection point which is the origin of coordinative system. Taking four different equations, constructing their respective lines, and using *Zoom In* tool, as many times as the program allows, to see if their positions are different we don't notice such thing. There is only one line passing through the or*igin. Thinking that the region we are looking at is very bounded and very close to the origin we use the *Move Graphic View* tool to move the geometry window on the left or on the right side and along the line. Moving on the left, and "far west", and checking the positions, we observe that all the lines y = kx, for which the angular coefficient satisfies the condition:

$$|k - (-0.5)| = |k + 0.5| \leq 10^{-4} \implies$$

$$-0.5001 \leq k \leq -0.4999,$$

take the same position. The lines coincide. Maybe there are other lines as well that are present here, so anyone can try by taking k: $-0.501 < k < -0.499$. Definitely, the computer program cannot demonstrate that any two lines are perpendicular or not.

2.4. Can the Program Demonstrate that Any Two Circles Can be Tangent

Consider the circles: $x^2 + y^2 = 4$ *and* $(x - 4)^2 + y^2 = 4$. They are tangent, but try using some computer program what they show. We have used GeoGebra. They look tangent in the normal view of Geometry window. Then, we use the *Zoom In* tool moving towards micro-world to see if it is true that they have one point in common. Without making such effort we know that the point is dimensionless, hence nobody has to expect that will find some extraordinary thing. Using *Zoom In* tool, as many times as the program allows, we see within the Geometry view only a common line of the two circles. We try to move deeper and deeper towards the micro-world, expecting to see a split of the curved parts of the two circles, but it doesn't happen. Furthermore, we come to a moment when the line disappears from our sight. Then, we move back, using *Zoom Out* tool, until the line appears again and try another movement. Using the *Move Graphic View* tool, we displace the view down in order to move up and "far-north". We continue moving up, hoping to see the split, until the ordinates of the points of the common line reach the value 2. We have a big part of the common points of the two circles that is checked using Geogebra software (their ordinates are between 0 and 2), and no split!!! It is enough to say that the program cannot demonstrate that the two circles have in common one point alone.

2.5. Can a Program Show that ANY Equation of Type $\frac{x^2}{a^2} + \frac{y^2}{b^2} = 1, a^2 \neq b^2$ is Represented by an Ellipse?

Consider the equation $\frac{x^2}{2.0009^2} + \frac{y^2}{2^2} = 1$.

Entering this equation in the Input field we get in the Geometry window a circle. Sure, this is depended on our sight ability. Therefore we rely on the program: what does it say? Constructing the intersection points of the geometrical representation of the equation with the coordinative axes we get the points: (2,0), (-2,0), (0,2), and (0,-2) which means that the two ellipse axes (major and minor) are equal. The program cannot make the difference between the given ellipse and the circle with equation $x^2 + y^2 = 4$. In general, the program does make a difference between this circle and the ellipses with equations $\frac{x^2}{a^2} + \frac{y^2}{2^2} = 1$ if $a^2 > 2.0009^2$ or $a^2 < 1.9991^2$. For instance, if $a^2 = 2.009^2$ then the intersection points of the ellipse with the coordinative axes are: (2.1,0), (-2.1,0), (0,2) and (0,-2).

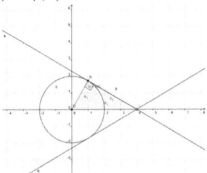

Fig 1. *Right angled triangle.*

2.6. Can be Proved or Disapproved by Using a Program that a Triangle is a Right Angled One?

We know that in a right angled triangle the longest side of the triangle is called "hypotenuse". So, the formal definition (based on Pythagoras' Theorem) is: In a right angled triangle, the square of the hypotenuse is equal to the sum of the squares of the other two sides. Using GeoGebra we construct the circle of radius 2 (look at Figure 1) and from point A = (4,0) are constructed its tangents. Consider the tangent AB and the triangle ABC. Using the *Angle* tool we measure the angle ABC. In Figure 1 is shown that the size of the angle is: $\alpha = 90°$. This fact is based on what we see and what the program shows. The only precise way of proving that a triangle is right angled is to check if the Pythagorean Theorem is true. In our case, using GeoGebra tools, we are given the lengths of hypotenuse AC = b_1 =4, of the sides AB = c_1 = 3.46 and BC = a_1 = 2. We check weather $b_1^2 = a_1^2 + c_1^2$ is valid, but $4^2 \neq 2^2 + 3.46^2$!!! This result depends on the size of the error done during the calculation of the length of the side c_1. Nevertheless, whatever small be the error, the program cannot demonstrate that the given triangle has a right angle!! We could take another example in which are given the lengths of the three sides of a triangle, and using the *angle* tool by measuring the biggest

angle we could find out that it is 90°!! This is not the right way to prove that a triangle is right angled.

2.7. The Optical Property of the Ellipse

Suppose a line a is tangent to an ellipse at a point T. Then, the angles between the line a and the two foci rays (TF1 and TF2), drawn from point T, are equal.

We can demonstrate this property using GeoGebra software (look at Figure 2) for the ellipse

$$\frac{x^2}{2.0009^2} + \frac{y^2}{2^2} = 1$$

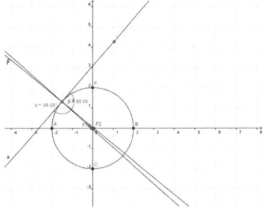

Fig 2. *The property of foci rays.*

This is also true for other ellipses for which the first semi-axis satisfies the condition: $a^2 > 2.0009^2$. But if we take another example like

$$\frac{x^2}{2.00009^2} + \frac{y^2}{2^2} = 1$$

or in general, satisfying the condition $a^2 < 2.0009^2$, then the foci are very close to the coordinative origin. The program does not help to demonstrate the above property of the foci rays because, in such cases, the foci rays are represented by a line alone: they are placed one on the other. In reality the situation is not so, they are different but the program shows one line.

2.8. The Difference between the Areas of a Circle and the Regular Polygon Inscribed in it (Case: the Side Length Decreases)

Consider the circle with radius r = 6. Before constructing the inscribed regular polygon of the circle we insert in the Geometry window a slider, named *n*, which has the function of changing the number of the sides of the regular polygon in order to observe what happens with the two areas when the number n of the sides is increased. To construct the regular *n*-gon, inscribed in the circle, we construct a vertex with coordinates:

$$M = \left(6cos\frac{360^0}{n}, 6sin\frac{360^0}{n} \right)$$

which falls on the circle. Construct the intersection point A of the circle with the x-axis on the positive side. Then we use the *Regular Polygon* tool referring the segment AM as one of its sides. Using the slider *n* we increase the number of the sides of the regular polygon to observe the difference between the area of the circle and the area of the regular *n*-gon. In this case the side length decreases. The first observations for the differences, where the number of sides is considerably great, are shown in the table below (Table 1): for greater values of *n* the difference remains zero. We use *Zoom In* tool for the regular 2000-gon to look closer at the relation between one side and the respective arc of the circle. The observation shows that they have different positions, meaning that there is a part of the circle which is outside the polygon. This is true for the other sides of the regular polygon and their respective arcs.

Table 1. *The difference between the area of the circle and the area of the regular n-gon inscribed in it*

n	50	100	300	500	1000	1500
Differences	0.3	0.08	0.01	0.01	0	0

So, there are 2000 small pieces of the circle that are outside the polygon, hence the difference between the circle area and the regular polygon, inscribed in, is not zero (it is very, very small but not zero). We get the difference zero because there are limitations in the program with respect to calculations. However sophisticated the program be it cannot give the answer for any problem in micro-world or in macro-world.

2.9. The Difference between the Areas of a Circle and the Regular Polygon Circumscribed around it (Case: the Side Length is Constant)

Consider a circle with radius *R* and a regular *n*-gon circumscribed around the circle (Fig. 3). Let the side of the regular polygon be of a fixed length denoted by *a*. We observe the difference between the area of the circumscribed regular *n*-gon and the area of the circle which is tangent with all the sides of the polygon. The observation is done using Geogebra software and for the case *a* = 4. The number of the sides is changed by using the slider *n*, as in the previous example. We have constructed the two objects in such a way that, when the number *n* of the sides is changed, the two objects change simultaneously and their relation is not affected. That is,

whatever be the value of *n*, the regular *n*-gon is circumscribed around the circle (both they represent one object). The results of the observation are presented in the following table (Table 2):

Table 2. *The difference between the area of the circle and the area of the regular n-gon circumcised around it*

n	18	120	500	1000	2000	3000
Differences	4.17	4.2	4.2	4.2	4.2	4.2

The observation shows that the different values of the difference stand for small values of *n*. As can be seen from the table, for great values of *n* there is no change.

The program does not help in observing this phenomenon. In other words, it cannot give the answer about what the series of differences is: decreasing or increasing? Analytical methods give the right answer. There is no place here to show that the differences of the areas represent a decreasing series. We just calculate the limit of the ratio of the area of the regular *n*-gon, circumscribed around the circle, with the area of the respective circle where, $R = GH$, $a = AB$ (*a* is the length of any side), *n* is the number

of sides and π is approximately 3.142, G is the center of the circle.

$$area(\Delta OAB) = \frac{a}{2} \cdot R = \frac{a^2}{4 \cdot tan\frac{\pi}{n}}$$

$$area\left(sector\ \frac{2\pi}{n}\right) = \frac{\pi \cdot R^2}{n} = \frac{\pi}{n} \cdot \frac{a^2}{4 \cdot \left(tan\frac{\pi}{n}\right)^2}$$

$$\lim_{n\to\infty} \frac{area(\Delta)}{area(sector)} = \lim_{n\to\infty} \frac{\frac{a^2}{4 \cdot tan\frac{\pi}{n}}}{\frac{\pi}{n} \cdot \frac{a^2}{4 \cdot \left(tan\frac{\pi}{n}\right)^2}} = \lim_{n\to\infty} \frac{n}{\pi} tan\frac{\pi}{n}$$

$$= 1$$

The result of the limit, which is 1, of the ratio (when the number of the sides is infinitely increased) shows that the areas of the circle and of the regular *n*-gon, circumscribed around it, tend to equalize with one another. Hence, it is understood that the series of the above observed differences is a decreasing one.

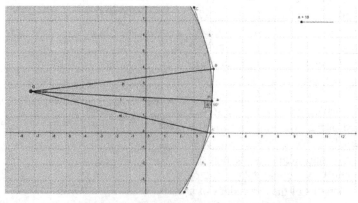

Fig 3. *The circle and the regular n-gon circumscribed around it.*

2.10. The area Problem of Circles in the Micro-World

Another example, showing that the computer program is limited, is the circle of a very small radius. Entering in the Input field equations of the form $x^2 + y^2 = r^2$ it is possible to take the constructions for the cases: $r^2 = 10^{-2},..r^2 = 10^{-4},....until..r^2 = 10^{-8}$. Applying *Zoom In* tool we can clearly see the circles for which $r^2 = 10^{-4}..and..r^2 = 10^{-5}$. In this micro-world they look big and very far from one another, but if we calculate their areas, they are zero.

3. The Medium in which the Program Operates is Really Discrete

The set of rational numbers has the property: between any two rational numbers there are also infinitely many rational and irrational numbers. This is called: property of being *"dense"*, because it means that we can find rational numbers in even the smallest gaps on the number line. Always can be answered the question: if are given two different rational numbers, is it possible to find another rational number that sits between them?

Let see if this property is supported by a computer program. We take the rational numbers 1/3 and 2/3 and explore how many different numbers between them can be found using GeoGebra software. Sure, can be found a lot, but to what scale can the program help? The best way to explore this property is to take segments with ends representing the rational numbers we are seeking. The dense property of the rational numbers can be formulated in a geometrical way: for any segment with ends in different rational numbers can be found segments (also infinitely many) with ends in rational numbers that are lied within the first segment. So, we start with the segment with ends at the points: (1/3, 0) and (2/3, 0) which is clearly visible in the Geometry window lied on the x-axis. Then, we take the segment with ends at the points: (7/15, 0) and (1/2, 0). It is visible that it is within the first segment, but too short. We color them with different colors in order to make the distinction. Then, we take the segment with ends at the points: (145/300, 0) and (148/300, 0). The segment is not visible in the normal view therefore we use the *Zoom In* tool to bring it to our sight. It becomes visible and lies within the second segment.

Continuing further by taking the segment with ends at the points (1456/3000, 0) and (1475/3000, 0) and using *Zoom In* tool we can detect that this segment lies within the third segment. For further exploration we take the segment with ends at the points: (146/300, 0) and (147/300, 0). Using *Zoom In* tool we can detect that this segment lies within the fourth segment. Trying to go deeper by selecting segments with ends within the last one is very difficult. There are still infinitely many of such segments but the program doesn't help to detect them. For instance, the segment with ends at the points: (1456/3000, 0) and (1460/3000, 0) cannot be shown by the program. Using *Zoom In* tool we cannot detect this segment, it

is missing. The result of this exploration is that between the points generated by the program there are vast gaps. Surely, the points, generated by the program, have a real size that is extremely big compared to very tiny elements of the micro-world. The mathematical meaning of the point is as a dimensionless object. This experiment fully confirms the results and conclusions of the former examples that the medium in which the program operates is discrete

4. Last Thoughts

We brought many examples or facts that show that the computer programs help for exploring mathematical issues down or up to a level, and moving further is impossible. Using the popular language we have reached a point where the saw has faced a nail or stuck in it.

It happens this way because many of our basic intuitions about numbers and the things that we can do with them are actually deeply connected with the limits of computation. There are also people of such arguments who try to invoke ideas about computation in misleading ways. In the history of mathematics are known the efforts done in the early 20th century to create a perfect complete mathematics, which meant a new formalization of mathematics in terms of a logic in which every true statement was probably true, every false statement was provably false, and for any given statement could be followed a completely mechanical process to find out whether it was true or false (Bruner, 21-32).

Gödel wrestled with his incompleteness theorems as well. Later, Alan Turing worked on defining the limit of what could be done by a purely mechanical computation process. What Turing showed about computability was really the same concept as what Gödel showed about logic with incompleteness: there are limits of mechanical/axiomatic processes (Michel Detlefsen, pp.26). By remembering this short history we want to emphasize that Turing did prove that there are things that cannot be computed. He did it by defining an easy to understand problem which cannot be solved by any mechanical device, and by showing how common non-computable things are.

The first of Turing's proofs is known as the Halting problem. The simplest version of the Halting problem is the following:

Suppose that some program P can be run on a computing machine M. Can someone write a program H which can determine whether the running P will eventually stop? In this case we have a computing machine which computes some function on its input. The halting problem (John Tabak, 59) is in fact the question: given a machine M, is there such a program H that at the end will result with the answer "YES" (return YES) if and only if M would halt, and will return "NO" if and only if M would not halt. Such a program H is called a halting oracle and the question is raised differently: is it possible to write a halting oracle?

The answer is no because no such program can possibly exist. It is very easy to write a program for which H is guaranteed to get the wrong answer. On the other side there are lots of things that can't be computed. Actually, most functions are not computable! Is the same thing with the numbers, most of which are irrational numbers. So, most of the functions are not computable. Let consider just the functions on the natural numbers: $\{f \mid f: N \rightarrow N\}$. It is an infinite set of such functions which is larger than the infinite set of natural numbers. Turning back to a computing machine, we can reflect each one of its programs to a natural number. Consequently, the computing machine can only have as many programs as there are natural numbers. So, there are values in that infinite set of functions that have no program that can compute them.

We have brought here facts that bring to light the limitations of the computer programs. Here it is important to turn that truth into understanding. This is linked with the interpretation of the data. Do we understand how the program runs or works? How precise and how well understood are the outputs of the program? These are results of explorations that are carefully done. The explorations or the experiments can, in fact, be wrong but the facts aren't wrong. It is possible to make mistakes in our interpretation of the facts. Good experimentalists usually do things right, but we all make mistakes. There are cases when we do everything right which is associated with something going on that we are not aware of it. We cannot know everything that is linked with our experiment or exploration. Once we have our experimental results, we set to the task of trying to understand them, trying to put them in context and turn them into something that we might call an understanding of some part of nature (Hulshof, pp. 27; Reimann P, pp.34). The ultimate goal is to develop a fruitful and working theory.

A theory is a framework for understanding how does the nature work, how a process works and it serves as means of predicting the results of experiments and observations (Klahr and Dunbar, 1-5). Such a theory works and is supported by the data, also it withstands myriad tests (Fiedler and Walther, pp.58). Science is more practical. When a theory works, and keeps working, we consider it right. It serves and works well for all practical purposes. Truth is that which science hopes to asymptotically approach (Orton Anthony, pp.77). Turning back to the main purpose of this research article we emphasize again that the machine and program capacities are limited. They derive from the human capacities which are limited in both directions: towards the extremes of the macro-world that are infinitely great in number and in dimensions; also, towards the extremes of the micro-world that are infinitely great in number and infinitely small in dimensions.

5. Conclusions

The computer programs are a very powerful and helpful tool for calculus, plotting, constructing geometric figures, studying the properties of different functions or equations, demonstration in teaching math and other fields of science and so on.

In using c*omputer programs the teachers must have into consideration that,

1. The potentials of the computer programs are limited
2. The space or the medium in which a computer program operates is discrete or discontinues
3. The students get knowledge regarding the behavior of a function, or the properties of different objects, or calculus, not for every case.
4. The analytical method in calculus gives the right answer, and a mathematically and only a logically shaped mind has the power to pierce the division between points, lines and curves and, discern the elements of the micro-world.

NOTE: Anyone can try him/herself the above examples or others by using GeoGebra software simply by downloading it from www.geogebra.org.

References

[1]   Bruner, J. S., "The act of discovery", *Harvard Educational Review*, 1961, pp. 21-32.

[2]   Fiedler Klaus and Walther Eva, "Stereotyping as Inductive Hypothesis Testing", *Psychology Press*, Great Britain, 2004, pp. 56-59.

[3]   Hulshof C.D., "Discovery of Ideas and Ideas about Discovery", Publisher: *Twente University Press*, Enschede, the Netherlands (www.tup.utwente.nl), 2001, pp. 16-42.

[4]   John Tabak, "Numbers: Computers, Philosophers and the Search for Meaning", *The History of Mathematics*, Printed in USA, 2004, pp.59, 173.

[5]   Josef Böhm, "Linking Geometry, Algebra and Calculus with GeoGebra", *ACDCA, DUG and Technical University of Vienna* (http://www.geogebra.org), 2008, pp. 3-8.

[6]   Klahr, D. and Dunbar, K., "Dual space search during scientific reasoning", *Cognitive Science*, 1988, pp. 12, 1-5.

[7]   Lu Yu-Wen Allison, "Linking Geometry and Algebra: A multiple-case study of Upper-Secondary mathematics teachers' conceptions and practices of GeoGebra in England and Taiwan", *Faculty of Education, University of Cambridge* (http://www.geogebra.org), 2008, pp. 1-2, 25-26.

[8]   Markus Hohenwartera and Judith Hohenwarter, "Introduction to GeoGebra." (*http://www.geogebra.org*), 2008, pp. 7-8

[9]   Michel Detlefsen, "Proof and Knowledge in Mathematics", Printed in USA and Canada, 1992, *Taylor and Francis e-Library*, 2005, pp.26.

[10] Orton Anthony, "Learning Mathematics: Issues, Theory and Classroom Practice", *British Library Cataloguing-in-Publication Data*, Third Edition, (www.continuumbooks.com), 2004, pp.71-84.

[11] Reimann P., "Problem solving models of scientific discovery learning processes", Published by *P. Lang in Frankfurt am Main*, New York, 1991, pp.15-45.

10

Designing a Machine Learning – Based Framework for Enhancing Performance of Livestock Mobile Application System

Herbert Peter Wanga[1], Nasir Ghani[2], Khamisi Kalegele[1]

[1]School of Computational and Communication Sciences and Engineering (CoCSE), Nelson Mandela African Institution of Science and Technology (NM-AIST), Arusha, Tanzania
[2]College of Engineering, Department of Electrical Engineering, University of South Florida, Florida, USA

Email address:
wangah@nm-aist.ac.tz (H. P. Wanga), nghani@usf.edu (N. Ghani), khamisi.kalegele@nm-aist.ac.tz (K. Kalegele)

Abstract: Smallholder livestock keepers live in rural areas where there is poor Internet connectivity. Many mobile based system designed do not function well in such areas. To address these concerns, an Android Mobile Application will be designed and installed on a smartphone. The application will have an easy to use Graphical User Interface (GUI) and request resources from the server through the Internet. This Intelligent Livestock Information System (ILIS) will be able to provide and predict feedback to the livestock keepers. This solution will also collect livestock data from livestock keepers through mobile phones. The data will then be sent to the database if connectivity is available or through synchronization if connectivity is poor. Livestock experts will be able to view data and respond to any query from livestock keepers. The system will also be able to learn and predict the responses using machine learning techniques. The goal of the ILIS is to provide livestock services to anyone at anytime, overcoming the constraints of place, time and character. Overall, this is a novel idea in the field of mobile livestock information systems. Along these, this paper presents the software, hardware and architecture design of the machine learning based livestock information system. Overall this solution embodies an artificial intelligence approach which combines hardware and software technologies. The design will leverage the Android ADK operating system and Android mobile devices or tablets. Our main contribution here is the intelligent livestock Information System, which is a novel idea in the field of mobile livestock information systems.

Keywords: Intelligent Information System, Machine Learning, Android ODK, Requirements, Modeling, Artificial Intelligence, Livestock App

1. Introduction

With the rapid increase in population and livestock economic development, poor exchange of livestock information is a cause for increasing concern. Many livestock keepers live in rural areas, where there is poor connectivity. Hence the provision of an intelligent livestock information system in such poor connectivity areas is of vital importance, and this is the focus herein.

In our design, we will use smartphone devices, installed with a developed Android application. The device will have SQLite for data synchronization with a remote database. Machine learning techniques will also be deployed in the device. By using these devices, information flow will be supported between livestock keepers, field officers, researchers, and district officers. The designed system will be also able to replicate from the remote database to the SQLite. Machine learning will be able to use experience and make predictions. We will use machine learning to program systems to automatically learn and to improve with experience, hence making intelligent decisions based on data. It will improve performance in some tasks using experience.

As per [1] machine learning addresses two interrelated problems, namely the development of software that improves automatically through experience and the extraction of rules from a large volume of specific data. Therefore systems capable of exhibiting such characteristics are important because they have the potential to reach higher levels of performance versus other systems that must be modified manually to deal with situations their designers did not anticipate.

In the design stage, given the number of requirements on software complexity and quality, it is important to present detailed requirements on software structure, on navigation by software, on design of user interfaces, on multimedia components of software, on usability, and on technical requirements [2]. This study gathered all necessary requirements towards designing and development of the intelligent livestock information system.

The intelligent program can be implemented on the client's mobile for the purpose of smooth working within the application program, in a fully or partially disconnected environment [3].

When the mobile clients do not have synchronized data, they are dependent on servers for continuous support because of the intermittent nature of the mobile networks. Hence in such cases, mobile clients must be capable of operating in the disconnected mode for some periods of time, depending on the critical need of the synchronized data. This program implementation eliminates the other system, which assumes constant connectivity [4].

During disconnected operation, updates are persistently logged by the system, using a variety of optimizations to reduce resource consumption. For example, if a file is created, renamed, and later deleted, none of those records need to be saved; i.e., it is as if none of the operations ever happened. When connectivity is re-established, the program should replay these updates at the servers through reintegration [3]

As a large amount of livestock data is handled by the server, the server will perform mining and analyze data. Hence by performing analysis and by using suggestions and information provided by the livestock experts, the server can learn and provide feedback automatically. Moreover as time goes on the server will be trained automatically by mining and analyzing data of all the possible livestock practice scenarios and become more and more intelligent.

Our main contribution here is the intelligent livestock information system, which is a novel idea in the field of mobile livestock information systems.

The remaining part of this paper is organized as follows. Section 2 briefly describes some related applications. Next, Section 3 presents the analysis on the requirements of a machine – learning based framework for enhancing performance of livestock mobile application system, Whereas Section 4 overviews the design of the proposed system. Section 5 concludes the paper, and explains the future work.

2. Related Work

This section deals with some of the existing works related to the proposed mobile solution, and their challenges.

2.1. Existing Works

This section reviews some studies related to the machine-learning based framework for enhancing

performance of livestock mobile application system.

2.1.1. Livestock Gestation Tables

This app helps with breeding decisions for the larger farm animals. It provides a gestation chart for the 5 main species of farm animals, included access to a calendar. Hence users can determine when they want to breed animals to have offspring at the best time of the year.

2.1.2. Cow Tracker

If the cow is pregnant it will calculate the approximate due date. It has ability to see what events are coming up in the next 7 days.   A user can also click on a cow within this view and it will take them to the cow's page. There is the ability to have notifications delivered for all three events as well and when the events will be delivered on a once per day basis. A heat check notification will arrive 3 days prior to the next heat date. A blood draw notification will arrive 5 days after the first time you can draw blood for testing. A calving notification will arrive 14 days prior to the estimated due date [5].

2.1.3. Mobile Cattle Tracker

While the majority of data on a beef cow-calf operation is collected seasonally at herd workings, certain data must be collected on an ongoing basis throughout the production year. Also, production data like birth records, weights and measurements and management activities needs to be entered real-time, so that it can be available for review when animals are gathered and worked. Mobile Cattle Tracker allows data to be collected in a consistent manner and on a timely basis so that meaningful information can be generated [6].

Figure 1. Mobile Cattle Tracker interfaces.

2.1.4. Willoughby Livestock

A one stop access to all divisions of Willoughby Sales through the convenience of a mobile device. This App makes it easy to interact with any of the live auctions. Features include: direct access to auction sites, GPS directions, detailed auction schedules, photo gallery, live forum and much more.

2.1.5. Livestock Feeding Made Easy

Authors in [7] say that this app allows one to enter the amount of livestock, e.g., such as dairy cows, beef cattle, cattle, and calves of all ages. Also information on sheep, deer and horses can also be entered. Then record the quality of the brass/silage or hay being fed can also be stored along with the amounts (if any) of concentrates being used. One can also find out how much they need to use to stretch that feed. Finally, detailed reports can also be generated detailing the amount of livestock units, the amount they consume per day (kilograms) and how much concentrates they get.

2.1.6. Livestock Information Management System

As per reference [8], at the NBAGR, Karnal, a menu-driven livestock information management system was developed for animal resources. All the date tables and report forms are designed in the form of a single package. The database has information on livestock population, genetic resources, infrastructure, production, products and utilization, farms, etc. Separate tables have also been defined for each parameter. The master tables have names and codes of fields, which are repeatedly used in other tables, and there are data tables, which are linked to master tables and contain actual data.

2.1.7. Livestock Information Management System (LIMS)

The LIMS software package is designed to facilitate the recording and processing of livestock data in developing countries. The package is not specialized for use with any particular species or production system, but can be used with data for any mammal species for a variety of purposes, such as research, extension and commercial production. The objective is to provide users with a computerized tool that allows them to manage complex livestock performance data set, and to provide help in livestock management without relying on specialist computer and data management support.

The LIMS software package has been designed to address six key issues in management of livestock performance data, i.e., balance of flexibility and standardization of data definition, documentation and definition of data sets, assistance in deriving non-observed data (breed, parity, mating-parturition connection), data validation and error correction, reporting for animal management, and data extraction and calculation of standard performance traits for statistical analysis. In order to address these various aspects of livestock data management, the proposed LIMS software has a modular design, with different modules addressing each of the above mentioned issues. A generic data set is distributed along with the LIMS software. LIMS is developed in the CLIPPER language. All data in a LIMS data set are stored in dBASE III + compatible data files [9].

2.2. Challenges of Current Information Systems

Most of the applications mentioned above require continuous Internet access. Moreover, they cannot use experience to build upon prior knowledge and better respond to user requests. As such, they do not address the specific issues and concerns facing Arumeru district livestock keepers.

3. Requirements Analysis

In this section, we discuss the requirements analysis for designing of the machine – learning based framework for enhancing performance of livestock mobile application system. Now requirements analysis involves defining customer needs and objectives in the context of planned customer use, environments, and identified system characteristics to determine requirements for system functions

System requirement is a need: a process or improvement that stakeholders want to realize through a system. It is a demand to a system: (functionality) or quality (performance) that a system must have to fulfill the need of the stakeholders [10].

3.1. Functional

Overall, the system should provide convenience and automation for both livestock keepers and livestock experts. It should also satisfy the following requirements:

a) The system should provide plenty of informative instructions or guidelines to help livestock keepers find available modern livestock practices.
b) The system should provide effective information to livestock experts and back to livestock keepers.
c) The system should provide suitable marketing information.
d) The system should provide powerful functions to help district livestock officers manage field livestock officers.
e) The system should be able to work and collect information in poor connectivity areas.
f) The system should be able to predict responses.
g) System should be able to improve performance of livestock keepers in some tasks basing on experience.
h) The systems should allow users to retrieve up-to-date livestock information.
i) Intelligent processing using machine learning techniques.
j) Developing system interfaces which can call and implement specific data processing in the system.

In accordance with the above requirements, the machine – learning based framework for enhancing performance of livestock mobile application system should require minimize human operation and supervision, so as to reduce the cost of manpower and the lost from human mistake and to enhance the extension services.

3.2. The Non-Functional Requirements Include

a) Ease of use, so that developers can use the tool to their benefit;
b) Ease of distribution and integration, making the tool available and ready for application;
c) Extendibility, allowing developers to add functionality according to their specific needs.

3.3. Data Flow Diagram (DFD)

As per [11], a data flow diagram (DFD) graphically describes the flow of data within an organization. It is used to document existing systems and to plan and design new ones. Generally, there is no ideal way to develop a DFD. However it is composed of the following four basic elements: data sources and destinations, data flows, transformation processes, and data stores. In this study, the DFD shows how information is delivered by the livestock keeper from various sources such as livestock researchers, field officers and livestock field officers.

3.3.1. Existing Data Flow Diagram

The existing model puts the livestock field officer at the middle between the livestock keeper and other actors. Hence all information passes through this individual.

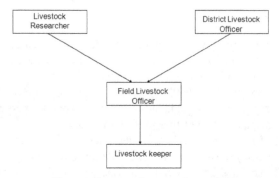

Figure 2. Existing information flow model.

Field livestock officers face challenges in dispersing useful information to livestock keepers who are geographically scattered. These officers generally do not have reliable means of transport and communication. Therefore there are barriers in conveying modern livestock practices and other extension services.

3.3.2. Proposed Data Flow Model

The proposed model will work in both internet connectivity and poor connectivity area basing upon machine learning techniques, see Figure 3 below.

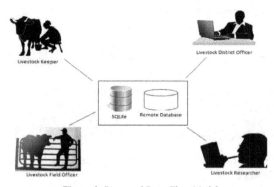

Figure 3. Proposed Data Flow Model.

The proposed data flow model has more advantages than the existing model. These include;

- Information is received by the livestock keeper directly from various stakeholders, as opposed to the existing one where data is received through the livestock field officers.
- Information is delivered through mobile phones.
- Field officers respond to queries on the system, not face to face.
- Researchers publish results on a central database which are accessible to every actor.
- System also works in poor connectivity areas.

- Machine learning responds to queries and can make predictions

3.4. Flowchart of the Information System

A flowchart is an analytical technique used to describe some aspect of an information system in a clear, concise, and logical manner. Flowcharts use a standard set of symbols to pictorially describe transaction processing procedures. Flowcharting symbols can be divided into the following four categories: input/output symbols, processing symbols, storage symbols, and flow and miscellaneous symbols [11]. Figure 4 below shows the flow chart of the proposed system.

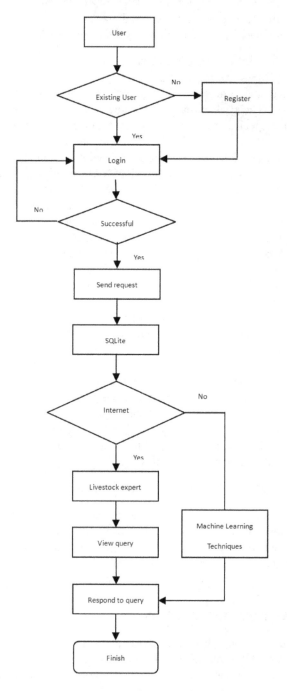

Figure 4. Flow chart diagram.

3.5. Differences Between DFDs and Flowcharts

According to [11], there are many differences between DFDs and flowcharts including:

- DFDs emphasize the flow of data and what is happening in a system, whereas a flowchart emphasizes the flow of documents or records containing data.
- A DFD represents the logical flow of data, whereas a flowchart represents the physical flow of data.
- Flowcharts are used primarily to document existing systems. DFDs, in contrast, are primarily used in the design of new systems and do not concern themselves with the physical devices used to process, store, and transform data.
- DFDs make use of only four symbols, whereas flowcharts use many symbols and thus can show more detail.

3.6. Use Case Diagram

A use case illustrates a unit of functionality provided by the system. The main purpose of the use case diagrams is to help development teams visualize the functional requirements of a system, including the relationship of "actors" (human beings who will interact with the system) to essential processes, as well as the relationships among different use cases [12].

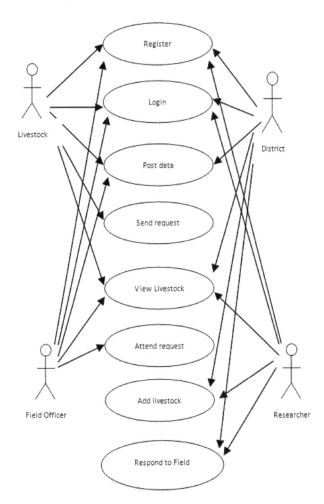

Figure 5. Information Flow Diagram.

3.7. Information Flow

An information flow model characterizes how information flows throughout an application by describing the kinds of processing that take place and how data flows between these stages.

In our study we will connect to a remote MySQL database via an Android application. Since these entities cannot communicate directly, we will use PHP. Namely, we will create a PHP-based web service that will allow our Android application to register a new user, login, and parse data within our application. Hence the design will need a server, a MySQL database, PHP knowledge, Eclipse, and the Android SDK.

3.8. Data Modeling

According to [13], data modeling is the process of learning about data, and the data model is the end result of the data modeling process. In addition, data modeling is a process used to define and analyze data requirements needed to support the business processes within the scope of corresponding information systems in organizations.

A data model organizes data elements and standardizes how the data elements relate to one another. As the name implies, the data model focuses on what data is required and how it should be organized rather than what operations will be performed on the data. The data model focuses on representing the data as the user sees it in the "real world".

According to [14], a data model is a way finding tool for both business and IT professionals, which uses a set of symbols and text to precisely explain a subset of real information to improve communication within the organization and thereby lead to a more flexible and stable application environment.

Data models are often used as an aid to communication between business people (defining the requirements for a computer system) and technical people (defining the design in response to those requirements). The data model can sometimes be referred to as data structure, especially in the context of programming languages. Data modeling comprises of Entity Relationship Diagrams (ERD) and Class Diagrams.

3.8.1. Entity Relationship Diagrams (ERD)

As per [15] an Entity-Relationship (ER) diagram provides a graphical model of the things that the organization deals with (entities) and how these things are related to one another (relationships). This approach presents a graphical representation of objects or concepts within an information system or organization and their relationship to one another. ER diagrams are typically used in computing to show the organization of data within databases or information systems. An entity is a piece of data, an object or concept about which data is stored. A relationship is how the data is shared between entities.

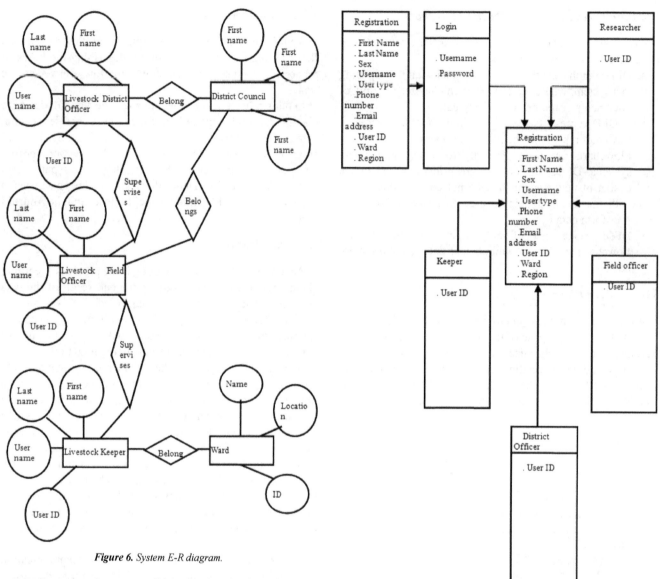

Figure 6. *System E-R diagram.*

E-R diagrams often use symbols to represent three different types of information. Boxes are commonly used to represent entities. Diamonds are normally used to represent relationships, and ovals are used to represent attributes.

3.8.2. Class Diagram

A class diagram describes the types of object in the system and the various kinds of relationships among them. The UML representation of a class is a rectangle containing three compartments stacked vertically. The top compartment shows the class's name. The middle compartment lists the class's attributes. Finally, the bottom compartment lists the class's operations. Class diagrams describe the types of objects in the system and the various kinds of static relationships that exist among them. It shows how the different entities (people, things, and data) relate to each other.

Figure 7. *System class diagram.*

3.9. Application Wireframe

Wireframes is an important design tool used in mobile app development. It is a visualization tool for presenting proposed functions, structure and content of the mobile app. It separates the graphic elements of the app from the functional elements in such a way that Android development teams can easily explain how users will interact with the app.

A key aspect of mobile applications development is building a good wireframe. Namely, we miss out on the layout configuration at the beginning, our development, thus the project costs could exceed the planned amounts. Nevertheless, changes in the specification are possible at any time. Here, some will change the mobile application price, whereas others will just re-use already allocated resources [16].

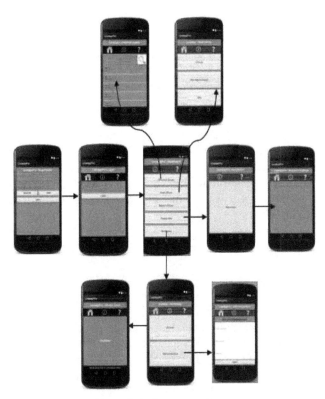

Figure 8. *Application wireframe.*

4. System Overview

In this section, we describe the design of our machine learning - based framework for enhancing performance of livestock mobile application system. First, we introduce the hardware components employed in our system. Next we discuss the software components of the system. Finally, we describe the overall architecture.

4.1. Hardware Components

Hardware comprises of all physical components that make up the intelligent livestock information system.

4.1.1. Smartphone

Smartphone are used to send queries and receive the requests. The user can request the modern livestock practices at any time from the server. The smartphone also has SQLite database to synchronize and store data.

4.1.2. Server

A server is a computer program that provides services to other computer programs (and their users) in the same or other computers. The computer that a server program runs in is also frequently referred to as a server (although it may be used for other purposes as well) [17].

4.1.3. Remote Database

A database is any collection of related data. The database stores details for all the users subscribed in the service with their locations. Hence the proposed system will use remote database to store data. The data replication will be done using

SQLite.

4.2. Software Components

These are the instructions that operate the functions of the information system.

4.2.1. PHP

PHP is a server-side scripting language designed for web development but also used as a general-purpose programming language [18]. It provides a powerful tool for building dynamic and interactive web page content. PHP is a widely-used, free, and provides an efficient alternative to competitors such as Microsoft's API [18].

4.2.2. Eclipse

Eclipse is an integrated development environment (IDE) which contains a base workspace and an extensible plug-in system for customizing the environment. It is written mostly in Java and can be used to develop applications in other programming languages as well [19]. Eclipse is used to design the Android system. It has XML side, which is used for designing the application, and Java side which is used for coding.

4.2.3. Android Software Development Kit (SDK)

We will use the Android Software Development Kit (SDK) to develop Applications in the Java programming language.

4.2.4. Android Application

Android is the world's most popular operating system for mobile devices and tablets. It is an open source operating system created by Google and is available to all kinds of developers with various expertise levels, ranging from rookie to professional [20].

4.2.5. SQLite

SQLite is the embedded database used for Android applications, which is a client-server relational database management system.

4.2.6. Matlab

We will use MATLAB as it has a number of built-in features that make machine learning easier. MATLAB is also very fast compared to other languages such as Mathematica and Python.

4.3. System Architecture

The ILIS framework will collect livestock data from keepers via mobile phones. The data will be sent to the database either through the regular Internet or via synchronization (in case of poor connectivity). Livestock experts will view data and respond to any query from the keepers. The system will be able to learn and predict the responses using machine learning techniques.

The application architecture and its working principle are centered on the use of machine learning techniques.

The centralized database provides a livestock database to the users. The purpose of choosing centralized data sharing is to reduce the storage overhead on each phone. Otherwise, each mobile may have its own local database stored on the device and sharing may be allowed between different users.

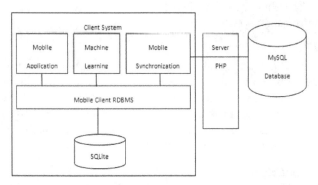

Figure 9. System Architecture.

4.3.1. Client System

The Android mobile application will be designed and installed on a smartphone and will provide an easy-to-use Graphical User Interface (GUI). The application will request resources from the server via the Internet or with a limited connectivity and will check connectivity state using a connection manager.

4.3.2. Typical Learning

Smartphone devices will be installed with a developed android application. The designed system will be able to replicate from the remote database to the SQLite. Machine learning will be able to use experience and make predictions. Server can learn to provide feedback automatically. Server will be trained automatically by mining and analyzing data of all the possible livestock practice scenarios and become a real intelligent one.

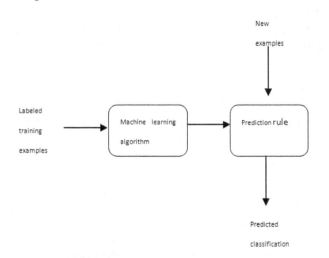

Figure 10. Typical learning.

4.3.3. Steps in Developing Machine Learning Application

Below are steps that will be used in developing machine learning application.

1) Collect data. Data will be collected from livestock keepers and livestock experts from fifteen wards of Arumeru district, Arusha region, in Tanzania.

2) Prepare the input data. We will prepare the input data in a useable format.

3) Analyze the input data. We will look at the data from the previous task to make sure steps 1 and 2 are actually working, and to see if we can recognize any patterns or if there will be anything obvious. We will plot data in graphs.

4) Train the algorithm. This is where the machine learning takes place. We will feed the algorithm good clean data from the first two steps and extract knowledge or information.

5) Test the algorithm. We will test it to see how well it is doing. We will use some known values to evaluate the algorithm.

6) Use it. Here we will make a real program to do some task, and see if all the previous steps work as expected.

5. Conclusion

This paper proposes the design of a machine learning - based livestock information system. It discusses different modeling diagrams, software, hardware descriptions, and architecture of the system. The system is designed to work in poor connectivity rural areas. The requirements of livestock keepers and livestock experts are analyzed to develop the main system functions and system architecture.

This Intelligent Livestock Information System (ILIS) will be able to provide and predict feedback to the livestock keepers. This solution will also collect livestock data from livestock keepers through mobile phones. The data will then be sent to the database if connectivity is available or through synchronization if connectivity is poor. Overall this solution embodies an artificial intelligence approach which combines hardware and software technologies. The design will leverage the Android ADK operating system and Android mobile devices or tablets.

Our main contribution here is the designing of intelligent livestock Information System, which is a novel idea in the field of mobile livestock information systems. It will be able to respond to user queries and make predictions. The System will provide livestock services to anyone at anytime, overcoming the constraints of place, time and character.

The ILIS will minimize human operations and supervisions, so as to reduce the cost of manpower and the lost from human mistake and to enhance the extension services.

6. Future Work

In the future we plan develop and implement machine learning – based application framework for enhancing performance of livestock mobile application systems. The application will cutter for the problem of decreasing performance of mobile apps when in poor connectivity areas. When completed, this system will enable users of an ILIS, in areas of poor connectivity, to experience same performance levels as in good connectivity areas.

Acknowledgement

We hereby express our gratitude to the Nelson Mandela African Institution of Science and Technology (NM-AIST), Livestock Training Agency (LITA-Tengeru), National Artificial Insemination Agency (NAIC), and Arumeru District Council for their support.

We acknowledge the input made by the anonymous peer reviewers.

References

[1] Weld, D.S., editor. (1995), The Role of Intelligent Systems in the National Information Infrastructure, American Association for Artificial Intelligence.

[2] Oksana Pomorova, Tetyana Hovorushchenko. Intelligent Assessment and Prediction of Software Characteristics at the Design Stage, American Journal of Software Engineering and Applications. Vol. 2, No. 2, 2013, pp. 25-31. doi: 10.11648/j.ajsea.20130202.11

[3] Noble, B. D., Satyanarayanan, M. C., Siewiorek, D. P., Zhang, H. and Katz, R. H., 1998. Mobile Data Access, School of Computer Science, Carnegie Mellon University, CMU-CS-98-118.

[4] Terry, D. B., Theimer, M. M., Petersen, K. and Demers, A. J., 1995. A Portable Multimedia, Terminal Weakly Connected Replicated Storage System, In Proceedings of the 15th ACM Symposium on Operating System Principles, 30(12), 64–76. PMid:10152743

[5] Applion, "cow tracker", accessed on 25th March 2015, from http://applion.jp/android/app/com.sbumpkin/

[6] Freapp, "Mobile cattle tracker", accessed on 25th March 2015, from http://app.freapp.com/apps/ios/775966992/

[7] Google play, "Livestock feeding made easy", accessed on 23rd March 2015, from https://play.google.com/store/apps/details?id=com.livestockfeed

[8] DARE/88 ARE/ICAR ANNUAL REPORT 2003–2004, "Livestock Information Management System", unpublished.

[9] Metz, T., Asfaw (1999), Livestock Information Management System, ILRI, Ethiopia.

[10] Joris Vanderschrick (2011), System Requirements Analysis: The first step to value-based system development, Uit: Handboek Requirements.

[11] Marshall B. Romney and Paul John Steinbart (2003), Accounting Information Systems, 9th Edition, Prentice Hall Business Publishing.

[12] IBM, "UML basics: An introduction to the Unified Modeling Language", accessed on 15th March 2015, from http://www.ibm.com/developerworks/rational/library/769.html

[13] Steve Hoberman (2009), Data Modeling Made Simple 2nd Edition, Technics Publications, LLC 2009.

[14] Steve Hoberman (2014). Data Modeling Master Class Training Manual 5th Edition. Technics Publications, LLC.

[15] Webopodia, "entity-relationship diagram (model)", accessed on 10th March 2015 from http://www.webopedia.com/TERM/E/entity_relationship_diagram.html

[16] Profi.co, Mobile Applications Development. Accessed on 20th March, 2015 on http://profi.co/mobile-applications-development/

[17] WhatIs, "Server", accessed on 19th March 2015, from http://whatis.techtarget.com/definition/server

[18] W3Schools, "Introduction to PHP", accessed on 20th March from http://www.w3schools.in/php/intro/.

[19] Wikipedia, "Eclipse (software)", accessed on 20th March 2015, from http://en.wikipedia.org/wiki/Eclipse_%28software%29.

[20] Cprogramming, "Developing for Android - An Introduction", accessed on 21st March 2015, from http://www.cprogramming.com/android/android_getting_started.html.

11

Model-based approach to design web application testing tool

Dalila Souilem Boumiza[1], Amani Ben Azzouz[1], Salma Boumiza[2]

[1]Applied Computer Science Department, National Engineering School of Sousse, Sousse, Tunisia
[2]Computer Science Department, Technical University of Sofia, Sofia, Bulgaria

Email address:

Dalila.souilem@yahoo.fr (D. S. Boumiza), amanibenazzouz@yahoo.com (A. B. Azzouz), salma.boumiza@yahoo.com (S. Boumiza)

Abstract: Software engineering is a systematic approach defined as a science of industrial engineering that measures the practical methods and working process of the software engineers. This approach is based on analyzing, designing, assessment implementing testing and reengineering processes of given software All those phases are very important and have a specific role in SE's cycle, especially software testing that acts as a significant element in this cycle and it represents also a fundamental key for software quality assurance. Software testing has as goal to test the software performance by measuring the gap between the expected behavior of the software under test and the test results. This comparison allows the tester to analyze errors and bugs in order to fix them and develop the software performance. As a critical factor in SQA, software testing is considered like a definitive review of the tool's specification: it permits the tester to redesign the tool specification after the test in case of failure. This procedure is also applied on web applications, in similar ways to obtain the same goal: applications quality assurance, but the web applications are more complicated to be tested because of the interaction of the application with the rest of the distributed system. In fact, in more precisely terms, web application testing is a process that measures the functional and non functional proprieties of a given web application to analyze its performance in order to fix errors or even to reach a better level of the application under test. The demand on web applications or generally on software testing tools groups up with the increase in applications or software failures and cost.

Keywords: Software Testing Tools, Software Quality Assurance, Web Application, Model-Based Testing

1. Introduction

The main idea of this paper is trying to improve the popular existing approach of testing web applications. In fact the most used technique to test web applications is the approach record and replay but we have proved that it is an unreliable technique so that an alternative solution must be taken. This settlement is the model based testing technique, and our project will be based in this fundamental perspective.

In fact, model based testing tool is an existing solution, but is it still a new approach that just some tools support. Our goal is to develop a tool that supports this technique and at the same time is simple and easy to be used by a regular user thanks to a graphical user interface GUI.

Our GUI will form a simple way to users to test web scenarios through the new "model-based testing" technique introducing a new and a simple way to perform test cases.

2. Record and Replay Approach [1]

This technique, as its name indicates, consists in recording a scenario from a web application then trying to replay it again in order to extract failure cases and to ensure right ones.

A web scenario is a group of a finite number of actions that the user can do manually. This group includes any action that can be performed by the mouse from a web page displayed in a browser like: clicking a button, clicking a link, filling a text field, dragging and dropping

The Scenario is recorded step by step, which means action after another, to form a test case. After being registered by the tool, this test case can be replayed so that the user can observe the generated results after the test execution and analyze them.

Most of web testing tools apply the "record/replay" function to create a test scenario, by following those steps: The user opens the Website to be tested, activates the record function, navigates into the website and select the desired actions, stops the record

The program saves the recorded actions as a file that can be opened at any time to replay the scenario.

3. Model-Based Testing [2] [3]

The model-based testing approach is not just specific for web applications only, but it is generally designed to fit all sorts of software.

Model-based testing is the testing process proceeding from a model that describes the comportment of the application that the user wants to test.

This model will be used in order to represent and simulate the behavior of the system under test (software, web application…).The model must be abstract to be faithful to the real system description. The key skill that is really required to make the model successful and derive from it good test cases is the design of a good and abstract model that captures only the essential aspects of the desired application or, in general terms, the SUT.

Model-based testing is a technique that reduces the amount of the user interaction by minimizing the manual tasks afforded by user, and producing tests automatically.

This technique only demand a well done model, that is indeed, the only part the user have to do; and the rest of procedure will be done by the tool itself automatically and basing-on this given model.

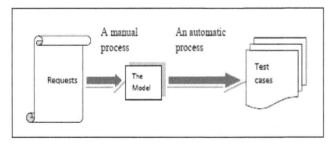

Figure 1. Process of Model-based testing approach.

4. Study of Existing Web Testing Tool

As a starting point of our project, a large study has been done while exploring the web testing tool's domain.

Many and various tools are provided; for that, users may wonder what tool to use when testing theirs applications. According to our research, we have selected a list of 20 web testing tools. The choice has been based on two major characteristics: At the first place, selected tools must be Java-based, afterwards, we have tried to figure out those between the large scale of Java based tools, what the most famous and most used are (this analysis has been concluded from the importance accorded to a given tool in professional forum discussions, web developers opinions, the total downloads number of the tool trial…).

Then, when actually trying to judge, in practical terms, the value of these pre-selected tools, some of them have been

illuminated. Indeed, many problems occur when trying to evaluate some tools: Some of them display errors even before any action is performed (like cubic test), other ones seem to be inefficient or very complicated and incomprehensible for the regular user (like GUI Dancer and Jubula)…

4.1. Research Methodologies [4] [5]

In order to proceed in analyzing an existing phenomenon, a research became obligatory to obtain satisfactory results.

Consequently, many methodological ways of research have appeared to saturate this need.

Indeed, three main research methodologies coexist: Quantitative, qualitative and mix research.

Every methodology exists to cover a special part of the sample that the researcher wants to examine.

So, before beginning any research process, the researcher is demanded to determine first of all its analyzing goals.

According to our case, our goal is to analyze the qualitative part of existing web testing tools, in order to achieve a quality product. Underlying this final goal, our research orients immediately, to the qualitative methodology.

Speaking about this research category, we can mention that it is characterized by analyzing textual data that can be an interview, a conversational analysis, a questionnaire…and then the collection of all provided information to measure the sample's quantitative value.

Coming back to our study that consists in examining existing web testing tools, the questionnaire methodology seems to be the most suitable solution for this case. A well done questionnaire, can easily measures the sample functionalities, and starting from this perspective, we have prepared an inclusive eight-question-based questionnaire.

These methodological questions are posed in a way to study the global characteristics of a web testing tool: This study allows comparing between those tools, detailing their features and most importantly their limits…

4.1.1. Questionnaire for the Qualitative Research Methodology [6] [7] [8] [9]

Questions are held in the following part in the format of eight separated paragraphs

4.1.1.1. Testing Ajax Applications

The first question has as an aim to test if the tool is able or not to support Ajax functions: It is able or not to record normally Ajax-based tests? In fact, we have chosen to accomplish a small simple test, Ajax-based, and repeat this test with the entire selected tool list.

4.1.1.2. Multisession

Here the question is: Is the tool able to record a same test from two different web browsers? And does it link between them in a same action?

This means, if the chosen testing tool is able to record a test divided in two different web browsers, some actions of the test are done in a browser; others are done in the other one, to form a whole one test.

In this level we have chosen to figure out whether a tool is able to record a chat action between two users from two different web browsers, in the same test. Accordingly, this test can be very useful to test web chatting pages, and it may be a critical measure to judge the tool.

4.1.1.3. Assertions

In this part we attempt to test if the tool is able or not to make assertions for HTML elements; we check if a user can be sure in a specific way that the desired HTML element exists or not in a specific web page.

Assertions are very important in the testing process. In fact, for some examples, the use of assertions is critical, like the case when a login process fails; the application returns a page indicating that the operation failed. This implies that no error has been detected. However, this is certainly an error condition. If the user has included additional pages dependent on successful login, an error would very probably occur later in one of these pages.

It is therefore, crucial to use assertions to detect such situations. Assertions help the tester to identify an error condition in the early scenario and to avoid analyzing incomprehensible errors, due to previous failures.

4.1.1.4. Report and Results

In this part, our goal is to explore the tool interface and see if it is able or not to offer a report or any type of result indications. Also, this is a very important point, because the report can ensure users from the test results: it passes or not; if not, what kind of errors occur, and how to fix them.

An efficient tool must be able to give the maximum details about a test especially when it fails, to guide users to the right way in order to get the satisfying results. Therefore, this point is a critical way to judge the tool efficiency.

4.1.1.5. Multi-Browser Support

The question here is: Is the tool able to works with more than just one web browser?

A multi-browser tool allows the user to test its web application in different platforms and that is very useful to examine how a browser reacts with this application in order to make it more efficient and convenient for all web browsers.

In some cases a web application can work with a web browser and fails with another one, so a multi-browser web testing tool can warn the user to this case, so that he can deal with this kind of problems.

4.1.1.6. Options of Extracting HTML Elements

The sixth question is: Does the tool provide the user with any option to pick how it searches and extracts the HTML elements when playing a test?

Methods of extracting HTML elements are many: by id, by label, by index…

Every tool has a default method to refer to a recorded HTML element. Indeed it is the manner how the tool recognizes a selected element to be able to re-call it again when playing the test. Some options are non methodological and fail re-finding the element frequently, so that we can pick this question as a measurement agent of the tool importance

and efficiency.

4.1.1.7. Error Handling

At this level, our question is how the tool handles with an error when it happens? Once again tools differ by their reaction in front of the error occurrence, and that may represent a factor of distinction between them.

Users may prefer a tool that allows them to choose how to react when an error occurs, for some purposes related with the test nature.

Some of them would prefer, for example, to stop the test execution and try to fix the error; others may want to know how the application continues in this case, so they pick the continuation mode when finding an error.

4.1.1.8. Exporting and Importing Options

Right here, we want to see if the web testing tool is able or not to import and export the test into a specific programming language.

Exporting projects or tasks are in some cases, very important, because that allows users to handle with the exported file: explore it, edit it…without being obliged to re-open the tool every time.

Besides, it can help them to translate the test into another programming language that can be very easy to work with for some users.

4.1.2. Analyzing of the Chosen Web Testing Tools [10]

The questionnaire methodology consists in analyzing some given samples and making conclusions in order to improve and develop those samples. We have chosen to illustrate all the quantitative study done before, in a small table that aims to allow a direct and easy comparison between deferent tried tools.

In our project we choose to focus on what we have considered as the most important and common limits: the problem of use of the dynamic ID while recording actions and saving HTML objects during the test, and the un-multisession issue.

Consequently to these major limits, we can conclude that the "record and replay" technique is unreliable technique. As a matter of fact, it is the "record and replay approach" that we have tried with all previous tools, and we have discovered that it contains many deficiencies.

5. The Proposed Approach [1]

To avoid all the record and replay approach problems, we have chosen to create a model-based testing application.

The most important benefit of model-based testing is that instead of performing many test cases manually the tester can replace this big effort by just designing a model that describes the expected behavior of the application that he wants to test.

From the user requests from a given application, the user has to generate all test cases manually with the traditional approach, but the model-based testing technique saves the tester effort by generating all tests cases automatically; only the model has to be done manually.

From a given model, the user can select a specific algorithm that permits the test case generation, so the tester can obtain different test cases depending on the used algorithm.

Our project relies on this approach because of its diverse benefits. In fact, model-based testing technique:

- Reduces time costs: Many published studies show that this technique reduces time while testing. It is a fact that an abstract model can take time to be well designed but in case of deriving many test cases of the same application, the automatic test generation will be faster and easier than the manual one even when including the model designing time.

- Helps to detect logical errors: Besides its natural role, detecting the functionality errors, model-based testing can help to detect some requirement errors in the application structure and design, which means that while designing the model, the tester can detect some errors or lacks in the application conception and this gives him the possibility to rectify and develop the application after or even while testing the model.

- Is easy to be update: One important advantage is that when the application requirements change, it will be very difficult to be done once again manually: In case of large amounts of test cases, it will take time and patience to repeat all test cases manually, one per one. In case of model- based testing the user has only to update his model and re-generate new test cases automatically from the new updated model.

The main disadvantage of the approach is the time that has to be spent while modeling an abstract model and also the necessity of the expertise of some programming language and modeling skills to achieve a good model

Our application will be in a flash representation a graphical user interface GUI that is divided into two parts:

- General test scenario creation: Based on, like explained before, the model-based testing approach to automate test case generation.

- Specific test scenario creation: That permits the user to generate a specific test case manually.

So, like that, our project will be like a combination between the two approach advantages:

- The possibility to automate test generation, especially in case of large amounts of test cases are needed, to profit from the model-based testing technique and the test automation. This technique will be faster and easier in our project by simplifying the model designing compared to the existing one. This plus will make models easier to be modeled by the user and will reduce the amount of errors in the test. The simplification of the existing model format will be explained later on the conception part to explain the conception of the new model standard and then in the realization chapter to demonstrate how we have realized the designed model.

- The possibility to pick the manually recording test in case of a specific test case, because if the tester wants to test just one specific case, the automatic mode will generate many test cases, and that will demand a long time to find the suitable and desired case if it exists. So, in this case, a manual test will be a faster, easier and more practical solution.

The case of a specific scenario creation will be also model-based, despite that we will not use the model to generate test cases automatically, but it will be used to build a step by step test case, in terms of the user choice.

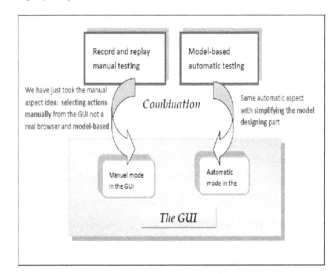

Figure 2. *The architecture of the GUI.*

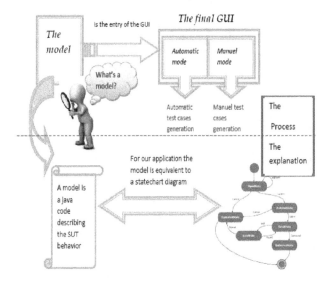

Figure 3. *General architecture of application.*

For web testing applications, models will be like a behavior's description of a given website. For that, the model can be considered as a group of states that represent all possible status of the application. Moving from a state to another is in fact a result of a specific action that leads the application from a status to another one.

So like that, a model can be regarded as a combination of states and actions that are related in a logical and sequential way to form a state chart diagram.

For more understanding the following figure can translate the internal components interaction in the application, relating the testing process to its logical explanation.

6. The Conception of the GUI [11]

6.1. Global Structure of the Application

The following figure recapitulates the application's behavior. Red boxes are the actions that have to be done by the user, and the green ones are those afforded by the application.

All user actions are afforded by simple mouse interactions with the tool. The only important action that the user has to do is the model designing.

After selecting the model describing the SUT behavior, the user can follow the previous steps indicated in the figure: First of all, the user has to select a testing mode through the first window of the application. Second, the GUI will automatically extract all the constitutions (states, actions and assertions) of the given model using the java reflection. If the selected mode is automatic, test cases generation will be done automatically after picking a specific generation algorithm (an algorithm is a specific manner that the application can follow to produce automatic testes). If the user choice is the manual mode, the tool will display all the possible actions in the model, and then the user can select a specific one between them.

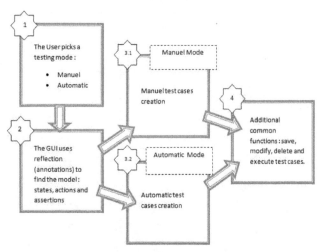

Figure 4. Structure of the GUI.

From this chosen action the tool will display the state that the action has led to. From the new state, the tool will display all the possible actions in this particular state so that the tester can pick another action leading to a new state and so one in order to form the desired test case (traveling in a state chart diagram). After creating automatic or manual test cases, the user can modify, save, execute or delete any test he wants.

7. Conclusion

In this paper we have tried to demonstrate the need of a new approach for testing web applications.

Previously while speaking about the adopted solution according to traditional testing ways, we have mentioned that we have improved existing models format, for the automatic testing mode. The old model has to handle with all the existing actions in the SUT independently, which means that the model designer has to produce all the possible actions and relate them to form a state chart diagram. This process can be very long and fatiguing when designing web application models, because they are complicated and rich. So, we have merged some related actions into one action. For example, to perform a login process to a specific website, the user has to accomplish three successive actions: entering the user pseudo name or email, then the password and finally clicking the submit button. By merging those three actions in a unique action, we can save the designer effort and time.

References

[1]   D. Souilem Boumiza and A. Ben Azzouz and F. Ben Brahim 2012 "Design and development of a user interface to customize web testing scenarios" *International Conference on Education & E-Learning Innovations ICEELI' 2012 , July 1-3 Sousse, Tunisia*

[2]   C. Eaton and A. M. Memon: "An Empirical Approach to Testing Web Applications Across Diverse Client Platform Configurations" by. International Journal on Web Engineering and Technology (IJWET), Special Issue on Empirical Studies in Web Engineering, vol. 3, no. 3, 2007, pp. 227–253, Inderscience Publishers.

[3]   T.Banner, H.Eicher, A.Rennoch. "Model-based testing in practice". 2nd workshop on model-based testing. In practice MOTIP 2009.

[4]   Sampath, R. Bryce, Gokulanand Viswanath, Vani Kandimalla, A. Gunes Koru: "Prioritizing User-Session-Based Test Cases for Web Applications Testing". Proceedings of the International Conference on Software Testing, Verification, and Validation (ICST), Lillehammer, Norway, April 2008.

[5]   Research methodologies: concluded from http://www.enge.vt.edu", on april 2012.

[6]   Testing anywhere: concluded from http://www . softwaretesting.net/ otherproducts/ testinganywhere .html , 2012.

[7]   Win Task: concluded from http://www .csscody.com/ resources / web -testing- tool -list , 20013.

[8]   Bad Boy: concluded from "http:/www.badbody.com.au/" 2012.

[9]   Sahi: "http:/www.sahi.co.in/w/" 2012

[10] Fabasoft app.test : concludes from "htt://en.wikipedia.org/ wiki/fabasoft_app.test" , April 2012.

[11] Unified Modeling Language: Extract from "http://en.wikipedia.org/wiki/ Unified_Modeling_Language" , May 2012.

[12] Softwareengineering: http://en.wikipedia.org/wiki/Software _engineering, on April 2012

[13] J. Ernits, R. Roo, J. Jacky, M. Veanes «http://research.microsoft.com/pubs/101196/extended_version .pdf » On August 9, 2012

[14] B. Hayduk, « http://searchsoftwarequality.techtarget.com /tip/Model-based-testing-for-Java-and-Web-based-GUI-applic ations » On August 9, 2012

An empirical study on the effectiveness of automated test case generation techniques

Bolanle F. Oladejo, Dimple T. Ogunbiyi

Department of Computer Science, University of Ibadan, Ibadan, Nigeria

Email address:

fb.oladejo@ui.edu.ng (B. F. Oladejo), ogunbiyidimple@gmail.com (D. T. Ogunbiyi)

Abstract: The advent of automated test case generation has helped to reduce the laborious task of generating test cases manually and is prominent in the software testing field of research and as a result, several techniques have been developed to aid the generation of test cases automatically. However, some major currently used automated test case generation techniques have not been empirically evaluated to ascertain their performances as many assumptions on technique performances are based on theoretical deductions. In this paper, we perform experiment on two major automated test case generation techniques (Concolic test case generation technique and the Combinatorial test case generation technique) and evaluate based on selected metrics (number of test cases generated, complexities of the selected programs, the percentage of test coverage and performance score). The results from the experiment show that the Combinatorial technique performed better than the Concolic technique. Hence, the Combinatorial test case generation technique was found to be more effective than the Concolic test case generation technique based on the selected metrics.

Keywords: Automated Test Case Generation Technique, Combinatorial, Concolic, Empirical Study, Software Testing, Software Metrics

1. Introduction

Software testing plays a very significant role in the software development process and serves as an important way to measure and improve software quality with its main intent on detecting defects in software. Software testing has been defined as a process of verifying and validating that a software program meets its business and technical requirements that guides its design and development and works as expected [2] therefore, it is a very important means of assessing software to determine its quality [11]. It is also heavily used to initiate, locate and remove software defects [13]. Software testing can be broken down into three fundamental procedures; design (generation) of test cases, execution of test cases and checking whether the output produced is correct based on the input given [10].

Test case generation is a process of creating or identifying test data which can satisfy a given testing criterion [8]. Test case generation is among the most labour-intensive tasks in software testing and its manual approach can take very long time to generate and execute test cases. Automated test case generation came into place to reduce the work load of testers

[1] with the intent of generating quality test cases to execute programs. In recent years, several techniques have been developed to enhance automated test case generation and it is important for testers/researchers to be conversant with current approaches to generating test cases automatically. Furthermore, it is also important to perform experiments on automated test case generation techniques in order to appraise their performances. Reference [15] encouraged researchers to carry out repeated experiments on tools and techniques in order to give the software testers knowledge on their strengths, weaknesses, effectiveness and functionalities. Hence, this study is aimed at evaluating the effectiveness of two major automated test case generation techniques, with its objectives stated as; identifying which technique achieves the highest test coverage; identifying the effect of program complexities on the test coverage of techniques and identifying which technique is most effective in general.

In this paper, we evaluate the Combinatorial and Concolic test case generation techniques. In addition, we compare and evaluate the techniques based on the number of test cases generated, complexities of the selected programs, percentage of test coverage and performance score for achieving each of the stated objectives. The results from the experiment shows that Combinatorial technique achieved a higher test coverage than the Concolic technique for the programs used. The results also show that the complexities of the programs used does not affect the Combinatorial technique in achieving high test coverage but affects the Concolic technique in achieving high test coverage.

The remaining part of this paper will present a brief description of the selected techniques in section 2, the related studies in section 3, the experimental procedure in section 4, the results in section 5 and the conclusion in section 6.

2. Description of Selected Techniques

This section presents a brief description of the operations of the techniques selected for evaluation. The techniques are; Concolic and Combinatorial techniques. The automated test case generation tools (referred to as test case generators) for each technique, were selected based on their features and functions. The techniques/tools are described in the subsections below.

2.1. Concolic Technique

The Concolic technique is a hybrid technique that combines Concrete execution (executes program using concrete inputs) with Symbolic execution (executes program using symbolic inputs). Concolic testing performs symbolic execution of a program along a concrete execution path. It executes a program starting with some specified or random concrete input and gathers symbolic constraints on inputs at conditional statements during the execution caused by the concrete input then it uses a constraint solver to create variants of the concrete input for the next execution of the program. This process will be repeated until all feasible execution paths are explored or a user-defined coverage criterion is met [16].

The Concolic test case generator used for the experiment is a publicly available tool named LIME Concolic Tester [7] and is available at http://www.tcs.hut.fi/Software/lime/.

2.2. Combinatorial (Pairwise) Technique

The Combinatorial technique generates test cases for a combination of parameters for programs. It places special emphasis on selecting a sample of input parameters covering a recommended subset of combinations of elements to be tested. For each pair of input parameters it will test all possible discrete combinations of those parameters, using chosen test vectors [9]. Pairwise testing is a prominent combinatorial strategy that reduces the number of test cases created. Pairwise testing strategy is defined as: Given a set of N independent test factors: $f_1, f_2, ..., f_N$, with each factor f_i having L_i possible levels: $f_i = \{l_{i,1}, ..., l_i, L_i\}$, a set of tests R is produced. Each test in R contains N test levels, one for each test factor f_i, and collectively all tests in R cover all possible pairs of test factor levels i.e. for each pair of factor levels $l_{i,p}$ and $l_{j,q}$, where $1 \leq p \leq$

L_i, $1 \leq q \leq L_j$ and $i \neq j$ there exists at least one test in R that contains both $l_{i,p}$ and $l_{j,q}$ [3]. The Combinatorial test case generator used for the experiment is also a publicly available tool named Test Case Generator, developed by Bulmahn M. in 2007 and is available at http://www.download.microsoft.com/download\.

3. Related Studies

Several experimental studies have been carried out on various automated test case generation techniques. This section presents the methods and results of some similar work that have been carried out on automated test case generation. Reference [6] conducted experiment on four test data generation techniques (Random technique, IRM based Method, Korel method and GA based method). The results of the experiment show that the genetic algorithm (GA)-based test data generation performs the best. Reference [5] carried out an experiment comparing a total of 49 subjects split between writing tests manually and writing tests with the aid of an automated unit test generation tool, EVOSUITE. The purpose of this study was to investigate how the use of an automatic test generation tool, when used by testers, impacts the testing process compared to traditional manual testing. Their results indicated that while the use of automated test generation tools can improve structural coverage over manual testing, it does not appear to improve the ability of testers to detect current or future regression faults. Reference [7] compared the effectiveness of Concolic testing and random testing. The experiment shows that Concolic testing is able to find significantly more bugs than random testing in the testing domain. Reference [4] presented an empirical comparison of automated generation and classification techniques for object oriented unit testing. Pairs of test-generation techniques based on random generation or symbolic execution and test-classification techniques based on uncaught exceptions or operational models were compared. Their findings show that the techniques are complementary in revealing faults. Some other experimental studies conducted are on the evaluation of tools [17], [14].

This study extends existing empirical studies by testing the effectiveness of two techniques that have been widely used over the years for test case generation and test coverage improvement. We present in this study an experimental structure describing the activities involved in evaluating the techniques, this can also serve as a framework for further experiments or can be advanced.

4. Experimental Procedure

This section presents the methods and procedures used for the experiment. It covers the programs selected, experimental processes and the metrics used for evaluation. In addition, we present an experimental structure that simplifies the description of the experimental procedure used in evaluating the test case generation techniques selected as shown in "Fig. 1".

We used three different java programs (test objects) based on some features such as; arrays, loops, branching statements method calls and complexity measure of the programs. The complexity of each program was measured using the cyclomatic complexity metric (see section 4.1.1.) and the test case generators were applied on the programs.

The Concolic test case generator was installed and executed on a Linux ubuntu environment. It was applied on the three programs. Each program was passed as input to the test case generator and the resulting test cases were generated and coverage measured automatically. However, during the course of carrying out the experiment, it was discovered that a limitation of the Concolic test case generator used is that it does not accept string parameters. Therefore, the test case generator was applied on only two of the programs out of the three selected programs as one of the programs accepts string inputs only.

"Fig. 2" shows a snapshot of the Concolic test case generator environment.

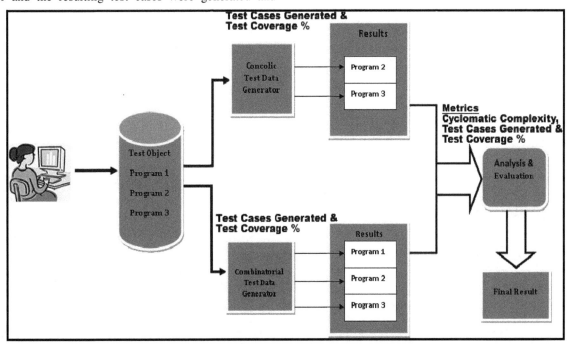

Figure 1. Experimental Structure for the Evaluation of Selected Techniques.

Figure 2. The Concolic Test Case Generator Environment.

The Combinatorial test case generator was installed and executed on a windows 7 environment. It was applied on three of the programs for individual results and applied on two of the programs for the compare results. The test cases were generated automatically from a list of user specified parameters, expected outcomes and rules for each of the programs. A combination depth of two (2) was selected because this study considers pairwise combinatorial strategy and the test coverage was determined from the test cases generated. "Fig. 3" shows a snapshot of the Combinatorial test case generator environment.

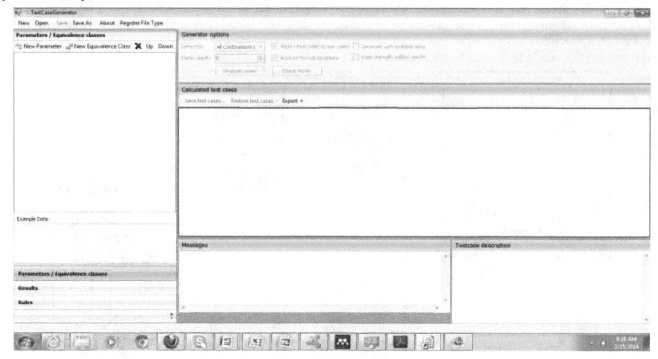

Figure 3. The Combinatorial Test Case Generator Environment.

4.1. Selected Metrics

This section presents the metrics used for comparison of the techniques. They were selected amongst other metrics in order to achieve the stated objectives of this study. Their descriptions are given in the following subsections:

4.1.1. Cyclomatic Complexity

We used the cyclomatic complexity metric to measure the complexity of each program used in this study. This complexity metric was selected because it quantitatively measures the logical capability of a program. The cyclomatic complexity was calculated from each program's control flow graph. A control flow graph shows the flow of control of statements and decisions in a program. It consists of nodes (used to represent statements and decisions in a program) and edges. The complexity of each of the programs was measured using the McCabe's cyclomatic complexity formula [12].

The formula is given as;

$$v(G) = E - N + 2P$$

where:

$v(G)$ = Cyclomatic Complexity
E = The number of edges of the graph
N = The number of nodes of the graph
P = The number of connected components

Table 1 shows the complexity values for the three programs with the range from a low complexity value to a high complexity value.

Table 1. Cyclomatic Complexity Value for Selected Programs.

Program	Cyclomatic Complexity
Program 1	3
Program 2	5
Program 3	25

The complexity values of the programs as shown in the table above ranges from the lowest complexity to the highest complexity. Some researchers have deduced that the complexity value of a program above ten (10) has a very high complexity. Furthermore, Reference [14], categorized the cyclomatic complexity value range of programs into three parts which include; LOW (complexity value range is 1- 4), MID (complexity value range is 5-10) and HIGH (complexity value range is above 10).

We used the cyclomatic complexity metric to test if the complexities of the programs would affect the test coverage of the automated test case generation techniques. An assumption is that the techniques should be able to achieve high coverage even with complex programs to prove that it is really effective.

4.1.2. Number of Test Cases Generated

The number of test cases generated for each program was gotten from the test case generators.

4.1.3. Test Coverage

We used the test coverage metric to determine the degree to which the programs have been executed by the test cases generated. The branch coverage criterion was determined for the Concolic technique while the state space coverage criterion was determined for the Combinatorial technique [9]. The average percentage of test coverage by each test case generator was calculated and their performances were compared.

4.2. Threats to Validity

Our initial intent was to apply the test case generators on the three selected java programs partially because of the complexity range of the programs but in the comparison phase, the techniques were applied on only two of the three selected programs because of the limitation of the Concolic test case generator stated earlier. Furthermore, the test case generators were chosen amongst others because they meet our hardware requirements and program construct specifications. However,

we believe that if the test case generators were applied on the third program, the result would still be the same or would be very similar to the present results. Also, if the third program was used for comparison of the techniques, the Combinatorial technique would have achieved an average test coverage of 89% which is still very reasonable and still makes it effective.

5. Results

The previous section gave a description of the methods and experimental procedures used in this study. This section presents and discusses the results gotten from the experiment performed on the automated test case generation techniques. We present the individual results for the techniques and the compared results. The compared results are presented based on the objectives of this study.

5.1. Individual Results Generated

Table 2 shows the individual results gotten for the Concolic and Combinatorial techniques. It includes the program names, the cyclomatic complexity value for each program, the number of test cases generated and the percentage of test coverage for each of the techniques.

Table 2. *Individual results for the two Techniques.*

Program	Cyclomatic Complexity	Concolic Technique		Combinatorial Technique	
		No. of Test Cases Generated	Test Coverage (%)	No. of Test Cases Generated	Test Coverage (%)
Program 1	3	-	-	18	67
Program 2	5	1	50	3	100
Program 3	25	400	41	8764	100
Total/Average Test Coverage	33	401	46	8785	89

The Concolic test case generator was applied on program 2 and Program 3 and generated a total number of four hundred and one (401) test cases and an average test coverage of forty six percent (46%) while the Combinatorial test case generator was applied on the three programs generating a total of eight thousand, seven hundred and eighty five (8785) test cases and an average test coverage of eighty nine percent (89%).

5.2. Compared Results

Only Program 2 and Program 3 were used for the comparison of the techniques. The results are presented based on the objectives of this study as follows.

Objective 1: Identify which technique achieves the highest test coverage

The test coverage is highly important in evaluating the techniques. A test case generation technique which achieves test coverage of 100% means that it has generated test cases which explored all the feasible paths of a program but does not mean that the program is free from defects. Table 3 and "Fig. 4", shows the results of the test coverage for the techniques.

Table 3. *Comparison of Test Coverage of Techniques.*

Program	Concolic Test Coverage (%)	Combinatorial Test Coverage (%)
Program 2	50	100
Program 3	41	100
Average Test Coverage	46	100

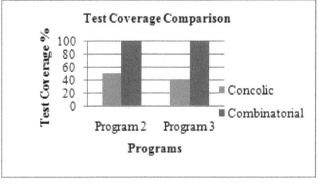

Figure 4. *Comparison of Test Coverage for Techniques.*

The chart above shows that the Combinatorial technique performs better than the Concolic technique in achieving a high test coverage because for the two programs used, it achieved a test coverage of 100% each. The Concolic technique achieved a lower coverage for the two programs compared to the Combinatorial technique. Hence, it can be inferred that the Combinatorial test case generation technique performs better than the Concolic test case generation technique in achieving high test coverage.

Objective 2: Identify the effect of program complexities on

the test coverage of techniques

Knowing if the complexities of programs will affect the test coverage of techniques is a very essential factor to measure their effectiveness. For *n* programs with different levels of complexities, the techniques should be able to achieve a substantial amount of test coverage to prove their strength. The result for the comparison of the effect of program complexities on techniques is presented in Table 4 and a chart describing the comparison is shown in "Fig. 5".

Table 4. Complexity Effect Comparison.

Program	Cyclomatic Complexity	Concolic Test Coverage (%)	Combinatorial Test Coverage (%)
Program 2	5	50	100
Program 3	25	41	100
Total/Average Test Coverage	30	46	100

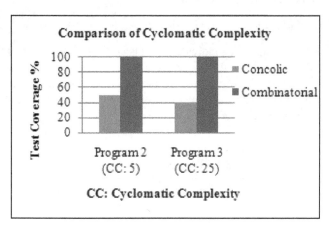

Figure 5. The Effect of Program Complexities on both Techniques.

The chart above compares the Concolic and the Combinatorial technique based on the effect of the complexity of two programs on the percentage of test coverage achieved. From the chart it can be stated that the Combinatorial technique performs better than the Concolic technique in achieving high test coverage for complex programs.

Objective 3: Identify which technique is most effective in general

We identified the technique that is most effective in general. By the word 'general' we mean the technique that performs best in meeting the objectives presented previously i.e. the technique that achieves the highest test coverage and the technique that program complexities have little or no effect on. We allocated a score to each objective and the total score was given as three (3), one for each objective. The Combinatorial technique scored the highest value of 3 because it performed better in all the objectives than the Concolic technique. The Concolic technique scored 1 for attaining at least level of test coverage. Table 4 shows the summary of the evaluation and it includes; the overall result for each technique based on the three metrics used in the study and the score for each technique.

Table 5. Summary of Evaluation.

Technique	Complexity Effect	Total Number of Test Cases Generated	Average Test Coverage (%)	Score
Concolic	Has Effect	401	46	1
Combinatorial	No Effect	8767	100	3

From the table above, it is possible that if the number of test cases generated by the Concolic test case generator increases then the average test coverage achieved would increase.

6. Conclusion

We have been able to evaluate two major automated test case generation techniques (Concolic and Combinatorial Techniques) through experiment. The results from the experiment show that the Combinatorial test case generation technique performed better than the Concolic test case generation technique and is thereby a more effective technique based on the evaluation criteria used. Hence, future works should be directed towards conducting further empirical studies on the Combinatorial technique with other major techniques and a large number of programs to validate its effectiveness.

References

[1] S. Anand, E. Burke, T. Y. Chen, J. Clark, M. B. Cohen, W. Grieskamp, M. Harman, M. J. Harrold, and P. McMinn, "An orchestrated survey on automated Software test case generation," Antonia Bertolino, J. Jenny Li and Hong Zhu, Editor/Orchestrators, Journal of Systems and Software 2013.

[2] J. E. Bentley, "Software testing fundamentals-concepts, roles, and terminology," Corporate Data Management and Governance, Wachovia Bank, 201 S. College Street, NC-1025, Charlotte NC 28210, 2001.

[3] J. Czerwonka, "Pairwise testing in real World: practical extensions to test case generators," Microsoft Corporation, One Microsoft way Redmond, WA 98052, 2006.

[4]   M. d'Amorim, C. Pacheco, T. Xie, D. Marinov, and M. D. Ernst, "An empirical comparison of automated generation and classification techniques for object-oriented unit testing," Department of Computer Science, University of Illinois, Urbana-Champaign, IL, U.S.A., 2006.

[5]   G. Fraser, M. Staats, P. McMinn, A. Arcuri, and P. Padberg, "Does automated White-Box test generation really help Software Testers,?" Department of Computer Science, University of Sheffield, United Kingdom, 2013.

[6]   S. Han and Y. Kwon, "An empirical evaluation of test data generation techniques." Journal of Computing Science and Engineering, vol. 2, No. 3, September, 2008.

[7]   K. Kahkonen, R. Kindermann, K. Heljanko and I. Niemela, "Experimental comparison of Concolic and Random Testing for Java Card Applets," Department of Information and Computer Science Aalto University, P.O. Box 15400, FI-00076 AALTO, Finland, 2010.

[8]   B. Korel, "Automated Software test data generation," IEEE Transactions on Software Engineering, Vol. 16, No. 8, 1990.

[9]   D. R. Kuhn, R. N. Kacker, and Y. Lei, "Practical Combinatorial Testing,". National Institute of Standards and Technology (NIST), U.S. Government Printing Office, Washington, U.S.A., 2010.

[10] K. Lakhotia, P. McMinn, and M. Harman, "Automated test data generation for coverage: haven't we solved this problem yet?," King's College, CREST centre, London, WC2R 2LS, U.K., 2009.

[11] L. Luo, "Software Testing Techniques," Institute for Software Research International, Carnegie Mellon University, Pittsburgh, PA15232, U.S.A., 2001.

[12] T. J. McCabe, "A complexity measure," IEEE Transactions on Software Engineering, Vol. Se-2, No., 4, 1976.

[13] J. Pan, "Software Testing, Dependable Embedded Systems," Electrical and Computer Engineering Department, Carnegie Mellon University, 1999.

[14] X. Qu, and B. Robinson, "A case study of Concolic Testing tools and their limitations," ABB Corporate Research 940 main campus drive, Raleigh, NC, U.S.A., 2010.

[15] M. Roper, J. Miller, A. Brooks, and M. Wood, "Towards the experimental evaluation of Software testing techniques," EuroSTAR '94, pp 44/1-44/10October 10-13, 1994, Brussels.

[16] K. Sen, "Concolic testing and constraint satisfaction," Proceedings, 14th International Conference on Theory and Applications of Satisfiability Testing (SAT'11), 2011.

[17] S. Wang, and J. Offutt, "Comparison of unit-level automated test generation tools," Software Engineering, George Mason University, Fairfax, VA 22030, USA, 2008.

13

Matrix Decomposition for Recommendation System

Jie Zhu, Yiming Wei, Binbin Fu

School of Information, Beijing Wuzi University, Beijing, China

Email address:

zhujie@bwu.edu.cn (Jie Zhu), talent_weiyiming@126.com (Yiming Wei), binbin6807@163.com (Binbin Fu)

Abstract: Matrix decomposition, when the rating matrix has missing values, is recognized as an outstanding technique for recommendation system. In order to approximate user-item rating matrix, we construct loss function and append regularization constraint to prevent overfitting. Thus, the solution of matrix decomposition becomes an optimization problem. Alternating least squares (ALS) and stochastic gradient descent (SGD) are two popular approaches to solve optimize problems. Alternating least squares with weighted regularization (ALS-WR) is a good parallel algorithm, which can perform independently on user-factor matrix or item-factor matrix. Based on the idea of ALS-WR algorithm, we propose a modified SGD algorithm. With experiments on testing dataset, our algorithm outperforms ALS-WR. In addition, matrix decompositions based on our optimization method have lower RMSE values than some classic collaborate filtering algorithms.

Keywords: Matrix Decomposition, Regularization, Collaborative Filtering, Optimization

1. Introduction

In the fields of e-commerce, online video, social networks, location-based services, personalized email and advertising, recommendation system has achieved great progress and success. At least 20% of Amazon's sales volume is benefit from recommendation system, according to its recommendation system developer [1].

Recommendation system can be categorized into: 1) content-based recommendation, which is based on products' characteristics. 2) Collaborative filtering (CF), which is based on historical records of items that users have viewed, purchased, or rated.

Collaborative filtering has been widely and maturely applied in e-commerce, as CF only needs user-item matrix, which records users rating information on items [2]. There are three primary approaches to facilitate CF algorithm: nearest neighbor model [3], matrix decomposition [4], and graph theory [5].

2. Rating Matrix

In this paper, R_{ij} records the rating information of user i on item j, and r_{ij} is prediction value. Higher value means stronger preference. For example, table 1 shows a rating matrix that records five users rating information on six items. As shown in table 1, the horizontal axis shows each item, and the vertical axis shows each user.

Table 1. User-Item rating matrix.

User_ID	Item_ID					
	Item1	Item2	Item3	Item4	Item5	Item6
User1		3	4		3	5
User2	4			2		
User3			3			
User4	2				4	
User5		3		5		1

The degree of missing values can be measured by equation (1)

$$R_{sparsity} = 1 - \frac{\sum\limits_{i \in U} \sum\limits_{j \in M} f_{ij}}{|U| \times |M|} \qquad (1)$$

$|U|$ is the number of users, and $|M|$ is the number of items. If the value of R_{ij} is missing, the value of f_{ij} is 0. When the value of R_{ij} has value, the value of f_{ij} is 1.

Collaborative filtering algorithm makes recommendation based on similarity calculation, which completely rely on the values of user-item rating matrix. Thus, recommendation accuracy is greatly affected by the sparsity of the rating matrix.

3. Matrix Factorization

In the fields of data mining and machine learning, matrix decomposition is used to approximate the original user-item rating matrix with low-level matrix. In this way, the missing value problem of recommendation system is solved. Thus, matrix factorization become a famous preprocessing step for collaborate filtering algorithm.

In the early stage of recommendation field, there are many approaches to conduct matrix factorization: probabilistic latent semantic analysis (pLSA) [6], neural networks, latent dirichlet allocation (LDA) [7], and the singular value decomposition (SVD) [8], and so on.

The basic idea of Singular value decomposition algorithm is using low-level matrix to replace original matrix. As there are several disadvantages of SVD in practical application, many modified algorithms are merged [6].

The academia proposes the latent factor model (LFM) algorithm, which is also named as implicit semantic model. Rating matrix R is decomposed into the form of matrix $R = P^T * Q$.

This approach maps both users and items into a latent feature space. Latent factors, though not directly measurable, often contains some useful abstract information. The affinity between users and items are defined by latent factor vectors. Take figure 2 for example, class can be explained as latent factor. P is user factor matrix, and Q is item factor matrix.

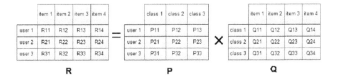

Figure 1. *Latent factor model (LFM).*

3.1. Loss Function

In order to accurately approximate the original user-item rating matrix, we construct loss function (2) to help finding proper user matrix and item matrix. The initialization of user matrix and item matrix are often using random number, and are proportional with $1 / \sqrt{factors}$ by experience.

$$C(u,m) = \sum_{(i,j)\in train} (R_{ij} - u_i^T m_j)^2 \tag{2}$$

To prevent overfitting, we add regularization constraint to (2). Thus, the loss function becomes an optimization problem. Many past studies have proposed optimization methods to solve (3), e.g. [11] [10]. Among them, alternating least squares (ALS) and stochastic gradient descent (SGD) are popularly used.

$$C(u,m) = \sum_{(i,j)\in train} (R_{ij} - u_i^T m_j)^2 + \lambda(\|u_{if}\|^2 + \|m_{uf}\|^2) \tag{3}$$

In (3), f is the number of latent factor, u is user factor matrix, and m is item factor matrix.

3.2. Alternating Least Squares with Weighted Regularization

The method of alternative least squares is originated from mathematical optimization technique. In the loss function, u and m are unknown. The basic idea of ALS-WR is assume that one unknown parameter is certain. Then the loss function can be regard as a least squares problem. After setting a stopping criterion, we can get a proper m or u with iteration method.

In addition, we use Tikhonov regularization to punish excessive parameters [10]. Thus, (3) is updated into (4), which is based on the weighted regularization of alternative least squares method (ALS-WR):

$$C(u,m) = \sum_{(i,j)\in train} (R_{ij} - u_i^T m_j)^2 + \lambda \left(\sum_i n_{ui} \|u_i\|^2 + \sum_j n_{mj} \|m_j\|^2 \right) \tag{4}$$

Input: original rating matrix R_{ij}, the number of feature f
Output: prediction matrix r^{ij}
Step 1: initial matrix m by assigning the average ratings as the value of first row, and complete remaining part of the matrix with small random numbers.
Step 2: fix item factor matrix, and calculate the derivative of function (4)

$$\frac{1}{2}\frac{\partial C}{\partial u_i} = 0 \Rightarrow \sum (u_i^T m_j - R_{ij}) m_j + \lambda n_{ui} u_i = 0$$

$$\Rightarrow u_{i.} = R_{i.} m_{ui} \left(m_{ui}^T m_{ui} + \lambda n_{ui} I \right)^{-1} \quad i \in [1, m]$$

Step3: fix user factor matrix, and calculate the derivative of function (4)

$$\frac{1}{2}\frac{\partial C}{\partial u_j} = 0 \Rightarrow m_{j.} = R_{.j} u_{mj} (u_{mj}^T u_{mj} + \lambda n_{mj} I)^{-1} \quad j \in [1, n]$$

Step4: Repeat step2 and 3, until a stopping criterion is satisfied (enough iterations or the result of equation (2) is converged), and return u and m.
Step5: Calculate $r_{ij} = u_i^T m_j$

When recommendation system need parallel computations, ALS-WR has high accuracy and stronger scalability. As in this algorithm, system can calculate item factor matrix independently without consideration of user factor matrix, or calculate user factor matrix independently without consideration of item factor matrix. Thus, there is high efficient in solving loss function (4).

3.3. Stochastic Gradient Descent Algorithm

Stochastic gradient descent (SGD) is based on gradient descent. The update rule of gradient descent is taking steps proportional to the negative of the gradient (or of the approximate gradient) of loss function at the current point. The basic idea of SGD is that, instead of expensively calculating the gradient of instance point in loss function (3), it randomly selects a R_{ij} entry from (3) and calculates the corresponding gradient. When the number iteration increase, user factor u_i and item factor m_j are updated by the following rules

$$u_{if} = u_{if} + \alpha(m_{jf}(R_{ij} - u_i^T m_j) - \lambda u_{if}) \quad (5)$$

$$m_{jf} = m_{jf} + \alpha(u_{if}(R_{ij} - u_i^T m_j) - \lambda m_{jf}) \quad (6)$$

In the rules of (5) and (6), Parameter α is learning rate. Its value is generally obtained by trial and error approach until the training model converges. Parameter λ is regularization coefficient for avoiding over-fitting.

Within each iteration process, user factor u_i and item factor mj are updated by calculating gradient descent value of a sequence of rating instances. $R(u)$ is a rating set of users, and each training instance is recorded in (r_{u1}, r_{u2}, r_{u3}, ... r_{uk}) .We use $u(0)$ to represent the initial value of user factor u_{if}, and $u(1)$ represent updated value after calculating instance r_{u1}.

$$u^{(1)} = u^{(0)} + \alpha(m_1^{(h1)}(r_{u1} - (u^{(0)})^T m_1^{(h1)}) - \lambda u^{(0)})$$
$$= u^{(0)}(1-\alpha\lambda) + \alpha(m_1^{(h1)}(r_{u1} - (u^{(0)})^T m_1^{(h1)})) \quad k = |R(u)| \quad (7)$$

In (7), $h1$ represent the temporary state of $m1$. After training instance from r_{u2} to r_{uk}, (7) will be updated into

$$u^k = u^{(k-1)}(1-\alpha\lambda) + \alpha m_k^{(hk)}(r_{uk} - (u^{(k-1)})^T m_k^{(h)}) \quad k = |R(u)| \quad (8)$$

After one round of iteration, u^k can be rewrite into (9). We use $c = 1 - \alpha\lambda$ in (9).

$$u^k = c^k u^0 + c^{k-1}\alpha m_1^{(h1)}(r_{u1} - (u^{(0)})^T m_1^{(h1)})$$
$$+ c^{k-2}\alpha m_2^{(h2)}(r_{u2} - (u^{(1)})^T m_2^{(h2)}) \quad (9)$$
$$+ ... + \alpha m_k^{(hk)}(r_{uk} - (u^{(k-1)})^T m_k^{(hk)})$$

In (9), $m_k^{(hk)}$ represent the temporary state of mk using instance r_{uk}. In the same way, we use $R(m)$ to represent rating set of items. The set of (r_{1m}, r_{2m}, r_{3m}, ... r_{hm}) records the sequences of instances that are select to calculate gradient descent ($h = |R(m)|$).After one round of iteration, m^h can be rewrite into

$$m^h = c^h m^0 + c^{h-1}\alpha u^{(k1)}(r_{1m} - (u_1^{(k1)})^T m^{(0)})$$
$$+ c^{h-2}\alpha u_2^{(k2)}(r_{2m} - (u^{(k2)})^T m^{(h2)}) \quad (10)$$
$$+ ... + \alpha u_h^{(kh)}(r_{hm} - (u^{(kh)})^T m^{(hk)})$$

Considering (9) and (10), we can see user factor u_i and item factor m_j are not only depend on initial value, but also

depend on temporary states of u^k and m^h. From the above iteration processes and update rules from (5) to (10), we can see that SGD is a serialization method.

4. Our Approach

As the gradient search processes traverse the entire rating instances, it can update user and item factor matrixes in every round of iteration. Thus, SGD can accurately describe the multiple features of the rating matrix. Matrix decompositions based on SGD have high precision of recommendation, and strong scalability.

However, the iteration process of SGD is depending on temporary state of item factor matrix m and user factor matrix u, and the update rules need the accumulated value of each iteration process in a serial mode. Thus, in some cases the training processes may experiences system deadlocks. In addition, in the multi-core environment, SGD method is low efficiency. In the contrary, ALS-WR algorithm doesn't have such problems, as it can update m and u independently.

Based on the advantage of ALS-WR, we modify SGD, and propose a parallel SGD algorithm (PSGD). The following is the training process of matrix factorization based on PSGD:

Input: original rating matrix R_{ij}, the number of feature f
Initial: matrix m and u
While stopping criterion is not satisfied
For each user
Do Allocate a new thread for user
For each train rating instance
Do Calculate loss function
Update matrix u
End for
End for
For each item
Do Allocate a new thread for user
For each train rating instances
Do Calculate loss function
Update matrix m
End for
End for
Output: updated latent factor matrix u and m

In above algorithm, the update rules are (5) and (6). Instance training processes are based on (8) or (9). As we can see from PSGD algorithm, the matrix u and m can be update separately. Thus, the rate of convergence will be accelerated, and the results will be more accurate.

5. Experimental Results of ALS-WR and PSGD

The accuracy of the recommendation model is measured by root mean square error (RMSE), and |train| represents the validation dataset. A lower value of RMSE indicates a higher accurate in recommendation system.

$$RMSE = \sqrt{\sum_{i,j \in train}(R_{ij} - r_{ij})^2 / |train|}$$

Apache Mahout is a project of the Apache Software Foundation to produce free implementations of distributed or otherwise scalable machine learning algorithms focused primarily in the areas of collaborative filtering.

In this paper we focus on the collaborative filtering algorithm based matrix decomposition. Thus, in order to simulate the real recommendation system environment, we run our experiment in Mahout Environment, which has been maturely adopted in a distribute Hadoop system in many commercial fields.

Our experiment uses the famous MovieLens datasets which is developed by the GroupLens Lab of Minnesota University. Our matrix factorization algorithms are test on MovieLens 100k dataset, which including 100,000 records of rating information that are given by 943 users on 1682 movies. The sparsity of dataset is 6.305%.

In the following experiments, MovieLens dataset is divided into two parts. 70% of it is training set, and the rest is testing set. In the following comparison, there are three parameters: number of hidden features, overfitting parameter and number of iterations. The parameter selections are derived by experience and cross validation. In the following experiments, the default settings are: 0.05(overfitting parameter), 20(number of iterations) and 30(number of hidden features)

5.1. Experiment 1

In figure 2, the horizontal axis represents the number of hidden features in LFM algorithm, and the vertical axis records values of RMSE. When the number of hidden feature is changing from 15 to 75, the RMSE value of ALS-WR is obviously higher than PSGD. In addition, with the increase of hidden features, the prediction matrix tends to be dense and have less missing values in user-item matrix. Thus, the RMSE values of them reach a stabilized state.

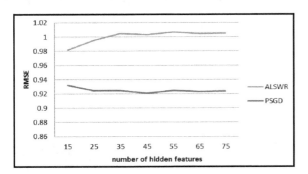

Figure 2. Comparison of ALS-WR and PSGD on hidden features.

In figure 3, the horizontal axis records the changes of overfitting parameter in loss function (3), and the vertical axis shows RMSE values. When the value of overfitting parameter is on the increase, the RMSE values of ALS-WR and PSGD are closer. From the overall look, the RMSE curve of ALS-WR is higher than PSGD.

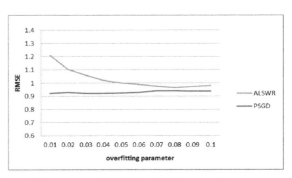

Figure 3. Comparison of ALS-WR and PSGD on overfitting parameter.

In figure 4, the horizontal axis shows the iteration numbers of matrix decomposition algorithm based on ALS-WR and PSGD optimization methods, and the vertical axis shows RMSE values. When the number of iterations is increasing from 10 to 80, the RMSE value of ALS-WR is high than PSGD. In addition, with the increase of iteration number, both optimization algorithms tend to convergence, and their RMSE are gradually stabilized.

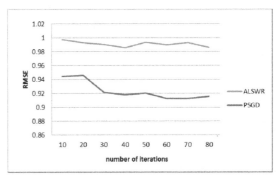

Figure 4. Comparison of ALS-WR and PSGD on number of iterations.

5.2. Experiment 2

In this experiment, we use the same datasets as experiment 1. Userbased and itembased are classic collaborate filtering algorithms, which are based on user or item similarity. SlopeOne algorithm uses linear regression to filter message and make recommendation. BiasMF is a modified version of LFM, with considering the influence of system inherent factors. For LFM and BiasMF, they are matrix decomposition algorithms. In the following experiment, LFM and BiasMF will be solved using PSGD method.

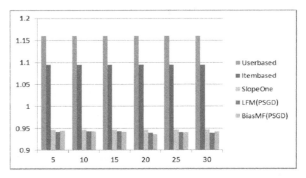

Figure 5. Comparison of algorithms on hidden feature.

In figure 5, Userbased, Itembased and SlopeOne algorithms are not matrix decomposition methods. Thus, their RMSE values are remaining certain.

According to the chart, the RMSE value of LFM(PSGD) and BiasMF(PSGD) are obviously lower than classic collaborate filtering algorithms of Userbased and itembased, and slightly lower than SlopeOne algorithms.

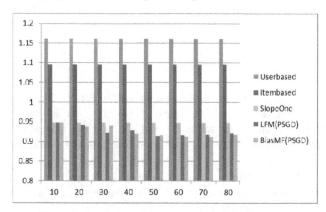

Figure 6. Comparison of algorithms on number of iterations.

In figure 6, with the number of iteration increases, their RMSE values tend to be stabilized. As we can see from figure 6, matrix decomposition based PSGD algorithms have better performances than classic collaborate filtering algorithms.

6. Conclusion

In this paper, we introduced recommendation system and collaboration filtering algorithm. When user-item rating matrix is sparse, matrix factorization is recognized as an efficient approach to approximate original rating matrix. Latent factor model (LFM) is a famous decomposition method, which related user and item to their implicit features. In order to get an accurate and proper prediction matrix, we construct loss function.

The loss function is an optimize problem, and alternating least squares with weighted regularization (ALS-WR) is an efficient and parallel method to solve it. However, the calculation of matrix decomposition based on ALS-WR involved with matrix inversion, thus it has great computation complexity.

Similar to ALS, Stochastic gradient descent (SGD) is another famous optimization approach. Calculation based on SGD is needs to obtain the gradient of each rating instance. Thus, it is easy to conduct matrix composition based on SGD. However, SGD is a sequential algorithm.

Based on the strengths of ALS-WR, we modify and propose a new algorithm PSGD based on SGD. The training processes of PSGD are twice than SGD approach, it seems to be a reduction in efficiency. However, PSGD can update user or item factor matrix independently, and thus provide the possibility of parallel performance. Based on experiment 1, PSGD has better performance than ALS-WR.

In addition, we compare two matrix decomposition

algorithms based on PSGD with classic collaborate filtering algorithms. In the real recommendation system, the sparse rating matrix increases the difficulty to calculate similarity between users or items, but matrix decomposition methods are survived of this problem. As experiment 2 shows, matrix decomposition algorithms based on PSGD arc out performance than collaborate filtering algorithms based on similarity.

Acknowledgements

This paper is supported by the Funding Project for Technology Key Project of Municipal Education Commission of Beijing (ID:TSJHG201310037036); Funding Project for Beijing key laboratory of intelligent logistics system ;Funding Project of Construction of Innovative Teams and Teacher Career Development for Universities and Colleges Under Beijing Municipality (ID:IDHT20130517), and Beijing Municipal Science and Technology Project (ID:Z131100005413004); Funding Project for Beijing philosophy and social science research base specially commissioned project planning (ID:13JDJGD013).

References

[1]   LINDEN G, SMITH B, YORK J. Amazon.com recommendations: Item-to-item collaborative filtering [J]. IEEE Internet Computing, 2003, 7(1): 76−80.

[2]   KOREN Y. Factorization meets the neighborhood: a multifaceted collaborative filtering model[C]//Proceedings of the 14th ACM SIGK-DD International Conference on Knowledge Discovery and Data Mining. New York: ACM, 2008: 426−434.

[3]   ALI K, WIJNAND V S. TiVo: Making show recommendations using a distributed collaborative filtering architecture[C]//KDD'04: Proceedings of the 10th ACM SIGKDD International Conference on Knowledge Discovery and Data Mining. New York: ACM, 2004:394- 401.

[4]   GOLDBERG K Y, ROEDER T, GUPTA D, et al. Eigentaste: A constant time collaborative filtering algorithm [J]. Information Retrieval, 2001, 4(2): 133−151.

[5]   SALAKHUTDINOV R, MNIH A, HINTON G. Restricted Boltzmann machines for collaborative filtering[C]//Proceedings of the 24th International Conference on Machine Learning. New York: ACM, 2007:791−798.

[6]   HOFMANN T. Latent semantic models for collaborative filtering [J]. ACM Transactions on Information Systems, 2004, 22(1) : 89−115.

[7]   BLEI D, NG A, JORDAN M. Latent Dirichlet allocation [J]. Journal of Machine Learning Research, 2003, 3: 993−1022.

[8]   DaWei C, Zhao Y, HaoYan L. The overfitting phenomenon of SVD series algorithms in rating matrix [J]. Journal of Shandong university (engineering science), 2014, 44(3): 15-21

[9]   XiaoFeng H, Xin L, Qingsheng Z. A parallel improvements based on regularized matrix factorization of collaborative filtering model [J]. Journal of electronics and information, 2013，35(6):1507-1511.

[10] Zhou Y, Wilkinson D, Schreiber R, et al. Large-scale parallel collaborative filtering for the Netflix prize [M]//Algorithmic Aspects in Information and Management. Springer Berlin Heidelberg, 2008: 337-348.

[11] I.Pil´aszy,D. Zibriczky, and D.Tikk. Fast ALS-based matrix factorization for explicit and implicit feedback datasets. In Proceedings of the Fourth ACM Conference on Recommender Systems, pages71–78, 2010.

14

Open source software selection using an analytical hierarchy process (AHP)

Yusmadi Yah Jusoh[1, *], Khadijah Chamili[2], Noraini Che Pa[1], Jamaiah H. Yahaya[3]

[1]Dept. of Software Engineering and Information Systems, Faculty of Computer Science and Information Technology, Universiti Putra Malaysia (UPM), Serdang, Selangor, Malaysia
[2]Centre of Information Technology, USIM, Nilai, Negeri Sembilan, Malaysia
[3]School of Computer Science, Faculty of Information Science and Technology, National University of Malaysia (UKM), Bangi, Selangor, Malaysia

Email address:
yusmadi@upm.edu.my (Y. Y. Jusoh), khadijah@usim.edu.my (K. Chamili), norainip@upm.edu.my (N. C. Pa),
jhy@ftsm.ukm.my (J. H. Yahaya)

Abstract: There are many potential and good open source software (OSS) products available on the market with a free license. However, with various choices, the adoption rate is still low among potential users because there is not an agreed acceptable set of criteria to evaluate and select various OSS. The criteria of selection may differ between the stakeholders within the organisations. There is a tendency that the user may have a biased perception of an OSS's characteristics or capabilities for solving problems when selecting OSS products. Other restrictions are caused by inadequate documentation and user manuals, and immature products. Therefore, the users need to consider how to improve their decision making when selecting the most suitable OSS products. In this paper, the background research on the proposed OSS adoption and criteria of selection are discussed and explored. Then the research methodology, processes and implementation of the My Open Source Software Toolkit (MyOSST) v1.0 are covered. The analytical hierarchy process (AHP) was applied on the selection process and for the purpose of assisting the potential user to decide on the OSS products based on their preferred selection criteria. MyOSST v1.0 was tested and validated by IT professionals in one of the Malaysian universities. The results show that the tool is capable of assisting the decision making process for selecting an appropriate OSS product.

Keywords: Open Source Software Selection, Selection Criteria, Analytical Hierarchy Process

1. Introduction

The adoption of open source software (OSS) is still growing all over the world, including within businesses, non-profits and public sector agencies because of the financial benefits. The criteria of selection may differ between the stakeholders within the organizations. Therefore, there is a tendency for the user to have a biased perception of an OSS's characteristics or capabilities for solving problems when selecting OSS products.

The OSS adoption rate in Malaysian public sector agencies was still low up until end of 2010 [1]. Therefore, the next step is to apply the suggested selection criteria to understand what is the best dimension to contribute to Malaysian public sector agencies in order to encourage the adoption and implementation of OSS products in their agencies [2] [3]. In other words, the proposed selection criteria may help to identify the characteristics to be considered by the users when adopting the OSS product. Hence, conducting a survey may give support to the identification of the main characteristics for the proposed OSS adoption model.

In our previous study, we identified all the possible OSS characteristics which referred to the ISO standard for comparison, better understanding and future enhancement purposes. We also proposed an additional quality characteristic which is the internal constraint to be included when agencies make decisions concerning OSS adoption. With these hierarchical characteristics of OSS, the selection criteria might benefit users by building confidence in OSS product adoption in the future [4].

Recently, there have been many potential and good OSS

products on the market with a free license, but yet they are still not popular among Malaysian public sector agencies. What are the constraints or limitations on adopting these good OSS products? What drives them to rely on proprietary software which costs them hundreds of thousands of dollars? To understand this scenario, a survey was conducted among technical and IT managerial personnel at selected public sector agencies. Identifying the preferred selection criteria will help to build confidence among users and a better understanding of their perception of OSS.

The remainder of the paper is organized as follows. In Section 2, the proposed OSS selection dimensions and criteria are presented, and section 3 discusses the methodology which includes the AHP, the selection processes and tool development. Sections 4 explain the MyOSST v1.0 implementation, a toolkit to assist the OSS product selection process. The results and discussion are presented in Section 5. Finally, in Section 6 the insights of the study are summarised and directions are given for future research.

The next section will explain the OSS selection dimensions. The selections are based on four dimensions: system quality, information quality, service quality, and another dimension which includes the potential internal constraints.

2. The OSS Selection Dimensions

The first step of our study was to explore the existing research on the selection criteria for the OSS product. Many researchers have suggested models and frameworks for their preferred list of important criteria for OSS selection. The detail of related studies was reported in a previous publication [4] [5].

It is important to note that in generating the selection criteria in this study, we referred mainly to four main sources: (i) the D&M IS Success Model [6] (ii) related work on the OSS quality model [7] [8] [9] [10] [11] and (iii) general standards for software quality, such as ISO 25010 [12] and (iv) the Malaysian Public Sector Open Source Software Initiative: OSS Implementation Guidelines [3].

The suggested selection criteria consist of four (4) dimensions: system quality, information quality, service quality and one other dimension. The additional dimension is named as other and its criteria and characteristics can be added by the organization from their own evaluation criteria such as internal technical competencies and knowledge. The proposed dimensions, criteria and characteristics for selecting the OSS product are as shown in Table 1.

Table 1. The dimensions, criteria and characteristics.

Dimension	Criteria	Characteristic
System quality	Reliability (C01)	Maturity
		Popularity
		Availability
	Usability(C02)	Learn-ability
		Operability
		Accessibility
		User interface aesthetics
	Performance efficiency (C03)	Time behavior
		Resource utilization
	Functionality (C04)	Functional completeness
		Functional correctness
		Functional appropriateness
	Maintainability (C05)	Modularity
		Modifiability
		Reusability
Information quality		Testability
	Security(C06)	Confidentiality
		Integrity
		Authenticity
	Tangible(C07)	Support
		Documentation
Service quality	Reliability (C08)	Version
	Responsiveness (C09)	Community
	Assurance (C10)	Competence
		Credibility
	Empathy (C11)	Communication
Others	Competence (C12)	Skill

The dimensions of the OSS product selection are organized in a hierarchy of two levels which are the criteria and characteristics. The dimensions include 12 criteria for selection. Each criterion has one or more characteristics. The characteristics also can be added by the organization to comply with their organizational requirements for the OSS products.

Both the criteria and the characteristics are considered to contribute in some way or other to each of the dimensions that they belong to. We also suggest the measurement for each of the sub-characteristics to ensure that these quality characteristics are ranked accordingly [5].

3. Methodology

In this section, we will describe the methodology of the proposed OSS selection dimensions which were included in the toolkit that was developed, and elaborate the AHP technique applied for the decision making for selecting the OSS products and the development environment of the toolkit, MyOSST v1.0.

3.1. Analytical Hierarchy Process (AHP)

The AHP was introduced by Thomas L. Saaty in the 1970s. It is a systematic decision making method which includes both qualitative and quantitative techniques. It has been widely used for a long time in many fields. The AHP is also a structured technique for organizing and analysing complex decisions based on mathematics and psychology [13] [14].

Rather than prescribing a "correct" decision, the AHP helps decision makers find one that best suits their goal and their understanding of the problem. It provides a comprehensive and rational framework for structuring a decision problem, for representing and quantifying its elements, for relating those elements to overall goals, and for evaluating alternative solutions.

The main advantage of the AHP is its ability to rank choices in the order of their effectiveness in meeting conflicting objectives. It is quite hard – but not impossible – to 'fiddle' the judgments to get some predetermined result as well as to detect inconsistent judgments.

The AHP can also be used by individuals working on uncomplicated decisions; it is most useful where teams of people are working on complex problems, especially those with high stakes, involving human perceptions and judgments, whose resolutions have long-term repercussions. It has unique advantages when important elements of the decision are difficult to quantify or compare, or where communication among team members is impeded by their different specializations, terminologies, or perspectives.

Users of the AHP first decompose their decision problem into a hierarchy of more easily comprehended sub-problems, each of which can be analysed independently. The elements of the hierarchy can relate to any aspect of the decision problem—tangible or intangible, carefully measured or roughly estimated, well- or poorly-understood—anything at all that applies to the decision at hand.

Once the hierarchy is built, the decision makers systematically evaluate its various elements by comparing them to one another two at a time, with respect to their impact on an element above them in the hierarchy. In making the comparisons (the pair-wise comparison), the decision makers can use concrete data about the elements, but they typically use their judgments about the elements' relative meaning and importance. Each of these judgments is assigned a number on a scale as shown in Table 2.

These pair-wise comparisons are carried out for all elements to be considered, until the matrix is completed. It is the essence of the AHP that human judgments, and not just the underlying information, can be used in performing the evaluations. The AHP converts these evaluations to numerical values that can be processed and compared over the entire range of the problem. A numerical weight or priority is derived for each element of the hierarchy, allowing diverse and often incommensurable elements to be compared to one another in a rational and consistent way. This capability distinguishes the AHP from other decision making techniques.

In the final step of the process, numerical priorities are calculated for each of the decision alternatives. These numbers represent the alternative's relative ability to achieve the decision goal, so they allow a straightforward consideration of the various courses of action.

Table 2. AHP Scale.

Intensity of Importance	Definitions	Explanations
1	Equal	Two factors contribute equally to the objective
3	Moderate	Experience and judgments slightly favors one over the other.
5	Strong	Experience and judgments strongly favor one over the other.
7	Very Strong	Experience and judgments very strongly favor one over the other. Its importance is demonstrated in practice.
9	Extreme	The evidence favoring one over the other is of the highest possible validity.
2,4,6,8	Intermediate values	When compromise is needed

3.2. The Selection Process

The processes for selecting the OSS products are proposed to identify the best alternatives or preferences by implementing the AHP. There are four processes involved as depicted in Figure1.

The first process of the selection is to establish the AHP structure by identifying the selected selection criteria. In this step the hierarchy of criteria and the alternatives are generated. Therefore, there are three important components which need to be identified: the goal/project, the criteria of the products, and the list of alternatives/products.

In the next process, human or user judgment is needed. The user needs to determine the relative importance of each criterion, which means ranking the criteria based on the priorities for each of the criteria using the matrix.

Next, the judgment exercise involves applying the pair-wise comparison for each of the criteria using the proposed AHP scale in Table 2. For example C02–System Usability is 3 times as importance as C01–System Reliability.

After completing the judgment matrix, the last process is to multiply the alternative weight by the criteria weight to obtain the best of all the alternatives. Finally, the result of the final ranking was computed and presented for decision making to the selection committee or users.

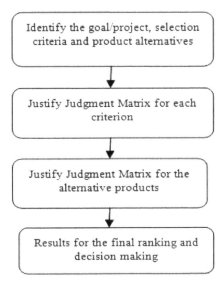

Figure 1. The Selection Process.

3.3. The Development

In developing the OSS selection criteria toolkit, a few requirements have been identified. First, the system should be a web based application to allow users to access it via the internet. The development uses the OSS environment – that is MySQL 4.1.14, PHP 5.0.5, and Apache HTTP Server.

MySQL is the world's most used open source relational database management system (RDBMS), which runs as a server providing multi-user access to a number of databases. MySQL ships with no GUI tools for administering MySQL databases or managing the data contained within the databases. Users may use the included command line or download MySQL front-ends from various parties that have developed desktop software and web applications to manage MySQL databases, build database structures, and work with data records. The data in MySQL is stored in database objects called tables. A table is a collection of related data entries and it consists of columns and rows. Databases are useful when storing information categorically.

PHP is a general-purpose server-side scripting language originally designed for Web development to produce dynamic Web pages. It is one of the first server-side scripting languages to be embedded into an HTML source document rather than calling an external file to process data. The code is interpreted by a Web server with a PHP processor module which generates the resulting Web page. It has also evolved to include a command-line interface capability and can be used in standalone graphical applications. PHP can be deployed on most Web servers and also as a standalone shell on almost every operating system and platform free of charge.

The Apache HTTP Server, commonly referred to as Apache, is web server software notable for playing a key role in the initial growth of the World Wide Web. In 2009 it became the first web server software to surpass the 100 million website milestone. Apache was the first viable alternative to the Netscape Communications Corporation web server (currently named Oracle iPlanet Web Server), and since has evolved to dominate other web servers in terms of functionality and performance. Typically, Apache is run on a Unix-like operating system.

4. The Implementation

MyOSST has been developed to implement all validated OSS selection criteria in order to assist potential users while making decisions on OSS products in their agencies. Below is a list of the scope and features of the system:

- web based application which allows users access via the internet.
- adopting the OSS selection dimension-criteria which are system-reliability (C01), system-usability (C02), system-performance efficiency (C03), system-functionality (C04), information-maintainability (C05), information-security (C06), service-tangible (C07), service-reliability (C08), service-responsiveness (C09), service-assurance (C10), service-empathy (C11) and other-competence (C12).
- allows single input (one person) for each project based.

Small group discussions are encouraged to determine the criteria weightage. MyOSST v1.0 was developed using the suggested methodology for AHP as depicted in Figure 1. The illustrations given are used only as an example on the implementation of the particular system.

4.1. Identify the Goal, Selection Criteria and Product Alternatives

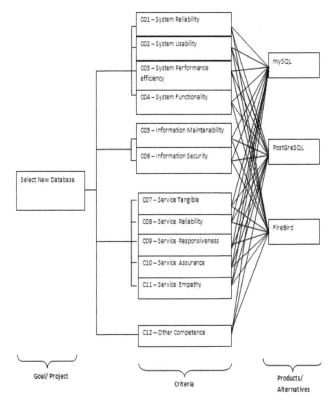

Figure 2. AHP Structure for Select New Database.

In MyOSST v1.0, the criteria have been defined which are applied from Table 1. Further to this section, we demonstrate how AHP is applied in MyOSST v1.0 as Select New Database, which is shown as the goal or project presented in this paper. The complete AHP structure for Select New Database is as depicted in Figure 2.

4.2. Judgment Matrix for Each Criterion

Using pair-wise comparison, the relative importance of one criterion over another can be expressed as depicted in Figure 3.

Matrix

	C01	C02	C03	C04	C05	C06	C07	C08	C09	C10	C11	C12
C01	1	1/3	1/7	1/5	2/1	1/9	1/5	1/2	1/2	1/5	1/2	1/5
C02	3/1	1	1/5	1/2	5/1	1/8	1/5	5/1	5/1	1/5	3/1	1/3
C03	7/1	5/1	1	3/1	7/1	1/2	1/2	7/1	7/1	5/1	7/1	5/1
C04	5/1	2/1	1/3	1	7/1	1/3	1/3	5/1	5/1	1/4	5/1	1/3
C05	1/2	1/5	1/7	1/7	1	1/9	1/8	1/2	1/2	1/7	1/2	1/5
C06	9/1	8/1	2/1	3/1	9/1	1	2/1	8/1	8/1	6/1	9/1	3/1
C07	5/1	5/1	2/1	3/1	8/1	1/2	1	5/1	7/1	2/1	3/1	2/1
C08	2/1	1/5	1/7	1/5	2/1	1/8	1/5	1	1/3	1/5	1/4	1/7
C09	2/1	1/5	1/7	1/5	2/1	1/8	1/7	3/1	1	1/5	1/2	1/5
C10	5/1	5/1	1/5	4/1	7/1	1/6	1/2	5/1	5/1	1	2/1	3/1
C11	2/1	1/3	1/7	1/5	2/1	1/9	1/3	4/1	2/1	1/2	1	1/5
C12	5/1	3/1	1/5	3/1	5/1	1/3	1/2	7/1	5/1	1/3	5/1	1

Calculate Cancel

Figure 3. The Pair-wise Matrix.

After completing the matrix for each criteria, AHP turns the matrix into a ranking of criteria. To obtain the ranking of priorities from the pair-wise matrix, an eigenvector solution is applied. Below is the step by step process to perform the eigenvector:

1) Converting the fraction value to the decimal number as shown in Figure 4.

Matrix

	C01	C02	C03	C04	C05	C06	C07	C08	C09	C10	C11	C12
C01	1.00	0.33	0.14	0.20	2.00	0.11	0.20	0.50	0.50	0.20	0.50	0.20
C02	3.00	1.00	0.20	0.50	5.00	0.13	0.20	5.00	5.00	0.20	3.00	0.33
C03	7.00	5.00	1.00	3.00	7.00	0.50	0.50	7.00	7.00	0.20	7.00	5.00
C04	5.00	2.00	1/3	1.00	7.00	0.33	0.33	5.00	5.00	0.25	5.00	0.33
C05	0.50	0.20	0.14	0.14	1.00	0.11	0.13	0.50	0.50	0.14	0.50	0.20
C06	9.00	8.00	2.00	3.00	9.00	1.00	2.00	8.00	8.00	6.00	9.00	3.00
C07	5.00	5.00	2.00	3.00	8.00	0.50	1.00	5.00	7.00	2.00	3.00	2.00
C08	2.00	0.20	0.14	0.20	2.00	0.13	0.20	1.00	0.33	0.20	0.25	0.14
C09	2.00	0.20	0.14	0.20	2.00	0.13	0.14	3.00	1.00	0.20	0.50	0.20
C10	5.00	5.00	5.00	4.00	7.00	0.17	0.50	5.00	5.00	1.00	2.00	3.00
C11	2.00	0.33	0.14	0.20	2.00	0.11	0.33	4.00	2.00	0.50	1.00	0.20
C12	5.00	3.00	0.20	3.00	5.00	0.33	0.50	7.00	5.00	0.33	5.00	1.00

Figure 4. Convert to Decimal Numbers.

2) Squaring the pair-wise matrix where the matrix is multiplied with itself. Each value of each column (C1, C2 ...C12) is multiplied with each value of each column (R1, R2 ...R12) to obtain a new value in each cell of the new matrix.
3) Sum each of the rows of the matrix
4) Sum the total rows of the matrix
5) Normalize by dividing each of the sum rows by the total rows. The value of the last step is the eigenvector of the pair-wise matrix. The computed eigenvector value gives us the relative ranking of our criteria.

4.3. Judgment Matrix for the Alternative Products

Once the eigenvector value is computed, users need to repeat the pair-wise comparison activities for the alternatives on each of the OSS selected criteria. In this activity, users determine the preferences for each alternative over another – such as for the criteria of system reliability (C01) with the fraction numbers for the pair-wise comparison on the alternatives.

After completing the pair-wise comparison on the alternatives, the weights for each alternative are generated using the eigenvector solution. Computing the eigenvector determines the relative ranking of the alternatives under each criterion.

4.4. The Final Ranking and Decision Making

Alternative Weightage

	C01	C02	C03	C04	C05	C06	C07	C08	C09	C10	C11	C12	Result
mySQL	0.2474	0.5239	0.2261	0.0993	0.6376	0.6804	0.1537	0.1714	0.1710	0.1090	0.5597	0.7079	0.3728
PostGreSQL	0.5981	0.3572	0.6746	0.2261	0.0739	0.2227	0.5564	0.6936	0.7274	0.5820	0.1208	0.2101	0.4211
FireBird	0.1544	0.1189	0.0993	0.6746	0.2884	0.0969	0.2899	0.1350	0.1016	0.3091	0.3195	0.0820	0.2000

End Process

Criteria Weightage

C01	0.016
C02	0.048
C03	0.188
C04	0.070
C05	0.012
C06	0.239
C07	0.146
C08	0.016
C09	0.020
C10	0.116
C11	0.029

Figure 5. Alternative and Criteria Weightage

Lastly, the tool will multiply the alternative weight with the criteria weight to obtain the winner amongst all the alternatives. The result of the selection is presented as shown in Figure 5.

5. Results and Discussion

MyOSST v1.0 was tested in one of the Malaysian public universities. The testing exercise was conducted within a half day session at the Data Centre Unit, Information Technology Centre in June 2012. The testing session is started by explaining the objective of the testing session to a small group from the Data Centre Unit which involves the Senior IT officer, the IT officer and the assistant IT officer. Coincidently, the team is currently evaluating three business intelligent (BI) tools. They have studied product alternatives and have already installed, tested and previewed the selected products. However, the selected products are not 100% open source products. They are a mix between open source and proprietary products.

The products/alternatives list for Business Intelligent (BI) tools consists of OracleBI (proprietary), Qlikview, and Pentaho (OSS). After some discussion, we decided to continue the testing session, which we believed could give better results when using MyOSST v1.0 for decision making concerning choosing the precise tool.

They were given a briefing on how to use MyOSST v1.0 and how to prepare the pair-wise matrix. The user was also informed of the employment of the AHP technique as a core function of the OSS decision making tool. The users were then given half an hour to understand the criteria and prepare the pair-wise matrix manually. Finally, they used MyOSST v1.0 by themselves with guidance from the instructor.

As a result, the group found that this toolkit was very useful and really helped them in selecting a product which was based on the pair-wise comparison and selection criteria. However, they found that it was quite difficult to prepare the pair-wise comparison, which needed them to understand and technically compare the criteria. But they agreed that this technique would give a more accurate result rather than the traditional way which they needed to choose based on a one-one product features comparison which may lead to unfair judgments.

Another suggestion highlighted by them is that they need to have a detailed discussion with other team members before creating the pair-wise comparison again, and obtain a consensus result for their proposal writing. In future it is suggested that the toolkit is capable of generating a pair-wise comparison based on multiple users for group decision making.

6. Conclusion

This paper describes the OSS selection criteria as well as the development tools and technique used. The Analytical Hierarchy Process (AHP) is one of the best decision making techniques used all over the world. This technique was adopted in MyOSST v1.0 in order to assist in the decision making of OSS products selection. MyOSST v1.0 will hopefully assist potential OSS users on selecting any products using the OSS selection criteria.

Based on the tool implementation at one of the data centres in one of the Malaysian universities, some positive feedback and suggestions for improvements were obtained. The next step is to make some modifications and then provide further exposure in other organisations.

The study of a methodology to improve the decision making concerning OSS selection may help to identify an appropriate OSS selection solution more easily. Therefore using fuzzy theory, those dimensions, criteria and characteristics can possibly be transformed into a hierarchical structure that represents the weight of importance for the users. Group decision making should also be considered in future, since several decision makers are involved [15].

Acknowledgements

We are grateful for the Universiti Putra Malaysia's (UPM) financial support for the project.

References

[1] OSS Adoption Statistics. 2010. Malaysian Public Sector Open Source Software Programme. OSCC MAMPU. http://www.oscc.org.my/content/view/227/139/. Accessed on Jan 8, 2012.

[2] Malaysian Administrative Modernization and Management Planning Unit (MAMPU). 2011. The Malaysian Government Interoperability Framework for Open Source Software (MyGIFOSS). http://www.oscc.org.my//content/view/185/245/. Accessed on Dec 25, 2011.

[3] Malaysian Administrative Modernisation and Management Planning Unit (MAMPU). 2011. Malaysian Public Sector Open Source Software (OSS) Initiative, Open Source Software (OSS) Implementation Guidelines. http://www.oscc.org.my/content/view/186/244/. Accessed on Dec 26, 2011.

[4] Khadijah Chamili, Yusmadi Yah Jusoh, Jamaiah H. Yahaya, Noraini Che Pa. 2012. Selection Criteria for Open Source Software Adoption in Malaysia. Asian Transaction on Basic and Applied Sciences. 2 (2). ISSN: 2221-4291. On-line Journal.

[5] Khadijah Chamili, Yusmadi Yah Jusoh, Jamaiah H. Yahaya, Noraini Che Pa. 2012. The Selection Criteria for Open Source Software Adoption in Malaysia. International Journal of Advancement in Computing Technology (IJACT). In press.

[6] W. H. Delone, E. R. McLean. 2003. The DeLone and McLean Model of Information Systems Success: A Ten Year Update. Journal of Management Information Systems. Springer. 19 (4): 9–30.

[7] N. Ahmad. 2011. A Systematic Approach to Evaluating Open Source Software. International Journal of Strategic Information Technology and Applications. 2 (1): 48-67. Doi: 10.4018/jsita.2011010104.

[8] J. Confino, P. Laplante. 2010. An Open Source Software Evaluation Model. International Journal of Strategic Information Technology and Applications. IGI Global. 1 (1): 60–77.

[9] E. Glynn, B. Fitzgerald, C. Exton. 2005. Commercial adoption of open source software: An empirical study. International symposium on Empirical Engineering. pp. 225-234.

[10] D. Spinellis, V. Giannikas. 2012. Organizational adoption of open source software. Journal of Systems and Software. 85 (3): 666-682.

[11] R. Uzma, M. J. Tretter. 2012. Defining and evaluating a measure of open source project survivability. IEEE Transactions on Software Engineering. 38 (1).

[12] ISO/IEC 25010:2011 Systems and software engineering-systems and software quality requirement and evaluation (SquaRE) – system and software quality models.

[13] T. L. Saaty. 1980. The Analytical Hierarchy Process. New York: McGraw Hill.

[14] T. L. Saaty. 1986. Axiomatic Foundation of the Analytical Hierarchy Process. Management Science. 32(7): 841-855.

[15] M. A. Azadeh, S. N. Shirkouhi. 2009. Evaluating simulation software using fuzzy analytical hierarchy process. In Proceedings of SpringSim, 2009.

15

Dynamic models for multiplication and division offered by GeoGebra

Lindita Kllogjeri[1, *], Pellumb Kllogjeri[1, 2]

[1]The General High School, 9-Year Cycle, Labinot-Fushe, Elbasan, Albania
[2]University of Elbasan, Department of Mathematics and Informatics, Elbasan, Albania

Email address:
peristerikllogjeri@gmail.com (L. Kllogjeri), pkallogjeri@gmail.com (P. Kllogjeri)

Abstract: One of the most important features of GeoGebra is the coordination of the geometric and algebraic representations, easily observed in GeoGebra window. Using GeoGebra software the teacher can geometrically and fruitfully teach the concepts and algorithms of arithmetic operations in the elementary school. Our paper focuses on two important operations: multiplication and division in the set of natural numbers. Using GeoGebra features we visually demonstrate the concepts of these two operations and help the students to develop the process of mastering multiplication and division facts. Our paper aims to achieve three objectives: Firstly, teach multiplication and division using an area model with base and height of 10 squares. The table designed for this special purpose can be considered as a platform where the arrangements of objects, pictures or numbers in columns and rows is done. Secondly, teach division by using the concept of sharing or partitioning. We have designed a particular dynamic model allowing the teacher to convey the meaning of division so that the students can have a better understanding of the division process. Thirdly, by creating dynamic models for teachers and students we want to: 1. Increase teacher pedagogical content knowledge and improve the instructional practice; 2. Promote student learning by improving teaching practices and providing capacity-building solutions; 3. Encourage the teachers engage themselves in research activity and innovative educational practices and teaching strategies

Keywords: Multiplication Model, Division Model, Technology

1. Introduction

We are witnesses of rapid technological developments and changings in the business world, in industry, in the organization and management of learning institutions etc. Information and Communication Technology (ICT) is continually adding values in the process of teaching and learning as well. Today are available many ICT resources, almost in every country and region, such as computer laboratories, internet access, computer softwares and so on. GeoGebra software is a very good and attractive one, useful for any level of the education system and free. Technology requires that the new skills and knowledge be frequently mastered and adopted. The teachers have to be focused on gaining the ICT competencies, on understanding how and when to use ICT tools. Understanding how and when to use ICT tools is a basic stage for all the educators, managers and specialists.

This stage implies the ability to recognize situations where ICT will be helpful, choosing the most appropriate tools for a particular task, and using these tools in combination to solve real problems. (INFORMATION AND COMMUNICATION TECHNOLOGY IN EDUCATION, pp.17)

Particularly, this stage is linked with the infusing and transforming approaches in ICT development. The teachers use ICT to manage not only the learning of their students but also their own learning.

In the infusing approach to ICT development, ICT infuses all aspects of teachers' professional lives in such a way as to improve student learning and the management of learning processes. The approach supports active and creative teachers who are able to stimulate and manage the learning of students, integrating a range of preferred learning styles and uses of ICT in achieving their goals.

In the transforming approach to ICT development, teachers

and other school staff regard ICT as so natural and part of the everyday life of schools that they begin to look at the process of teaching and learning in new ways. The emphasis changes from teacher-centred to learning centred. (INFORMATION AND COMMUNICATION TECHNOLOGY IN EDUCATION, pp.20)

GeoGebra is a dynamic software package allowing teachers and students to visualize geometric transformations and explore geometric properties. It incorporates algebra, calculus and geometry. GeoGebra can be used by teachers and students: teachers providing step-by-step instructions for the students and the students by independently using GeoGebra tools and commands to construct and explore different objects and properties and generate knowledge. Since the time GeoGebra software has been introduced and ongoing there is a huge amount of materials, tutorials and experiences and a great number of GeoGebra trainers, specialists and educators with web-based monitoring. GeoGebra provides a seamless link between the various mathematical sciences and, between mathematics and other sciences. It promotes the study of mathematics, technology, physics, biology, engineering etc. It encourages exploration, creativity and learning, by doing, in any science and in any level of the school.

One of the most important features of GeoGebra is the coordination of the geometric and algebraic representations, easily observed in GeoGebra window. Using GeoGebra software the teacher can geometrically and fruitfully teach the concepts and algorithms of arithmetic operations in the elementary school. Our paper focuses on two important operations: multiplication and division in the set of natural numbers. Multiplying and dividing are two very important math skills that all students should have. Using GeoGebra features we demonstrate and visualize the concepts of these two operations and help the students to develop the process of mastering multiplication and division facts. The students learn to use patterns and property theories as strategies for recalling the facts related to multiplication and division. They develop, by personal manipulation and exploration of patterns in multiplication and division, computational fluency. Our paper aims to achieve three objectives:

Firstly, teach multiplication and division using an area model with base and height of 10 squares. The table designed for this special purpose can be considered as a platform where the arrangements of objects, pictures or numbers in columns and rows is done.

Secondly, teach division by using the concept of sharing or partitioning. We have designed a particular dynamic model that allows the teacher to convey the meaning of division so that the students can have a better understanding of the division process.

Thirdly, by creating innovative and professional dynamic models for teachers and students we want to:

- Increase teachers pedagogical content knowledge and improve their instructional practice
- Allow the schools to use technology effectively to improve and enhance teaching and learning
- Promote student learning by improving teaching practices and providing capacity-building solutions
- Encourage the teachers engage themselves in research activity and innovative educational practices and teaching strategies

2. The Dynamic Multiplication Model and the Benefits

2.1. The Dynamic Multiplication Model

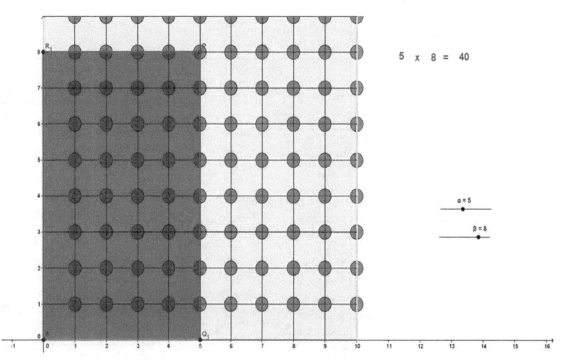

$5 \times 8 = 40$

$a = 5$

$\beta = 8$

Fig. 1. Multiplication Table

In the case of multiplication: students are given length and width of a rectangular to find its area which is the product (length x (times) width or factor x (times) factor). The figure above shows the case of calculating the area of the rectangular (red color) of base: $\alpha = 5$ units and hight: $\beta = 8$ units. The respective area is: $a = \alpha\beta = 5 \times 8 = 40\ square\ units$. Instead of calculating the area can be assigned the task of finding the number of the circles arranged in a rectangular array of 8 rows and 5 columns, or arranged in a rectangular array of 5 rows and 8 columns (this relates to another figure).

The table designed for this special purpose can be considered as a platform where the arrangements of objects, pictures or numbers in columns and rows is done (Look at Fig. 1). This is an array method of explaining the multiplication. On the other side, this array is used for the concept of division related to multiplication as its inverse operation. In the case of division: students are given area and the length in order to find the width (that is: given dividend and the divisor let be found the quotient). Also, the students learn how to use arrays to show the relationship between multiplication and division.

2.2. Procedure of Constructing the Multiplication Table

1. Construct a square 10 x 10 with left lower vertex at the origin of the coordinative system and fill it with a colour (for example, gold).
2. Construct its respective coordinate grid 10 x 10 (the crossed segments coincide with the coordinative lines).
3. Insert two sliders:
   - α with min = 1, max = 10 and increment 1
   - β with min = 1, max = 10 and increment 1
4. Insert into the Input field the point P = (α, β)
5. Construct the rectangle with diagonal OP (OQ_1PR_1) and fill it with red colour.
6. Insert into the Input field, one at a time, the variables α and β and the equation $v = \alpha \cdot \beta$ (α and β represent the factors of the product: $v = \alpha \cdot \beta$).
7. Insert the following texts (each one separately):
   - α (representing factor)
   - β (representing factor)
   - X (representing the multiplication operation)
   - = (representing the equality sign)
   - v (representing the product)
8. For each text choose properties to select the colour (blue), the size of the text etc.
9. Arrange the texts on the right side of the square grid to be on a row, and form the equation $\cdot \beta = v$.
   The value of the product corresponds to the respective values of α and β on their respective sliders.
10. Change the values of α and β on their respective sliders and observe their product at the equation (for example: 5 X 8 = 40).

Interpretation and observation: interpret the result of the product referring to the number of the unit squares consisting the rectangle OQ_1PR_1, or refer to its area. Manipulate the sliders and observe the product at the equation and the respective rectangle with diagonal OP. You can change the

position of point P and observe the change of α and β on their respective sliders. The dependence between the product *d the values of α and β* , in our case, is bidirectional.

2.3. Another Interpretation of the Multiplication Operation

Additional procedure:
1. Using the virtual tool for circle, construct *circles with radius* 0.2 and with centre at each intersection point of the grid (look at figure above). There are 100 such circles.
2. Using *object properties* of each circle, colour them blue.

Interpretation and observation: interpret the result of the product of the whole numbers m and n as the total number of the circles (objects) arranged in a rectangular array, consisted of m horizontal rows of n circles (objects) each and n vertical columns of m circles (objects) each, e.g. interpret 5 x 8 as the total number of the circles in 8 horizontal rows of 5 circles each.

Differently, interpret the result of the product of the whole numbers as the total number of the circles (objects) in 5 vertical rows of 8 circles (objects) each.

Note: The multiplication model can be used to compute the product of decimal numbers of our base-ten number system, as well. For numbers having one digit to the right of the decimal point choose at the sliders increment 0.1. For numbers having two digits to the right of the decimal point choose at the sliders increment 0.01 and so on. In this case the product result relates to the approximate area of the rectangle OQ_1PR_1.

The multiplication model can be used as a calculator. If we want to approximately calculate 3.4 X 5.6 then choose the values $\alpha = 3.4$ and $\beta = 5.6$ at the sliders and read the approximate product at the equation in geometry window or at poly 2, or at v in algebra window. Another way: using *Move* tool displace the point P in such a way that its coordinates be 3.4 and 5.6. Check the result at the equation.

Visit http://tube.geogebra.org/material/show/id/134094 to play with the model.

2.4. The Benefits of Using the Multiplication Model

The teachers:
- Provide professional development
- Improve teaching practices
- Use innovative educational practices and technologies
- Provide capacity-building solutions through the use of GeoGebra software
- Integrate mathematics pedagogy and technology
- Engage in research activity in the areas of educational content, instruction and technology
- Improve and enhance teaching and student learning
- Help in developing policies and programs
- Extension activities: construct multiplication table through 12 x 12, 15 x 15 etc.
- Design multiplication games

The students:
- Get clear meaning about the result of the multiplication

- Develop computational fluency
- Master multiplication facts: *zero* property, *one* property, *commutative* property, multiples of 2, multiples of 5 etc.
- Model their thinking and develop mind patterns for multiplication operation
- Develop fluency in multiplying whole numbers
- Use and develop strategies to estimate the results of multiplication and judge the reasonableness of such results.
- Understand and apply the properties of multiplication operation

3. The Division Model

3.1. Partition Model

The division can be thought of in two ways: partitioning and measurement. We will build a model related to the first concept, partitioning. This relates to the case of finding the number of objects in each group when the total number of the objects is shared in equal quantities. The performed operation is called fair sharing or partitioning. The other case relates to finding the number of groups and the division is called measuring or repeated subtraction. For instance, we keep subtracting 3 objects from 15 objects until we reach zero. Each 3 subtracted is a group.

Let us be concentrated on partitioning. Using the following model we can convey the meaning of the first kind of division in order the students have a better understanding of the division process. The model presented is valid for the interpretation of the whole-number quotient of a whole number. For every case of a division "whole-number quotient of a whole number" must be designed a model which helps to interpret the case. We have chosen the case of partitioning the set of 12 objects into:

(a) 2 groups of equal shares in each one, symbolically denoted as 12÷2
(b) 3 groups of equal shares in each one, symbolically denoted as 12÷3
(c) 4 groups of equal shares in each one, symbolically denoted as 12÷4

The 12 objects are represented by 12 blue circles (look at Fig.2). The respective model for the division interpretation is constructed using GeoGebra software with its effective virtual tools and the excellent periodic properties of the trigonometric functions. The model of this case and the respective procedure serve as a demonstrative model for the teachers to use in their classroom, equipped with computers, or in computer laboratories. By watching this case the students are able to figure out and build in their minds similar models for other cases of division "whole-number quotient of a whole number". Manipulatives and visual aids are very important when teaching multiplication and division.

On the other side, the teachers can use the presented procedure to construct models for other cases of the division. Furthermore, they can design and develop other procedures using GeoGebra software and the properties of the trigonometric functions or recursive sequences.

$$12 : 1 = 12$$

Fig. 2. *The set of 12 objects grouped together*

3.2. The procedure for the Division Model

Case: 12÷n; n = 2, 3, 4
1. Open GeoGebra window
2. Construct a slider with parameter n; interval [1, 4], increment 1
3. Successively enter in the Input field the following points:

$$A = \left\{1, 8 - 2 \cdot \left[1 - \left(sin\left(\frac{n\pi}{2}\right)\right)^{2n} - \left(cos\left(\frac{n\pi}{2}\right)\right)^{2n}\right]\right\}$$

$$B = \left\{2, 8 - 2 \cdot \left[1 - \left(sin\left(\frac{n\pi}{2}\right)\right)^{2n} - \left(cos\left(\frac{n\pi}{2}\right)\right)^{2n}\right]\right\}$$

$$C = \left\{3, 8 - 2 \cdot \left[1 - \left(sin\left(\frac{n\pi}{2}\right)\right)^{2n} - \left(cos\left(\frac{n\pi}{2}\right)\right)^{2n}\right]\right\}$$

$$D = \left\{4, 8 - 2 \cdot \left[1 - \left(sin\left(\frac{n\pi}{2}\right)\right)^{2n} + \left(cos\left(\frac{n\pi}{2}\right)\right)^{2n+1}\right]\right\}$$

$$E = \left\{5, 8 - 2 \cdot \left[1 - \left(sin\left(\frac{n\pi}{2}\right)\right)^{2n+1} + \left(cos\left(\frac{n\pi}{2}\right)\right)^{2n+1}\right]\right\}$$

$$F = \left\{6, 8 - 2 \cdot \left[1 - \left(sin\left(\frac{n\pi}{2}\right)\right)^{2n+1} + \left(cos\left(\frac{n\pi}{2}\right)\right)^{2n+1}\right]\right\}$$

$$G = \left\{7, 8 - 2 \cdot \left[1 - \left(sin\left(\frac{n\pi}{2}\right)\right)^{2n+1} - \left(cos\left(\frac{n\pi}{2}\right)\right)^{2n+1}\right]\right\}$$

$$H = \left\{8, 8 - 2 \cdot \left[1 - \left(sin\left(\frac{n\pi}{2}\right)\right)^{2n+1} - \left(cos\left(\frac{n\pi}{2}\right)\right)^{2n+1}\right]\right\}$$

$$I = \left\{9, 8 - 2 \cdot \left[1 - \left(sin\left(\frac{n\pi}{2}\right)\right)^{2n} - \left(cos\left(\frac{n\pi}{2}\right)\right)^{2n+1}\right]\right\}$$

$$J = \left\{10, 8 - 2 \cdot \left[1 - \left(sin\left(\frac{n\pi}{2}\right)\right)^{2n} + \left(cos\left(\frac{n\pi}{2}\right)\right)^{2n}\right]\right\}$$

$$K = \left\{ 11, 8 - 2 \cdot \left[1 - \left(sin\left(\frac{n\pi}{2}\right) \right)^{2n} + \left(cos\left(\frac{n\pi}{2}\right) \right)^{2n} \right] \right\}$$

$$L = \left\{ 12, 8 - 2 \cdot \left[1 - \left(sin\left(\frac{n\pi}{2}\right) \right)^{2n} + \left(cos\left(\frac{n\pi}{2}\right) \right)^{2n} \right] \right\}$$

4. Using the virtual tool "Circle with Centre and Radius" construct the circles with centre at each above point and radius 0.3

5. Using "Object Properties" select the colour and the

opacity of each circle (blue). This is achieved by clicking on the equation of each circle that are shown on Algebra window.

Demonstration: play with the slider by moving at the values 2, 3 and 4 and observe the dynamic of partitioning the set of 12 objects into 2, 3 and 4 groups, respectively. For each value of n, each group contains the same number of objects (Look at Fig.3).

Fig. 3. *Twelve objects partitioned into 4 groups of equal size*

3.3. Representing the Equation of the Division in GeoGebra Window

Show separately on GeoGebra window the following texts:
1. Using the virtual tool "ABC-Text" register the number 12 (representing the dividend) and the division operation, that is 12:
2. Use again the "ABC-Text" tool to register variable n as follows: open "Text" and, on the open window, click at *Objects*. On the displayed window of *Objects* choose the letter n (representing the divisor). If you register variable n in any other way (e.g. by typing n) then it is not possible for n to take its values 1, 2, 3 and 4.
3. Using the virtual tool "ABC-Text" register the symbol of equality.
4. Enter in the Input field the function j = 12/n or use the command *Product [12, 1/n]* in order to display it on Algebra window.
5. Use again the "ABC-Text" tool to register letter j in the same way: open "Text" and on the open window click at *Objects*. On the displayed window of *Objects* choose the letter j (representing the quotient).
6. Arrange the texts in order they form the equation of the division by selecting the place, their size and their colour as desired.

When played with the slider and observed the dynamic of partitioning of the set of 12 objects into 2, 3 and 4 groups, respectively, simultaneously are shown the respective equations of the division.

Note 1: the respective applet is shared on GeoGebra tube.

You can download the free application from the GeoGebra Web site- www.geogebra.org and play with it by visiting http://www.geogebratube.org/material/show/id/134087 .

Note 2: since the division is the inverse of multiplication we can use the array table of multiplication to help students understand how division and multiplication are related. In multiplication is found the product of two factors, whereas in division is found the missing factor when the other factor and the product are known.

3.4. The Measurement Division Modelling or Strategy

Let see now the model related to the second concept of division, measurement. This is the case of determining the number of groups in which a given number of objects is equally shared or spread. In other words, the task is to find the number of groups (which is unknown) when the total number of the objects is shared in equal quantities (which is known).

The common strategy the students use is: they create sets containing the given number of objects (this number represents the equal quantity in each set) until they have used all the objects. Finally, they count how many sets they made. Recall that this is not an easy task for the students of elementary school. The strategy is based on using trial and error method to determine the right number of sets: the number of sets determined by the students can be less than the right one (there are objects left out), the number of sets determined by the students can be greater than the right one (there are sets with no objects) or, they can hit the right number of sets since the first trial. This type of strategy used by the students is called the measurement strategy, because the students in each trial measure (count) the number of sets they have created.

The measurement strategy relates to the common practice applied to find the number of containment of a given stick in a given straight part of a road, of a given segment in another bigger segment when the smaller segment is contained in it a whole number of times. The common practice is measuring the length of the straight part of the road, starting from one edge to the other, by the use of the stick as a unit. Assume our task is to find out how many times the segment (stick) OA is

contained into the segment OP given that the length of segment OP is 14 units and the length of the stick is 2 units. The equivalent problem is: find out how many times number 2 is contained to number 14, or what is 14 : 2 ? To solve the problem we measure the length of OP, starting from point O, and using the stick OA. The model and the respective strategy of answering the above question is shown in Fig.4.

The respective applet is shared on GeoGebra tube: http://tube.geogebra.org/material/show/id/165465

Read the instructions and download the applet to play with it.

Fig. 4. The measurement model representing the division 14 : 2

4. Conclusions

Our research and practice drives our previous work. Our purpose is to conduct and utilize applied research in special areas of educational content, instruction and technology to improve student learning and enhance teaching and learning and meet the needs of diverse learners. Working alongside with the other researchers and GeoGebra specialists, the main objectives are:

- Help the teachers to use technology effectively in their teaching process to improve student learning
- Promote student learning by improving teaching practices and providing capacity-building solutions
- Increase teacher pedagogical content knowledge and improve instructional practice
- Encourage the teachers engage themselves in research activity and innovative educational practices and teaching strategies
- Encourage the teachers to use designed models, develop other models and share their works and results within GeoGebra community and with other education communities.
- Contribute in the professional development programs

Any teacher can learn and be equipped mostly on his/her own by experimentation, adding here the help from suggestions on GeoGebra wiki, Twitter, and googling stuff from the online help.

Acknowledgement

Lindita Kllogjeri thanks her husband, Pellumb Kllogjeri, for leading the Special Issue, titled "Growing GeoGebra Environment and Use", for the American Journal of Software Engineering and Applications, creating this way the opportunity that her contribution in teaching with technology be publicized.

References

[1]   Carl Stitz, Ph.D. Jeff Zeager, Ph.D., "College Trigonometry" , Lakeland Community College and Lorain County Community College, August 2010, pp. 600-700

[2]   GeoGebra. Available via: http://www.geogebra.org; [Accessed 27 February 2009].

[3]   HOHENWARTER JUDITH, HOHENWARTER MARKUS: "Introduction to GeoGebra", 2008, pp. 3 – 20.

[4]   Hohenwarter M. & Preiner J., "Dynamic mathematics with GeoGebra", TheJournal of Online Mathematics and its Applications, ID1448 ,vol. 7, 2007

[5]   Hohenwarter, M., &Lavicza, Z., "The strength of the community: How GeoGebra can inspire technology integration in mathematics teaching", Mathematics, Statistics, Operation Research Connections, 9(2), 2009, pp. 3-5.

[6]   INFORMATION AND COMMUNICATION TECHNOLOGY IN EDUCATION (A CURRICULUM FOR SCHOOLS AND PROGRAMME OF TEACHER DEVELOPMENT), Division of Higher Education © UNESCO 2002, Printed in France, pp. 8-22.

[7]   Paul A. Foerster ,Trigonometry: Functions and Applications, published by Prentice Hall, USA 1990

16

Towards a Framework for Enabling Operations of Livestock Information Systems in Poor Connectivity Areas

Herbert Peter Wanga, Khamisi Kalegele

School of Computational and Communication Sciences and Engineering (CoCSE), Nelson Mandela African Institution of Science and Technology (NM-AIST), Arusha, Tanzania

Email address:

wangah@nm-aist.ac.tz (H. P. Wanga), khamisi.kalegele@nm-aist.ac.tz (K. Kalegele)

Abstract: Livestock farming is one of the major agricultural activities in the country that is contributing towards achieving development goals of the national Growth and Reduction of Poverty (NSGRP). Smallholder livestock keepers depend on the information from the livestock field officers for sound decision making. Mobile application based solutions, which are currently widely proposed to facilitate the process, fail to perform in poor connectivity areas. This study proposes a machine learning based framework which will enhance the performance of mobile application based solutions in poor connectivity areas. The study used primary data, and secondary data. The primary data were collected through surveys, questionnaires, interviews, and direct observations. Secondary data were collected through books, articles, journals, and Internet searching. Open Data Kit (ODK) tool was used to collect responses from the respondents, and their geographical positions. We used Google earth to have smallholder livestock keepers' distribution map. Results show that smallholder livestock keepers are geographically scattered and depend on the field livestock officers for exchange of information. Their means of communication are mainly face to face, and mobile phones. They do not use any Livestock Information System. The proposed framework will enable operations of Livestock Information System in poor connectivity area, where majority of smallholder livestock keepers live. This paper provides the requirements model necessary for designing and development of the machine learning-based application framework for enhancing performance of livestock mobile application systems, which will enable operations of livestock information systems in poor connectivity areas.

Keywords: Livestock, Information System, Machine Learning, Mobile Application, Technology, Smartphone

1. Introduction

This section introduces the study by providing the general overview. It covers the information system development, livestock in Tanzania, usefulness of machine learning (ML), and objective of the study.

1.1. Information System Development

Usually, information system development projects start with textual requirements descriptions and transform these into a conceptual schema based on a particular conceptual model (e.g., using the UML) [1].

Use case analysis is one particular technique that has shown value for specifying requirements for many different types of systems. Use case analysis has gained prominence due to its inclusion in the Unified Modeling Language (UML) and therefore has gained particular prominence in the construction of object oriented systems [2].

The UML supports a standard notation for use cases and actors. Participation in a particular use case by an actor is shown by a line between the actor and the use case. The notation allows for requirements to be abstracted and encapsulated in a structure that is logical and concise [2].

The process of requirements gathering and analysis has, according to [3] main objectives: To provide system developers with a better understanding of stakeholder needs, which are the professionals directly involved with the project from the end user to responsible for approving the project development; Define the limits of the system (system scope); provide a basis for planning the technical content of the stages of development; provide a basis for estimating cost and development time of the system; define a user interface for the system, focusing on the needs and goals of the users; Establish and maintain compliance with customers and other stakeholders about what the system should do.

1.2. Livestock in Tanzania

According to [4], Livestock farming is one of the major agricultural activities in the country that is contributing towards achieving development goals of the national Growth and Reduction of Poverty (NSGRP). The livestock industry contribution to the Agricultural Gross Domestic product is about 13%, and contributed 4.0% of the National Gross Domestic product in 2009 compared to 4.7% in 2008.

Despite of its contribution to the economy of the country, the livestock sector faces a number of challenges, including geographical dispersion of livestock stakeholders, inadequate number of livestock workers, and poor access of agricultural information.

1.3. Usefulness of Machine Learning (ML)

Machine learning is a field that is at the intersection of computer science, statistics, and applied mathematics. It is the study of algorithms that improve their performance based on experience. It is a branch of Artificial Intelligence which focuses on the construction and study of systems that can learn from data. It is a science of getting computers to act without being explicitly programmed. Machine Learning enables computers to learn and act based on their knowledge.

We use Machine Learning in our daily lives, sometimes without our knowledge: our email service uses machine learning to identify spam or malicious emails and removes them from our inbox, the search engines use machine learning to analyze and evaluate websites and answer our queries etc.

Employing machine learning techniques to livestock information systems in poor connectivity areas, allow the system to intelligently predict the user's demand, provide services accordingly and save the human users' attention cost significantly.

Their implicit predictive ability could be embedded in automatic processes such as expert systems, or they could be used directly for communication between human experts and for educational purposes [5].

One of the practical problems in applying machine learning is that it is hard to acquire a variety of learning tools and experiment with them in a uniform way. We describe a software workbench, called WEKA, which collects together a number of schemes and allows users to run them on real-world data sets and interpret and compare the results [5].

Most learning techniques that have actually been applied assume that the data are presented in a simple attribute-value format in which a record has a fixed number of constant-valued fields or properties [5].

Machine learning techniques will allow the android application to respond to the livestock keepers in poor connectivity area, where majority of them live. In addition, it will assist the application to make predictions.

1.4. Objective of the Study

The objective of the study is to improve farm-level decision making in poor connectivity areas using a machine learning based framework.

This study was conducted in the Arumeru district, Arusha region, which is found in the northern zone of Tanzania. Data were collected from fifteen wards, namely Poli, Sing'isi seela, Makiba, Maroroni, Mbuguni, Akheri, Kikatiti, Kikwe, King'ori, Maji ya chai, Nkoanrua, Nkoaranga, Nkoarisambu, Songoro, and Usa river.

The study identified four key user groups of the system, namely smallholder livestock keepers, field livestock officers, district livestock officers, and livestock researchers. Generally, field livestock officers, district livestock officers, and livestock researchers are called Livestock experts.

This paper presents users and system requirements as a result of data analysis obtained from questionnaires, interviews, direct observations, and document reviews.

It was observed that, majority of smallholder livestock keepers depend on the information delivered from livestock field officers.

The remaining part of this paper is organized as follows. Section 2 briefly describes literature review, Next, Section 3 presents methodology, and Whereas Section 4 covers results and discussion. Section 5 concludes the paper, and explains the future work.

1.5. Our Contribution

Our main contribution here is the intelligent livestock Information System, which is a novel idea in the field of mobile livestock information systems. This system will work in both internet and poor internet connectivity areas.

The study paves a way for a machine learning based framework which will enhance the performance of mobile application based solutions in poor connectivity areas.

2. Literature Review

The study went through the related works. It covers a number of aspects, which are requirements definition, importance of requirements gathering, attributes of good requirements, requirements analysis, and studies of livestock information systems.

2.1. Requirements Definition

Reference [6] suggests that requirement is what the system must be able to do. It is a process or improvement, which stakeholders want to realize through a system. Requirements are for users, stakeholder customers, service providers, development team, testers/ validation.

Requirements definition is a careful assessment of the needs that a system is to fulfill...must say why a system is needed, based on current and foreseen conditions, which may be internal operations or an external market...must say what system features will serve and satisfy this context...must also say how the system is to be constructed [7].

A requirement is a description of a system feature, capability, or constraint. Requirements generally focus on what a system should do, rather than how it should do it [8].

Classes of Requirements are functional, and nonfunctional (constraints)

2.2. Importance of Requirements Gathering

According to [9], user requirements play a fundamental role in restricting the area of interest for data analysis and in choosing facts, dimensions, and measures for system design and implementation.

Requirements are the primary focus in the systems engineering process because the process's primary purpose is to transform the requirements into designs.

Requirements analysis involves defining customer needs and objectives in the context of planned customer use, environments, and identified system characteristics to determine requirements for system functions [10].

2.3. Studies of Livestock Information Systems

A number of mobile phone information systems (IS) in the area of agriculture were studied. Agriculture includes, but not limited to, livestock, aquaculture, crop production, and forestry. Below are some of the IS that were studied.

2.3.1. ICOW

iCow is an Agricultural Information Service with a variety of products available as a subscription service through *285# to help farmers enhance productivity.

The app is a mobile phone cow calendar, which prompts farmers in Kenya on vital days of cows' gestation period. Helps them find the nearest Veterinary and Artificial Insemination providers. In addition, it collects and stores farmers' milk and breeding records, and it sends farmers best dairy practices.

2.3.2. Kilimo Salama

It is a mobile phone service that enables smallholder farmers to insure their agricultural inputs against adverse weather conditions.

2.3.3. Kuza Doctor

They call it 'A farmer's mobile toolkit from farm to fork'. It provides knowledge to farmers using SMS.

2.3.4. SALI

Sustainable Agricultural Livelihood Innovation (SALI) done in Mbeere, Embu by Christian Aid. It uses mobile phone technology to notify farmers of weather updates.

2.3.5. Sangonet

Sangonet is involved with an application that allows small-scale dairy farmers in East Africa to record the lactation history of their cows.

2.3.6. Esoko

Esoko is an information system that gives farmers, traders, agribusiness, and development projects tools to collect and share market information via SMS.

2.3.7. Livestock Information Network and Knowledge System (LINKS)

LINKS is a Livestock Information Network and Knowledge System which provides regular livestock prices and volume information on most of the major livestock markets in Ethiopia, Kenya and Tanzania. It provides market information that is available on request via SMS.

2.4. Mobile Phone Technology in Tanzania

The rapid expansion of mobile phone usage in Tanzania has been triggered by a highly competitive market and service diversification, with the operators now providing different mobile phone services such as voice and message transmission, data services, paging as well as Internet services. In terms of market shares, different companies, namely Vodacom and Zain (former Celtel) Zain/Airtel, tiGO and others are faring quite well [11].

The completion of the National ICT Broadband Backbone (NICTBB) and the booming number of mobile phone users has attracted and increased the number of Internet users in Tanzania to nine million [12]. However, Tanzania has a population of forty five (45) million people.

Historically, Internet services in Tanzania started in 1995. Five years later, in 2000, the country had only 115,000 people connected to the Internet. Since then the number has kept growing significantly –reaching 9.3 million users in 2014; equivalent to 20 per cent of the 45 million people in Tanzania [12].

3. Methodology

The study used qualitative methodology. It is a research method used extensively by scientists and researchers studying human behavior and habits. Qualitative techniques are extremely useful when a subject is too complex to be answered by a simple yes or no hypothesis. These types of designs are much easier to plan and carry out. They are also useful when budgetary decisions have to be taken into account. Qualitative research methods are not as dependent upon sample sizes as quantitative methods.

3.1. Research Methods

The study used primary data, and secondary data. The primary data were collected through surveys, questionnaires, interviews, and direct observations. Secondary data were collected through books, articles, journals, and Internet searching.

Open Data Kit (ODK) tool was used to collect responses from the respondents, and geographical position.

3.2. Description of the Study Area

Arumeru district is found in Arusha region, in the northern zone of Tanzania. Researchers collected data from fifteen wards, namely Poli, Sing'isi seela, Makiba, Maroroni, Mbuguni, Akheri, Kikatiti, Kikwe, King'ori, Maji ya chai, Nkoanrua, Nkoaranga, Nkoarisambu, Songoro, and Usa river.

3.3. Research Design

The research design refers to the overall strategy that you choose to integrate. The different components of the study in a coherent and logical way, thereby, ensuring you will effectively address the research problem; it constitutes the blueprint for the collection, measurement, and analysis of data [13].

This study used a case study research design. According to [14], a case study is an in-depth study of a particular research problem rather than a sweeping statistical survey or comprehensive comparative inquiry. We used Arumeru District as a case study.

3.4. Sampling Design

Sampling design covers all aspects of how the samples are specified and selected. The study used Simple Random Sampling without replacement, which is under the Probability Sampling, in a finite population. Under this sampling design, every item of the universe has an equal chance of inclusion in the sample.

In selecting sample design a researcher must pay attention to the following points: type of universe, sampling unit, source list, size of sample, parameters of interest, budgetary constraint, and sampling procedure [15]. We have considered these points in selecting the sampling design.

Advantages of simple random sampling include; bias is generally eliminated, and sampling error can be estimated.

3.5. Inclusion/ Exclusion Criteria

Inclusion criteria are characteristics that the prospective subjects must have if they are to be included in the study, while exclusion criteria are those characteristics that disqualify prospective subjects from inclusion in the study. Inclusion and exclusion criteria may include factors such as age, sex, education, and profession.

This study used inclusion criteria whereby prospective subjects were supposed to be livestock keepers, who lived in Arumeru district.

3.6. Population

As of the 2012 census, Arumeru district has a population of 368,144 people. Livestock keepers are 102,134.

3.7. Sample Size

Sample size can be determined using different methods such as; sample size from a similar study, sample size table, and sample size calculator.

According to [16], using a population of 102,134 subjects, margin of error 5%, confidence level 95%, response distribution 50%, the sample size is 383.

In terms of the numbers we selected above, the sample size n and margin of error E are given by

$$x= Z(c/100)2r(100-r) \qquad (1)$$

$$n= N\ x/((N-1)E2 + x) \qquad (2)$$

$$E= Sqrt[(N - n)x/n(N-1)] \qquad (3)$$

where N is the population size, r is the fraction of responses that you are interested in, and Z(c/100) is the critical value for the confidence level c.

A total of 210 smallholder farmers and 30 livestock experts were sampled to represent the population. The livestock experts included fifteen (15) field livestock officers, one from each ward. Ten (10) District livestock officers, and five (5) livestock researchers from Nelson Mandela African Institution of Science and Technology (NM-AIST), Livestock Training Agency (LITA), and National Artificial Insemination Center (NAIC).

Similar studies were conducted by [17], [18]. They used similar sample sizes.

3.8. Analysis of Data

Data analysis was conducted using Statistical Package for Social Sciences (SPSS). Data were previously collected using Open Data Kit (ODK) tool and exported to SPSS.

3.9. Case Study Area Mapping

Open Data Kit (ODK) tool helped in collecting data and geographical position of the respondents during requirements gathering. Positions were recorded, exported to KML file format, and plotted using Google Earth, see Figure 1 below. Geographical positions of the respondents show importance of using mobile phones for exchange of information.

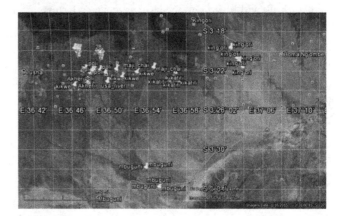

Figure 1. Distribution of the respondents in the research area.

Figure 2 below shows the frequency distribution of respondents in fifteen wards that are located in Arumeru district, Arusha region.

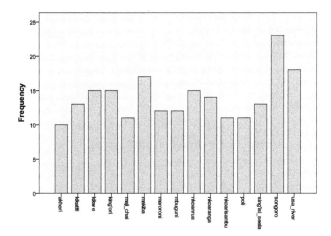

Figure 2. Frequency distribution of the respondents in the wards.

Among the livestock keepers who were interviewed, males were 103 (49%), while females were 107 (51%). Age distribution was 2 (1%) below 20 years, between 20 and 39 were 68 (32.4%), between 40 and 55 were 103 (49%), and above 55 were 37 (17.6%).

4. Results and Discussion

This section shows results and discussion of the study basing on the challenges facing field livestock officers, types of information shared, how they share information, how often livestock keepers communicate with livestock field officers, how they record data, access to marketing information, mobile phone usage, advantages of a proposed framework, system requirements, quantifiable benefits, and requirements model.

4.1. Challenges Facing Field Livestock Officers

Field livestock officers face a number of challenges, which impair their routine activities. These include; they serve a large number of livestock keepers who are far and scattered; lacking means of transport; lack of enough funds to support extension services; difficulties in accessing published research findings;

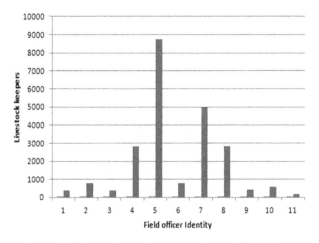

Figure 3. Number of livestock keepers per livestock field officer.

On average each field officer serves 2078 livestock keepers. However, the ideal ratio is one livestock field officer to seven hundred (700) livestock keepers. This increases challenges to the field officers to serve livestock keepers.

4.2. Types of Information Shared

User requirements gathering process was conducted among the livestock keepers and livestock experts. The livestock keepers mentioned market information, disease outbreaks, vaccinations and treatments, weather, and modern livestock husbandry. On the other hand, livestock experts mentioned market information, disease information, and weather.

4.3. How They Share Information

The study shows that, smallholder livestock keepers mainly share information through the field livestock keepers. They use face to face mechanism. This is a challenge as livestock keepers are geographically dispersed, and the field livestock officers do not have reliable means of transport. Another way that they use is to make a phone call. However, solving the livestock problems on a phone is also another challenge.

Sometimes the smallholder livestock keepers share information through neighbors, and mass media such as radio and television.

4.4. How Often They Communicate with Livestock Field Officers

Analysis shows that majority of livestock keepers 116 (55.2%), communicate with the livestock field officers when problems arise, followed by 46 (21.9%), who communicate monthly. Others communicate either weekly, or do not communicate at all.

Livestock keepers communicate with livestock field officers when the problems arise because the livestock field officers do not follow the regular visit timetable. Some livestock keepers do not know their field officers, and some do not even know if they exist.

4.5. How They Record Data.

In most of the farms, data is recorded on hard copy and then it is posted to herd registers for compilation, recoding and feeding in computer for analysis. This is often not a regular process even in many institutional farms. The study observed the same trend in Arumeru district; however some livestock keepers kept their data by mere memorizing.

4.6. Access to Marketing Information

Livestock keepers need market information to sell their products and by products, or buy the commodities. Study found that, they access market information through face to face, mobile phones, and visit to markets. There is no livestock information system which is necessary for exchange of information.

4.7. Mobile Phone Usage

Among the livestock keepers 206 (98.1%) own phones. Only 4 (1.9%) do not own phones. However, only 11 respondents own smart phones. They use their mobile phones for Short Message Services (SMS), making and receiving calls, and mobile money transfer.

They support the idea of using mobile phones for exchange of information among the livestock stakeholders.

4.8. User Requirements

The study came up with the following requirements; receive prices of their products and byproducts, buyer information, livestock auctions, feed and fodders, insecticides, pesticides, and communication with livestock field officers, milk production, milk sales, disease outbreaks, Vaccinations, Births, Deaths, and slaughter.

4.9. Quantifiable Benefits

Below are some of the quantifiable benefits that smallholder livestock keepers will receive;
(1) Less time wasted in search for livestock information.
(2) Better prices for their products and by-products.
(3) Increasing profit.
(4) Reduced product and by-product losses.
(5) Fewer journeys in search for information.
(6) More volume production.
(7) Better livestock keeping practices.

4.10. Requirements Model

Requirements model captures functional requirements from user perspective. It makes use of Use Case diagrams. It has inputs and outputs. Inputs are system requirements specifications, documentations of existing systems, and practices that are to be followed, exchanges between developers and users and specifiers. Outputs are use case model, and concise descriptions of use case.

4.10.1. Existing Data Flow Diagram

The existing model puts the livestock field officer at the middle between the livestock keeper and other actors. Every information passes through the livestock field officer.

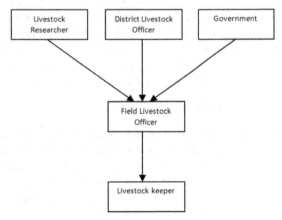

Figure 4. Existing data flow model.

Field livestock officers face challenges in dispersing useful information to livestock keepers, who are geographically scattered. The field livestock keepers do not have reliable means of transport and communication. Therefore there are barriers in conveying modern livestock practices and other extension services.

4.10.2. Use Case Model
Use case model is a collection of use cases.

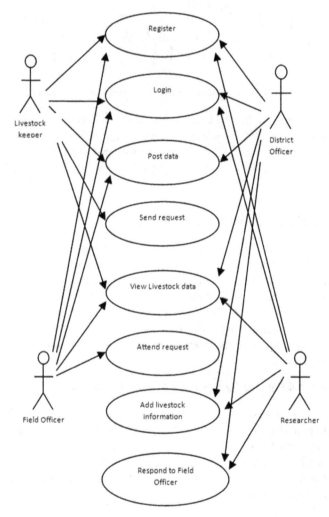

Figure 5. Use case model.

The model has four actors who are livestock keeper, livestock field officer, livestock researcher, and livestock district officer.

Livestock keeper wants to register in the system, login using his/ her username and password, post data, send request or query to the livestock field officer, and view livestock information on various aspects such as feed and fodder, disease outbreak, pesticides, and market prices.

Livestock field officer, apart from registering and logging in the system, he/ she needs to receive livestock data from livestock keepers, post data, view livestock data from livestock keepers, livestock district officers, and livestock researchers.

Livestock researcher registers and logs in to the system.

He/ she needs to view livestock data from livestock keepers and do data analysis so as to come up with scientific solutions to the problems.

Livestock district officer supervises the livestock field officers, view livestock data from the livestock keepers, view research findings from researchers, and can respond to livestock field officers.

4.11. Advantages of a Proposed Framework

Findings show that, many frameworks were addressing issues of crop production, and their value chain. The emphasis was in the marketing of crops. In addition, the apps are using SMS to receive information. The study did not find the frameworks which address difficulties and challenges of smallholder livestock keepers.

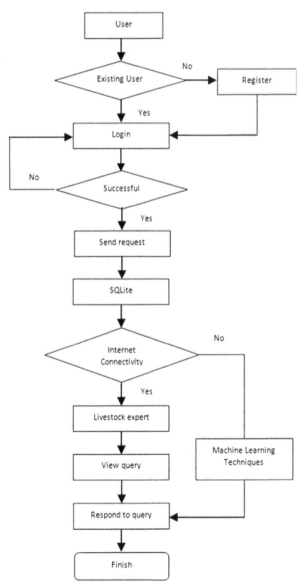

Figure 6. *Data flow diagram.*

Smallholder livestock keepers need the framework that will enable them receive prices of their products and byproducts, buyer information, livestock auctions, diseases,

feed and fodders, insecticides, pesticides, and communication with livestock field officers.

The existing mobile phone solutions fail to work in poor connectivity areas. They only work where there is constant connectivity. They do not use machine learning techniques to respond to the queries. They are not able to make predictions that can assist operations of livestock information systems.

The proposed framework will enable operations of livestock information systems in poor connectivity areas through making use of machine learning techniques. It will be capable of responding to queries from livestock keepers without assistance from the livestock field officers.

5. Conclusion

Mobile application based solutions, which are currently widely proposed to facilitate the process, fail to perform in poor connectivity areas, and do not address issues that smallholder livestock keepers face. This study does the requirements analysis and comes up with requirements model. It paves a way for a machine learning based framework which will enhance the performance of mobile application based solutions in poor connectivity areas.

Results show that smallholder livestock keepers are geographically scattered and depend on the field livestock officers for exchange of information. Their means of communication are mainly face to face, and mobile phones. They do not use any Livestock Information System. The proposed framework will enable operations of Livestock Information System in poor connectivity area, where majority of smallholder livestock keepers live.

Future Work

In the future we plan to design Machine learning based framework for enhancing performance of livestock mobile application system. We will use that design to develop and implement machine learning – based application framework for enhancing performance of livestock mobile application systems

Acknowledgement

Appreciations are expressed to the Nelson Mandela African Institution of Science and Technology (NM-AIST), Livestock Training Agency (LITA-Tengeru), National Artificial Insemination Agency (NAIC), and Arumeru District Council, for making this study a success.

We would like to thank the anonymous reviewers for their valuable feedback.

References

[1]   C. Rolland et al., "A proposal for a Scenario Classification Framework", Journal of Requirements Engineering, Vol. 3 No. 1, 1998, Springer Verlag, pp. 23–47.

[2]   Schneider, G. and J. Winters, "Applying Use Cases - A Practical Guide", Object Technology Series, ed. J. Booch, Rumbaugh. 1998: Addison Wesley.

[3]   Leffingwell, D. and Widrig, D. (2003) "Managing Software Requirements". 2nd Edition, Addison-Wesley, Boston, MA, USA.

[4]   Ministry of Livestock and Fisheries Development (2010), "Livestock Sector Development Strategy", Tanzania.

[5]   Robert J. Mcqueen (1994), "Applying Machine Learning to Agricultural Data", Management Systems, University of Waikato, Hamilton, New Zealand.

[6]   Joris Vanderschrick (2011), "System Requirements Analysis: The first step to value-based system development", Verhaert – Embedded Systems Development, Belgium.

[7]   Jaelson Castro and John Mylopoulos (2002), "Information Systems Analysis and Design",

[8]   S. Pfleeger and J. Atlee (2006), "Software Engineering - Theory and Practice", Third Edition, Prentice Hall.

[9]   Rai, A., Dubey, V., Chatuverdi, K. K., Malhotra, P. K., (2008). "Design and development of data mart for animal resources", Journal of Computers and Electronics in Agriculture. 64 (2), p111-119.

[10] Defense Acquisition University (2001), "Systems Engineering Fundamentals", Defense Acquisition University Press, Fort Belvoir, Virginia.

[11] Bhavnani, A A., Won-Wai Ciu, R., Janakiram, S. and Silarszky, P. (2008), "The Role of Mobile Phones in Sustainable Rural Poverty Reduction", Report for the World Bank ICT Policy Division, Global Information and Communications Department, Washington DC.

[12] The Citizen, 2014, "Tanzania's Internet users hit 9m", published online, Wednesday October 1, 2014.

[13] De Vaus, D. A. (2001), "Research Design in Social Research", London: SAGE.

[14] Yin, R. K. (2003), "Case Study Research: Design and Theory", Applied Social Research Methods Series. CA: Thousand Oaks.

[15] Kothari, C. R. (2006), "Research Methodology, Methods and Techniques", New Delhi, India: New Age International Publishers.

[16] Calculator, R. (2014, December 17), "Raosoft", Retrieved December 17, 2014, from http://www.raosoft.com/samplesize.html:

[17] Bernard Mussa, Zaipuna Yonah, Charles Tarimo, (2014), "Towards a Mobile – Based DSS for Smallholder Livestock Keepers: Tanzania as a Case Study", International Journal of Computer Science and Information Security, Vol. 12, No. 8, August 2014.

[18] Gladness Mwanga, Zaipuna Yonah, (2014), "ICT as a tool for improving information flow among livestock stakeholders: a case study of Tanzania", International Journal of Computer Science and Information Security, Vol. 12, No. 8, August 2014.

17

PID DC motor drive with gain scheduling

Wasif Abdel Aziz Saluos[1], Mohammad Abdelkarim Alia[2]

[1]Faculty of Engineering Technology, Zarqa University, zarqa Jordan
[2]This research is Supported by Zarqa University, zarqa-Jordan

Email address:

Saluos2000@yahoo.com (W. A. Saluos), makalalia2000@yahoo.com (M. A. Alia)

Abstract: In this work software-based PID controller with gain scheduling is implemented to drive a DC motor. LabVIEW PID controller tool with its associated gain scheduling VI was used. Motor start up interval was experimentally analyzed and divided into three regions with three related PID gains sets. Gain scheduling selection criterion was based on the dynamic error absolute value, and it was realized by using case structures. Experiments show that speed overshoot was eliminated and drive system response became faster. Generally it is possible to auto tune the PID controller to achieve a response with the required static or dynamic specifications.

Keywords: PID Control, Gain Scheduling, PWM, Adaptive Controller

1. Introduction

Although PID controllers are by far the most widely used controllers in industry , they are not always well suited for every process control system. One important drawback of PID control is the frustration often involved in reaching the correct tuning parameters for a given operation. Because of that academics have been working on countless alternatives.

As an example of these attempets is our work (2), where aself-tuning software based PID controller was designed . This work may be considered as continuation of the previous one aiming at exploring the possibility of realizing an adaptive controller with gain scheduling.

The advent of microprocessors and advanced computing platforms has catalyzed the shift to adaptive model-free PID controllers for its ability to improve the performance of mechanical and electromechanical systems (1, 2).Recently , gain scheduling technique is benefiting from the advances in PC computing dedicated software and is used generally in non-linear control systems successfully. One of the inherent characteristics of DC motor drives is the undesirable speed overshooting when it is required to design a dynamic-mode high speed motor drive systems. In order to get a high speed motor drive with minimum overshoot , gain scheduling is suggested to be used in this work. In this case one can tune the PID controller for different sets of controller parameters . Depending on the value of the dynamic error during the transient period , and by using an if – then statement(case

structure) the corresponding set of PID parameters shall be called by the controller in order to achieve the required performance. In order to realize this idea LabVIEW gain-scheduled and PID software are utilized. Experimental results show that system performance has improved compared with tuning PID controller only with one set of parameters.

2. Description of the Motor Drive System

The block diagram of the drive system is shown in figure NO (1). The main hardware components are a DC motor , tacho- generator , a PC , NI DAQ board and power interface circuit which includes a MOSFET- static power switch. The controller is software- based using LabVIEW PID tool with its associated gain scheduler. The output

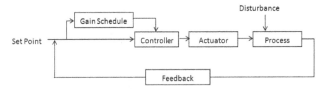

Figure NO (1). *Block diagram of the control system*

Of the PID is the driving signal of a pulse width modulator(PWM)which is generated internally within LabVIEW. The PWM output is fed to the power interfacing circuit. As the PID output signal changes the PWM duty cycle changes proportionally regulating by that the average voltage which feeds the motor armature,. Consequently the motor speed is controlled. As the block diagram shows , the gain scheduler is connected in a feed forward channel and functions depending on the value of the dynamic error. As seen, the general setup of the drive system is quazi -invariant with a feed forward and feedback configurations. Such a drive system may be viewed as a feedback system in which the feedback gains are adjusted by using feed-forward compensation.

Although the feedback configuration helps to compensate for variation of system parameters and system components non-linearity , the inclusion of an adaptive feed forward channel will also reduce the effects of parameter variation which makes the control system more robust.

3. Software Components

The block diagram of the control system is shown in figure NO(2) . It includes the following components. The DAQ assistant express VI , PID controller ,numeric functions, case structures , mean value VI , comparison functions, waveform chart and simulate signal VI.

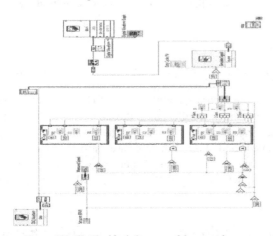

Figure NO (2). *The block diagram of the control system*

The front panel of the control system is given in figure NO (3). It includes the controls and indicators .

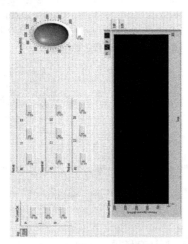

Figure NO (4). *Front panel widow of the control system*

The DAQ assistant is in charge of reading the voltage from the tacho-generator output. Morover the mean component takes the average of the read voltage every 20 samples.

Some numeric and logic functions(comparison) are involved in order to convert the feedback voltage into a speed measured in rotations per minuite(RPMs). This is shown in figure NO(3).

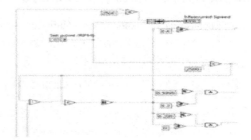

Figure NO (3) Mathematic & Comparisons Operations

For the gain scheduling selector to function, speed error is found as the difference between the set point and the process variable i.e. the instantaneous speed. $\varepsilon = SP - PV$. The absolute value of the error is divided by the set point to get a ratio

$$x = \frac{SP - PV}{SP} = \frac{\varepsilon}{SP} \; ; 0 \le x \le 1$$

For gain scheduling we used three sets of PID parameters which correspond to three sets of ratio x such that :
- For the first PID parameters set $0.6 \le x \le 1$
- For the second PID parameters set $0.3 \le x \le 0.599$
- For the third PID parameters set $0 \le x \le 0.295$

Concerning the case structure , the selector of the desired set is connected to case structure. The case structure has two states (True , False) states. For the False state the value (0) is inserted in it. For the True state we entered the values of (x) sets. Thus we have one case structure for each set as shown in figure NO (5).

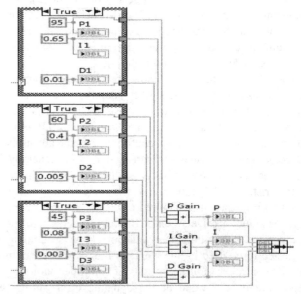

Figure NO (5). *Details of the case structure connections*

The PID virtual instrument has three inputs :
- The set point , which is connected to a dial control that is located at the front panel.
- Process variable , which is represented by the data coming from the DAQ assistant.
- PID parameters(gains) which are the data coming from the output of bundle component.

The output of the PID VI is utilized in order to control the duty cycle of the PWM signal. The PWM signal is generated internally using Simulate Signal

Express VI .In order to get the control signal out of the DAQ device the DAQ assistant with some conversion signal tool was utilized.

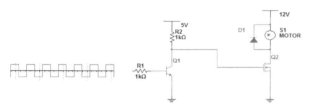

Figure NO (6). Power interface circuit.

Concerning power interfacing , simple power interfacing

circuit is given in figure NO (6).

4. Experimental Results

Initially the values of the set point and process variable are zero. When the desired speed is set through the dial control in the front panel , the motor starts running and motor speed keeps increasing until it reaches the set point. During the rise time the speed error begins decreasing from the maximum value up to zero.

At the first stage , when the error is maximum(the ratio of the error to the set point is between 0.6 and one, the system will select the first set of gains , which is immediately displayed on the Operating Set Indicator. When the speed reaches the middle of the rise time the ratio (x) will be in the second range and the gain scheduling selector will select the second set of gains. At the final portion of the rise time the third set of PID parameters is selected and the speed creeps closer towards the set point.

For an open loop control circuit Figure NO (7) shows the PWM and steady state speed for a duty cycle of 20% and a speed of 1209 RPM.

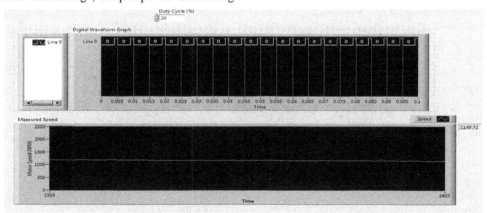

Figure NO (7). PWM signal and motor speed at 20% duty cycle

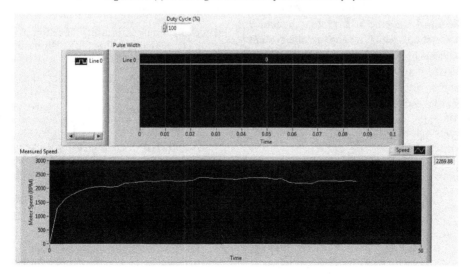

100% of duty cycle

Figure NO (8). Showes the PWM signal and motor speed at 100% duty cycle.

Figure NO (8) PWM signal and motor strat up speed at 100% duty cycle

For a closed loop system figure NO (9) shows the values of the gains for the three sets of PID gains.

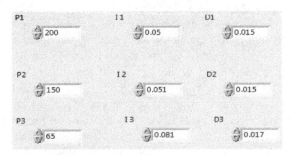

Figure NO (9). Indicator of the values of used PID gains

Figure NO (10) shows motor speed at start up and steady state regions for a closed loop system when three PID gain settings are used. The figure shows that the over shoot is not existing.

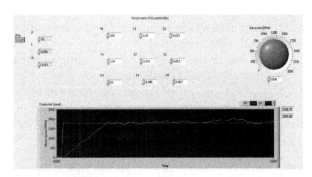

Figure NO (10). Start up speed curve when three PID gain settings are used

In order to compare between gain scheduled and one gain setting PID controller , curve NO (11) shows the start up curve for the first set of PID gains only.

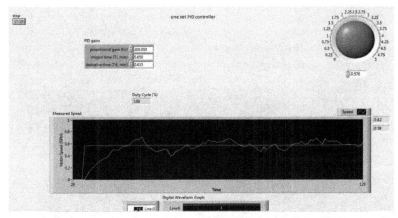

Figure NO (11). Motor start up with the first set of PID gains

5. Conclusions

Using a PID controller with gain scheduling improves the performance of the control system. The system becomes faster with minimum overshoot, which means that the system becomes more robust with a higher stability margin.

Using PID gain scheduling is applicable for linear or nonlinear control systems. By dividing the system working interval into a specific number of regions with the appropriate sets of PID gains , controller tuning becomes an automatic process and the iterative tuning procedure is eliminated.

References

[1] Simulation of auto-tuning PID controller for DC motor using Ziegle-Nichols method. Aina Azliyana bt Mohamd. Thesis of B.SC degree. University Malaysia Pahang. June – 2012

[2] A design of a PID self-tuning controller using LabVIEW. Mohammad A.K.Alia , Tariq M.Younes , Shebel A.Alsabbah. Journal of software engineering and applications. March-2011 , 4 , 161-171

[3] Comparison performance of different PID controllers for DC motor. Abidoun H.Shellal. Diyala Journal of engineering sciences. June -2012, Vol. 5 NO 01 Diyala University.

[4] Study on auto tuning controller for servo system. Nguyen Hoang Giap, Jin-Ho Shin , Won –Ho-Kim. Intelligent control and automation . July 2014, 5 , 102-110. Graduate school of Dong-eui University. Busan-Korea

[5] Adaptive PID controller for DC motor speed control. A Taifour Ali, Eisa Bashier M and others International journal of engineering inventions. Sept 2012 , Vol. 1 , issue 5

[6] Refinments of Ziegler – Nichols tuning formula . Hang C-C K.J Astrom and W.K Ho. IEE proc . part D , Vol. 138, NO 2pp , March 1991

[7] PID control system analysis , design and technology.IEEE transactions on control systems technology. Vol. 13 , NO 4 July2005.

18

Student Database System for Higher Education: A Case Study at School of Public Health, University of Ghana

Wisdom Kwami Takramah[1], Wisdom Kwasi Atiwoto[2]

[1]Department of Epidemiology and Biostatistics, School of Public Health, University of Health and Allied Sciences, Ho, Ghana
[2]Department of Biostatistics, School of Public Health, University of Ghana, Accra, Ghana

Email address:
takramah@uhas.ed.ug (W. K. Takramah)

Abstract: The success of any organization such as School of Public Health, University of Ghana hinges on its ability to acquire accurate and timely data about its operations, to manage this data effectively, and to use it to analyze and guide its activities. Integrated student database system offer users (Student, Registrar, HOD) with a unified view of data from multiple sources. To provide a single consistent result for every object represented in these data sources, data fusion is concerned with resolving data inconsistency present in the heterogeneous sources of data. The main objective of this project is to build a rigid and robust integrated student database system that will track and store records of students. This easy-to-use, integrated database application is geared towards reducing time spent on administrative tasks. The system is intended to accept process and generate report accurately and any user can access the system at any point in time provided internet facility is available. The system is also intended to provide better services to users, provide meaningful, consistent, and timely data and information and finally promotes efficiency by converting paper processes to electronic form. The system was developed using technologies such as PHP, HTML, CSS and MySQL. PHP, HTML and CSS are used to build the user interface and database was built using MySQL. The system is free of errors and very efficient and less time consuming due to the care taken to develop it. All the phases of software development cycle are employed and it is worthwhile to state that the system is very robust. Provision is made for future development in the system.

Keywords: Relational Database, Interoperability, Database Management System, phpMyAdmin, MySQL Server, Data Redundancy, Middleware

1. Introduction

The registrar of the School of Public Health, University of Ghana is responsible for handling student information and gathering them during enrollment. This information includes each student's background information, student medical history, courses taken student attendance at lectures grades, performance record, and other information needed by the school.

Today, the success of School of Public Health, University of Ghana depends on its ability to acquire accurate and timely data about its operations, to manage this data effectively, and to use it to analyze and guide its activities. Phrases such as the information superhighway have become ubiquitous, and information/data processing is a rapidly growing multibillion dollar industry.

Several forms and reports are used in day to day processing of results. A database can integrate these several components hence resulting in improved and more efficient operations (Greenwald et al., 2005; Connolly and Begg, 2004).

Student Database System deals with all kind of student details, academic related reports, college details, course details, curriculum, batch details and other resource related details too. It tracks all the details of a student from the day one to the end of his course which can be used for all reporting purpose, tracking of attendance, progress in the course, completed semesters years, coming semester year curriculum details, exam details, project or any other assignment details, final exam result; and all these will be available for future references too.

1.1. Problem Statement

Information plays a vital role in the development and growth of every organization. Currently, the various departments manage student information independently in their own ways. There are no common, standardized process and program for capturing, processing and storing student's information. This has kept student information disintegrated in different departments and information provided to the various departments by the students is characterized with discrepancies.

The various departments have systems in place to store and process student data but the systems are not able to talk to each other (Interoperability). This makes it difficult for the registrar to collate information of students across departments. For instance, if the registrar wants information about students with respect to their academic performance urgently, he must go to all the departments and collect the required data. On occasions where the department is not able to produce the needed information immediately, the business or activity at that particular time would come to a standstill. On the other hand, time is being wasted going round the various departments to solicit data. This situation is very frustrating and impedes smooth operations and decision making process.

One of the policies of School of Public Health, for that matter University of Ghana is the fact that students must not fail in three or more courses. Referrals in three or more courses will warrant expulsion from the school. The current information system is incapable of providing students with exams result before courses are registered for the next semester.

A past student who needs a transcript will have to travel all the way to the school before he could access it because the current system is so weak to the extent that it is unable to provide this document online.

The problems facing the current manual system are data redundancy, difficult to update and maintain, inconsistent data, insecurity, difficult to impose constraints on various data file and difficult to backup.

It is against this backdrop that automated Student Database System is being developed to address the problems catalogued above.

1.2. Project Objective

The main objective is to develop a robust Student Database Management System for School of Public Health.
Specific Objectives
- To identify the problems involved in the implementation of the current student information system;
- To develop a database system that allows the registrar to list and update students information;
- To develop a system that permits authorized student to view their result online;

- To develop the prototype of an integrated Student Database System that can be implemented.

1.3. Purpose of Project

The proposed system is intended to make life easy. The main purpose of the project is to build an integrated student database system to facilitate easy access of records of students across departments. The Student Database System will allow the registrar of School of Public Health, Legon to edit, update and list personal and academic details of students. It will also enhance efficient management of student's information.

The proposed system is also intended to allow students to view their results on line. This will go a long way to help students decide on what courses to register.

1.4. Scope

The proposed system is intended to manage specific information of students such as personal details, course details and exam details etc. It is not Student Information Management System which has a broader application. It is only a part of Student Information Management System.

This project when completed will provide comprehensive Student Database System for School of Public Health, University of Ghana. The system should be able to capture, validate, sort, classify, calculate, summarize, store, retrieve, reproduce and communicate operational data. Student Database System will store semester details, course details, department details and all the details of students including their background information, educational qualifications and personal details etc.

The proposed system will have the following features:
- Login module: Login module will help in authentication of user accounts. Users who have valid login id and password can only login into their respective accounts;
- Search module: This model allows one to search for a particular student or group of students using search criteria such as name of student, Index number, course code etc;
- Registration Module and Account Management: This module will help the student get registered from anywhere if internet is present .This module will really simplify the task of the manual registration. Also after successful registration the user can update information and change their password as and when required;
- User Management: This module will help the registrar in enabling/disabling a user account and updating user information as required.

2. Literature Review

A project on Student Information Management system which was carried out by Kapil Kaushik Ankur Agarwal Tushar Somani, an IT student of Institute of Engineering and Technology, Maharishi provides a simple interface for maintenance of student information. It can be used by any educational institute or colleges to maintain records of students easily. Achieving this objectives is difficult using a manual system as the information is scattered, can be redundant and collecting relevant information can be very time consuming. All these problems are solved using this project. Throughout the project the focus has been on presenting information in an easy and intelligible manner. The project is very useful for those who want to know about Student Information Management Systems and want to develop software/websites based on the same concept. The project provides facilities like on line registration and profile creation of student thus reducing paper work and automating the records generation process in an educational institution.

The goal of this chapter is to explain the theory of database management system development which will be applied in the development of student database management system for school of public health, University of Ghana. The following issues will be presented respectively.

1. Integrated information system
2. Database and DBMS
3. Student records/data management
4. Web technology
5. Conclusion

This will give an insight into the project area and help to get information that will enhance the development of the student database management system.

2.1. Integrated Information System

Integrated Information Systems offer users with a unified view of heterogeneous data sources. To provide a single consistent result for every object represented in these data sources, data fusion is concerned with resolving data inconsistencies present in the sources. Querying the heterogeneous data sources, combining the results, and presenting them to the user is performed by the integration system.

When multiple sources are to be integrated into a single and consistent view, at least the following three steps need to be performed:

- One needs to identify corresponding attributes that are used to describe the information items in the source. The result of this step is a schema mapping that is used to transform the data present in the sources into a common representation;
- The different objects that are described in the data sources need to be identified and aligned. In this way, using duplicate detection techniques, multiple, possibly inconsistent representations of some real world objects are found;
- As a last step, the duplicate representations need to be combined and fused together into a single representation while inconsistencies in the data need to be resolved;

There are two main kinds of inconsistencies in data integration:

- First, there are schematic inconsistencies between

sources, tables not having the same attributes, attributes meaning the same concept but having a different name, or stored data in a different structure and;
- Conflicts is another kind of data inconsistency

There are two types of conflicts in data integration; Uncertainties and contradictions

Uncertainty is a conflict between a non-null value and one or more null values that are used to describe the same property of an object. Usually it occurs as a result of missing information. Null values present in tables can have different meanings. Three interpretations of null values can be distinguished as follows:

1. Value unknown: The value exist but whoever entered the data did not know it
2. Value inapplicable: The corresponding property is not applicable for the object represented by this tuple.
3. Value withheld: The data exist but we are not allow to see it.

The other type of conflicts is contradiction. It is the conflict between two or more different non-null values that are used to describe the same property of an object. An example is the case if two or more data sources provide two or more different values for the same attribute on the same object.

One good reason for regarding uncertainty as a special case of conflict is the fact that it is easier to deal with uncertainty than contradiction.

Several forms and reports are used in day to day processing of documents. A database can integrate these several components hence resulting in improved and more efficient operations (Greenwald et al., 2005; Connolly and Begg, 2004).

2.2. Database and Database Management System

A database is an integrated collection of data, usually so large that it has to be stored on secondary storage devices such as disks or tapes. This data can be maintained as a collection of operating system files, or stored in a DBMS (database management system).

A Database Management System (DBMS) is computer software designed for the purpose of managing databases based on a variety of data models. A DBMS is a complex set of software programs that controls the organization, storage, management, and retrieval of data in a database. DBMS are categorized according to their data structures or types, sometime DBMS is also known as Database Manager. It is a set of prewritten programs that are used to store, update and retrieve a Database (Gerald C. Okereke, 2009).

When a DBMS is used, information systems can be changed much more easily as the organization's information requirements change. New categories of data can be added to the database without disruption to the existing system. Organizations may use one kind of DBMS for daily transaction processing and then move the detail onto another computer that uses another DBMS better suited for random inquiries and analysis.

Database servers are specially designed computers that

hold the actual databases and run only the DBMS and related software. Database servers are usually multiprocessor computers, with RAID disk arrays used for stable storage. Connected to one or more servers via a high speed channel, hardware database accelerators are also used in large volume transaction processing environments.

Advantages of DBMS
- Improved strategic use of corporate data
- Reduced complexity of the organization's information systems environment
- Reduced data redundancy and inconsistency
- Enhanced data integrity
- Application-data independence
- Improved security
- Reduced application development and maintenance costs
- Improved flexibility of information systems
- Increased access and availability of data and information
- Logical & Physical data independence
- Concurrent access anomalies.
- Facilitate atomicity problem.
- Provides central control on the system through DBA.

2.3. Student Records/Data Management

According to student records manual prepared by University of South Florida (office of the registrar) the creation and maintenance of records relating to the students of an institution are essential to:
- managing the relationship between the institution and the student;
- providing support and other services and facilities to the student;
- controlling the student's academic progress and measuring their achievement, both at the institution and subsequently;
- providing support to the student after they leave the institution.

In addition, student records contain data which the institution can aggregate and analyze to inform future strategy, planning and service provision.

A student is an individual who is registered for a university credit course or program.

A student record/data contains information directly related to a student, which means that the record is personally identifiable. Personal identifiers that relate a record to a student include student name, student ID, student address, parent/family member names, and a list of personal characteristics. Student records could be maintained in multiple media including handwriting, print, microfilm/fiche, computer's main memory, magnetic tape, cassette, disk or diskette.

Student records/data may be presented by the student, submitted on behalf of the student, or created by the University. These records are used to assist offices in their support of basic institutional objectives and to document student progress and achievement in the educational process of the University.

Educational institutions and agencies are required to conform to fair information practices. This means that persons who are subjects of data systems (i.e., students at an institution) must:
- be informed of the existence of such systems
- have identified for them what data about them are on record,
- be given assurances that such data are used only for intended purposes
- be given the opportunity to request an amendment or correction to their record and
- be certain that those responsible for data systems take reasonable precautions to prevent misuse of the data.

2.4. Web Technology

The web is a hypermedia-based system that provides a means of browsing information on the Internet in a non-sequential way using hyperlinks. The web is a compelling platform for the delivery and dissemination of data-centric, interactive applications. The web's ubiquity provides global application availability to both users and organizations. Because the architecture of the web has been designed to be platform-independent, it has the potential to significantly lower deployment and training cost. Organizations are now rapidly building new database applications or reengineering existing ones to take full advantage of the web as a strategic platform for implementing innovative business solutions, in effect becoming web-centric organization.

The World Wide Web (web for short) provides a simple point and click means of exploring the immense volume of pages of information residing on the Internet (Berners-Lee 1992; Berners-Lee et al.. 1994). Information on the web is presented on the web pages which appear as a collection of text, graphic, pictures, sound and video.

2.5. Conclusion

Finally, since the data generated in day to day transactions by School of Public Health increase geometrically according to the registrar, it is worthwhile and holistic to develop robust student database management system for the school to hold the large amount of data that is generated. The proposed system, SDMS, should be able to stand the test of time because student records should be kept as long as is necessary to:
- fulfill and discharge the contractual obligations established between the institution and the student, including the completion of any non-academic disciplinary action;
- provides information on the academic career and achievements of the student to employers, licensing/regulatory bodies and other organizations, as well as to the student as part of their lifelong learning record.

The information gathered whilst reviewing existing literature on student information management system has been very useful in the development of the proposed system.

The project when completed will provide an efficient way to store and organize data than spreadsheet. It will also serve as a centralized facility that can easily be modified and quickly shared among multiple users. The proposed system will have a well-designed interface that allows users to interact with the system via internet connection and a web browser.

3. Methodology

This Chapter gives a brief description of the methodology used to develop the proposed system. The main methodology involves feasibility study, data collection, system analysis and design, developing and implementing Student Database Management System. The data considered necessary to build the system were collected and analyzed. The methodology is very important to ensure that the new system would give benefits to the school.

3.1. Data Collection

The required data including department details, course details, student personal details, semester details, exam details etc. were collected. The data collected would help identify attributes, relationships, classes, entities/objects that describe, relate and interact with the system.

The data collection tools and techniques that were used are as follows:

3.1.1. Interview

Interview is a powerful tool for data gathering since it allows the interviewer to probe and clarify a number of issues. Face to face interview was used to interact with the registrar and the users of the proposed system to obtain the data required for the database management system.

3.1.2. Analysis of Current Student Information System

Purposes of the current Student Information System analysis are:
- To identify problems inhibiting the current student information system
- To know how data is being managed
- To examine the methods used in current student information system
- To know the data flow in the system

The current student information system was studied to get some useful information for developing an effectual Student Database System. Currently, the various departments manage student information independently in their own ways. There are inadequate common, standardized process and program for capturing, processing and storing student's information. This has kept student information fragmented in different departments and information provided to the various departments by the students is characterized by discrepancies.

The various departments have systems in place to store and process student data but the systems are not able to talk to each other (Interoperable). This makes it difficult for the registrar to collate information of students across departments. On the other hand, students are unable to view their result online for them to know whether they are continuing the program and also to know the courses they can register for the next semester.

3.2. Proposed System will Consist of the Following Modules

3.2.1. Security

The Student database management system will ensure that the data are secured by assigning a unique password and username. The registrar and student of school of public health will be allowed to access the system. The administrator account can be accessed by the registrar and student account can be accessed by the student using their registration number. The respective student database management system will be encoded by the system administrator. In case the user forgot their password, the system offers a forgot password module in which the user can select this menu and answer the secret question or code that the user only knows. A log component that chronicles information about users who login and logout will be provided.

3.2.2. Registration and Verification

This module allows users to enter the required information including username, password, first name, last name, address, birth date and position. This will serve as the personal record of the users. The system will verify this information first before the authorized users can enter the system. Duplication of users in the system will completely be eliminated due to a very rigid verification method.

3.3. Functions of the Proposed System

Three different user categories will be allowed access to the system
1. registrar who can view and edit the details of any students
2. head of department who can add courses, departments and exams details as well as edit and delete details
3. students who can view and modify their details .

The proposed system will provide the following features to the registrar:
- The registrar can login into the system and execute any of the available tasks;
- Can enable/disable student;
- Can edit student information in the database;
- Can make search for a specific student;
- Can access all the details of the student.

The features that are available to the student are:

Student can login into the system and can perform any of the available options.
- Can view his/her personal details.
- Can edit his/her personal details
- Can upload his/her project topics.
- Can upload his/her image.

3.4. Specific Requirement

Use-Cases are a scenario based technique in the Unified Modelling Language which identify the actors in an interaction and which describe the interaction itself. Use cases were used to describe all possible interactions of the entities with the system.

Organizing Student Records Flow of Event
The registrar is mandated to manage student records
Use Case: Login in to the SDMS
Summary: This use case is used when the registrar wants to access the SDMS to add/update the personal details of the student.

Actors: Registrar

Pre-condition: Registrar's account must be active on the system

Main Flow:

MF-001: The system displays the login page and prompts the registrar for the Login_Id and Password

MF-002: The registrar provides values for the Login_Id and password fields.

MF-003: The registrar hits the submit button

MF-004: The system verifies (authenticates) the password and sets the registrar's authorization. (AF-1.1, AF-1.2)

MF-005: The Administrator is given access to the SDMS to perform his tasks.

ALTERNATE FLOW 1.1 (AF-1.1):

AF-1.1.1: The registrar enters invalid LoginId and password then he will not be allowed to enter the system

AF-1.1.2: Go to MF-002

ALTERNATE FLOW 1.2 (AF-1.2):

AF- 1.2.1: The system fails to authenticate user after a default of 2 continuous unsuccessful attempts

ALTERNATE FLOW 1.3 (AF-1.3):

AF- 1.3.1: The system fails to authenticate user after a default of 3 continuous unsuccessful attempts

AF-1.3.2: The system deactivates user account

AF-1.3.3: System notifies the user of account deactivation via a system prompt

AF-1.3.4: The user acknowledges system prompt by clicking OK button

Post-Condition: The registrar login successfully

Use Case Report- Register student on SDMS

Use-case: Login into the SDMS

Goal: Gain access to the website

Summary: This use case is used when the student wants to access the web site

Preconditions: The registrar must enable the particular student onto the website in order for this use case to begin.

Main Flow:

MF-001: The system displays the login page and prompts the student for the Login_Id and Password.

MF-002: The student provides values for the Login_Id and password fields.

MF-003: The student hits the submit button

MF-004: The system verifies (authenticates) the password and sets the student's authorization. (AF-1.1, AF-1.2)

MF-005: The student is given access to the SDMS to perform his tasks.

ALTERNATE FLOW 1.1 (AF-1.1):

AF-1.1.1: The student enters invalid LoginId and password then he will not be allowed to enter the system

AF-1.1.2: Go to MF-002

ALTERNATE FLOW 1.2 (AF-1.2):

AF- 1.2.1: The system fails to authenticate user after a default of 2 continuous unsuccessful attempts

AF-1.2.2: The system triggers image verification for any further login attempts

AF-1.2.2: Go to MF-002

ALTERNATE FLOW 1.3 (AF-1.3):

AF- 1.3.1: The system fails to authenticate user after a default of 3 continuous unsuccessful attempts

AF-1.3.2: The system deactivates user account

AF-1.3.3: System notifies the user of account deactivation via a system prompt

AF-1.3.4: The user acknowledges system prompt by clicking OK button

Post-Condition: The student login successfully

3.5. Non-Functional Requirement

3.5.1. Safety Requirement

Operating system failure or virus can cause the database to crash at any point in time. Database backup is very important.

3.5.2. Security Requirement

Secured database system was developed. There are three categories of users namely registrar, faculty and student who would view either all or some specific information from the database. Depending upon the category of user the access rights are decided.

This means that if the user is a registrar then he can be able to modify the data, append etc. Other users can only retrieve information.

3.5.3 Performance Requirement

The proposed system would serve as the main performance system which will go a long way to help School of Public Health manage and maintain the database of student. All specified requirements are expected to be met by the proposed database.

3.6. System Design

The purpose of the system design phase was to develop a clear blueprint that would satisfy all documented requirement for the system.

The overall system design objective was to provide an efficient, modular design that will reduce the system's complexity, facilitate change and result in an easy implementation. This blueprint provided interface design models that are consistent, user friendly and will provide straightforward transition through the various system functions.

3.6.1. System Architectural Design

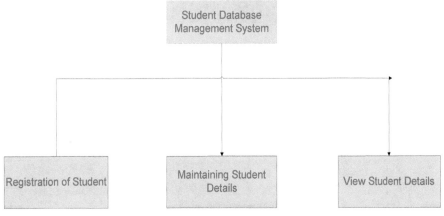

Fig 3. *Architecture Diagram*

The SDS is system which has major components such as student detail, department detail and course detail. One of the available options is selected as an input to the system. The system acts and the rest of the functions are performed respectively based on the input by the user. The registrar has automatic access right to manage and maintain student detail. The student can only view their details.

3.6.2. Data Design
Entity Relationship Diagram

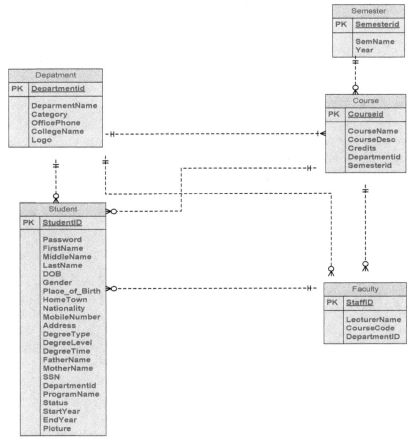

Fig 3.1. *Entity Relationship Diagram*

3.6.3. Functional Design Description
Dataflow Diagram

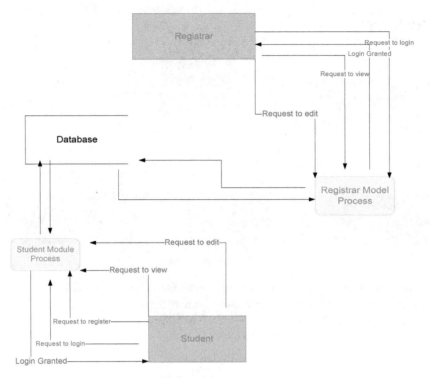

Fig 3.2. *Dataflow Diagram*

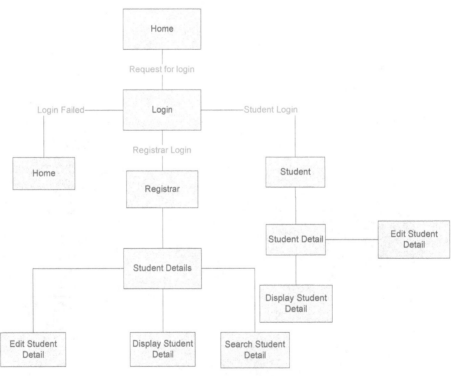

Fig 3.3. *Decision Tree Diagram*

Finally the design phase provides enough information with respect to all the entities and their relations.

3.7. Technology Overview

The technology selected for implementing Student Database System is PHP/MYSQL. Apache is used as the HTTP server.

3.7.1. PHP

PHP is a general-purpose scripting language that is especially suited to server-side web development where PHP generally runs on server. PHP code is embedded into HTML source document. Any PHP code is a requested file executed by the PHP runtime, usually to create dynamic web page content. It can also be used for command-line scripting and client-side graphical user interface (GUI) applications. PHP can be deployed on many web servers and operating systems, and can be used with many relational database management systems (RDBMS). It is available free of charge, and the PHP Group provides the complete source code for users to build, customize and extend for their own use.

3.7.2. MySQL

MySQL is a relational database management system (RDBMS) that runs as a server providing multi-user access to a number of databases. MySQL is a popular choice of database for use in web applications and is an open source product. The process of setting up a MySQL database varies from host to host, however we will end up with a database name, a user name and a password. Before using the database, a table must be created. A table is a section of the database for storing related information. In a table, different fields must be set up which will be used in the table. Table creation in phpMyAdmin is not difficult. SQL statement can also be executed to create databases and tables.

3.7.3. Apache

The Apache HTTP Server is web server software notable for playing a key role in the initial growth of the World Wide Web. In 2009 it became the first web server software to surpass the 100 million web site milestone. Apache is developed and maintained by an open community of developers under the auspices of the Apache Software Foundation. Since April 1996 Apache has been the most popular HTTP server software in use. As of November 2010 Apache served over 59.36% of all websites and over 66.56% of the first one million busiest websites.

3.7.4. XAMPP

XAMPP is a small and light Apache distribution containing the most common web development technologies in a single package. Its contents, small size, and portability make it the ideal tool for students developing and testing applications in PHP and MySQL. XAMPP is available as a free download in two specific packages: full and lite. While the full package download provides a wide array of development tools, XAMPP Lite contains the necessary technologies that meet the Ontario Skills Competition standards. The light version is a small package containing Apache HTTP Server, PHP, MySQL, phpMyAdmin, Openssl, and SQLite.

4. Result

A web based student database system intended to track and store student records is the outcome of the project after a critical analysis, design, building and testing of the system. Evaluation was properly done to ensure that the system meet all the requirements and specifications.

A stringent plan to monitor the implementation of the new system is laid-out and the entire project documented. Finally, the new system is deployed and users will receive some training to understand the new system. The new system would run alongside the old system until the new system is

proven to be effective and efficient.

4.1. Technologies Used

HTML, CSS and PHP programming language are used to create an interface that allows the front end user to interact freely with the system. PHP is an object oriented programming language and it is flexible and user friendly because it allows the software developer to design the system with less code using Cascading Style Sheet (CSS), manipulate and graphically design the system. PHP is an HTML-embedded scripting language and is very powerful behind the scenes scripting language that visitors would not see. When you visit the PHP webpage, the web server processes the PHP code. It then sees which part it needs to show to visitors (contents and pictures) and hide the other stuff (file operations math calculations, etc.) then translate the PHP to HTML. After the translation into HTML it sends the webpage to the visitor's web browser.

MySQL is also chosen to create the database for the back end user since it is extensively used third generation database management system.

4.1.1. Steps Involved in Database Creation

The following steps were followed to create the database in MySQL:
- Create the database file in PHPMyADMIN
- Create a table in PHPMyADMIN
- Set up different fields which will be used in the table
- Insert dummy data into table
- Browse to view records in the table

4.1.2. Forms Creation and Connection to the Database

HTML is used to create the forms and the 'filename.php 'file created will process the HTML form information.

Before data can be accessed in a database, a connection to the database must be created. In PHP this is done with MySQL_Connect() function.

For example:
```
<? php
$con=mysql_connect ("localhost", "root","")
If(! $con)
//Some data here
{
Die ('could not connect' .mysql_eror(());
}
?>
```
The example above is a simple PHP script used to connect to the MySQL database server. The die part will be executed if the connection fails.

4.1.3. Hardware Requirements
- Processor: Pentium IV
- Ram: 512 MB RAM
- Hard Disk: 80 GB Hard disk

4.1.4. Software Requirements
- Operating System: Microsoft XP/VISTA
- Database: Mysql database Server

- Application Software: Hypertext Preprocessor(PHP)

4.2. Linking Internal Database to the Web

A series of middleware and other software products has been developed to help users gain access to organization's legacy data through the web. For example, a user with a web browser might want to search the web based student database for student information.

The figure below illustrates how the user might access the database over the web. The user would access the student database website over the internet using web browser on his or her personal computer. The user's browser would request data from the student database, using HTML commands to communicate with the web server. Because many back-end databases cannot interpret commands written in HTML, the web server would pass this request for data to special software that translate HTML commands into SQL so that they could be processed by the DBMS working with the database. The DBMS receives the SQL request and provides the required data. The figure also shows that the middleware working between the web server and the DBMS is an application server running on the dedicated computer.

Fig 4. *Linking internal database to the web.*

4.3. Implementation

Implementation includes all the activities that take place to convert from the old system to the new. A proper implementation is required to provide a dependable system to meet the requirements. An improper installation may affect the success of the automated system. The most appropriate approach used was to run the old and new system in parallel. This offers high security, because even if there is a flaw in the automated system, the manual system can be depended on.

4.4. How to Access the System

- Mozilla or Internet Explorer can be used to access the web based student database system
- Follow the steps below to access the homepage:
- The page can be displayed by typing the URL address in the address field on the browser.
- The system has three type of accessing modes, registrar, student and head of department.
- Valid password and login Id are required on the login page to access the system

4.5. Testing

Thorough testing was done to ensure that the system produces the right results. It was time consuming to test the system because data must be carefully prepared, results reviewed and corrections made in the system.

4.6. Maintenance

The system will be maintained periodically through effective monitory and evaluation. This will go a long way to help identify and debug emergency production problems and address them accordingly. A considerable amount of time would be spent to effect changes in data, files, reports, hardware and software.

5. Conclusion

Information is an indispensable tool many schools and other organization use to advance decision making. Large amount of student's data are generated either manually or electronically on daily basis.

When population of student in a school is less than a hundred, the manual system can work perfectly but it is not the best method of managing records of students. The manual and disintegrated electronic systems have numerous disadvantages because these methods of capturing and managing data about students are prone to data inconsistency, data redundancy, difficult to update and maintain data, bad security, difficult to impose constraint on various data file and difficult to backup.

An integrated student database system provides prudent solutions to address problems associated with manual system. In order to assess the performance of the school and students overtime, there is the need to use past records of students without any missing data. The integrated student database system which captures and maintains longitudinal data of students would provide an accurate and reliable data about current and past students.

The system is free of errors and very efficient and less time consuming due to the care taken to develop it. All the phases of software development cycle are employed and it is worthwhile to state that the system is very robust. Provision is made for future development in the system.

5.1. Recommendation

Since student database system is very broad, the scope of this project covers only a small aspect of student information system due to the fact that the stipulated three month within which the project is expected to be executed is too short.

Students who are interested in building database system should be encouraged to work on other aspect of student information system in that all the available related student database system could be linked together.

The department of biostatistics should add programming to the courses offered and it should be made compulsory and run for both semesters. Health informatics students should be encouraged to work in a team to develop a software application system so that they will be well equipped with database and programming skills. This move will go a long way to help them do their project without any difficulty.

This report could be useful to any person who wants to do a project on similar topic.

Appendix A

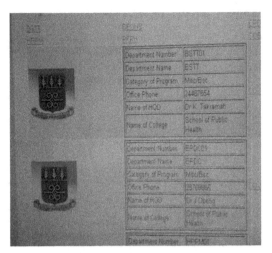

Fig 1. Department Details

Appendix B

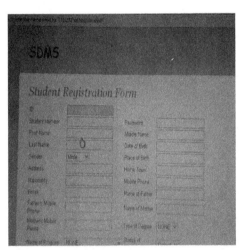

Fig 2. Student Registration Form

Appendix C

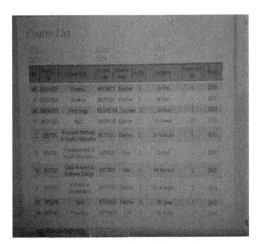

Fig 3. Course List Page

Appendix D

Fig 4. Student List Page

Appendix E

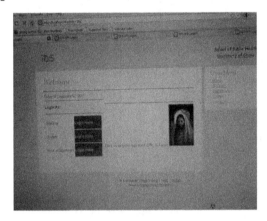

Fig 5. Home Page for Student Database System

References

[1] Connolly, T.M. and C.E. Begg, 2004. Database System: A Practical Approach to Design, Implementation and Management. 4rd Edn., Addison Wesley; ISBN: 10: 0321210255, pp: 1236

[2] Adams, C., Beath, C. M, Bolan, R., Branin, J., D'Elia, G., Rhode, N.L. & Straub, D. 1991. Issues Relating to the Implementation and Management of an Integrated Information Centre. Journal of the American Society for Information Science.

[3] Adman, P. & Warren, L. 1996. Information systems management: Perspectives for Higher Education. Lancs: Mir Press

[4] Angell, I. O. & Smithson, S. 1991. Information Systems management: Opportunities and Risks. London: Macmillan Education Ltd.

[5] Association for the Development of Education in African. 2001. Technology as a Management Tool: A New Approach and Implementation. http//www.technologia.org/ [accessed on 23rd May 2011].

[6]   Greenwald, R., R. Stackowiak, G. Dodge, D. Klein, B. Shapiro and C.G. Ghelliah, 2005. Professional Oracle Programming. Wrox, ISBN: 10: 0764574825, pp: 790

[7]   Blaha M Rumbaugh 2005 (2nd ed.) Object-Oriented Modeling and Design with UML. [Basically this is the second edition of Rumbaugh et al 1991]. Prentice Hall

[8]   Fry B. G. 1997. The Family Educational Rights and Privacy Act of 1974. In Student Records Management, edited by M Theresa Ruzicka and Beth Lee WeckMulle. London: Greenwood Press, 43-76.

[9]   Higgins, J.C. 1976. Information Systems for Planning and Control: Concepts and Cases. London: Edward Arnold.

[10]   Husain, K.M. 1977. Information Systems: Basic Concepts, Management Information Systems for Higher Education. Paris: The Organization for Economic Co-operation and Development.

[11]   Gerald, C.O. 2009. Database Management System. Nigeria National Open University.

[12]   Kroenke, D. & Hatach, R. 1994. Management Information Systems, 3rd edition. New York: McGraw-Hill.

[13]   Oliver, R. (2000). Creating Meaningful Contexts for Learning in Web-based Settings. Proceedings of Open Learning 2000. (pp 53-62). Brisbane: Learning Network, Queensland.

[14]   Jonassen, D. & Reeves, T. (1996). Learning with technology: Using computers as cognitive tools. In D. Jonassen (Ed.), Handbook of Research Educational on Educational Communications and Technology (pp 693-719). New York: Macmillan.

[15]   Lebow, D. (1993). Constructivist values for instructional systems design: Five principles toward a new mind set. Educational Technology, Research and Development, 41(3), 4-16.

[16]   Berners-Lee, T. J. 1992. "World-Wide Web: Information Universe", Electronic: Research, Applications and Policy. www.w3.org/People/Berners-Lee/Longer.html [accessed on 24th May 2011]

[17]   Collis, B. (2002). Information technologies for education and training. In Adelsberger, H., Collis, B, & Pawlowski, J. (Eds.) Handbook on Technologies for Information and Training. Berlin: Springer Verlag.

19

Metrics for Quantification of the Software Testing Tools Effectiveness

Pawan Singh[*], Mulualem Wordofa Regassa

School of Informatics, IOT, Hawassa University, Awassa, Ethiopia

Email address:
pawansingh3@yahoo.com (P. Singh), dr_pawansingh@hu.edu.et (P. Singh), jimpowerdire@gmail.com (M. W. Regassa)

Abstract: An automated testing tool helps the testers to quantify the quality of software by testing the software automatically. To quantify the quality of software there is always a requirement of good testing tools, which satisfy the testing requirement of the project. Although there is a wide range of testing tools available in the market and they vary in approach, quality, usability and other characteristics. Selecting the appropriate testing tool for software there is a requirement of a methodology to prioritize them on the basis of some characteristics. We propose a set of metrics for measuring the characteristics of the automated testing tools for examination and selection of automated testing tools. A new extended model which is proposed provides the metrics to calculate the effectiveness of functional testing tools on the basis of operability. The industry will be benefited as they can use these metrics to evaluate functional tools and they can further make selection of tool for their software required to be tested and hence reduce the testing effort, saving time and gaining maximum monetary benefit.

Keywords: Software Testing, Software Metrics, Automated Testing Tools, Tool Evaluation

1. Introduction

Testing is a tedious part of the software development process. There are lots of different automated software testing tools currently available in the market. Some of these tools are only able to perform specific kind of testing and other products support a wide range of applications and offer more features and functionality. Automated testing tools help the testers to quantify the quality of software by testing the software. To quantify the quality of software, there is always a requirement of appropriate testing tool, which satisfy the testing requirement of the project. Although there is a wide range of testing tools available in the market and they vary in approach, quality, usability and other characteristics. Selecting a right testing tool is very cumbersome. To select the appropriate testing tool there is a requirement of a way to prioritize them on the basis of characteristics. Through this paper we proposed a set of metrics for measuring the characteristics for examination and selection of automated testing tool. This set of metrics will help to quantify the quality of automated software tools. Using this set of metrics the evaluation of effectiveness of testing tools can be done. With the help of the metrics the comparison of characteristics of different available testing tools can be performed to select the best suited for the corresponding project. In the development process the evaluation of software testing tools effectiveness has become an important factor to be considered for software testing and assessment, especially for critical software. A new extended model which is proposed provides the metrics to calculate the effectiveness of functional testing tool on the basis of operability. Students are studying only the traditional metrics to evaluate the software quality but this set of metrics will help them to understand the fundamentals of selection of exact and suitable tool for software testing. The industry will also be benefited; they can use the metrics to evaluate tools and reduce the testing effort hence saving time and extracting maximum benefits.

2. Metrics

In software engineering, any sort of quality can be quantified in terms of metrics. Software metric a measurable property, is an indicator of one or more of the quality criteria that we are seeking to measure. There are a number of conditions that a quality metric must meet. The history of software metrics began with counting the number of line of codes. It was assumed that more line of codes implied more complex programs, which shows a possibility of having more errors. However software metrics have evolved well beyond the simple measures introduced in the 1960s.

2.1. Traditional Metrics

The traditional metrics are those which is been taught to the students from a long period of time and it only quantifies the quality of the software.

2.1.1. Cyclomatic Complexity (CC)

It measures the amount of decision logics in a single software module. The use of CC [1] is in two related purposes in the structured testing methodology. First, it provides the number of optional tests for software. Second, the use of CC is during all phases of the software development lifecycle, starting with design, to maintain software reliable, manageable and testable. The structure of software's control flow graph is the basis of Cyclomatic complexity. The word "cyclomatic" derives from the number of fundamental or basic cycles in connected, undirected graphs. More essentially, CC also provides the number of independent paths through strongly connected directed graphs. In strongly connected graph each node can be reached from any other node by following directed edges in the graph. The cyclomatic number in graph theory is defined as:

$$CC = e - n + 2P \qquad (1)$$

Program control flow graphs (CFG) are not strongly connected, but they become strongly connected by adding a virtual edge connecting the exit node to the entry node. The CC definition for program control flow graphs is resultant from the cyclomatic number formula by merely adding one to represent the contribution of the virtual edge. According to this definition the cyclomatic complexity equals the number of independent paths through the standard control flow graph model, and avoids explicit declaration of the virtual edge.

$$M = V(G) = e - n + 2P \qquad (2)$$

Where V(G) is the cyclomatic number of G, e is the number of edges, n is the number of nodes, and p is the number of unconnected parts of G.

2.1.2. Function Point (FP)

It is a metric that may be applied independent of a specific programming language, in fact, it can be determined in the design stage prior to the commencement of coding. To determine FP, an Unadjusted Function Point Count (UFP) is calculated [2]. UFP is found by counting the number of external inputs (user input), external outputs (program output), external inquiries (interactive inputs requiring a response), external files (inter-system interface), and internal files (system logical master files). Each member of the above five groups is analyzed as having either simple, average or high complexity, and a weight is associated with that member based upon a table of FP complexity weights. UFP is then calculated via:

$$UFP = \sum_{i=1}^{15}(\text{number of items of variety i}) * (\text{weight of i}) \quad (3)$$

Next, a Complexity Adjustment Factor (CAF) is determined by analyzing fourteen contributing factors. Each factor is assigned a score from zero to five based on its criticality to the system being built. The CAF is then found through the equation:

$$CAF = 0.65 + 0.01 \sum_{i=1}^{14} Fi \qquad (4)$$

FP is the product of UFC and CAF. FP has been criticized due to its reliance upon subjective ratings and its foundation on early design characteristics that are likely to change as the development process progresses.

2.1.3. Halstead

Halstead [3] created a metric founded on the number of operators and operands in a program. His software-science metric (a.k.a. halted length) is based on the enumeration of distinct operators and operands as well as the total number of appearances of operators and operands. With these counts, a system of equations is used to assign values to program level (i.e., program complexity), program difficulty, potential minimum volume of an algorithm and other measurements.

2.2. Object Oriented Software Metrics

Object-oriented design and development has turn out to be popular in present software development environment. There exists wide recognition of benefits of object-oriented software development. Object-oriented development needs not only diverse approaches to design and implementation; it also requires different approaches to software metrics [4]. The metrics for object-oriented systems are different from structured system due to the difference in program paradigm and language itself [5]. An object-oriented program paradigm and structure are different from procedural languages; it uses localization, inheritance, information hiding, encapsulation, object abstraction and polymorphism. There are quite a few sets of proposed metrics for object-oriented software in the literature. The definition of six different metrics is specified in this text.

2.2.1. Weighted Methods per Class (WMC)

WMC is a sum of complexities of methods of a class. Consider a Class C1 with Methods $M_1 \ldots M_n$ that is defined in the class. Let $c_1 \ldots c_n$ be the complexity of the methods. Then:

$$WMC = \sum_{i=1}^{n} c_i \qquad (5)$$

WMC measures size as well as the logical structure of the software. The number of methods and the complexity of the involved methods are predictors of how much time and effort is required to develop and maintain a class. The bigger the count of methods within a class larger the potential impact on inheriting classes. Consequently, more effort and time will be needed for maintenance and testing. Furthermore, classes with large number of complex methods are likely to be more application specific, limiting the possibility of reuse [4], [7],

[8], [9]. Estimation of usability and reusability of the class can be done using WMC. If all method complexities are considered to be unity, then WMC equals to Number of Methods (NMC) metric.

2.2.2. Depth of Inheritance Tree (DIT)

The depth of a class inside the inheritance hierarchy is the largest length from the class node to the root of the tree, calculated by the number of ancestor classes [4], [8] and [10]. The deeper a class is in the hierarchy, the larger the number of methods it is likely to inherit, making it more difficult to forecast its behavior. Deeper trees constitute higher design complexity, since more methods and classes are concerned. The deeper a particular class is in the hierarchy, the larger prospective reuse of inherited methods. The longest path is usually considered for languages that allow multiple inheritances. The large DIT is as well associated to understandability and testability. The complexity can be decreased using inheritance by reducing the count of operations and operators, but this abstraction of objects can create maintenance and design complicated.

2.2.3. Number of Children (NOC)

Number of children metric equals to number of immediate subclasses subordinated to a class in the class hierarchy. Greater the number of children, greater the reuse, since inheritance is a form of reuse [4], [7], [8], [9]. If greater the number of children than more is likelihood of improper abstraction of the parent class. If a class has a large number of children, it may be a case of misuse of sub classing. The number of children gives an idea of the potential influence a class has on the design. If a class has a large number of children, it may require more testing of the methods in that class. In addition, a class with a large number of children must be flexible in order to provide services in a large number of contexts.

2.2.4. Coupling between Object Classes (CBO)

CBO for a class is a count of the number of other classes to which is coupled. CBO relates to the notion that an object is coupled to another object if one of them acts on the other, i.e., methods of one uses methods or instance variables of another [4], [9], [10], [11]. Excessive coupling between object classes is detrimental to modular design and prevents reuse. The more independent a class is, the easier it is to reuse it in another application. In order to improve modularity and promote encapsulation, inter-object class couples should be kept to a minimum. Direct access to foreign instance variable has generally been identified as the worst type of coupling. The larger the number of couples, the higher the sensitivity to changes in other parts of the design, and therefore maintenance is more difficult. A measure of coupling is useful to determine how complex the testing of various parts of a design is likely to be. The higher the inter-object class coupling, the more rigorous the testing needs to be.

2.2.5. Response for a Class (RFC)

The response set of a class is a set of procedures that can potentially be executed in response to a message established by and object of that class. RFC evaluate both external and internal communication, but particularly it comprises procedures called from outside the class, so it is also a gauge of the potential communication between the class and other classes [4], [8], [9]. RFC is more perceptive evaluation of coupling than CBO since it take into account procedure instead of classes. If a huge count of procedures can be invoked in account to a message, the testing and debugging of the class turn out to be more problematical since it requires a greater level of perceptiveness required on the part of the tester. The greater the count of routines that can be invoked from a class, the greater the complication in the class. A worst-case value for possible reaction will assist in suitable allocation of testing time.

2.2.6. Lack of Cohesion in Methods (LCOM)

The LCOM is a calculation of the number of procedure pairs whose resemblance is "0" minus the count of procedure pairs whose resemblance is non zero. The larger the count of number of alike procedures, the greater cohesive the class, which is consistent with conventional notions of cohesion that calculate the inter-relatedness between segments of a program [4], [7], [10]. If none of the procedure of a class reflects any instance performance, i.e., do not use any instance variables, they consists no resemblance and the LCOM value for the class will be zero. Cohesiveness of procedures inside a class is desirable, since it encourages encapsulation. Short of cohesion indicates classes should most likely be divided into two or more subclasses. Any calculation of disparateness of procedure helps recognize flaws in the design of classes. Low cohesion augments complication; thereby it increases the probability of errors at some stage in the development process.

3. Prior Work on Metrics

The Institute for Defense Analyses (IDA) made available two survey information on tools for testing software. Although the tool explanations provided in those reports are dated, the examination provide a historical frame of reference for the current progress in testing tools and recognize a great count of quantity that may be utilized in evaluating testing tools [12], [13]. For every tool, the report specifies diverse types of analysis carried out. Software Technology Support Center (STSC) works with Air Force software organizations to recognize assess and accept technologies to advance product quality, augment production effectiveness, and hone cost and schedule forecast capability [14]. Section four of the report tells about numerous issues that should be addressed when examining testing tools and offers a model tool-scoring matrix.

Brett Daniel [6] has provided a broad summary of the process he suggested to calculate effectiveness of an automatic test production tool. The method has two parts: instructing a decision tree by means of code with identified coverage characteristics and using the tree to forecast coverage on new code. It starts with a big amount of source code, which we say as the training code. It provides two data sets from the training code. First, extract many metrics that characterize method structure. Second, run the automatic testing tool to produce a suite.

A thorough analysis was conducted by J. Thatcher in Evaluation and repair tools [15]. His examination of six accessibility testing tools was focused at calculating the cost/benefit ratio and supporting probable customers to choose the most suitable tool. In submission to allowing for costs, availability, and accuracy, the examination scope was quality of use. The procedure he used is highly influenced by manual and methodical inspection of the results formed by the tools on chosen test pages, and is consequently less generally relevant than the procedure suggested in his paper, as it needs carefully generated test files and a lengthy and subjective analysis of the results.

In a current paper, Ivory and her colleagues focused at examining quality of use of testing tools [16]. They carry out an experiment where web designers were required to use testing tools and to amend web sites as a result to what tools suggested. Afterward in second experiment, the authors extract how effective such modifications were for disabled web site visitors.

The criteria proposed by Poston and Sexton [17] aimed on company precise criteria or on criteria demanding an intense effort to be evaluated e.g. test effort or test quality, these criteria do not narrate for a pre-selection of the test tools. In addition to it, criteria precise to test tools is stated without a validation for their derivation. The criteria stated by Poston and Sexton signify a subset of the criteria methodologically derived in our approach.

4. Our Approach

The project suggests some of the metrics which can be used to discover the suitable automated software testing tool. These metrics are been derived on the functional and operational basis. The metrics are designed so they produced different values when applied to different testing tools. They can produce similar values also for different metrics and different testing tools. The suite of metrics to evaluate and select software testing tools carries the following properties: the metrics reveal smoothness in that they generate unlike values when applied to different testing tools. The metrics is finite in count and in very few cases they may provide similar values for few tools; usually they provide different values when applied to unlike testing tools.

4.1. Operational Metrics

These metrics are used to quantify the effectiveness of testing tools on the basis of the capability of and ease to operate. The testing tools are desired to be easy to use in all terms and it must be popular if it is giving good results in terms of working. The vendor's responsibility includes making it simple and informative as well. On the basis of some of the operational properties there are few metrics provided by us which can help the tester to select the appropriate tool for his projects:

4.1.1. Toughness of Interface (ToI)

To start testing with automated software testing tool one need to configure it first. If any tool is designed in a proper manner than the human interface with the tool will lead to simple, efficient and correct setting of tool configuration but if the design is inadequate then the number of keyboard to mouse switches will be large, number of input fields provided will be large with long input strings and required output fields will also be large in number.

$$\text{ToI} = \frac{1}{\sum F}\left[\sum\left(\frac{\text{SKM}}{t}\right) + \sum\left((\text{IF} * \text{TLIF}) + \text{OF}\right)\right] - \text{BBF} \tag{6}$$

In (1) SKM / t is the number of switches from keyboard to mouse per unit time, IF is the average number of input fields, TLIF is the total string length of input fields, OF is the number of output field required, BBF is the number of buttons based functions. The values of SKM, IF, TLIF, OF is calculated per function. A large value of ToI indicates the toughness in learning the tool due to complicated interface. This can also lead to possibility of errors if we use the tool for a long time. A tool with lesser value of ToI must be selected.

4.1.2. Customers Affection and Tool Age (CATA)

There exist a number of designers of automated testing tools carrying different approaches and experiences. If the tool is properly designed and having good customer satisfaction of testing their software on the tool, then this satisfaction level can be used to motivate other users to use that testing tool. The maturity of a software counts to suggest the same tool as it shows customers having trust on that tool from a long period of time.

$$\text{CATA} = \text{CA} + \text{TA} \tag{7}$$

In (7) CA customer affection is the number customers of that tool and they are using tool from more than one year. TA tool age is the number of years the tool is in use including its previous versions. A tool with a larger value of CATA is selected for testing software.

4.1.3. Projects Handled (PH)

There In making the decision to select a testing tool for a software of known expected size the major factor will be the experience of tool in dealing with similar sort of project with same size and different size. The tool having good experience of dealing with similar size will be the preferred one but the tool having experience in dealing with big in size project will also be better than the tool dealing with small projects.

$$\text{PH} = \alpha * \text{STSS} + \beta * \text{STBiS} + \gamma * \text{STSiS} \tag{8}$$

In (8) $\alpha < \beta < \gamma$, STSS is the number of projects of same type and same size tested previously on that tool, STBiS is the count of projects with same type and big in size tested previously on that tool and STSiS is the count of projects with same type and small in size tested previously on that tool. A tool having a large value of PH is the suggested.

4.1.4. Inconvenience of Use (IU)

An automated testing tool is desired to be easy in terms of using it first time and in subsequent attempt. The tool which is better to learn in first will be given preference to the tool easy to use in subsequent attempts. The desired property of a testing tool is its retainability of use means the procedure of using can be easily remembered by either a casual user or by the frequent user. If the time required using a tool for testing by either a casual user or frequent user is less it will be the preferred one.

$$IU = (\: 0.75 * LTFTU + 0.25 * LTExUPV \:) - (\: RoPc + RoPf)$$

$$+ \: (\: AOTc + AOTf \:) \qquad (9)$$

In (9) LTFTU is the learning time for first users in days, LTExUPV is the learning time for the experienced user of previous version in days, RoPc is the retainability of procedure knowledge for casual users, RoPf is the retainability of procedure knowledge for frequent users, AOTc is the average operational time for casual users in hours and AOTf is the average operational time for frequent users in hours. The tool having a less value of IU is better.

4.1.5. Documentation Support (DS)

To have the efficient implementation and use of tool a proper documentation must be provided. A user of a tool may need certain information at different time for reference this information is usually provided by the vendor in the form of documentation. The tools effectiveness is influenced by the time required to search some information and by the number of ways the information can be accessed. It is negatively supported if the documentation is inadequate.

$$DS = WIA - (ID + ASTD) \qquad (10)$$

In (10) ASTD is the average search time of documentation, WIA is the number of ways the information can be accessed and ID stands for the inadequacy in documentation which is measured as the number of unsuccessful searches of documentation. The higher value of DS is expected for a good tool.

4.1.6. Tools Reliability (TR)

Tool reliability of any system is defined as inverse of number of failure per unit time. Lesser the value of number of failure better the tool is as reliable tool.

$$TR = \frac{1}{N/T} \qquad (11)$$

In (11) TR is tool reliability, N is the number of failure of testing software and T is the total time. It is expected that the tool must be with high value of TR.

4.2. Functional Metrics

These metrics are used to quantify the effectiveness of testing tools on the basis of the capability of testing the software programs. The operational simplicity and informativeness are not the only factors which must be included in the decision to select the testing tool but there are some more functional properties required to be included. Functional metrics incur some cost in terms of some sort of pre testing required to analyze the tools. The functional testing may be better utilized to prepare the data regarding the tools for the further projects to be evaluated. On the basis of functional properties there are some metrics provided by us which can help the tester to select the appropriate tool for his projects:

4.2.1. Tool's Completeness (TC$_m$)

Tool's Completeness is a computation of how many accessibility defects present in the software are noticed and revealed to the user. Completeness is associated to how well the tool is capable to seize defects. Completeness is a complex property to distinguish operationally. In fact it requires knowing the true problems in advance. Therefore determining the true problems means accurate usability investigations through some means of testing.

$$TC_m = DCS/TDP \qquad (12)$$

In (12) DCS is the number of defects of software caught and shown by the tool to the user. TDP is the total number of defects actually present in the software. The value of TC$_m$ is required to be high for a better selection.

4.2.2. Tool's Correctness (TC$_r$)

Tool's Correctness is the fraction of problems reported by the tool that are certainly true problems and the actual total number of defects actually present in the software. Correctness is associated to how well a tool reduces actual defects. It requires the potential and knowledge of true and false defects shown by the tool otherwise it may lead to wrong decision.

$$TC_r = (DCS - FDCS)/TDP \qquad (13)$$

In (13) DCS is the number of defects of software caught and shown by the tool to the user. FDCS stands for false defects of software caught and shown by the tool to the user. TDP is the total number of defects actually present in the software. TCr value must be bigger for a tool to be selected.

4.2.3. Tool's Coverage (TC$_v$)

Tool's Coverage is defined as the number of different types of defects possible to detect and described by a tool. The larger this set the more capable is the tool of providing specific warnings and suggestions, and therefore the more useful it is for the developer. It is not an easy property to be determined and not necessarily related to the tool effectiveness. It is good to have high value of TC$_v$.

5. Experimental Setup

To validate our proposed set of metrics for examination and selection of software testing tools, we have selected two automated software testing tools QTP 9.0 and WinRunner 7.6 to apply our metrics. In the following section we have described the working of these tools.

5.1. Quick Test Professional 9.0 (QTP 9.0)

It is an automated functional Graphical User Interface based testing tool generated by HP subsidiary Mercury Interactive that permit the automation of user actions on the web or client based and desktop computer application. It is principally used for functional regression test automation QTP requires a scripting language built on top of VBScript to indicate the test method and to update the object and control of application under test.

As a part of functional test suite, it performs together with Mercury Interactive Winrunner and HP Quality Centre and support project Quality Assurance.

Quick Test Professional 9.0 is an automated functional testing tool for diverse environments. It is having graphical point and click interface to record and play tests, add synchronization points and verification steps as well as create multiple action tests. As Quick Test runs test it simulates a human user by moving the cursor in a webpage or application window, clicking GUI objects and entering keyboard inputs; however Quick Test does this faster than any human.

5.2. WinRunner 7.6 (WR 7.6)

It offers an organization a power full tool for enterprise-wide functional and regression testing. Mercury WinRunner captures, verifies and replay user interactions automatically to identify defects and ensure that business processes work flawlessly upon deployment and remains reliable. Its intuitive recording process allows us to produce robust functional tests.

To create a test it simply records a typical business process by emulating user actions, such as ordering an item or opening a vender account. It executes tests and operates the application automatically, as though a real user is performing each step in business process. Its interactive reporting tool helps us interpret results by providing detailed, easy to read report that lists errors and their origination. It enables to build reusable tests to use throughout an application lifecycle.

For validation of our metrics we have selected 1047 small projects (codes) for testing using the two tools. For every code we have generated 20 to 73 test cases depending on the size of code and its complexity. The sizes of codes are ranging from 37 to 109 lines of codes.

In calculating the metrics the average values of the factors involved in the metrics are considered. The values calculated for different factors and finally the metrics are shown in the tables 1 to 7.

Table 1. Calculation for ToI.

Factors	QTP 9.0	WR 7.6
$\frac{1}{\sum F}\sum (SKM/t)$	4.3	6.4
$\frac{1}{\sum F}\sum (IF * TLIF)$	32	47
$\sum OF$	2	2
BBF	6	5
ToI	32.3	50.4

In the tables from 1 to 7 different factors are calculated and the metrics for both the tools QTP 9.0 and WR 7.6. In table 1 ToI metric value for QTP is less means it is less tough in using its interface by all types of users.

Table 2. Calculation for CATA.

Factors	QTP 9.0	WR 7.6
CA	25	15
TA	14	19
CATA	39	34

In table 2 the tool age of WR is shown more even then the customer of QTP is more than the WR so the overall value of CATA is greater and reflects preference of QTP.

Table 3. Calculation for PH.

Factors	QTP 9.0	WR 7.6
α * STSS	7.5	3
β * STBiS	2	1.25
γ * STSiS	.5	1
PH	10	5.25

As it is suggested that the project experience of same type and same size is better than the project of same type and big in size as well as project of same type and small in size so the values considered of α= .5, β= .25 and γ= .25. This gives the PH high value (as shown in table 3) to QTP hence upper hand with respect to WR.

Table 4. Calculation for IU.

Factors	QTP 9.0	WR 7.6
0.75 * LTFTU	5.25	7.5
0.25 * LTExUPV	.75	.75
RoP_c	.25	.20
RoP_f	.78	.66
AOT_c	.75	.75
AOT_f	.33	.416
IU	6.05	8.556

The high value of IU indicated in table 4 for WR shows that it not easy to learn, operate and remember the working of WR than QTP.

Table 5. Calculation for DS.

Factors	QTP 9.0	WR 7.6
WIA	4	4
ID	0	0
ASTD	1	2
DS	3	2

As per the value of DS computed in the table 5 it is clear that the information provided and ease in access of information is better supported in the QTP than WR so any one will wish to have QTP for his project.

Table 6. Calculation for TR.

Factors	QTP 9.0	WR 7.6
N	3	3
T	2	2
TR	.66	.66

The statistics of table 6 indicates that both tools are similarly good in terms of reliability.

Table 7. *Calculation for TC_m AND TC_r.*

Factors	QTP 9.0	WR 7.6
TDP	76	76
DCS	61	56
FDCS	3	4
TC_m	.8026	.7368
TC_r	.7631	.6842

The high values computed for QTP in table 7 for the metrics tools completeness and tools correctness gives an idea of better functionality of QTP and it suggest to use QTPunless until not specified or mandatory for tester to use WR.

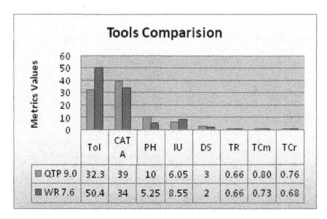

Figure 1. *Comparison of metrics for tools QTP and WR.*

From Fig. 1 it is shown that the metrics computed for both the tools indicates the high hand of QTP over WR.

6. Summary and Future Scope

In the current trend most of the software is required to be evaluated for two reasons. One the customer wants to get satisfied from the quality of the product which he will be going to use because he has invested a lot of amount to get the product. Two the developers want to quantify the quality so that his effort in further stages and in maintenance must not increased due to low quality. The testing is required to be fast and with less effort that is through the automated testing tools. The setback is confusion of way of selection of tool. The positive side of the paper is that it helps the developer in deciding the best testing tool as per his project by calculating the metrics value for the available tools in hand. The weakness of the proposed work is that it required a bit of time and effort in doing calculations for evaluating the tools and some data may also be needed in calculation of metrics.

As per the experience we have during the work, we would like to mention our view for the further extension of this work. The upper and lower bound of the tools metrics must be investigated. The more number of tools must be exposed to metrics to have the further empirical analysis. The categorization of the tools on the basis of functionality is required and the specification of particular metric for that type may be suggested. An algorithmic approach may be

generated to have the fast automated evaluation of metrics which may reduce the effort to calculate the metrics and automated suggestion for the better tools may also be a work piece.

7. Conclusion

To evaluate a tool it is highly required to check its functionality and operational potential. In our presented work the metrics are working on the operational and functional factors. The operational factors indicate the capability and easiness of handling the tool. The functional metrics are the reflection of ability of tool in tackling the software testing, its function. The operational metrics are almost static in nature as they can be calculated without performing any testing on tools to be selected, whereas the functional metrics needed some basic efforts to evaluate the tool's effectiveness.

In our work, the metrics proposed are applied on two tools QTP and WinRunner, here by comparing the calculated values of the metrics for the tools we came to have two conclusion. As per the first conclusion QTP is better tool with respect to WinRunner. The second conclusion is about our metrics which clearly discriminate the tools on different basis and these metrics are useful for developers as well as researchers to quantify the effectiveness of tools to get the help in decision of tool's selection. Using these metrics will help the tester to select the appropriate tool for his project it will save his time and removes his confusion.

References

[1]   J. T. McCabe, "A complexity measure," IEEE Trans. Software Eng. SE-2, 4, pp. 308-320, Dec 1976.

[2]   C. Dekkers, "Demystifying Function point: Lets understandsome terminology," IT metrics strategies, Oct 1998.

[3]   M. H. Halested, "Elements of software science, " New York: Elsevier Science, 1977.

[4]   S. R. Chidamber and R. F. Kemerer, "Ametrics suite for object-oriented design," IEEE Trans. Software Eng.vol. 20, 6, pp. 476-493,June1994.

[5]   W. Li and S. Henry, "Object oriented metrics that predicts maintainability," Journal of System and Software, vol. 23, 2, pp. 111- 122, Nov 1993.

[6]   B. Daniel and M. Boshernitsan, "Predicting and explaining automated testing tool effectiveness," University of Illiois at Urban- Campaign, Tech. Rep. UIUCDCS-R-2008-2956, April 2008.

[7]   M. Lorenz and J. Kidd, "Object Oriented Software Metrics," Printice Hall Publishing, 1994.

[8]   McCabe & Associates, McCabe Object Oriented Tool Usre's Instruction, 1994.

[9]   Linda H. Rosenberg, "Metrics for Object Oriented Environment," EFAITP/AIE Third Annual Software Metrics Conference, December 97.

[10] R. Hudli, C. Hoskins and A. Hudli, "Software Metrics for Object Oriented Design," IEEE, 1994.

[11] Y. Lee, B. Liang and F. Wang, "Some Complexity Metrics for Object Oriented Program Based on Information Flow," Proceedings: CompEuro, pp. 302-310, March 1993.

[12] C. Youngblut and B. Brykczynski, "An examination of selected software testing tools: 1992," IDA Paper, Inst. For Defense Analyses, Alexandria, Va., pp -2925, Oct. 1993.

[13] C. Youngblut and B. Brykczynski, "An examination of selected software testing tools: 1993," Supp. IDA Paper, Inst. For Defense Analyses, Alexandria, Va., pp -2769, Dec. 1992.

[14] G. T. Daich, G. Price, B. Ragland, and M. Dawood, "Software test technologies report," Software Technology Support Center, Hill AFB, Utah, Aug. 1994.

[15] J. Thatcher, "Evaluation and Repair Tools," posted on http://www.jimthatcher.com, June 2002.

[16] M. Y. Ivory, R. R. Sinha and H. A. Hearst, "Empirically validated web page design metrics," In Proceedings of the Conference on Human Factors in Computing Systems, pp. 53-60, New York, NY, ACM press, 2001.

[17] R. M. Poston and M. P. Sexton, "Evaluating and selecting testing tools," IEEE Software, vol. 9, 3, pp. 33-42, May 1992.

20

A Framework for Requirements Engineering for Oil and Gas Pipeline Systems Modeling

Japheth Bunakiye Richard[1], Asagba Oghenekaro Prince[2]

[1]Department. of Mathematics/Computer Science, Faculty of Science, Niger Delta University, Yenagoa, Nigeria
[2]Department of Computer Science, Faculty of Physical Science and Information Technology, University of Port Harcourt, Port Harcourt, Nigeria

Email address:
rb.japheth@ndu.edu.ng (J. B. Richard), asagba.prince@uniport.edu.ng (A. O. Prince)

Abstract: Domain specific modeling services, especially when made available to pipeline systems that transport oil and gas, constitute an interesting but very challenging domain. It poses fundamental problems for requirements engineering, software architecture, and their relationship. We propose a novel, domain-based framework for requirements engineering for this class of applications. The framework addresses the key concepts in this field, such as changing complexities for design platforms and domain specific requirements. We report experimental lessons learned on this framework and suggest requirements analysis products for documentation and future system design directions.

Keywords: Requirements Specification, Oil and Gas Pipeline, Domain Analysis, CAD Models, Stakeholders Intents

1. Introduction

Models are human concepts that explain systems in the real world, they are simply outcomes from abstractions, and one good example is the use of computer graphics to model a system. A typical oil and gas pipeline system is one good example of such computer graphics created from the interactive aggregation of graphics primitives, graphics assemblies and subassemblies of CAD systems [17]. These graphics models then represent the pipeline design from the domain of pipeline engineering. The transformation (modeling) of the model which is now domain specific to a complete artifact is made possible because of a constrained language definition that could address specific needs of the problem space of the domain. Such a possibility is usually referred to as domain specific modeling (DSM) [7]. The domain specific modelling approach is model centered and requires the construction of a domain specific modeling language that can provide a means for expressing domain concepts in a model. This domain model is capable of being transformed into other formats that represents all aspects of a systems understanding in the domain [8]. Modeling goals arise when stakeholders establish interests along lines of disciplines, intents, and design bases such as physical attributes, and environmental and materials-related factors.

There are competing design requirements among stakeholders; each one has their own set of constraints, objectives and responsibilities resulting to varying designs. These determining facts have to be gathered and accommodated in a language formalism to come up with an optimal solution. These goals can be achieved by capturing critical aspects of the domain, the expressions of stakeholders design intent and the requirements analysis; reflecting the domain characteristics and then integrated as concepts to the policies and mechanics of software architecture. This paper is about modeling requirements, and is targeted at oil and gas pipeline engineering domain analysis and requirements for a cost effective and timely modeling by domain experts to achieve desired products in their line of business. It is expected that the contribution of these requirements analysis framework will result in a new layer of reusable software capable of processing these graphics models to produce desired artefacts [5]. A collection that supports further layers of accessible software connected through interfaces for productivity centred configurations. The requirements of course will make sense only if the design goals can be met. This means in general that computer aided design systems have a complex representation of domain concepts and as such are not applicable to any specific domain [15]. For all these reasons, we argue that a new approach is needed to tackle this kind of complexities associated with these indispensable tools stakeholders must use. Such an approach is the subject of this paper, and will be described as follows. Section 2 will provide the reader with some background information. Section 3 explains the requirements engineering framework that will be used throughout the work. Section 4 outlines the specifications, while Sect. 5 sets out some of the key experimental lessons learned as well as requirements documentation for the design issues.

2. The Approach

The purpose of this section is to highlight the influence associated with requirements engineering in the area of modelling engineering systems. In order to properly define concepts in the domain of oil and gas pipeline engineering, we will adopt Jackson's terminology in his work on the "world and machine [4]. The requirement, which focus on the problem, is in the world; the machine is the solution we construct. In his paper Jackson [4] identifies four facets of the relationship between the world and the machine that represents a foundation in understanding the relationships between a software artefact and the surrounding world. The modelling facet is concerned with a model of some aspect of the world within the machine. The interface facet is concerned with interaction between the machine and the world. The engineering facet is concerned with the control the machine applies on the world, which allows us to distinguish between requirements, the environment, and specifications. Finally, the problem facet is concerned with the relationships between the structure of the world and the machine, where the nature of the problem and the shape of the world influence the shape of the machine and of the solution. The discussion of all the facets is useful to us; with a pipeline context model, the operational standards, environment and concepts of the pipeline domain can be modelled within the machine. The engineering facet concerns us particularly on the distinction between requirements, which identify the characteristics of processes in the world of oil and gas pipeline engineering, the environment surrounded with the processes, which implement the required support needed for the models, and specifications, which identify the collective occurrences between the requirements and the programs. This obvious distinction is hardly made in research on domain specific modelling software processes [16]. We have therefore clearly exemplified where requirements are concerned solely with the world of the domain; in this case with a model representing domain concepts, programs are concerned solely with the machine for design execution, specifications are bridging the requirements and the design. We will use these ideas in working out the boundaries within our framework.

3. Related Work

This section looks at related work on how requirements are defined and represented. It is common to express

requirements by describing the component elements in a framework. Anthony and Andrea [1] defined and presented a framework for requirements engineering for context-aware services. In their presentation, they described requirements for context-aware services, when made available to mobile devices. Requirements for the domain of mobile services, though an interesting study but constitutes lots of challenges. They therefore came up with a novel, reflection-based framework for requirements engineering for this class of applications that addresses the key difficulties such as changing context and changing requirements. We are more concerned with requirements for tackling platform complexities associated with conventional modelling systems. Comparing requirements analysis methods for developing reusable component libraries Alistair et al. [5] advocated the use of domain theory as a means of domain analysis for creating a reusable library of software components for constructing telemedicine applications. Reported in their work is the experience of applying each approach as a domain analysis method to specify abstract components that produced detailed specifications at different levels of abstraction. Instead of a comparison of approaches and analysing domains at different levels of abstraction, we are analysing domain as an integral part in the requirements engineering process to come up with abstractions that can meet the requirements goal. The World and the Machine by Jackson [4] clearly identifies the usefulness of the machines (i.e. the software solutions) developers make and the world, in which the machine serves a useful purpose. But there has to be a balance between the competing demands and attractions of these two concerns, and this balance can only be possible with requirements to solving a particular problem, which is in the world. We have clearly adopted this methodology in working out the boundaries within our framework. In his work on domain understanding the key to successful system development Ray [11] posited the need for developers to always look at the very significant advantages offered by developing a prior and adequate understanding of the surrounding application domain. He further argued that most practising engineers, be they pipeline, aeronautical, electrical, or maritime etc., would accept without argument that a clear, concise and unambiguous understanding of a development project's specific application domain is an essential precursor to successful systems development. This suggestion is quite useful to us because our requirements engineering framework is a necessary first step into eliciting knowledge about pipeline engineering and how a modelling system can be developed to ease technical work for the stakeholders in that domain. Charles et al. [12] presents a framework for security requirements elicitation and analysis, based upon the construction of a context for the system and satisfaction arguments for the security of the system. They started with enumeration of security goals based on assets in the system. They described the system context using a problem-centred notation, and then a satisfaction argument was constructed to validate the context against the security requirements. The satisfaction argument, which is in the form of a formal argument now, verifies if the system can meet its security requirements.

4. The Framework

The requirements framework described in figure 1

addresses the problems of a lack of distinction between requirements specifications and programs in software processes targeted at modelling engineering designs, and a general lack of a clear pathway for deriving requirements for modelling oil and gas pipeline systems from business goals in the pipeline engineering domain [19].

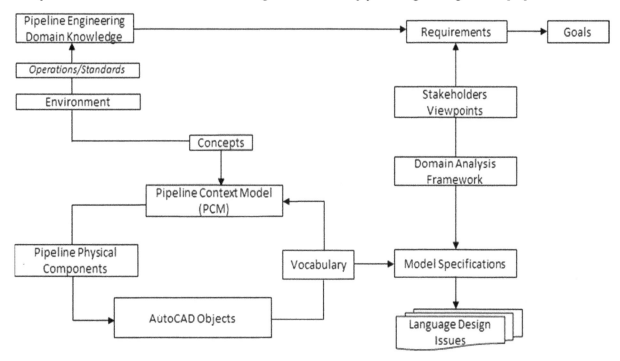

Figure 1. Requirements Engineering Framework.

The rest of this section is dedicated to the explanation of the elements of the framework [7]. As depicted in the framework, we will start with the goals and domain expert operational standards and environment, which are available in the world. The next will be the description of concepts, i.e. the salient technical characteristics prevalent in the domain of oil and gas pipeline engineering, all of which still belongs in the world. This concept description will follow a precise path that facilitates an understanding of the elicitation and formation of the pipeline context model (PCM) from AutoCAD objects and other domain knowledge. Integrating the concepts with the specifications, Will invariably be the bridge between the world and the machine for a modelling system [17].

4.1. Goal

The goal of modeling oil and gas pipeline systems is to provide domain engineers with hands on modeling tool with which they can build pipeline designs and related systems. It is a long-term objective achieved through cooperation of elements in the proposed software and in the environment. Essential aspects in the construction and coordination of the modeling software mechanism is [20] the application of domain specific modelling methodology (DSM) on the development of a domain specific modeling language (DSML) that can transform stakeholders input through

guided notations of the pipeline systems to desired artifacts. In our interpretation the goals do not change with the changing development context, and must represent the ultimate objective the modeling software system is meant to achieve through the cooperation of all the elements in the requirements engineering framework [15].

4.2. Domain Knowledge

Domain knowledge here refers to the specific information needed from stakeholders in the oil and gas pipeline engineering domain. Inputs regarding pipeline components physical attributes and design criteria are sequenced through the acquisition of qualitative information from pipeline enginneers in their fields of operation. This was necessary in order to set the boundaries of the new system. The environment was taken into account because of its strong influence on the elicitation of the domain knowledge [19]. Environment in this context means the scope and operational standards of pipeline engineering basic work flow. A few of which entails Isometric or orthographic pipeline drawings and system descriptions based on functions, intents and major features such as design foundations, operating modes, performance ratings, and control concepts. Feature oriented domain analysis (FODA) of the domain detailed the common and variable parts of the embodiment of the entire relationships and associations of the features and attributes of the pipeline context model in the problem space [18]. The problem space in its generic form refers to established feature constraints and their composition rules that guide the process of transforming the user requirements into a modelling language that satisfies the requirement goals. Figure 2 is the domain analysis subsystem in the requirements engineering framework that determine the degree of correctness between the realization steps of the pipeline model.

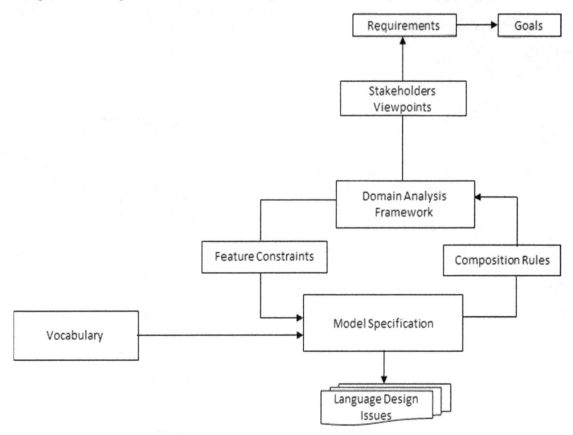

Figure 2. Domain Analysis Subsystem.

4.3. Description of Concepts

A typical oil and gas pipeline systems modeling formalism is expected to offer, through appropriate notations and abstractions, expressive power restricted to, the oil and gas pipeline design problem domain. Consequently this can be achieved only by taking advantage of specific properties of the pipeline engineering application domain that pertain to transmission [19]. The description of these specific properties therefore represents the domain concepts, which will be useful in creating the familiar notations and in the semantic mappings of the elements of the modeling platform. The design of a pipeline system requires the application of theory from a number of engineering principles [16]. It also requires the knowledge and application of a number of codes and standards such as physical attributes, loading and service conditions and environmental and materials factors that relate to pipeline design. Physical attributes are those parameters that govern the size, layout, and dimensional limits or proportions of the pipeline [2]. Dimensional standards have been established for most pipeline components such as fittings, flanges, and valves, as well as for the diameter and wall thickness of standard manufactured pipes. Physical piping

components in a pipeline project includes pipe, flanges, fittings and joints, bolting, gaskets, valves, and the pressure containing portions of other piping components. It also includes pipe hangers and supports and other items necessary to prevent over pressurization and overstressing of the pressure-containing components [19]. It is evident that pipe is one element or a part of piping. Therefore, pipe sections when joined with fittings, valves, and other mechanical equipment and properly supported by hangers and supports results into a pipeline system. A Pipe is a tube with round cross section conforming to the dimensional requirements of the American Society of Mechanical Engineering (ASME) B36.10M Welded and Seamless Wrought Steel Pipe and ASME B36.19M Stainless Steel Pipe [19]. Hangers and supports include elements which transfer the load from the pipe or structural attachment to the supporting structure or equipment. Pipeline valves are dedicated for controlling the flow of the fluid transported along the pipeline. Joint is a connection between two lengths of pipe or between a length of pipe and a fitting. There are quite a lot of types of joints in a pipeline system, each dependent on the service orientation in the pipeline project. Pressure containing components such as gauges and meters carries sufficient pressure metrics for the inputted fluid /pipe surface relationships.

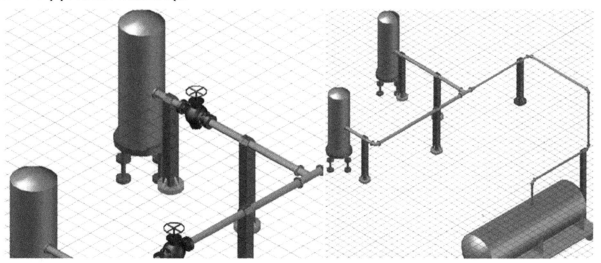

Figure 3. A Typical Pipeline Model with Fittings.

Figure 3 is a a typical pipeline model with fittings that can convey oil or gas from oil wells and storage facilities to tank farms for storage and to points of utilization or to refineries for processing. A pipeline context model (PCM) can be achieved with AutoCAD or any CAD system by careful selection of appropriate fittings as specialized pieces that connects other pieces together [17]. The description of the concepts i.e. the pipeline physical components and necessary design parameters are often represented as AutoCAD objects. Two basic reasons for this are:

1. to make sure all the objects are collectively seen to be the model for the modelling system definition.
2. to make sure the vocabulary necessary for the subsequent modelling platform specifications are captured

4.4. Vocabulary of Components

Domain specific modeling (DSM) approach to language development involves the logical use of models as core entities throughout development. This usually results into the language metamodel where the model is specified in some formal notation. In our view this model at the core of development is the pipeline context model (PCM). Consequently the model offers insight into the needs that when met, oil and gas pipeline systems modeling is made possible productively through a modeling language platform [3]. It is again evident that models are simply outcomes from levels of abstractions, so developing a modelling language is an effort in creating a platform where the domain concepts can be mapped to the abstraction levels. Once this mapping is achieved, it will create a stakeholder or domain expert user friendly interface with notations from the concepts description; it will also hide all the syntax and semantic complexities associated with programming and CAD platforms [6]. The vocabulary of components captured as origin, termination, length, diameter_inner, diameter_outer, material type, points of intersection, slope, colour etc. serves

a useful purpose of mapping these concepts to the abstractions in the form of attributes of the AutoCAD objects representing the pipeline physical components as described in the pipeline context model (PCM). Shown in Figure 4 is a technical diagram explaining the typical real life pipeline fitted with the components. It is an example of the pipeline context model where all the necessary attributes such as size, shape, direction of loops, layout, and dimensional limits or proportions of the pipeline are captured and represented as the vocabulary of components.

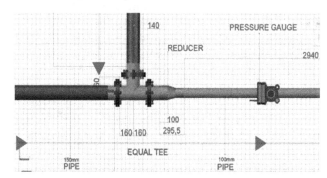

Figure 4. Technical Diagram Explaining Vocabulary Capture.

5. The Specifications

The modeling language specifications and design solution can be constructed in the sense of pipeline engineering product families of a set of basic items, in which the characteristically distinctive aspects of the products that are visible to various stakeholders are represented as features in the software framework [12].

The software framework or platform, embeds all feature variability and commonalities, and provides services common to all applications of the product family. While the variability indicates precisely what evidence is needed to specify an instance of a feature that could fit into a particular modeling scenario; the commonalities in this respect define the set of common operations and primitives of the language

[13]. Features such as fittings, joint and support, whose parent is the pipeline root concept, are common features. Then component dimensions and types, fitting dimensions and types, piping support features, points of joints and joint types and dimensions are the variabilities [10]. The piping components can be atomic or compound, access to the components as a service can be triggered by a design and modelling intent of a typical stakeholder; the variability and commonalities are considered as first step in designing the modelling language, and are therefore both built into the execution mode. The feature model of the composite forms enable transformation and for interactive configurations; interactive configuration implies possible assignment of features given the current state of the system, and propagating information whenever new choices are made [9]. These internal interactions adhere to the composition rules about configurability of the features that corresponds to the language definition.

6. Lessons Learned

The syntax and semantic complexities associated with programming and CAD platforms examined in the previous section represent a formidable challenge for any domain engineer [17]. One of the key issues in these systems is that stakeholders have competing design requirements. Therefore, requirements and system behaviour must adapt themselves to accommodate these determining factors. In order for this to be feasible, the vocabulary of CAD objects representing the domain specific oil and gas pipeline components must be specified in a domain specific language formalism for easy and timely artefact orientation of the pipeline systems configurations [14]. This representation must take place in a way that is both readily understandable by stakeholders and easily manipulatable by the machine, which means a suitable software architecture design phase should always precede the actual implementation. In other words, as far as experts could see through to a design scenario, the system will be able to capture it and evolve a design that meets their needs. The user could make some input through guided notations from the interface, and the system can then match these inputs with a parsing grammar specification to produce desired designs. Internal communication among the architecture components is enforced and made possible by utilizing the running system that implements a specification. This architecture, invariably defines the scope and environment of the new requirements. But some very important questions such as the ones listed below may arise [1].

1. What is the trade-off of switching from a CAD system to using the proposed language?
2. Could the benefits of expressing every detail of the pipeline overcome the simplicity that normally is associated to a CAD system in terms of usability for the user?
3. What clear benefit can be gained using the approach over existing approaches?
4. Why is a DSML needed at the first place?

The trade-off of switching to using this language is reduction in design time and cost of operations. For example, some trained CAD software professionals whose job is to oversee and attend promptly to varying engineering designs and fabrication considerations [20]. The simplicity in usability of this language is clearly exemplified in the vocabulary of components. Having captured the vocabulary and then translated into a modelling platform, the users need not any engineering design expertise to get their design intents achieved. In optimal cases, programming expertise must be needed to achieve some design intents [18]. The clear benefit is that in this language, the metamodel is a repository of concepts from the oil and gas pipeline domain. The models are constructed using these concepts and not the concepts of a given programming language. Therefore there is no semantic gap between design intent and the expression of this intent in several lines of codes [20]. The users have the freedom of expressing their intents through familiar domain representations; without facing any difficulties of how the policies are mapped onto the underlying mechanisms implementing them.

The obvious is that all the services in the framework cannot complete implementation cycle on its own. However, our current thought is that it should be possible to characterize stakeholders design intent as the view points of the input parameters; so that a complete requirements analysis products and system workflow can be documented. The term design intent refers to identified interests and disciplines of all the stakeholders of this system as it relates to pipeline design and highlights physical attributes that must be considered in completing a modelling process [15]. Figure 5 illustrates an overall view of the requirements analysis products for the requirements documentation and system workflow.

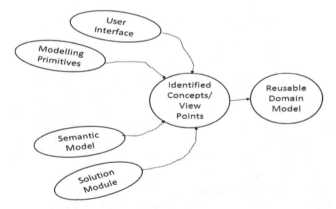

Figure 5. Requirements Analysis Products.

Some of the key requirements for the system work flow are described below.

1. A semantic model should be included as a feature of the new system. The semantic model in this instance is an abstraction that describes the meaning of the model instances that makes up the language metamodel. It also defines the way the model instances relate to the real world examples. It should be able to showcase the

expressive power to interpret meaning (semantics) from the instances.

2. The software has to have a user interface component with familiar notations, permitting its users to represent their mental models about their design intents. It should contain pipeline engineering features that can promote enhanced engineering design modelling for stakeholders without programming or CAD software expertise, and without being burdened by its syntactic or semantic refinements.

3. Users should be able to define modelling parameters in line with pipeline engineering principles. For example, if a pipeline design is constructed from the selection of a number of modelling primitives such as instrument components and support, then the artefact orientation may be considered as corresponding to the variability and commonalities of the primitives. Whereas the variability indicates precisely what evidence is needed to specify an instance of a feature that could fit into particular design intent, the commonalities define the set of common operations and primitives of the language.

4. Users should be able to interpret artefacts. For example, the system should have a knowledge based rule processing solution module, which can allow processing to generate products that reflect oil and gas pipeline real life operations.

7. Conclusion and Future Work

This paper has presented a framework for requirements engineering for oil and gas pipeline systems modeling where the domain of pipeline engineering is analysed and a requirements documentation effected to the goals of a modelling platform capable of transforming pipeline models to stakeholders and domain experts desired artefacts. Development of reusable software will necessitate advances beyond the current generation of programming and computer aided design systems. These systems provide little or negligible design and process guidance for expressing domain specific concepts; the contribution of this paper has been to apply a requirements engineering framework to the pipeline engineering domain for platform simplicity and for improving specification of domain specific libraries. In the future the experimental lessons learned on this framework will be used for design and implementation of a simplified modeling platform and for reuse of domain libraries.

References

[1] Anthony Finkelstein, Andrea Savigni A Framework for Requirements Engineering for Context-Aware Services Department of Computer Science University College London Gower Street London WC1E 6BT United Kingdom.

[2] M. Feather, S. Fickas, A. van Lamsweerde, and C. Ponsard. Reconciling System Requirements and Runtime Behavior. In *Proceedings of IWSSD'98 - 9th International Workshop on*

Software Specification and Design, Isobe, Japan, April1998. IEEE Computer Society Press.

[3] S. Fickas and M. S. Feather. Requirements Monitoring in Dynamic Environments. In *Proceedings of the Second IEEE International Symposium on Requirements Engineering*, pages 140–147. IEEE Computer Society Press, 1995.

[4] M. Jackson. The World and the Machine. In *Proceedings of the 17*th *International Conference on Software Engineering*, pages 283 – 292, Seattle, Washington, USA, April 24 – 281995.

[5] Alistair Sutcliffe, George Papamargaritis, Liping Zhao Comparing requirements analysis methods for developing reusable component libraries; The Journal of Systems and Software 79 (2006) 273–289.

[6] Hall, J. G., Jackson, M. J., Laney, R. C., Nusibeh, B., Rananotti, L., 2002. Relating software requirements and architectures using problem frames. In: Greenspan, S., Saddiqui, J., Pohl, K. (Eds.), Proceedings of RE 02, 1st International Conference on Requirements Engineering. IEEE Computer Society Press, Los Alamos, CA, pp. 137–145.

[7] Jarzabek, S., Ong, W. C., Zhang, H., 2003. Handling variant requirements in domain modeling. Journal of Systems and Software 68 (3), 171–182.

[8] MA. Lam, W., McDermid, J. A., Vickers, A. J., 1997. Ten steps towards systematic requirements reuse. In: Proceedings ISRE _97: 3rd IEEE International Symposium on Requirements Engineering (AnnapolisMD). IEEE Computer Society Press, Los Alamitos CA, pp. 6–15.

[9] Levi, K., Arsanjani, A., 2002. A goal-driven approach to enterprise component identification and specification. Communications of the ACM 45 (10), 45–52.

[10] Mannion, M., Kaindl, H., Weadon, J., 1999. Reusing single system requirements from application family requirements. In: Proceedings of the International Conference on Software Engineering, ICSE 99. IEEE Computer Society Press, Los Alamitos CA.

[11] Ray Offen Domain Understanding is the Key to Successful System Development Division of ICS, Macquarie University, New South Wales, Australia Requirements Eng (2002) 7:172–175_ 2002 Springer-Verlag London Limited.

[12] Charles B. Haley Milton Keynes Jonathan D. Moffett A Framework for Security Requirements Engineering *SESS'06*, May 20–21, 2006, Shanghai, China. 2006 ACM 1-59593-085-X/06/0005...$5.00.

[13] McMenamin, S. M., Palmer, J. F., 1984. Essential Systems Analysis. Yourdon Press, Englewood Cliffs, NJ.

[14] Papamargaritis, G., Sutcliffe, A. G., 2004. Applying the domain theory to design for reuse. BT Technology Journal 22 (2), 104–115.

[15] Van Lamsweerde, A., 2001. Goal-oriented requirements engineering: aguided tour. In: Proceedings of the RE_01—5th IEEE International Symposium on Requirements Engineering, Toronto, August, 2001.IEEE Computer Society Press, Los Alamitos, CA, pp. 249–263.

[16] Alessandro NADDEO, Cad Active Models: An Innovative Method in Assembly Environment, Journal of Industrial Design and Engineering Graphics Volume 5 Issue No. 1 – 2010.

[17] Autodesk Inc. (2013) *AutoCAD Release 2013 Programmers Reference Manual.*

[18] Feature-Oriented Domain Analysis (FODA http://www.sei.cmu.edu/reports/90tr021.pdf.

[19] Nayyar, Mohinder L. Piping handbook / [edited by] Mohinder L. Nayyar.—7th ed. p. cm. ISBN 0-07-047106-1 *McGraw-Hill* 2000.

[20] Markus Voelter, Eelco Visser: Product Line Engineering using Domain-Specific Languages Independent, acm.org 2011 15th International Software Product Line Conference 978-0-7695-4487-8/11 2011 IEEE DOI 10.1109/SPLC.2011.25.

21

Implementation of Egypt Sat-1 Satellite Test Center Using LabVIEW

Mohamed Elhady Keshk, Mohamed Ibrahim, Noran Tobar, Hend Nabil, Mohamed Elemam

Testing and Devleopment of Satellites Systems Group, Egyptian Space Program, NARSS, Cairo, Egypt

Email address:
m.elhady@narss.sci.eg (M. E. Keshk), m.ibrahim@narss.sci.eg (M. Ibrahim), N.Tobar@narss.sci.eg (N. Tobar),
H.Nabil@narss.sci.eg (H. Nabil), M.Emam@narss.sci.eg (M. Elemam)

Abstract: In each stage of any satellite design cycle, it is required to have test system that verifies the operational functions of each satellite subsystem and the integration operation among the satellite subsystems. Usually, these test systems consist of many hardware's and these hardware's are very complicated and occupied large space. The first Egyptian satellite, Egypt Sat-1, has a test center; a place where the satellite integration test sequences are carried out. This center consists of complicated hardware. In this paper a new trend, using LabView tool with National Instrument (NI) chassis, is used to build a satellite test center (STC) prototype that reduce the cost, complexity and occupied area of the STC. So the new trend tests the ability to replace the Egypt Sat-1 test center. The results of this paper shows that the quality of the new trend compared to the existed Egypt Sat-1 test center.

Keywords: Satellite Test Center, Space, Engineering Model

1. Introduction

The entrance of the space field is surrounding by the risks. One of them is the failure of the satellite subsystem operation after launching. So every satellite design process must be tested and verified before the launching of the satellite. To achieve that it is required to have a test center that has the capabilities to perform pre-launching tests. In addition to pre-launching tests that applied to each subsystem during the design procedures of the satellite, it is also required to test new operation plans on the ground before applying it on the satellite during its life time. So test center has two important functions one is pre-launching tests and post-launching tests.

The Satellite Test Center (STC) of Egypt Sat-1 satellite consists of control machine that initiates and performs all test programs, checkout equipment (CoE) for each subsystem on the satellite and a satellite mockup. Each CoE performs some functions to implement and analyze the test program contain complex hardware that need in order complex data exchange and interface among CoE and the control machine.

Many studies are implemented in different fields using Labview; labview can be used in simulation of satellite camera (payload) subsystem [4], also NASA used labview in automated testing of Micro shutters [5], labview can also used in Building a Satellite Navigation Test Platform Using the NI Vector Signal Transceiver [6], in channel modeling of mobile systems [7], used for testing satellite GPS receiver [8], [9] and in FPGA application[10].

The remainder of the paper is organized as follows. Section II has an overview on the proposed STC. Section III defines the Integration Test Machine (ITM). Section IV defines the basic functions of Telemetry Control (TC) CoE. Section V defines the basic functions of Payload CoE. Section VI defines the basic functions of and mathematical model of the Power CoE Section VII defines the basic functions of Satellite simulator. Section VIII conclusion of the proposed STC work.

2. STC

A new implementation of STC using LabView tool with less hardware is proposed in this paper which performs the same functions of the Egypt sat-1 STC but with less complexity, development time, and cost within small area.

For simplicity, the control machine (ITM) will be implemented to perform the same functions as the configuration control console (CCC) that in Egypt Sat-1 STC. To verify the proposed STC; Payload, Power, Telemetry control (TC) CoE's will be simulated using LabView tool in addition to a satellite simulator. Each subsystem will be implemented using LabView program running on NI machine.

A. STC Structure

The concept of the proposed STC is to make integration test among satellite simulator and Check Test Equipment CoE's under the control of ITM as in figure 1, i.e. the ability to replace the existing engineering model by the proposed STC system.

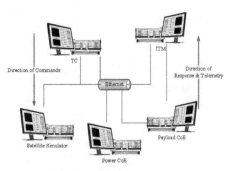

Fig. 1. *STC System Structure.*

B. Data Exchange Interfaces

- TCP/IP, to transfer the commands between TC and satellite simulator.
- FTP, to transfer Telemetry file from satellite simulator to ITM.
- Reflected Memory Card, to adjust the synchronization among the whole system parts and to transfer the image from satellite simulator to Payload CoE.

3. ITM

ITM is the main part of the Satellite Test Center (STC), which is used for managing and monitoring of complex integration test (CIT) before, during and after the test program. Figure 2 illustrates the flow chart of ITM sequence operation.

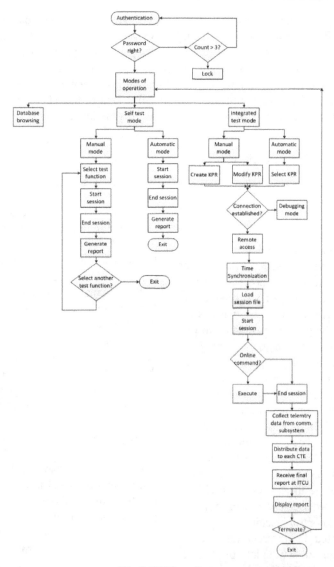

Fig. 2. *ITM flow chart.*

Before the test program, the ITM functional requirements are network administration, access authentication, checking of connection presence with subsystem CoE's, selecting the operational mode type, selecting the test type (integrated or Self-test), selection of the test program, Loading the initial data for the test program session and exchanging the data between the ITM and the CoE's.

During the test program session; TC CoE monitors the CoE's and Satellite subsystems status. After test program session; ITM receives the telemetry data from the simulator then send them to their CoE's by using file transfer protocol (FTP), Receives, displays & archives the test results from satellite CoE's. Figure 3 illustrate GUI of the ITM.

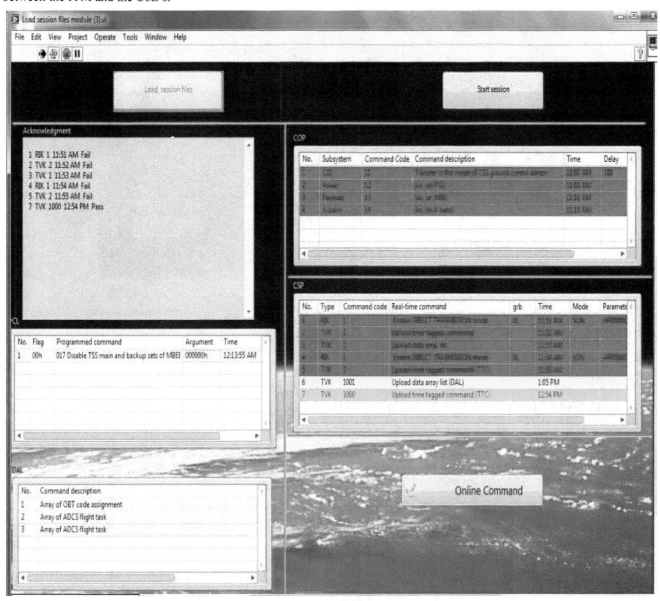

Fig. 3. ITM GUI.

4. TC CoE

After the reception of the test program session from ITM, TC CoE plays an important role in the execution of the test program session and monitoring each test program command. After the test program session, TC CoE sends the collected telemetry to ITM. First, TC Start the session then monitoring the execution of the session, receiving the acknowledgments of the session program and also it has the ability to sending on-line commands during session, Measuring of CE

operating time and measuring of S-BAND OBE operating time.

5. Payload CoE

The main function of the Payload CoE is to receive a pre-stored image in the satellite simulator to analyze, verify and compare this with the one stored in it. The verification of the received image is depending on the comparison result of the two images, and the comparator factor is the resolution.

Figure 4 illustrate GUI of the Payload CoE.

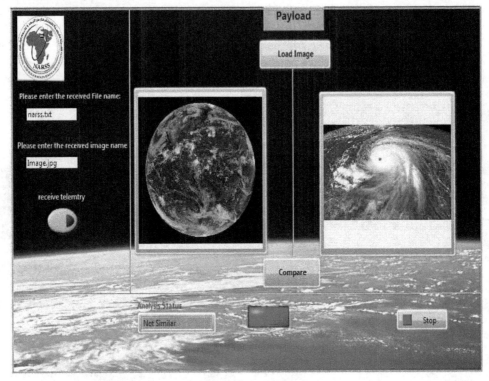

Fig. 4. *Payload GUI.*

6. Power CoE

The purposes of the power CoE are; Switch on the satellite simulator, provide the whole system by the required power needed and receiving the telemetry of the power subsystem from satellite simulator and analyzing them. Figure 5 shows the solar array simulator analysis report under the variation of temperature between 5Co and 40 Co seen that as temperature increase the voltage decrease and current increase until the temperature reaches 40 Co, the temperature decreases again till 5 Co, to simulate temperature variation in orbit.

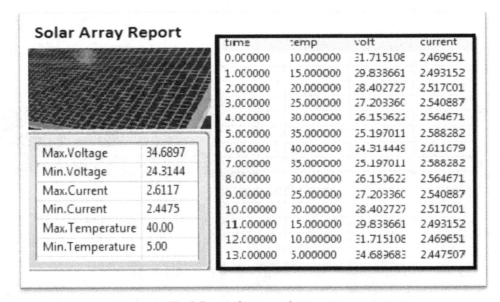

Solar Array Report

Max.Voltage	34.6897
Min.Voltage	24.3144
Max.Current	2.6117
Min.Current	2.4475
Max.Temperature	40.00
Min.Temperature	5.00

time	temp	volt	current
0.000000	10.000000	31.715108	2.469651
1.000000	15.000000	29.833661	2.493152
2.000000	20.000000	28.402727	2.517001
3.000000	25.000000	27.203360	2.540887
4.000000	30.000000	26.150622	2.564671
5.000000	35.000000	25.197011	2.588282
6.000000	40.000000	24.314449	2.611079
7.000000	35.000000	25.197011	2.588282
8.000000	30.000000	26.150622	2.564671
9.000000	25.000000	27.203360	2.540887
10.000000	20.000000	28.402727	2.517001
11.000000	15.000000	29.833661	2.493152
12.000000	10.000000	31.715108	2.469651
13.000000	5.000000	34.689683	2.447507

Fig. 5. *Power subsystem analysis report.*

7. Satellite Simulator

Satellite simulator contains the following subsystems; Payload and Power for simplicity.

The simulation of the power subsystem is divided into two parts; Solar Array and Battery.

A. Solar Array Simulation

The selected functions of solar array simulator can be described as following; Get maximum power point voltage, current & operating temperature, send this values instantaneously to Power CTE, graph represents VI-Curve at each temperature, create telemetry file (TDMS) and send it to power CTE using FTP.

The following equations are used To model the solar array mathematically using Egypt Sat-1 satellite solar array as reference [1]:

$$I = Iph - Is\left(e^{\frac{q(v+iRs)}{AKNsTc}} - 1\right) - \frac{(V+IRs)}{Rsh} \qquad (1)$$

$$Is = Irs\left(\frac{Tc}{Tr}\right)^3 * \left(e^{\left(\frac{qEg}{AK}\left(\frac{1}{Tr}-\frac{1}{Tc}\right)\right)}\right) \qquad (2)$$

$$Irs = \frac{Ish - \frac{Voc}{Rsh}}{\left(e^{\frac{qVoc}{AKNsTr}} - 1\right)} \qquad (3)$$

$$Voc = \ln\left(\frac{Isc}{Io} + 1\right)\left(\frac{AKTc}{q}\right) \qquad (4)$$

The symbols are defined as in Table 1.

B. Battery Simulation

The selected functions of solar array simulator can be described as following;It Simulate Charging and discharging of the battery, representing battery current ,Volt & temperature, send this values instantaneously to Power CTE ,it shows where battery charging or discharging and if it is ready to used or not, create telemetry file(TDMS) and send it to power CTE using FTP.

A NiCd battery is simulated with the following characteristics; Range of CB operational voltages: 24-34, Number of CB used: 1, Range of temperature: -5 to +50°C [3].

In Figure 6, a portion of GUI that represent power subsystem.

The second simulated subsystem is Payload which send taken image to payload CoE using FTP, receive command (CSP/Online) using TCP and execute this command, create telemetry file and send it to Payload CTE using FTP. Figure 7 shows Payload subsystem simulator.

Table 1. *Symbols Definition [1].*

Parameters	Attributes		
	Table column subhead	Value	Unit
Iph	Photo current of the SPV module	2.561176	Amp
Irs	Diode reverse saturation current	1.73071*10^-13	µAmp
Rs	Series resistance in the equivalent circuit of the module	0.294	mΩ
Rsh	Shunt resistance in the equivalent circuit of the module	639.302495	mΩ
A	Diode quality factor	1.3	
Voc	Open circuit voltage of the module	43.532	V
Ish	Short circuit current of the module	2.56	Amp
Vmp	Maximum power point voltage	38.032	Volt
Imp	Maximum power point voltage and current	2.412	Amp
Ki	Boltzman's constant	1.381×10-23	J/K
Eg	Band gap energy	1.1	EV
qe	Electron Charge	1.602×10-19	C

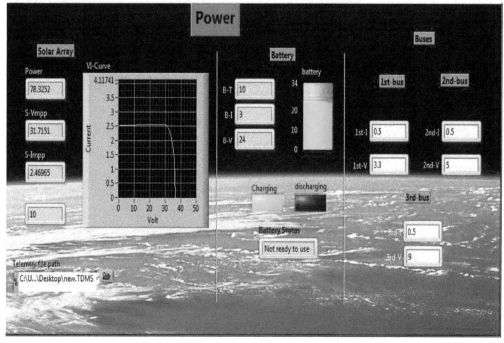

Fig. 6. *Power subsystem GUI (included into satellite simulator).*

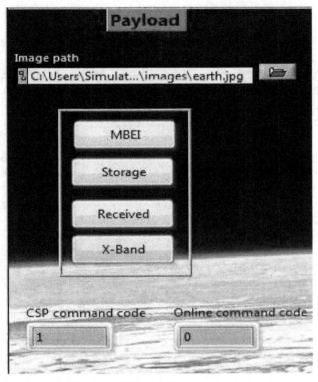

Fig. 7. Payload GUI (included into satellite simulator).

8. Conclusion

In this paper a new trend that using LabView program running on NI machine is used to implement satellite test center prototype with less hardware, development time, manpower and cost. From the results it is found that the new trend capable of replacing the existed STC. As a prototype, one subsystem is completely implemented (ITM) and the other test center subsystems are simulated with some of its functions and from the session that done and the results, it is found that the proposed STC is work properly.

References

[1]   M.S. El-Negamy, M.B. Eteiba 1 and G.M. El-Bayoumi, "Modeling and Simulation of Egyptsat-1 Satellite System Powered by Photovoltaic Module", Journal of American Science p. 110-116, Vol. 9, No.1, 2013.

[2]   Dr. J. Abdul Jaleel, Nazar. A, Omega A R, "Simulation on Maximum Power Point Tracking of the Photovoltaic Module using LabVIEW", International Journal of Advanced Research in Electrical, Electronics and Instrumentation Engineering, Vol. 1, Issue 3, p.190-199, September 2012.

[3]   M. Zahran, M. Okasha and Galina A. Ivanova, "Assessment of Earth Remote Sensing Microsatellite Power Subsystem Capability during Detumbling and Nominal Modes", Journal of Power Electronics, Vol. 6, No. 1, January 2006.

[4]   "Flight and Camera Electronics for a Satellite System - A NI Multisim National Lab Application", www.ni.com/white-paper/7829/en/, access: Oct 06, 2013.

[5]   F. Musso, F. Bresciani, L. Bonino, S. Cesare, "NASA uses NI LabVIEW to save time, reduce costs in automated testing of Micro shutters", military aerospace solutions Conference, pp. 60-62, 2007.

[6]   "Building a Satellite Navigation Test Platform Using the NI Vector Signal Transceiver"www.sine.ni.com/cs/app/doc/p/id/cs-16256.

[7]   G. Huang, A. Soghoyan, D. Akopian, P. Chen, A. Samant, "A Land Mobile Channel Modeling in LabVIEW", IEEE SMC, San Antonio, TX, pp. 4575-4580, 2009.

[8]   "Galileo Receiver Testing Based on LabVIEW and NI RF Hardware", www.sine.ni.com/cs/app/doc/p/id/cs-15551.

[9]   Arpine Soghoyan, Grant Huang, Jayanthi Narisetty, David Akopian, "A Comprehensive Labview-Based A-GPS Receiver and Integrated Development, Simulation and Testing Platform", www.researchgate.net/publication/258567337, jan.2011.

[10] National Instruments FPGA, www.ni.com/fpga/.

22

An MDA Method for Automatic Transformation of Models from CIM to PIM

Abdelouahed Kriouile, Najiba Addamssiri, Taoufiq Gadi

LAVETE Laboratory, Hassan 1 University, Settat, Morocco

Email address:

kriouile1970@gmail.com (A. Kriouile), addam.naji@gmail.com (N. Addamssiri), g.taoufiq@yahoo.fr (T. Gadi)

Abstract: The Model Driven Architecture (MDA) approach introduces a clear separation of the business logic from the implementation logic that's less stable. It uses the models that are more perennial than codes. It puts the models at the centre of the development of software and of the information systems. The MDA approach consists at, firstly, developing the CIM Model, secondly, obtaining the PIM model from the CIM, and finally generating the PSM model from the PIM which facilitates the generation of code for a chosen technical platform. In the literature, several works have summarized the MDA approach to the passage from PIM to PSM then from the PSM to code. Yet, very little work has contributed in the axis of the CIM to PIM transformation, and their approaches generally propose a CIM model which does not cover the different specifications of the Object Management Group (OMG) and/or the CIM to PIM transformation that they define is in the most cases manual or semi-automatic. Thus, our proposal aims at providing a solution to the problem of constructing CIM and its automatic transformation at the PIM using the QVT transformation rules. The approach proposes to represent CIM by two models: The business process model reflecting both the static and the behavioral views of the system, and the functional requirement model defined by the use case model reflecting the functional view of the system. The transformation of the CIM allows us to generate the PIM level represented by two models: The domain classes model which gives a structural view of the system at this level, and a model that describes the behavior of the system to each use case.

Keywords: MDA, CIM, PIM, Model Transformation, BPMN, QVT

1. Introduction

The discipline of software engineering has allowed the development of computer systems for more and more complex and requiring enormous investments. Yet, the sustainability of these systems is questioned whenever a new technology appears, since each new technology put in place a set of tools that, generally, does not support the older technologies.

However, in response to this difficult situation, we should reconsider the reduction of the cost of development work that is done independently from the target technology and which is, therefore, connected to the business logic of the application. The MDA approach (Model Driven Architecture) [1] is called by introducing a clear separation of the business logic -which is stable and undergoes little changes over time- from the implementation logic that's less stable; models are more perennial than codes. This MDA approach fits into the overall context of the Model Driven Engineering (MDE),

which puts the models at the centre of the development of software and of the information systems.

The principle of the MDA approach is based on the use of models and metamodels for the various phases of the software development lifecycle. Specifically, it recommends three types of models from different viewpoints) [1]: The Computation Independent Model (CIM), the Platform Independent Model (PIM) and the Platform Specific Model (PSM).

The MDA approach consists, at first, to develop the CIM Model. Secondly, to obtain the PIM model from the CIM, and finally to generate the PSM model from the PIM which facilitates the generation of code for a chosen technical platform. The passage from CIM to PIM and from PIM to PSM represents models transformations, while the generation of code from PSM is not regarded as a model transformation. Ideally, according to [1], the code generation can be done automatically by successive transformations of models: CIM to PIM, PIM to PSM and PSM to code.

In the literature, several works have summarized the MDA approach to the passage from PIM to PSM then from the

PSM to code. Yet, very little work have contributed in the axis of the CIM to PIM transformation, and their approaches, generally, propose a CIM model which does not cover the different specifications of the Object Management Group (OMG) and/or the CIM to PIM transformation that they define is in the most cases manual or semi-automatic.

Thus, our proposal aims to be a new solution to the problem of constructing CIM and its automatic transformation at the PIM. This problem can be divided into two sub-problems:

- Elaborate a CIM model conforms to the various specifications outlined by the OMG.
- Define an automatic model transformation allowing generating the PIM model conform to the various specifications outlined by the OMG.

Thus, our initiative aims at solving or at least mitigating - in the context of the MDA approach- the problems related to the sustainability of the applications. This sustainability cannot be ensured only through models that are sustainable and productive, independent from computing and independent from any technological platform. Our contribution seeks to solve this problem at top level of the MDA; it will specifically focus on modeling the CIM and define the transformation rules allowing generating the suitable PIM Model from the CIM Model. The transformations rules are expressed through language QVT.

In our approach, we propose to represent CIM by two models: The business process model (BPM) reflecting both the static aspect (Static View) and the behavioral aspect (Behavioral View) of the system, and the functional requirement model defined by the Use Case model (UC) reflecting the functional aspect (Functional View) of the system.

The transformation of the CIM allows us to generate the PIM model represented by two models: The domain classes model corresponds to the context in which the system should be applied which gives a static view of system (Structural View), and the Behavioral Model that describes the behavior of the system to each use case providing a behavioral view of system (Behavioral View).

The rest of this paper is organized as follows. In section 2, background and related work for this research are explained. Section 3 and section 4 depict respectively how the CIM and PIM will model. Section 5 presents the different steps of our method to construct CIM and to transform it automatically into PIM using the QVT transformation rules. In section 6, we shall present an illustrative case study. The analysis of the evaluation results of our proposal is explained in section7. Finally, in section 8, we briefly provide a conclusion and present our plan for future works.

2. Background and Related Work

2.1. Levels of Modeling in MDA

The OMG announced its initiative MDA (Model Driven Architecture) in November 2000, then proposed its first

version in 2001 and in 2003 adopted the final specification of the approach [2]. The MDA approach fits into the overall context of the model driven engineering (MDE), which puts the models at the centre of the development of software and of the information systems.

Since the models are more perennial than codes, and in order to enable the organizations to evolve their application models independently of the evolution of the technology platforms, MDA advocates the elaboration of perennial models by distinguishing models which are independent from the platforms of the models that are specific to platforms. Thus, its principle is to separate the functional specifications from the implementation specifications on a particular platform.

The MDA approach offers three types of models from three different points of view [1]:

- CIM (Computation Independent Model): It's a model independent of any computerization. The CIM Model does not show the details of the system structure. It describes the product independently of any computer system. It focuses on the requirements of the system as well as the environment in which it operates without going into the details of its structure and its implementation. It is sometimes called a domain model and serves as the vocabulary for system domain practitioners. However, a CIM is more than a domain model; it expresses also the requirements of the system.
- PIM (Platform Independent Model): It refers to a view of system or sub-system at an abstraction level allowing an independence from any technical platform. The role of the PIM is to be perennial and to make the link between the CIM and the PSM model. The MDA approach advocates the use of UML as a language to model the PIM. But it gives neither any indication of the number of models to develop at the PIM level nor the method to be used for developing it.
- PSM (Platform Specific Model): It is the dependent model of the technical platforms. It mainly serves as a base for generating an executable code on the chosen technical platform. It indicates how the product will be used on these platforms. A good PSM must incorporate enough features and concepts (data types, classes, interfaces, patterns, etc.) of the platform chosen to make the code generation easy.

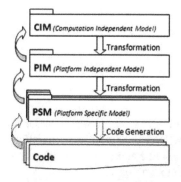

Figure 1. MDA software lifecycle

2.2. Model Transformations in MDA

The main artifacts of the MDA are models and model transformations. Generally, we call transformation of models any program which its inputs and outputs are models respectively conform to their metamodels. A model transformation matches, according to the transformation rules, the concepts of the source and the target metamodel. The transformation rules are described at the transformation models conform in turn to the metamodel that defines the transformation language. Thus, the elements of the target models can be generated from those of the sources models by applying transformation rules that are already defined.

In the MDA architecture the MOF (Meta Object Facility) allows the definition of modeling languages, as well as the definition of the transformation rules. It is normalized by the OMG in its current version 2.0 [3]. It is used to specify the structure and syntax of metamodels. It also specifies mechanisms for metamodel interoperability, allowing its comparing and its linking. Thanks to these exchange mechanisms, the MOF cohabit different metamodels.

The OMG proposes the standard MOF 2.0 QVT (Query View Transformation) [3] as language to define the transformation of models.

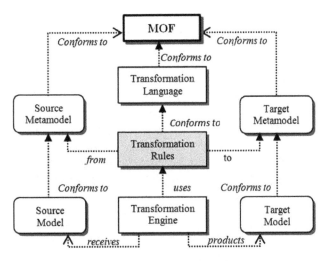

Figure 2. *MDA processing Process*

2.3. Business Process Modelling

BPMN and UML activity diagram are two competing standards, both maintained by the OMG, allowing to model business processes.

BPMN is based on a single Business Processes Diagram, called BPD [4]. It is easy to use and to understand, allowing modeling the complex business processes.

The UML AD specification does not deal with the business process modeling. It mentioned that the activities can be applied to organizational modeling for business processes engineering and workflows [5]. But practically UML activity diagrams can be used to model business processes, or the dynamic part of a model (e.g. an algorithm of an operation). They can represent a process, or the behavior of an operation.

A comparison between the Business Process Diagram (BPD) and the UML Activity Diagrams for modeling of twenty-one workflows patterns are introduced in [6]. It shows enough similarity between the two diagrams in terms of notations and the representations. However, other benefits are provided by the BPMN, its mathematical foundations designed to easily transform it in a business language. Furthermore, BPMN can be translated into UML and provide a solid modeling mean.

2.4. Related Work

Several methods of modeling and transformation of models have been proposed in the context of the MDA. However, through the bibliographical study that we have conducted only seven methods seem to address the modeling of the CIM level and its transformation to the PIM level.

The authors in [7] proposed a disciplined method for transformation of CIM to PIM. The CIM model uses two activity diagrams to represent business processes and system requirements. The business process model represents all the activities of the organization independently of their automation; while the requirements model specifies the system supporting such activities, by representing their use cases and considering it as a one actor. The PIM model is represented by the class diagram obtained from the requirements model. This last model is transformed into component models of the system that provide a first sketch of the structure of the system: a set of business archetypes that helps to transform, in detail, the components system into PIM. This approach is based on modeling the CIM using the UML 2.0 Activity Diagrams as a single technique, and the PIM behavioral aspect is not specified.

The method in [8] proposed a CIM to PIM transformation using a method oriented by the features and based on components. The requirements in the CIM model are represented by a model that includes a set of features and relations between them. And the PIM model is represented by a software architecture that includes a set of components and their interactions. This method uses an intermediate model that is neither CIM nor PIM, which does not consider business processes.

In the papers [9, 10, 11], the authors present a CIM composed by a business processes model, using a secured business process with the BPMN. This CIM is transformed, with the help of the QVT rules (Query/View/Transformation), checklists, and refinement rules into two models composing the PIM level: the use cases diagram and the class diagram. The use cases are detailed in order to obtain the activities and the class diagram that is considered an initial analysis model. Use cases diagram is moved, in this method, into the PIM level. Furthermore, the diagrams of the PIM that are obtained by transformation of the CIM, do not communicate the PIM behavioral structure.

Paper [12] presents an analytical solution for the

modeling of CIM and its transformation to the PIM model. To model business processes, the authors used at the CIM level the Data Flow Diagrams (DFD). Whereas the PIM level is covered by four UML diagrams: The Use Cases Diagram, The Activities Diagram, The Sequence Diagrams and the Domain Models.

Paper [13] tackles a semi-automatic method for building web applications from the high level of requirements, expressed as use cases in accordance with the model-driven architecture (MDA). The first step of the method is to transform the CIM model to the PIM model. It considers that the CIM is represented by the description of use cases as well as the default domain objects. The PIM model includes State Machines, the User Interface Model and the refined domain model. This method does not consider business processes.

In paper [14] the authors present a systematic method for MDA transformations, including the creation of the platform independent model (PIM) from the CIM, the transformation of the PIM to the platform specific model (PSM) and the generation of code from the PSM model. The CIM in this method is composed of the use cases diagram, the activity diagram and the robustness diagram. While, the PIM is modeled by two parts: the behavioral part by a sequence diagrams and the structural part by a class diagram.

The method in [15] allows, first, to build the CIM model and to transform it (semi-) automatically to the less abstraction level (PIM).The CIM level is covered by two models; on one hand the business process model (BPM) characterizing both the behavioral and the static aspects representing the different activities and resources used by them in the business processes. On the other hand, the use cases model representing functional aspect of system. While, the PIM level is modeled with the domain classes diagram (DCD) and the external behavior sequence diagram of the system (SDSEB). The later is an UML sequence diagram that demonstrates interactions between the actors and the system seen as unique entity represented by a one line of life, without focus on the interactions of the objects system. This method calls the business rules to generate the DCD PIM level.

It should be noted that in the literature we have found two other proposals that are limited only to the modeling of the CIM level, without giving details on its transformation into PIM. The method in paper [16] presents a method for modeling CIM based on the artifacts and the concepts of the RUP methodology. This method presents a CIM which covers two aspects: the business processes and requirements. It is composed of three models: A business use cases model, a business analyses model and the use cases model. Moreover, the method in the papers [17, 18, 19], called TFMfMDA (Topological Functioning Modeling for Model Driven Architecture) using formal mathematical foundations of topological functioning model. The CIM level is modeled with use cases model and the conceptual class diagram presenting the domain concepts and their relations to establish.

3. CIM Architecture

The creation of the CIM is the first task in the MDA development process. It must be developed in collaboration with the domain experts. The CIM is of great importance for the rest of the development process; any changes driven by new requirements at the CIM level will reflect the PIM and the PSM levels.

3.1. Specifications of CIM According to the OMG

According to the definition given by the OMG [1], we have deduced that the CIM model must verify the following requirements:

- CIM represents a point of view of the system independently of the computation.
- CIM should not show the details of the structure of the system.
- CIM is sometimes called domain model or a business model, using for its specification, the current vocabulary of practitioners of domain in question.
- Since the primary user of the CIM -the practitioner of domain- is generally not a know-all of models or of the artifacts used to make features for which the requirements are identified in the CIM. The CIM must play an important role in bridging the gap between the domain experts with its requirements and the experts of the design and construction of objects which must satisfy the domain requirements.
- The system requirements are modeled in the CIM.
- CIM describes the situation in which the system will be used.
- CIM is independent of the system implementation. It hides many or all of the information on the use of data automatic processing systems.
- CIM represents a source of common vocabulary to use in other models of the MDA.
- The requirements of the CIM must be traceable to the artifacts of the PIM and the PSM, and vice versa.
- CIM can include several models, some providing more details than others or focused on specific preoccupations.

3.2. Architecture of CIM in our Approach

According to Xavier Blanc [20], in a wider context, the requirements model (CIM) is considered as a complex entity, constituted by a glossary, the definitions of business processes, the requirements, and the use cases as well as a systemic view of application.

By analyzing the related works previously presented, there is no consensus on the number and types of elements constituting the CIM. In order to propose an appropriate CIM from previous requirements, our proposal suggests that the CIM must compose of two models: the BPMN Diagram, to describe the different business processes represented by different sequences of activities, and the use cases diagram

(UCD) allowing in turn the description of the requirements in the CIM level.

The system, at this level, is seen as black box to ensure the independence of any computation by hiding the details of the structure of the system.

A refinement between the two models (BPMN and UC) allows us, on one hand, to have the same vision between domain experts and technological ones and on the other hand to validate the CIM level before any transformation into the low levels of MDA.

3.2.1. Business Process Diagram (BPD)

A business process represents the interactions in the form of exchange of information between various actors: humans, applications or services and third-party processes.

Business Process Model and Notation (BPMN) is a graphical notation used to specify and to model business processes. Its main objective is to provide a standard notation that is easily understandable by all actors of the organization. It is a business model using a simple notation for domain practitioners, facilitating communication between experts of the domain and requirements, and technical experts. It shows the system in its environment.

The BPMN model called BDP (Business Process Diagram) consists of a small set of graphic elements classed into four categories: Flow Objects, Connecting Objects, Swimlanes and Artifacts [21].

Figure 3 illustrates the main fragment of the BPMN metamodel.

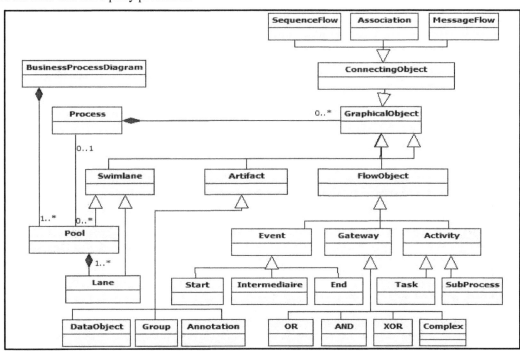

Figure 3. Main fragment of the meta-model BPMN

3.2.2. Use Cases Model (UML UC)

Use case diagrams allow identifying the features of a system and the conditions for their good functioning. They show functional elements, actors and objects in interaction. To this end, a use case diagram contains actors and use cases.

An actor is an entity that can interact with the system; whereas, a use case is a set of interactions between some actors and the system under development.

UML (Unified Modeling Language) defines a use case as : "the specification of a set of actions performed by a system, which yields an observable result that is, typically, of value for one or more actors or other stakeholders of the system" [5].

The use cases are not enchained. There is no temporal representation in a use case diagram. Each use case can be described in detail, describing the interactions between actors and the system, and the order in which they occur.

Several techniques exist for the detailed description of a use case, such as state machines, activity diagrams, or informal text. For our proposed method, we use the textual description (TD) of use cases that we formalize using SBVR (Semantic Business Vocabulary and Business Rules) [22].

We adopt the use cases diagrams for several reasons:

- Use cases diagrams play a very important role for the identification of the requirements of the users. They describe exhaustively the functional requirements of the system.
- Because of their simplicity, the analysts and the developers are familiar with the use of the use cases diagrams.
- The existence of the development process guided by the different cases, such as the Unified Process (UP) described by the authors of UML [23] and the Rational Unified Process (RUP) [24] that adheres to good

development practices observed in the industry for their success.

A simplified version of the metamodel of a use case

diagram is shown in figure 4, and the figure 5 illustrates the main fragment of the SBVR metamodel.

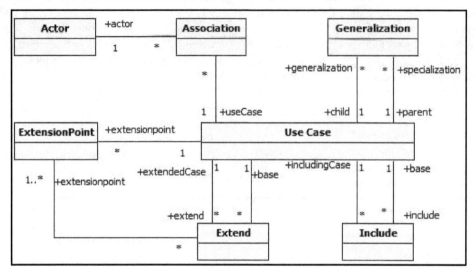

Figure 4. *Main fragment of the meta-model UC*

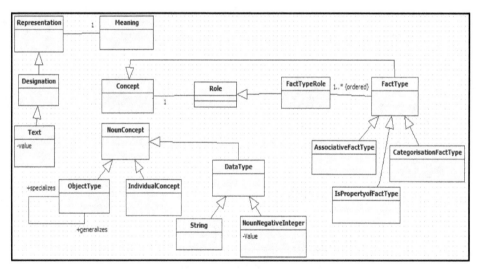

Figure 5. *Main fragment of the meta-model SBVR*

4. PIM Architecture

In previous section, we have presented the structure of the CIM proposed for our method, but the goal of our approach does not stop here. It must identify also the structure of the PIM, which can be used as a result of the development process, and define the transformation enabling to generate it automatically from the CIM. In this section, we define the adequate structure of the PIM that can easily integrate the development process. This PIM should be generated automatically through a transformation mechanism that we are going to define in section 5. Also, it must be generic capable of being transmitted to the PSM model.

4.1. Specifications of the PIM Model According to the OMG

According to the OMG [1], the PIM model must meet the

following requirements:

- The PIM represents a viewpoint of the system independently of any platform. Therefore may be appropriate for use with the similar platforms.
- The PIM describes the system, but doesn't show details on the use of its platform.
- A PIM can be adapted to a particular architectural style or more.
- The independence of PIM with respect platform can be achieved using a "technology-neutral virtual machine".
- The PIM will be transformed to the PSM.

In summary, the PIM is a view of a system without any knowledge of the implementation details. It describes the information system, but hides the details on the use of technologies that will be used to deploy the application. There are several levels of PIM but all are independent of any platform. PIM can integrate technological and architectural aspects but always without platform-specific details. It can contain, for example, information about security, persistence, etc. That allows more precisely to project the PIM model towards a specific model PSM.

4.2. Architecture of the PIM Model in Our Approach

The PIM, called Model of analysis and design, represents the business logic specific for a system. It depicts the functioning of entities and services. It must be sustainable over time.

The UML language is imposed today as a reference for realizing all analysis and design models. At this level we are interested in an abstract design, realizable without any knowledge of the techniques implementation. Thus, the application of the design patterns or the GoF (Gang of Four) is part of this stage of design. Nevertheless, the application of technical patterns, specific for some platforms, corresponds to a next step [20].

So, an adequate PIM should represent two aspects of the system:

- The structural aspect (static) of the system using classes, objects, attributes, operations, relations, etc.
- The behavioral aspect of the system showing the interactions between objects, etc.

At this level, the formalism used to express the PIM is a domain class diagram coupled with a system sequence diagram expressed in UML.

4.2.1. Domain Classes Diagram (DCD)

A domain model is not a description of software objects but a visualization of the concepts of a real-world domain. We speak about the analysis objects. It is possible that an analysis object becomes a software object during the design, but this is not systematic.

Domain class diagram should not be confused with a design class diagram. A domain class diagram can be enriched with methods obtained from the different interaction diagrams, such as the sequence diagram or a state-machine diagram for obtaining the design class diagram that contains classes with the signatures of their methods.

An UML class diagram will be used to represent the domain model. It can contain only the classes and some attributes without specification of the operations.

The domain class diagram represents in our approach the static view of the PIM.

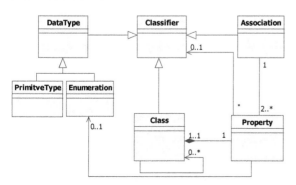

Figure 6. *Simplified metamodel of Domain Class Diagram*

4.2.2. System Sequence Diagram (SSD)

The objective of the system sequence diagrams (DSS) is to describe the behavior of the system where it is seen as a 'black box' (from the analysis point of view). The system is thus seen from the outside (by actors) without prejudice to how it will be achieved. The 'black box' will be open (described) to a subsequent design phase. The process of a use case will be described as a sequence of messages exchanged between the actors and the system.

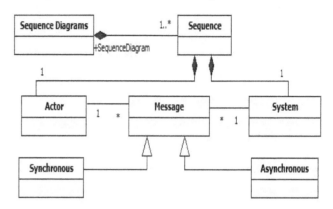

Figure 7. *Main fragment of the System Sequence Diagram Meta-model*

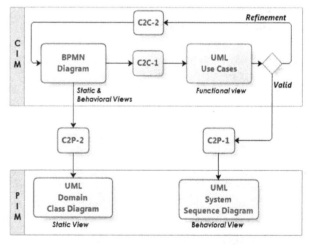

Figure 8. *Overview of the process of transformation of the CIM to PIM*

5. Steps of Transformation Approach from CIM to PIM

This section presents the approach for CIM modeling and its transformation to the PIM model.

Our approach consists of three steps:

- Step 1: Modeling CIM through the BPMN model (BPD) and the of use cases model (UML UC) obtained by the horizontal transformation CIM2CIM (figure 9) from the first model BPD.
- Step 2: Obtain from the CIM, the behavioral view of the PIM represented by a System Sequence Diagram (UML SSD). This step is assured by the vertical transformation CIM2PIM noted C2P1 in the remainder of the paper, as shown in figure 8. This step has been detailed in our

contribution [25].

- Step 3: Generate the static view of the PIM that is represented by a Domain Class Diagram (UML DCD) from the CIM. This part of the PIM is the result of a vertical transformation CIM2PIM designated C2P2 in this paper, as shown in figure 8. This step was presented in our article [26].

Any stage of transformation in our approach will be carried out as follows:

- Defining the rules of transformations of the source to the model target.
- Expression of the transformation rules.
- Application of transformation rules.

Thus, the transformation process takes as input a source model, performs the transformation rules and produces output as a target model.

It has opted for the use of the QVT standard for the expression of the transformation rules. An example of written language QVT transformation rule is presented as an example in table 99.

5.1. CIM Modelling

At the CIM level, two essential roles are distinguished. The business analyst is responsible for developing business processes diagrams without taking into account the technical aspects, and the computer expert that takes the responsibility to add the information necessary for the transcription of models in an execution language.

The CIM modeling begins with the representation of business processes via a BPMN diagram, then its horizontal transformation towards a use cases diagram detailed (UML UC), through the C2C1 transformation.

In order to have a common understanding of the system by business experts and technical experts, and do not drop system requirements, we propose a CIM refinement by a second exogenous horizontal transformation C2C2 of the UML-UC model to BMPN model (BPD). By this step, we try to validate the CIM model before any vertical transformation to the PIM level.

5.1.1. Business Processes Representation in Our Approach: BPD

For our approach, business processes are supposed to be defined. They should be formalized (modeled) if they are not already realized. We propose for that purpose to use the BPMN specification for modeling the business processes. It is done by grouping the components of the various business processes in one diagram of process BPD (Business Process Diagram).

5.1.2. Transformation from BPD to UCD: C2C1

The C2C1 is a horizontal and exogenous transformation that consists of transforming a BPMN model conforms to its metamodel towards a use cases model conforms to its meta-model.

This transformation is based on transformation rules written in the QVT standard. The transformation process takes as input a source model, executes the transformation rules and produces output as a target model. This consists of:

- Defining a mapping between the elements of the BPD and the elements of the use cases diagram.
- Performing the mapping using the model transformation language QVT.

The proposed mapping rules are based on the equivalence between the BPMN concepts and the UC concepts. The mapping used for this transformation is presented in table 1.

A detailed description of the first rule presented in table 2.

Table 1. BPMN2UC Transformation Rules

Rule	Transformation Rule	Source Model Element	Target Model Element
1	Pool2Actor	Pool	Actor
2	Lane2Actor	Lane	Actor
3	Lane. within. Pool 2 Generalization	Pool that contain Lanes	Actor(Pool) is a generalization of Actor(Lane)
4	Activity2UC	Activity (Sub-Process or Activity of type task)	Use Case
5	Activity. In. Swimlane 2Association	Activity (Sub-Process or Activity of type task) within a swimlane	Association between actor corresponding to swimlane and UC corresponding to Activity
6	Sequence Flow Or Message Flow 2 include	Flow	include
7	Gateway2extend	Decision Gateway	Extend between the related activities
For each activity type sub-processes			
8	Task. In. Actor. Swimlane 2 Message From Actor ToSys	Task in Actor swimlane performed by Actor	System Event (Message sent to System)
9	Task. In. System. Swimlane 2 System Response	Task in System Swimlane oriented Actor	System Response (Response Message from the System to Actor)
After each Decision Gateway within sub-processes			
10	Successful Flow 2 Event	Successful Flow	System Event Or System Response (Rules 8 & 9)
11	Alternative Flow 2 Alternative Scenario	Alternative Flow that terminate Sup-Process correctly	Alternative Scenario
12	Error Flow 2 Error Scenario	Error Flow that terminate Sup-Process with errors	Error Scenario

Table 2. QVT code of the first rule

Rule 1: Pool2Actor

Source Model Element	: Pool
Target Model Element	: Actor

Description:

In BPMN 2.0 [21] a "Pool" is a participant in a collaboration diagram. It can contain details or not. With details, it is a process. Without details, it acts as a simple 'black box '.

An actor is a user type that always has the same behavior to a use case. The same physical person may behave in as many different players as the number of roles it plays towards the system. Thus for example, a messaging system administrator might also be the same mail user. It will be considered as an actor of the system: in the role of administrator, in the first hand, and in the role of user in the second hand. An actor can also be an external system with which the use case will interact (Gabay & Gabay, 2008).

Therefore each "Pool" of the BPMN will be transformed into an "Actor" actor in the UC.

QVT Rule:

```
mapping Pool::PooltoActor (): Actor
{result.name: = self.name;}
result.UseCase += self.Activities.map
ActivitytoUseCase();
result.ChildActor += self.lanes.map
LanetoActor(); }
```

5.1.3. Transformation from UCD to BPD: C2C2

The C2C$_2$ is a horizontal and exogenous transformation that consists of transforming a use cases model conforms to its meta-model to a BPMN model conforms to its metamodel. Table 3 summarizes the rules used for C2C$_2$ transformation.

Table 3. Use-Case to BPMN transformation QVT rule

Rule	Transformation Rule	Source Model Element	Target Model Element
1	Actor2Lane	Actor	Lane
2	UC2Activity	Use Case	Activity (Sub-Process or Activity of type task)
3	Include2 SequenceFlow	include	Sequence Flow
4	Include 2MessageFlow	Include	Message Flow

5.2. Obtaining the PIM Behavioral Model from the CIM

The use case model obtained in the first step constitutes the source of the CIM2PIM transformation, subsequently noted C2P$_1$, allowing the production of the model representing the dynamic part of the PIM.

C2P$_1$ is an exogenous and vertical transformation which consists of transforming the UML-UC that is conformed to its metamodel to a system sequence model which is conformed to its metamodel. Thus, this transformation consists of defining a mapping between the elements of the UC model and elements representing the system sequence diagram, and then to express the corresponding QVT transformation rules. The proposed mapping rules are based on the equivalence between the concepts of UML UC and the concepts of the SSD. This mapping is presented in table 4.

Table 4. UC2SSD Transformation Rules

Rule	Transformation Rule	Source Model Element	Target Model Element
1	UseCase2SSD	Use Case	SSD
2	Principal Actor 2Actor	Actor that directly operates on the System	Actor
3	System Event 2 System Message	System Event (Message sent to System)	Message sent From Actor to System
4	Sys Response 2SystemMessage	System Response (Response Message from the System to Actor)	Message sent From System to Actor
5	Internal Task 2 Internal Message	Non-related system task to actor	Internal System Message
6	Alternative Scenario 2 Alt	Alternative Scenario	Interaction Fragment 'Alt'
7	Error Scenario 2 Break	Error Scenario	Interaction Fragment 'Break'

5.3. Obtaining the PIM Static Model from the CIM

The CIM2PIM transformation, noted subsequently C2P$_2$, is defined by 6 transformation rules illustrated in table 4. This exogenous and vertical transformation aims at transforming the BPMN model that is conformed to its metamodel to a domain classes model (UML DCD) which is conformed to its metamodel. It specifies how one or more elements of the BPMN model (source model) are transformed into one or more elements of the UML-DCD model (target model).

The proposed mapping rules are based on the equivalence between the concepts of the BPMN and the concepts of the DCD. This mapping is presented in table5.

Table 5. BPMN2DCD Transformation Rules

Rule	Transformation Rule	Source Model Element	Target Model Element
1	Pool 2 Class	Pool	Class
2	Lane 2 Class	Lane	Class
3	Lane. within. Pool 2 Aggregation	Pool that contain Lanes	Aggregation relationships between the Class derived from Pool And the Classes derived from Lanes
4	DataObject2Class	Data Object	Class
5	Activity 2 Operation	Activity	Operation attached to the corresponding analysis class at the container (Lane, Pool or Group)
6	Group 2 Class	Group	Class

6. Case Study

With the aim to illustrate our method by an example, we have taken our case study presented in our previous works [25, 26]. This example is based on a business process of enrollment system for training in a school. It models the interaction between customers and the school.

We have a one swimlane corresponding to 'customers' and another one for the 'school side'. However, since there are two actors involved in the former, we use a pool with two lanes, one for each actor. Thus, within the school pool there is a lane for an 'Assistant' and another for 'Financial Services'. Figure 9 depicts the process of our case study, whereas figure 10 presents the detail of the first Sub-Process 'Choose Training' using Data Objects as an example. It employs two Pools, one for a customer and another one for a system. In the same way we can represent the other sub-processes: 'Order Training', 'Payment', and 'Training Schedule'.

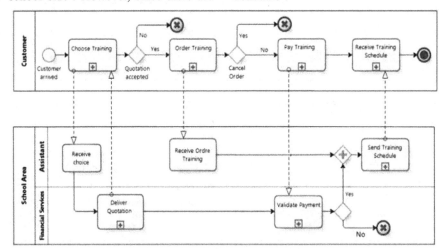

Figure 9. Business Process Diagram of the case study "enrollment system for training"

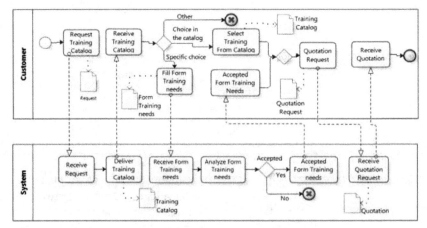

Figure 10. Diagram of Sub-Process "Choose Training"

Table 6. BPMN2UC Transformation Rules for the case study

Rule		Use Cases Element
1	Pool 2 Actor	Customer, School Area
2	Lane 2 Actor	Assistant, Financial Services
3	Lane. within. Pool 2 Generalization	'School Area' Actor is a generalization for 'Assistant' actor and 'Financial Services' actor
4	Activity 2 UC	Choose Training, Order Training, Pay Training, Receive Training Schedule, Receive Choice, Receive Order Training, Send Schedule, Deliver Quotation, Validate Payment
5	Activity. In. Swimlane 2 Association	Each UC is associated at the Actor corresponding to the Swimlane. (For example : 'Choose Training' is associated at 'Customer')
6	Sequence Flow Or Message Flow 2 include	'Receive Choice' include 'Choose Training' 'Deliver Quotation' include 'Receive Choice'', …
7	Gateway 2 extend	'Choose Training' extend 'Order Training' 'Order Training' extend 'Pay Training' 'Validate Payment' extend 'Send Schedule'
8	Task. In. Actor. Swimlane 2 Message From Actor ToSys	Request Training Catalog Fill Form Training needs Quotation Request
9	Task. In. System. Swimlane 2 System Response	Deliver Training Catalog, Accepted Form Training, Quotation Deliver
10	Successful Flow 2 Event	Choice in Catalog
11	Alternative Flow 2 Alternative Scenario	Specific Choice
12	Error Flow2 Error Scenario	Cancel Choice

The Use Cases Diagram obtained by applying the C2C$_1$ transformation rules is shown in figure 11 below. Table 12 shows the C2P$_1$ transformation rules corresponding to a Sub-Process "choose training".

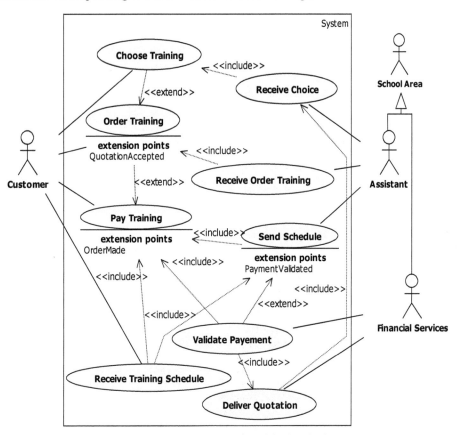

Figure 11. Use Cases Diagram of the Case Study

Table 7. UC2SSD Transformation Rules for the case study corresponding at the UC "Choose Training"

Rule		SSD Element
1	Use Case 2 SSD	SSD_ Choose_ Training
2	Principal Actor 2 Actor	Customer
3	System Event 2System Message	se1. Request Training Catalog() se2. Form Training Needs() se3. Quotation Request()
4	Sys Response 2 System Message	sr1. Deliver Training Catalog() sr2. Accepted Form Training() sr3. Qoutation Deliver()
5	Internal Task 2 Internal Message	se2.1. Analyze Form()
6	Alternative Scenario 2 Alt	Interaction Fragment 'Alt'
7	Error Scenario 2 Break	Interaction Fragment 'Break'

Figure 13 depicts the SSD obtained from a Use Cases Diagram by applying the C2P1 transformation rules.

Figure 12. The SSD of the Pay Training Use Case

The C2P transformation rules corresponding to our case study are presented in table 8 below.

Table 8. BPMN2DCD Transformation Rules for the case study

Rule		DCD Element
1	Pool 2 Class	Customer
2	Lane 2 Class	Assistant, Financial Service
3	Lane. within. Pool 2 Aggregation	Aggregation relationships between School Area And Assistant Aggregation relationships between School Area And Financial Service
4	Data Object 2 Class	Request Training Catalog, Training Catalog, Form Training Needs, Quotation Request, Quotation, Order Training, Payment, Training Schedule
5	Activity 2 Operation	*Operations of Customer :* Choose Training(), Order Training(), Receive Training(), *Operations of Assistant :* Receive Choice(), Receive Order Training(), Send Training(); *Operations of Finance Service :* Deliver Quotation(); Validate Pay()

Figure 14 show the Domain Class Diagram obtained by applying the C2P2 transformation rules.

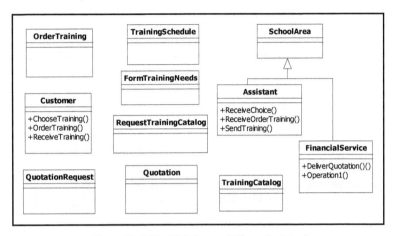

Figure 13. DCD of Sub-Process "Choose Training"

7. Analysis and Evaluation

According to our previous work [27], we have announced that an ideal method for modeling the CIM and its transformation into PIM should have the following characteristics:

- The CIM modeling should cover the different views of the business domain: static, dynamic and functional.
- Generating the PIM model -representing the structural and behavioral aspects of the system- from the CIM

- The CIM to PIM transformation should be automated, taking into account the traceability and offering the entire transformation rules.

The evaluation is based on the criteria that we have defined in the paper [27] in order to evaluate different methods which propose to model CIM and transform it into PIM.

The results of the evaluation are presented in table 9. The rows in the table design the studied methods and each column in the table represents an evaluation criterion.

Table 9. Results of the evaluation

Methods Studied	CIM coverage			PIM completeness		CIM to PIM transformation		
	Business Objects (Static View)	Business Process (Behavioral View)	Requirement (Functional View)	Structural aspect	Behavioral aspect	Automation	Traceability CIM to PIM	Completeness of transformation Rules
Kherraf and al. [7]	N	Y	Y	Y	N	P	P	N
Bousetta and al. [15]	P	Y	Y	Y	Y	P	P	P
Kardoš and al. [12]	N	P	N	Y	Y	P	N	N
Rodríguez and al. [9, 10, 11]	N	Y	Y	Y	Y	P	P	P
Wu and al.[14]	P	Y	Y	Y	Y	N	N	P
Zhang and al. [8]	N	Y	N	Y	N	P	Y	P
Fatolahi and al. [13]	Y	N	Y	Y	Y	P	N	N
Sharifi and al. [16]	Y	N	Y					
Erika and al. [17, 18, 19]	Y	N	Y					
Our Approach	Y	Y	Y	Y	Y	Y	Y	Y

Legend: Y: Yes; N: No; P: Partial

By analyzing the different results obtained, we conclude that only the method of the paper [15] which remains close to the ideal description of a method allowing the building of the CIM and transforming it to the PIM. Our proposal complements this method, by satisfying all the requirements needed during the construction of the CIM and its transformation into PIM.

8. Conclusion and Future Work

This paper proposes an approach for CIM modeling and its

transformation into PIM based on three steps:

- Representing the CIM by BPMN model and use cases model that covers the static, the behavioral and the functional views of the system. The transition from one model to another is provided by a horizontal model transformation.
- Obtaining from the CIM the behavioral view of the PIM. This step is assured by a vertical transformation from use cases model to a system sequence diagram.
- Generating from the PIM the static view of the PIM. This step is the result of a vertical transformation from

BPMN model to a Domain Class Diagram.

In order to make transformations automatic, we have developed all the transformation rules involved in this paper using the QVT language.

Future works aim at developing a tool that supports all the transformations performed in this paper.

References

[1]   J. Miller and J. Mukerji, "MDA Guide Version 1.0.1.," OMG, 2003.

[2]   R. Soley, «Model driven architecture (mda), draft 3.2. Rapport technique, disponible sur: http://www.omg.org/cgi-bin/doc?omg/00-11-05,» 2000.

[3]   OMG, "Meta Object Facility (MOF)2.0 Query/View/Transformation Specification, http://www.omg.org/spec/QVT/1.0/PDF," 2009.

[4]   S. A. White, "Introduction to BPMN," *IBM Cooperation,* pp. 2008-029, 2004.

[5]   OMG, "OMG Unified Modeling LanguageTM (OMG UML), Superstructure, http://www.omg.org/spec/UML/2.4.1/Superstructure," August 2011.

[6]   S. A. White, "Process Modelling Notations and Workflow Patterns, http://www.omg.org /bp-corner/bp-files/Process_Modeling_Notations.pdf," IBM Corporation, 2004.

[7]   S. Kherraf, E. Lefebvre and W. Suryn, "Transformation from CIM to PIM Using Patterns and Archetypes," in *19th Australian Conference on Software Engineering*, 2008.

[8]   W. Zhang, H. Mei, H. Zhao and J. and Yang, "Transformation from CIM to PIM: A Feature-Oriented Component-Based Approach," in *Model Driven Engineering Languages and Systems volume 3713 of Lecture Notes in Computer Science, pages 248–263*, Springer Berlin / Heidelberg, 2005.

[9]   A. Rodríguez, E. Fernández-Medina and M. Piattini, "Towards obtaining analysis-level class and use case diagrams from business process models," *Advances in Conceptual Modeling–Challenges and Opportunities. Springer Berlin Heidelberg.,* pp. 103-112, 2008.

[10]   A. Rodríguez, I. G.-R. de Guzmán, E. Fernández-Medina and M. Piattini, "Semi-formal transformation of secure business processes into analysis class and use case models: An mda approach," in *Information and Software Technology, 52(9):945– 971,* 2010.

[11]   A. Rodríguez, E. Fernández-Medina, J. Trujillo and M. Piattini, "Secure business process model specification through a UML 2.0 activity diagram profile," *Decision Support Systems,* vol. 51, no. 3, pp. 446-465, 2011.

[12]   M. Kardoš and M. Drozdová, "Analytical method of CIM to PIM transformation in Model Driven Architecture (MDA)," *Journal Of Information And Organizational Sciences,* vol. 34, pp. 89-99, 2010.

[13]   A. Fatolahi, S. S. Somé and T. C. Lethbridge, "Towards a semi-automated model-driven method for the generation of web-based applications from use cases," in *4th Model Driven Web Engineering Workshop (p. 31)*, 2008.

[14]   J. H. Wu, S. S. Shin, J. L. Chien, W. S. Chao and M. C. Hsieh, "An extended MDA method for user interface modeling and transformation," in *The 15th European Conference on Information Systems (pp. 1632-1641).*, June 2007.

[15]   B. Bousetta, O. El Beggar and T. Gadi, "A methodology for CIM modelling and its transformation to PIM," *Journal of Information Engineering and Applications,* vol. 3, no. 2, pp. 1-21, 2013.

[16]   H. R. Sharifi and M. Mohsenzadeh, "A New Method for Generating CIM Using Business and Requirement Models.," *World of Computer Science and Information Technology Journal (WCSIT),* vol. 2, no. 1, pp. 8-12, 2012.

[17]   J. Osis, E. Asnina and A. Grave, "Computation Independent Modeling within the MDA," in *Software-Science, Technology & Engineering, 2007. SwSTE 2007. IEEE International Conference on (pp. 22-34). IEEE,* October 2007.

[18]   J. Osis, E. Asnina and A. Grave, "Formal computation independent model of the problem domain within the MDA," in *Proceedings of the 10th International Conference on Information System Implementation and Modeling (pp. 23-25),* April 2007.

[19]   J. Osis, E. Asnina and A. Grave, "Computation independent representation of the problem domain," in *MDA. J. Software Eng, 2(1), 19-46.,* 2008.

[20]   B. Xavier, MDA en Action : Ingénirie Logicielles Dirigée par les Modèles, Paris: Eyrolles, 2005.

[21]   OMG, «Business Process Model and Notation (BPMN), Version 2.0.1,» OMG, http://www.omg.org/spec/BPMN, September 2013.

[22]   OMG, "OMG Unified Modeling LanguageTM (OMG UML), Superstructure, http://www.omg.org/spec/UML/2.4.1/Superstructure," August 2011.

[23]   OMG, «Semantics of Business vocabulary and Rules,» 2008. [En ligne].

[24]   I. Jacobson, G. Booc et J. Rumbaugh, Le Processus unifié de développement logicie, Eyrolles, 2000.

[25]   P. Kruchte, The rational Unified Process An introduction, Addison-WESLEY, 2000.

[26]   A. Kriouile, T. Gadi, N. ADDAMSSIRI et A. El Khadimi, «Obtaining behavioral model of PIM from the CIM,» *Multimedia Computing and Systems (ICMCS), 2014 International Conference on. IEEE,* pp. 949-954., 2014.

[27]   A. Kriouile, N. Addamssiri, T. Gadi et Y. Balouki, «Getting the Static Model of PIM from the CIM,» chez *3rd Colloquium IEEE on Information Science and Technology (CiSt'14)*, Tetuan, 2014.

[28]   A. Kriouile, T. Gadi and Y. Balouki, "CIM to PIM Transformation: A criteria Based Evaluation," *IJCTA,* vol. Vol 4 (4), no. ISSSN:2229-6093, pp. 616-625, July-August 2013.

23

Comparisons Between MongoDB and MS-SQL Databases on the TWC Website

Chieh Ming Wu[1], Yin Fu Huang[2], John Lee[3]

[1]Dept. of Computer Science, Taiwan Water Corporation, Taichung City, Taiwan
[2]School of Computer Science & Information Engineering, National Yunlin University of Science and Technology, Douliou, Yunlin, Taiwan
[3]Dept. of Sales, Formula Chemicals Corporation, New Taipei City, Shulin District, Taiwan

Email address:
g9210822@gmail.com (C. M. Wu), huangyf@yuntech.edu.tw (Y. F. Huang), jtlinternational@hotmail.com (J. Lee)

Abstract: Owing to the huge amount of data in websites to be analysed, web innovative services are required to support them with high scalability and availability. The main reason of using NoSQL databases is for considering the huge amount of data and expressing large-scale distributed computations using Map-Reduce techniques. To enhance the service quality of customers and solve the problems of the huge amount of data existing in the websites such as Facebook, Google, and Twitter, the relational database technology was gradually replaced with the NoSQL database to improve the performance and expansion elasticity in recent years. In this paper, we compare both NoSQL MongoDB and MS-SQL databases, and discuss the effectiveness of the inquiry. In addition, relational database cluster systems often require larger server efficiency and capacity to be competent, but it incurs cost problems. On the other hand, using NoSQL database can easily expand the capacity without any extra costs. Through the experiments, it shows that NoSQL MongoDB is about ten times efficient for reading and writing than MS-SQL database. This verifies that the NoSQL database technology is quite a feasible option to be used in the future.

Keywords: NoSQL, MS-SQL, MongoDB, Relational Database

1. Introduction

The term "NoSQL" first made its appearance by Carlo Strozzi in the late 90s as the name of an open-source relational database and there is no relationship between and NoSQL currently in use. The usage of "NoSQL" that we recognize today traces back to a meetup on June 11, 2009 in San Francisco organized by Johan Oskarsson, a software developer based in London. They want to organize a discussion of the different ways of data storage, that can make these people interested in brainstorming together, "NoSQL" name eventually provided by Eric Evans made a name for this party [9].

NoSQL is a non-relational database management systems, it really means "Not Only SQL" and significant difference from traditional relational database management systems (RDBMS) in some ways. It is designed for distributed data stores where very large scale of data storing needs. The data object model may not require fixed schema, avoid join operations and typically scale horizontally. In other word, we can use both SQL and NoSQL database to achieve optimal results. For example, we can use NoSQL database to store huge amounts of unstructured data and store structured data using SQL database, so that can make good use of SQL syntax.

The main reason we have chosen MongoDB to do in this paper is that MongoDB is a document-oriented database and it uses JSON objects for data storing. In the Hadoop platform, regardless of the huge or small amount of data, all can be effective by management. If it's a small amount of data, then the performance of a single node has faster performance than in a multi-node cluster, and vice versa, which means that we must be manually set to one or more nodes in the cluster. MongoDB is stored in JSON format in the database, including tables are called collections and rows of JSON objects are stored as documents, so we can use MongoDB to store structured data, MongoDB also supports query operation for database, so for the relation database management system has a better alternative [7].

This paper uses MongoDB to store website message and implement the user interface. Finally, we compare the reading and writing performance between NoSQL MongoDB and MS-SQL, and found the NoSQL MongoDB is faster (efficient) than MS-SQL in speed through the experiment data.

2. Related Work

Data aggregation is one of the important functions used in the database, especially in the face of business intelligence (such as ETL, OLAP) and Data Mining applications. In relational database, aggregation is used for more in-depth analysis in visualizing data. However, it is very difficult for the memory consumption on the huge amount of data and the calculation time [9].

As in [1], the authors use the files in the NoSQL MongoDB database [3], using its MapReduce algorithm to assist in processing large amounts of data. MapReduce [2] is a very popular program mode; 2004 Google use it to manage large amounts of data. This model has two primitive functions: Map and Reduce. Map is a function, and the value of the input is a single aggregation, while the value of the output is a key-value pairs. These applications are independent of each other, so you can build efficient and safe Map tasks that are parallelized operations on each node.

MongoDB can store huge amount of website information, and these messages can be unstructured. Compared to the relational database in the practical applications, MongoDB is more flexible. Same as the relational database, MongoDB entity may have multiple databases and for each database can have multiple collections. There is a big challenge for traditional relational database in face the rapid development of internet web 2.0 technologies. In [4], the authors propose the MongoDB Auto-Sharding architecture in order to response to the rapid development of internet web 2.0 technology in the cloud environment. The Auto-Sharding main objective is that it does not require a larger or stronger machine and is able to take responsibility for split data on distribution and automatic balancing to store more data and handle more load. They propose a FODO algorithm to improve the balance of the original algorithm so you can balance between effective data server and enhance the cluster effectiveness of parallel reading and writing.

In [10], the authors propose a mechanism for automatic load balancing MongoDB, and using heat-based automatic load balancing mechanism to reduce costs. Some studies have proposed a NoSQL MongoDB allow seamless support for JDBC SQL on the MongoDB database queries, and provide a virtual architecture allowing users to query and merge information from NoSQL and RDBMS. The main approach is to convert a single SQL query syntax to the APIs on NoSQL [5]. There is research study parsing LINQ query into MongoDB collection and rewrites them for MongoDB API format. The rewritten query execution on MongoDB and the returned results are converted to in-memory data structure, and then processed by JSINQ, reached the capacity by query MongoDB with LINQ [6]. Some studies explore the MongoDB data insertion time performance, in [7], the authors point out that both in writing or reading on the job, MongoDB performance come much better than MySQL.

3. Methods

3.1. Motivation

Because of the rapid growth rate of the huge amount of data in web application, the traditional RDBMS cannot be applied for several GB of data growth, and therefore NoSQL has been used to solving RDBMS Problem when maxed above limit. There are many management information systems in Taiwan Water Corporation (TWC). Some systems will also face the problem of huge amount of data bursts. NoSQL provides a much more elastic, schemaless data model that suitable maps to an application's data organization and simplifies the interaction between the application and the database resulting in less code to write, debug, and maintain. That is why we choose the best NoSQL solutions for this job.

3.2. Background

Learn MongoDB can help us to manage the huge amounts of data from a web application; a document-oriented database. We also found the MongoDB is indeed a reliable and efficient system. MongoDB allows almost unlimited horizontal expansion. This paper uses JAVA to deal with JSON file that is language-independent configuration files. To process records in MongoDB is simpler than in RDBMS and more flexible. MongoDB is very powerful and use the document to the basic unit of database, and it is a collection of schema-free database. An independent MongoDB entity can manage multiple databases and it has a powerful JavaScript command line interface.

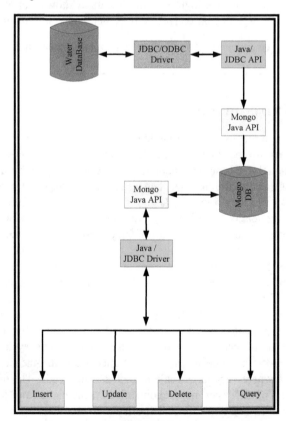

Fig. 1. System Framework.

This paper uses of JAVA programming language to read the related messages from the website in TWC, and insert the messages into the MongoDB database to further implement the relevant data processing functions, such as insert、query、delete and update functions. Fig.1 uses the JAVA JDBC DRIVER to capture the data from TWC website, using the JAVA DRIVER and MongoDB API to insert data into MongoDB database and implement various functions. Fig.2 shows the insert、update and delete functions by use JAVA syntax.

```java
public void INSERTforMongoDB() throws UnknownHostException
{

    BasicDBObject doc=new BasicDBObject();
    doc.put("NOs", nost.getText());
    doc.put("reason", reasont.getText());
    doc.put("range", ranget.getText());
    doc.put("bulletin", buetint.getText());
    doc.put("restore", restoret.getText());
    coll.insert(doc);
    coll.setWriteConcern(WriteConcern.SAFE);
    text.append(doc+"\n");
    text.append("Data Inserted OK \n");


}
```

```java
public void DELETEforMongoDB() throws UnknownHostException
{

    BasicDBObject QueryDel=new BasicDBObject();
    QueryDel.put("NOs", nost.getText());
    DBObject removeObj=coll.findAndRemove(QueryDel);
    text.append(removeObj+"\n");
    text.append("Above Data Deleted OK \n");
    mongodbCONNECTION();

}

public void UPDATEforMongoDB() throws UnknownHostException
{

    BasicDBObject QueryUPDATE=new BasicDBObject();
    QueryUPDATE.put("NOs", nost.getText());
    DBObject findObj=coll.findOne(QueryUPDATE);
    findObj.put("NOs", nost.getText());
    findObj.put("reason", reasont.getText());
    findObj.put("range", ranget.getText());
    findObj.put("bulletin", buetint.getText());
    findObj.put("restore", restoret.getText());
    coll.update(QueryUPDATE,findObj);
    text.append(findObj+"\n");
    text.append("Above Data Updated OK \n");

}
```

Fig. 2. *The insert delete update function for JAVA.*

3.3. Query

MongoDB provides find and findOne function to perform the ad hoc query in the database. We can use $lt, $lte, $gt, $gte comparison operator to do the scope of the query. It may also use $OR, $NOT. etc to enhance criteria query. Fig.3 shows use of $OR to query the water suspension number and/or reason and range of influence, and as long as one of the inputs meet the conditions, you can find the relevant information.

```java
public void QUERYforMongoDB() throws UnknownHostException
{

    DBObject clause1 = new BasicDBObject("NOs", nost.getText());
    DBObject clause2 = new BasicDBObject("reason", reasont.getText());
    DBObject clause3 = new BasicDBObject("range", ranget.getText());
    text.append(clause1.toString());
    text.append(clause2.toString()+"\n");
    text.append(clause3.toString()+"\n");
    BasicDBList or = new BasicDBList();
    or.add(clause1);
    or.add(clause2);
    or.add(clause3);
    DBObject query = new BasicDBObject("$or", or);
    text.append(query.toString()+"\n");
    cur = coll.find(query);
    DBObject str1= cur.next();
    String NOS=(String) str1.get("NOs");
    String reason=(String) str1.get("reason");
    String range=(String) str1.get("range");
    String stop=(String) str1.get("stop");
    String bulletin=(String) str1.get("bulletin");
    String restore=(String) str1.get("restore");
    setFText(NOS,reason,range,stop,bulletin,restore);

}
```

Fig. 3. *Using $OR condition to query.*

3.4. Indexing

Like a book's index that allows us to become more efficient in querying instead of looking through the whole book. Indexing database is to create an entry point of a query. For example, you will often query the user name in the database, so there is necessary to build an index on the key of user name to speed up queries. The index of MongoDB and traditional relational database is almost the same (query optimization; index tuning, etc.) which requires some skills to do. This generates the command for this query as follows.

>db.people.find({"username":"wjamin"})

We can create an index based on the above query of the key (shown below).

>db.people.ensureIndex({"username":1})

The index needs to be set only once per collection. If you try to establish the same index again, nothing will happen. Indexes in MongoDB make queries run faster and more efficiently. However, indexes have their cost: for every write includes insert, update, or delete will take longer for every index you add. This is because MongoDB has to update all your indexes whenever your data changes, as well as the document itself. Thus, MongoDB limits to build 64 indexes per collection. As shown in Fig.4, we have the username index, but the server have to scan all the collection, then it can find the date. Hence, it is very time consuming for a large collection. For example, the index on "username" wouldn't help much for this sort:

>db.people.find({"date":date1}).sort({"date":1, "username":1})

So we should be indexed on the date and the username.

>db.people.ensureIndex({" date":1, "username":1})

Fig. 4. *Compound query results with increasing/decreasing sorting.*

3.5. MapReduce

MongoDB provides aggregation tools in several basic query functions. These tools starts from simple task of calculating the number of documents to complex data analysis. MongoDB provide group function which allows us to perform more complex aggregation (similar to SQL's GROUP BY). In addition, the MapReduce functions are super useful in the aggregation tool and uses JavaScript as its "query language" so it can express arbitrarily complex logic. MapReduce is an aggregation method, which can be easily on multiple servers in parallel operation. The problem will be decomposition by different nodes to solve. When all the solutions return after the completion of the node, the answers will be merged into one complete answer [3].

MapReduce uses the map and reduce. With map being a kind of corresponding relation, it will correspond to the collection of each document. A little like separating into groups. The reduce will use the map list for induction, until the list of each key reduces it to a single element. This element is returned to the shuffle step until each key has a list containing a single value. In the map corresponding to use a special emit function to return values, emit function give MapReduce a key and a value. We use average water quality of purification plant in Taiwan Water Corporation counties as an example to illustrate how to use the powerful MapReduce functions.

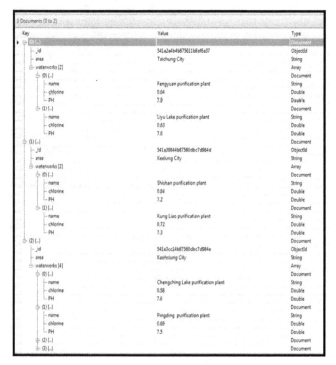

Fig. 5. *The average water quality in the JSON format.*

As shown in Fig.5, this is an average water quality data. For the convenience of description, we only input partial data and use the TAICHUNG city, KEELUNG city and KAOHSIUNG city as the key values. We want to get the average value of water quality in various PH and CHLORINE per county, and with the key values of PH and CHLORINE.

Fig. 6. *Calculate the average water quality using the MapReduce function.*

Such as Fig.6, in the Map function, that emit gives MapReduce a key like the one used by group and a value in the collection. In this case, we emit a count and some items of how many times a given key appeared in the document. The map function uses an emit function to return values that we want to process later.

>   map=function()   {for   (var idx=0;idx<this.waterworks.length;idx++){emit(this.area,{count: 1,   chlorineV: this.waterworks[idx].chlorine,PHV:this.waterworks[idx].PH})}};

Now we have little documents that associated with a key from the collection. An array of one or more of these documents will be passed to the reduce function. The reduce function is passed two arguments:key, which is the first argument from emit, and an array of one or more documents that were emitted for that key:

>Reduce=function(key, values) {var reduced = {count:0, C:0, P:0}; values.forEach(function(val) {reduced.C += val.chlorineV; reduced.P += val.PHV; reduced.count += val.count; });return reduced;}

We use the "finalize" function to send reduce's output to calculate their average value:

>Finalize=function(key, reduced) {reduced.avgchlorine = reduced.C reduced.count;reduced.avgPH = reduced.P reduced.count;return reduced;}

The result shown in Fig.7, which is grouped by counties respectively and calculating the average value. The value of "count" is the number of water purification plant. The symbol "C" is the sum of residual chlorine effectively; "P" is the sum of PH; "avgchlorine" is the average residual chlorine effectively; and "avgPH" is the average PH in the corresponding county city.

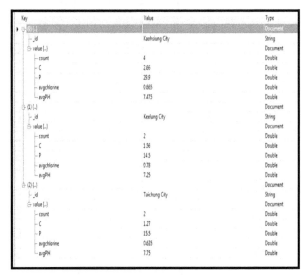

Fig. 7. *The execution result of MapReduce Function.*

4. Experimental Results

4.1. Experimental Environment and Data Sources

In this section, we evaluate the performances on a ASUS PC with Intel® Core™2 Quad CPU 2.5GHZ and 2GB main memory running Windows 7 enterprise. All the experimental data were generated randomly and stored on a local 200GB Disk. We also install the MongoDB 2.6.3 、 SQL Server 2005 Express and Eclipse IDE for Java Developers. The version is

Juno Service Release 1, the data source comes from the TWC website.

4.2. Experimental Analysis

In this paper, we use Java language to develop SQL Server and MongoDB algorithm in the Eclipse integrated environment. Fig.8 compares the efficiency of data written between MS-SQL and MongoDB under the different operation times. Through the experiments under the indexed condition, MongoDB shows itself to be nearly 10 times faster than MS-SQL in writing ability.

In Fig.9, through experiment under the indexed condition and the different operation frequency, the ability to read data in MongoDB is nearly 10 times faster than MS-SQL.

In Fig.10 and Fig.11, we have found that under the 1,000,000 operating frequency, whether MS-SQL or MongoDB, the writing performance is far better than reading. Through the experiments, we have found the performance of writing is 3-4 times faster than reading.

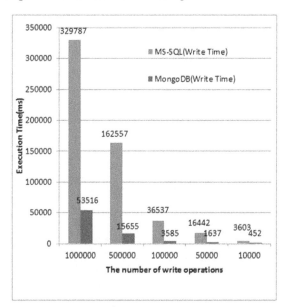

Fig. 8. *Compare the efficiency between MS-SQL and MongoDB on writing.*

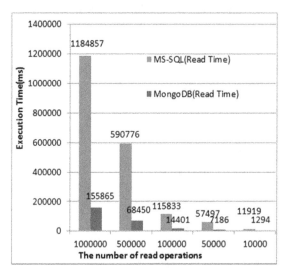

Fig. 9. *MS-SQL and MongoDB performance comparison on reading.*

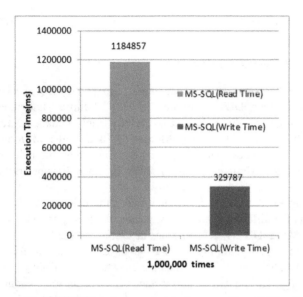

Fig. 10. *MS-SQL performance comparison on reading writing.*

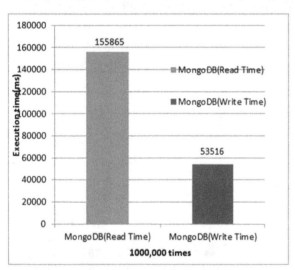

Fig. 11. *MongoDB performance comparison on reading/writing.*

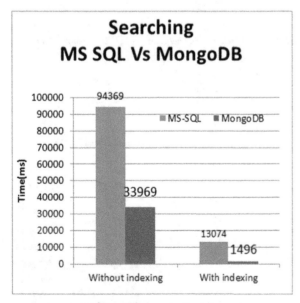

Fig. 12. *The influence of search efficiency in indexing.*

MongoDB insert or search for information is very fast. And the write performance of MongoDB or MS-SQL is better than reading efficiency. In Fig.12, under the indexed condition, the performance of searching is naturally better, especially in the MongoDB database.

In experiments using multithreading way to simultaneously read and write data to calculate their literacy effectiveness (whether it is reading or writing), Fig.13 shows that MongoDB in execution is still more efficient than MS-SQL. The experiment also found that MongoDB in a multi-threaded execution will remain stable. However, MS-SQL thread on Thread10 spends a considerable amount of time when writing, resulting in very inconsistent situations. Fig.14 effectively expresses the Thread10 exception; the maximum Y-axis set to only 100,000 in order to effectively reflect their differences.

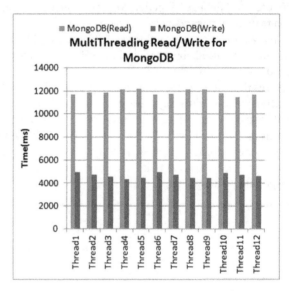

Fig. 13. *MongoDB multithreading read write performance.*

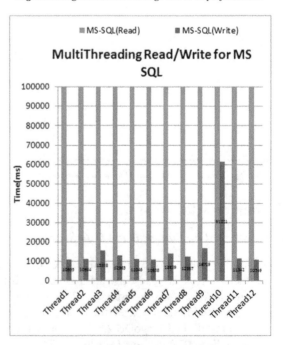

Fig. 14. *MS-SQL multithreading read write performance.*

5. Conclusions and Future Work

This paper mainly discusses the effectiveness of NoSQL; using the document-oriented NoSQL MongoDB database application to operate website message in Taiwan Water Corporation. We also use the open data of average water quality from the Taiwan Water Corporation website to illustrate MapReduce example.

We experimented various practical ways in MongoDB and use JAVA program to implement the task. In addition to the practical solution that MongoDB offers, it also has most of the internet application functions like index, replication, sharing, rich query syntax, and super elastic data model. We also compare the performance between MongoDB and MS-SQL. The results confirm the NoSQL MongoDB does have a better efficiency than MS-SQL.

Due to the popularity of the big data, the future trend for NoSQL will be based on integration. This integration will take place among the different varieties of NoSQL technologies and between SQL and NoSQL options. The convenience and the effectiveness of that integration will determine the big data applications in the enterprises (not just NoSQL technology).

References

[1] Bonnet, L.;Laurent, A.;Sala, M.;Laurent, B., REDUCE, YOU SAY: What NoSQL can do for Data Aggregation and BI in Large Repositories, 22nd International Workshop on Database and Expert Systems Applications (DEXA), pp. 483-488, 2011.

[2] J. Dean, S. Ghemawat. Mapreduce: simplified data processing on large clusters, Commun. ACM, pp.107-113, 2008.

[3] Kristina Chodorow & Michael Dirolf, MongoDB: The Definitive Guide , O'Reilly Media, 2012.

[4] Liu Yimeng; Wang Yizhi; Jin Yi, Research on The Improvement of MongoDB Auto-Sharding in Cloud Environment, 7th International Conference on Computer Science & Education (ICCSE), pp. 851- 854, 2012.

[5] Lawrence, R., Integration and Virtualization of Relational SQL and NoSQL Systems including MySQL and MongoDB, International Conference on Computational Science and Computational Intelligence, pp.285-290, 2014.

[6] Nakabasami, K.; Amagasa, T.; Kitagawa, H., "Querying MongoDB with LINQ in a Server-Side JavaScript Environment", 16th International Conference on Network-Based Information Systems (NBiS), pp.344-349, 2013.

[7] Nyati, S.S. ; Pawar, S. ; Ingle, R., Performance Evaluation of Unstructured NoSQL data over distributed framework, International Conference on Advances in Computing, Communications and Informatics (ICACCI), pp. 1623-1627, 2014.

[8] Okman, L. ; Gal-Oz, N. ; Gonen, Y. ; Gudes, E. ; Abramov, J., "Security Issues in NoSQL Databases", IEEE 10th International Conference on Trust, Security and Privacy in Computing and Communications (TrustCom), pp. 541 – 547, 2011.

[9] Pramod J. Sadalage, Martin Fowler, "NoSQL Distilled: A Brief Guide to the Emerging World of Polyglot Persistence", Addison-Wesley Professional, 2012.

[10] Wang Xiaolin ; Chen Haopeng ; Wang Zhenhua, "Research on Improvement of Dynamic Load Balancing in MongoDB", IEEE 11th International Conference on Dependable, Autonomic and Secure Computing (DASC), pp.124-130, 2013.

24

Adaptation of Rigid Registration Algorithm to the Fingerprints Identification

Mostafa Boutahri*, Samir Zeriouh, Said El Yamani, Abdenbi Bouzid, Ahmed Roukhe

Optronic and Information Treatment Team, Atomic, Mechanical, Photonic and Energy Laboratory, Faculty of Science, Moulay Ismail University, Zitoune, Meknès, Morocco

Email address:

boumost-1980@hotmail.fr (M. Boutahri)

Abstract: In this paper, we present an automated system for the recognition and identification of fingerprints based on rigid registration algorithms. Indeed, after preprocessing carried on a fingerprint database collected in the laboratory, we have built maps of minutiae for each fingerprint. Subsequently, we applied a rigid registration algorithm based on iterative search for closed points ICP (Iterative Closest Point), which allowed us to compare shifted fingerprints serving as test with the fingerprints of the reference database. This comparison gives convincing results and shows high accuracy.

Keywords: Recognition, Identification, Fingerprints, Rigid Registration, Minutiae, ICP

1. Introduction

Nowadays, authentication becomes one of the essential points at the security access controls in informatics systems. It is based on the recognition that verifies the presumed user identities [1].

The identification is generally based on several criteria and according to the extent of the investigation. It may be an identification by DNA search, by using images from surveillance cameras, for removal of odors and scents or most often by use of fingerprints [2]. This process remains in our day, the most reliable and most cost especially that the police have fingerprint database of all citizens holder a national identity card.

The important progress experienced by the fingerprint verification area in recent years have required new image processing tools, especially for multimodal image (from different sources). The registration algorithms are part of these tools. There are many, both within the rigid or non-rigid registration. However, these algorithms are difficult to validate in the absence of a reference standard for verifying the fields obtained.

In this context, our work proposes adapting rigid registration algorithm variants, allowing a more effective comparison. Indeed, after scanning fingerprints, object of study, we conducted a binarization and thinning of fingerprints to finally build the maps corresponding to each minutiae fingerprint. Subsequently, we established a mathematical modeling of the registration problem to fit these data based on iterative method ICP. The simulation results obtained after several tests resulted in the recognition of fingerprint test in a reference database with largely optimized errors.

2. Extraction of Fingerprint's Biometric - Signature

To build our database, we proceeded to the taking of fingerprints on different people; these fingerprint images were enhanced by a pretreatment process to extract the corresponding signature to each fingerprint. Thus, these signatures are stored in a reference database.

2.1. Preprocessing of Captured Fingerprints

In this step, we proceeded the acquisition of fingerprints of different people with a scanner of type Ko-UF100 500- dpi, performed in our laboratory. The resulting images are hence stored as grayscale with the appropriate format. However these images often present a noise during the acquisition phase that require a adapted filtering, which the goal is to strengthen the contrast by eliminating redundant points [3].

Then, these images are binarized by thresholding process

that associates the number 0 to the pixel if its value is below a predetermined threshold value and the number 1 if the pixel value is equal to or greater than this threshold value. This last, varies according to the quality of the captured image and was therefore set to a gray level equal to 160.

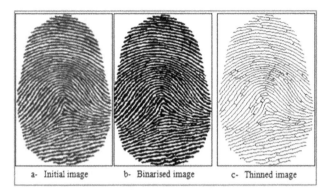

Figure 1. Fingerprint pretreatment process.

To facilitate its exploitation, the image must undergo a thinning treatment that consist to obtain a schematic image of the fingerprint, in which all the lines have the thickness of a pixel [4] [5].

The simulation results was carried out using Matlab software-R2014a (Figure. 1).

2.2. Extraction of Minutiae

To extract the fingerprint minutiae (bifurcations and endings), the calculation method used allows to detect them according to the neighborhood of each pixel following the continuity or discontinuity of the different lines [6] [7]. Once this step is completed, false minutiae are eliminated from the picture for finally have a two-dimensional minutiae map, containing the two values 0 or 1 (where 1 indicates the presence of the minutiae and 0 his absence) [8]. (Figure 2)

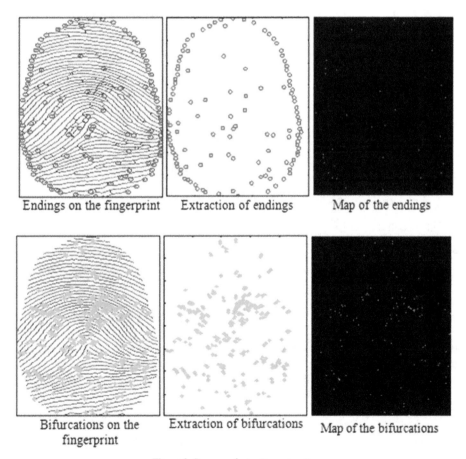

Figure 2. Process of minutiae extraction.

2.3. Data validation

The biometric signatures obtained are stored in a reference database. During the identification and authentication phase, a biometric signature is extracted from the fingerprint, object of recognition, and is compared to the signatures of the reference database using the iterative algorithm of fingerprints rigid registration.

3. Registration of Fingerprints Images by ICP

The ICP algorithm applied on fingerprints is based on the iterative matching of minutiae of a test fingerprint with their nearest neighbors on the next reference fingerprint.

Meanwhile, a least squares technique is used to estimate the transformation from these correspondences. Indeed, at the end of each iteration, the algorithm provides a list of matched points, and an estimate of the registration transformation, this transformation is used in the next iteration for updating the list of matched points. They used their towers to calculate a new estimate of the transformation. These steps are repeated until convergence of the algorithm.

3.1. Modeling of the Problem

The registration problem can be laid more formally by introducing the different notations used throughout this work and describing the general principle of the registration procedure (figure 3).

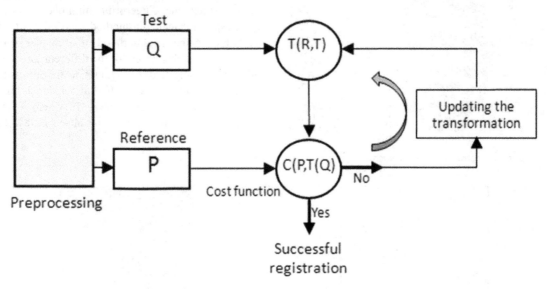

Figure 3. The principle of registration process.

Given two fingerprint images (Two maps of minutiae):

$Q = \left\{ q_i / i = 1 : N_q \right\}$; The source image to register;

$P = \left\{ p_j / j = 1 : N_p \right\}$; The reference Image.

We consider the rigid registration of a source image $Q : \Omega_s \rightarrow \mathbb{R}$ to a target image $P : \Omega_c \rightarrow \mathbb{R}$

The domains Ω_s and Ω_c of the two images Q and P are subsets of $\mathbb{R}^2$.

3.2. ICP Algorithm Applied to the Fingerprints

The proposed registration method is an iterative method ICP, which takes as input two point clouds of two-dimensional, and outputs an optimal estimate of the transformation between the two sets.

Therefore, the purpose of this algorithm is to find the parameters of the transformation (rotation and translation) which aligns a test fingerprint Q to another as reference P.

The cost function used is given by:

$$C = \min_{R,t,j} \left(\sum_{i=1}^{N_q} \left\| \left(R\vec{q}_i + \vec{t} \right) - \vec{p}_j \right\| \right)^2 \begin{array}{l} R.R^T = R^T.R = I_2 \\ \det|R| = 1 \\ j = 1 : N_p \end{array}$$

With R and $\vec{t}$ are the parameters of the transformation (rotation and translation respectively).

The ICP algorithm reaches its speed and precision performance by iterating the following two steps:

1. First, we establish the correspondences linking the two sets of points:

$$C_k(i) = \arg\min_{j=1:N_p} \left(\left\| \left(R_{k-1} \vec{q}_i + \vec{t}_{k-1} \right) - \vec{p}_j \right\|^2 \right) i = 1 : N_q$$

2. Then, we calculate the new rotation and translation minimizing the least square criterion:

$$\left(R_k, T_k \right) = \arg\min_{R,\vec{t}} \left(\sum_{i=1}^{N_q} \left\| R\vec{q}_i + \vec{t} - \vec{p}_{c_k(i)} \right\|^2 \right)$$

Note that at each iteration, ICP method uses the results obtained at the last iteration to yield a better result. That is until the result converges or that we have exceeded the maximum number of iterations allocated to the algorithm[9].

3.2.1. Matching Step

In first step of the algorithm, the matching is done by a simple algorithm to search neighborhood, which consist to pass on all the points Np of P and to see if it's nearer or not that one of the already selected close neighbors, and if so, insert it. We then obtain a linear calculation time in the size of P. This method is called linear search or sequential search. However, this method suffers from a problem of slowness if the set P is too large, then it is extremely expensive to test Np points in space. Fortunately, in our case of fingerprints, the number of matching minutiae points does not exceed a few dozen.

This search algorithm will be used as reference to compare other algorithms that use more complex data storage structures like Delaunay triangulation Matlab [10][11], Kd-tree [12], etc...

- Delaunay triangulation invented by the Russian mathematician Boris Delaunay in 1934. This triangulation is applied for each of the two sets (source and target), then they are merged afterwards.
- The Kd-Tree introduced in 1975, the principle is to try to place each point of the source image in the tree, and up until one gets to the root of the tree while searching closest neighbors.

Still in the same step, looking for the nearest point is an important part if you want to get a method, which is robust as well as efficient. This is why the detection of the existence of aberrant points (outliers) is significant. The existence of outliers in point sets to match is very detrimental to our algorithm because when we seek the transformation between the two sets, we assume that we have the same cloud of points at different positions, assumption that's violated in presence of outliers.

To solve the problem of outliers, we sort in ascending order all pairings by comparing the distances between paired points. Then we select the $n_r = r * n_q$ first pairings with r is a parameter called overlay coefficient including in the interval $[r_{min}, r_{max}]$, and obtained by minimizing the function:

$$\psi(r) = \frac{e(r)}{r^{1+\lambda}} \text{ ; (See figure 4)}$$

Such as

$$e(r) = \frac{1}{n_r} \sum_{i=1}^{n_r} \left(d_i^{k+1}\right)^2, d_i^{k+1} = \left\| R_k \vec{q}_i + \vec{t}_k - \vec{p}_{c_{k+1}(i)} \right\|$$

$\lambda = 2$, and typically ($r_{min} = 0.4$ and $r_{max} = 1$)

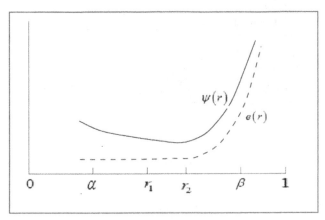

(Golden Section Method) [13]

Figure 4. *Golden Section Method.*

These pairings will be those that we will use to estimate the transformation between the two clouds following the

approach of the ICP method without outliers. The other points are dismissed as outliers.

3.2.2. Transformation Update

In the second step of the algorithm, the used approach is that of the singular value decomposition (SVD) applied in 2D. The idea is this:

1. Calculate the center of mass p_c and q_c of the two point clouds $\{p_i\}$ and $\{q_i\}$:

$$P_c = \frac{1}{n_r} * \sum_{i=1}^{n_r} p_i \text{ and } Q_c = \frac{1}{n_r} * \sum_{i=1}^{n_r} q_i \quad (i = 1... n_r)$$

2. Construct the covariance matrices:

$$P' = \{p_i - p_c\} = \{p_i'\} \quad and \quad Q' = \{q_i - q_c\} = \{q_i'\}$$
$$(i = 1... n_r)$$

3. Calculate the matrix $K \in \mathbb{R}^{2*2}$ such as $K = P'.Q'^T$

$$\left(P', Q' \in \mathbb{R}^{2*n_r}\right)$$

4. Write the matrix K as $K = U.S.V^T$, this decomposition is done by the SVD function predefined in Matlab by writing $[U.S.V] = SVD(K)$ where U and V are orthogonal matrices of orders 2 and S a diagonal matrix of size 2 * 2 whose diagonal contains the singular values of K.

5. The parameters of the transformation are deduced by:
$R = U.V^T (Rotation)$

$T = p_c - R.q_c (Translation)$

Note that if $\det(R) < 0$

$$R = V * B * U^T \text{ where } B = \begin{pmatrix} 1 & 0 \\ 0 & \det(V.U^T) \end{pmatrix}$$

3.3. Evaluation of the Method on Real Data of Fingerprints

We tested our approach by taking an incorporated reference database of 20 fingerprints taken from different people and another database for test containing 10 fingerprints, which six are taken from people already on the database with different positions of those carried out beforehand, whereas the remaining four are removed from people not included in database. (Figure 5)

- Preprocessing stage:

For simplicity, we limit ourselves to such minutiae endings. After pretreatment and extraction of minutiae, we clearly observe the presence of outliers, this is where the parameter r is automatically updated with each iteration.

The figure 6 shows two samples of fingerprint images taken from the reference and test database respectively and this, before and after the preprocessing stage.

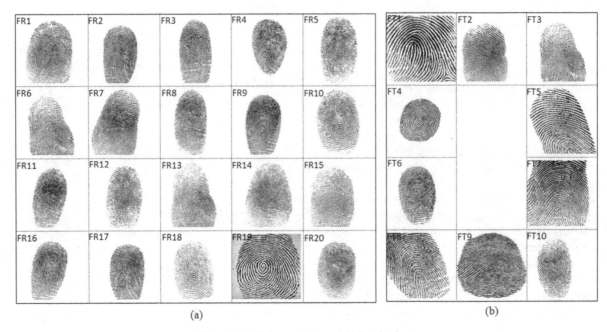

(a)   (b)

Figure 5. (a) Reference database; (b) Test database.

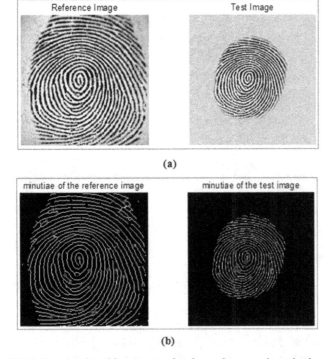

(a)

(b)

Fig. 6. Two samples of fingerprints taken from reference and test database respectively. (a) Before pretreatment; (b) After pretreatment.

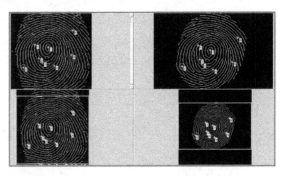

Fig. 7. Extraction of the two point clouds without outliers.

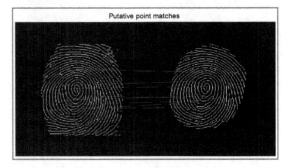

Fig. 8. Appariements between the two point sets of extracted minutiae.

• Alignment step of fingerprint images:

This stage includes the matching based on the naive method of searching the nearest neighbor cited in (3.2.1), then an intermediate step is to reject false comparison points (outliers) to reach finally the calculation of the new transformation (rotation and translation) minimizing the cost function. (Figures 7, 8, 9 and 10)

4. Results and Discussions

The confrontation results of the test fingerprints (FTi[1] /i=1, 2...10) to those of the reference (FRj[2] /j=1,2...20) by the studied method are provided in the following table (Table 1).

---

1 FTi: Test fingerprint number i where i=(1,2,...,10);
2 FRj: Reference fingerprint number j where j=(1,2,...,20).

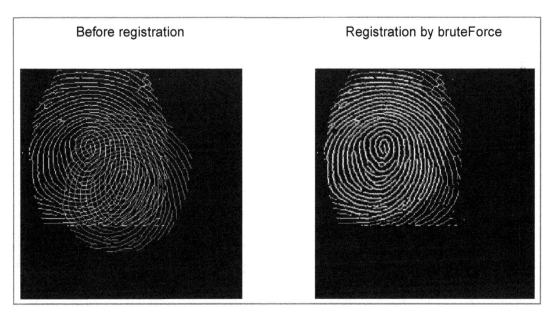

Fig. 9. *Fingerprint images before and after registration by ICP.*

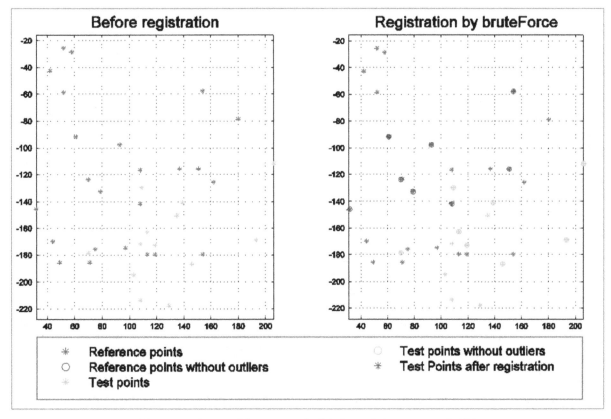

Fig. 10. *Visualization of the two point clouds before and after registration by ICP.*

Table 1. *Least squares error between the set of minutiae in the test and reference database.*

	FT1	FT2	FT3	FT4	FT5	FT6	FT7	FT8	FT9	FT10
FR1	1.841e2	2.241e2	0.705e2	3.510e2	3.001e3	2.110e2	2.143e2	1.726e3	7.520e1	7.021e2
FR2	2.245e2	7.217e1	1.235e2	0.271e3	4.231e-3	3.237e1	3.125e3	3.115e2	4.112e3	3.210e3
FR3	7.210e1	4.378e2	0.710e1	5.143e2	2.800e2	1.628e3	2.620e1	2.720e2	7.520e1	5.200e1
FR4	4.387e2	1.435e3	1.804e2	1.780e3	3.478e1	1.443e2	1.376e2	4.890e2	0.370e2	3.760e2
FR5	1.405e3	0.807e2	1.403e3	6.607e1	0.115e2	7.617e1	3.450e3	4.450e2	1.214e3	2.850e3

	FT1	FT2	FT3	FT4	FT5	FT6	FT7	FT8	FT9	FT10
FR6	0.867e2	1.023e2	6.035e-4	1.073e2	5.011e4	5.022e2	3.257e4	8.215e2	7.125e2	0.453e4
FR7	1.035e2	2.720e1	9.072e2	9.702e1	3.712e1	6.420e1	5.112e-4	9.100e1	6.034e3	7.500e2
FR8	2.721e1	0.860e3	0.770e3	0.896e3	6.823e0	1.031e3	1.750e3	6.750e3	3.712e2	3.230e2
FR9	0.864e3	1.075e3	4.800e1	0.089e3	2.700e2	1.912e1	3.719e2	5.300e-2	5.072e1	1.067e3
FR10	1.750e3	2.307e2	3.840e3	3.790e2	3.021e2	5.027e2	4.730e2	0.160e4	3.650e3	3.177e2
FR11	2.300e2	1.924e1	1.043e2	2.103e2	7.750e1	1.204e3	1.072e2	1.083e3	5.363e2	4.150e3
FR12	1.942e1	5.872e2	5.072e1	9.325e1	1.100e4	6.112e2	3.061e1	5.642e1	1.642e3	6.628e2
FR13	5.824e2	1.107e3	2.004e-2	6.300e2	8.114e2	5.117e1	7.194e2	3.414e2	9.100e2	3.110e3
FR14	1.177e3	2.450e2	1.487e3	1.622e1	2.810e2	1.092e2	1.037e4	2.657e3	1.847e3	4.720e2
FR15	2.450e2	1.380e-3	1.253e3	4.281e2	1.276e3	1.380e3	1.253e3	2.493e3	8.431e2	9.070e2
FR16	4.237e1	8.641e2	4.237e3	1.322e1	1.097e2	7.311e2	4.237e2	4.270e2	2.340e-2	5.017e2
FR17	8.654e2	9.045e1	5.301e1	4.623e1	3.654e-2	1.045e2	5.301e3	0.511e3	3.110e3	6.533e2
FR18	9.046e1	0.809e2	2.086e3	3.280e2	7.053e1	5.119e2	2.029e2	3.019e2	7.216e2	7.100e1
FR19	0.807e2	7.475e1	4.750e2	5.620e-4	2.381e2	7.041e2	4.712e2	4.312e1	5.327e3	5.970e2
FR20	7.450e1	4.273e1	8.310e1	6.211e2	4.610e2	1.323e3	4.623e2	0.610e3	1.972e1	1.410e3

These results demonstrate that people whose fingerprints FT1, FT6 and FT10 are not listed on the reference database because the value of the Least squares error is in the range of 10^1 to 10^4.

As to persons whose fingerprints FT2, FT4, FT7, FT8 and FT9, they are identified in the reference database and correspond to people whose fingerprints are respectively FR15, FR19, FR7, FR9 and FR16. Indeed, the errors stored vary in the range of 10^{-2} to 10^{-4}.

Still based on the table, we note that the fingerprint FT3 corresponds well to the reference fingerprints FR6 and FR13 with respective errors $6,035.10^{-4}$ and $2,004.10^{-2}$. This demonstrate that the fingerprints FR6 and FR13 are taken from the same person. Similarly for the test fingerprint FT5 that matches the person suffering the two prelevements FR2 and FR17 with respective errors in the range of 10^{-2} to 10^{-3}.

5. Conclusion

Thus, the work proposed in this paper is based on a purely geometric approach by implementing a system of identification or verification by rigid registration of fingerprints, with the main objectives processing speed and eliminating subjectivity based in particular on mathematical criteria to evaluate the results, this approach includes a chain of operations ranging from preprocessing fingerprints to rigid registration and based on the minutiae extracted. Indeed, we have chosen the minutiae type terminations as information to consider for guiding the registration. Then, after formalization of the general problem of registration, a registration method by ICP algorithm was proposed. At the rate of its sensitivity to noise and outliers, this algorithm has been improved by the introduction of a parameter, which acts on the selection of pairings. The latter are used to estimate the transformation between the two fingerprint images following the approach of the ICP method without outliers.

The results thus obtained in our study are compelling and indicate the effectiveness of the method in the field of identification of persons based on their fingerprints.

References

[1] Lorène, "La biométrie multimodale: stratégies de fusion de scores et mesures de dépendance virtuelle". Thèse de doctorat de Al Mutaz M. Abdalla, Safaai Dress, Nazar Zaki, "Detection of Masses in Digital Mammogram Using Second Order Statistics and Artificial Neural Network", International Journal of Computer Science & Information Technology (IJCSIT), Vol 3, No 3, pp. 176-186 June 2011.

[2] Morizet, "Reconnaissance biométrique par fusion multimodale du visage et de l'iris", Thèse de doctorat Télécom 2009.

[3] Doublet, Revenu, Olivier, "Reconnaissance biométrique sans contact de la main intégrant des informations de forme et de texture", France Telecom.2003.

[4] Salil Prabhakar, Anil K. Jain, "Learning Fingerprint Minutiae Location and Type", International Conference on Pattern Recognition (ICPR), 2000.

[5] Chaohong, "Advanced feature algorithms for automatic fingerprint recognition system", University of New Yorkatbuffalo.2007.

[6] A. Chaari, S. Lelandais, M. B. Ahmed, "Face classification scheme simplifying identification in biometric databases", Transactions on Systems, Signals & Devices (TSSD), Shaker-Verlag, sous presse, 2009.

[7] LIU L., JIANG T., YANG J., and al., Fingerprint Registration by Maximization of Mutual Information, IEEE Transactions on image processing,15(5), 1100-1110, 2006.

[8] M. Boutahri, S. El Yamani, S. Zeriouh, A. Bouzid and A. Roukhe, Fingerprint Identification by Artificial Neural Network, Journal of Physical Science and Application (David publishing), pp.381-384 Jun 2014.

[9] D. Maltoni, D. Maio, A.K. Jain, S. Prabhakar Handbook of Fingerprint Recognition Springer, New York, 2003.

[10] E. M.Gross , D. Wagner, KD trees and Delaunay-based linear interpolation for function learning: a comparison to neural networks with error backpropagation, pp.649 – 653 Nov 1996.

[11] Barber, C. B., Dobkin, D. P., Huhdanpaa, H., The quickhull algorithm for convexhulls. ACM Trans. Math. Software 22 (4), 469–483, 1996.

[12] Nuchter, A., Lingemann, K., Hertzberg, J., Cached k–d tree search for ICP algorithms. In: Proc. Sixth Internat. Conf. on 3-D Digital Imaging and Modeling(3DIM), pp. 419–426, 2007.

[13] D. Chetverikov, D. Stepanov, P. Krsek, Robust Euclidean alignment of 3D point sets: the trimmed iterative closest point algorithm, Vol 23, Number 3, pp. 299-309, March 2005.

25

The Research of Middleware Architecture of Intelligent Logistics System Based on SOA

Jie Zhu, Ruoling Zhang

School of Information, Beijing Wuzi University, Beijing, China

Email address:
zhujie@bwu.edu.cn (Jie Zhu), 422122281@qq.com (Ruoling Zhang)

Abstract: Prime minister, Keqiang Li, chaired a state council executive meeting in 2014 in which the medium and long term planning of development of logistics industry was discussed and passed. It put forward to set up modern logistics service system until 2020, enhancing the level of standardization, informatization, intellectualization, intensification of logistics, improving overall efficiency and benefits of economy [1]. At present, the vigorous development of a new generation of Internet technologies and the intelligent logistics equipment technology such as the Internet of things, cloud computing, big data, mobile Internet, smart logistics and Internet plus is driving the change of China's smart logistics [2].Internet of things technology brings convenience to the life. It also brings new problem. The data is collected by the sensors.It maps out all aspects of the physical world. At the same time, it will produce huge amounts of heterogeneous data. Aimed at the above problems, this paper puts forward the research of middleware architecture of intelligent logistics system which is based on SOA. It provides an unified and structured data for the upper application system through shielding the complex acquisition equipment and heterogeneous data.

Keywords: Intelligent Logistics Middleware, IOT Middleware, SOA Middleware Architecture

1. Introduction

Now IOT middleware software has been widely applied to each link of logistics. Because intelligent logistics system is composed of multiple subsystems collaboratively, this paper draws on the design style of SOA architecture to design this middleware system in order to better play the role of middleware and make subsystems which work in different platforms can use middleware system. The system can be loosely coupled and can real-time update of data to adapt to the flexible dynamics of intelligent logistics system.

Table 1. The advantages of SOA.

advantages	describe
The independence of the function of the entity	Emphasize completely independent ability of the function of the entity which provides services in the framework: The traditional component technology requires a host to store and manage these function entities, when there are some problems in the host itself or other functions, other application service that run on the host will be affected. Emphasizing the ability of self management and resilience of entities: Common technologies for self-recovery, such as transaction processing, message queues, redundant deployment and cluster system, play a crucial role in the SOA [4]. Recommend exchanging information with the method of large amount of data at once.
A huge amount of data	For those traditional distributed computing models, the service is carried out by means of function calls, the completion of a function often requires many times function calls between the client and server function. The influence of these calls for the response speed and stability of system is the key determinants to determine whether the system can work normally under the Internet environment.
Textual message passing	The existence of a large number of heterogeneous systems (including different languages and different platforms for data, and even some difference of basic data types defined) in the Internet determines that the SOA systems must use text messaging mode instead of binary messaging mode [5]. Based on text messaging, data processing software can only selective processing part of the data which itself understands and ignore other data, so as to get ideal compatibility.

2. An Overview of SOA

SOA (Service Oriented Architecture, SOA) a software system Architecture which can be achieved by connecting to an independent function entity that can complete specific tasks in order to solve the needs of the business integration in the Internet environment. SOA (service-oriented architecture) is a component model. It links the different functional units of application through well-defined interfaces and contracts between these services [3].

Interface is defined with the method of neutral. It should be independent of operating system, programming language and services hardware platform which can achieve services. Services which are built in different kinds of systems can interact by a unified and general way. Table 1 lists the advantages of SOA architecture.

3. IOT Middleware Architecture Design

This paper puts forward the overall architecture based on SOA middleware as shown in figure 1. Three layer structures are device access layer, the event processing layer, application interaction layer.

Device layer can collect related data of entity. It doesn't have function of simple data processing and filtration. Equipment layer is made up of IOT perception like barcode, RFID, ZigBee, sensors, PDA, wireless network and so on. These devices can make the physical world information real-time display in the computer world and information system in the form of digital. But different types, different manufacturers and different models of devices increase the difficulty of program development. Addition or decrease of all kinds of equipment can make a lot of changes of system [6].

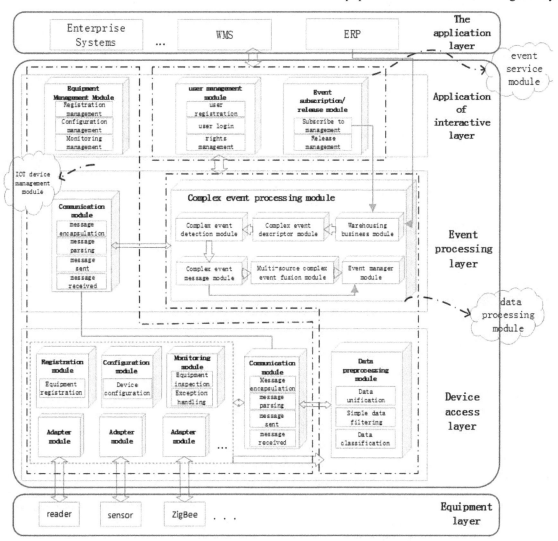

Figure 1. *Middleware whole architecture.*

Middleware layer can manage uniformly multiple data sets the source device and unified or block agreement between different multi-sources. At first time process collected

information of data, label and environment [7], and then process based on the application system or user requirements for secondary processing, and store information that has been dealt for the upper application to subscribe to. The layer is made up of the device access layer, information processing layer and application interaction. It is connected by a Web interface between different layers.

Application layer is made up of ERP, the enterprise business system and each link of the subsystems of the intelligent logistics system including the intelligent management system that is based on UHF RFID technology, intelligent shelves system, storage environment monitoring system and intelligent inventory system.

ERP or other business systems provide business orders to the middleware system, each subsystem of warehouse system coordinate with each other homework, each subsystem also request and subscription business orders to the middleware system according to the different operations, middle ware system Release the corresponding incident report to the users after completing the corresponding business operations.

3.1. The Hierarchical Structure of the Middleware

Differentiate from the level, middleware system is divided into three levels include device access layer, the event

processing layer and application of interactive layer like black solid line box in the figure bellow.

(1) Device access layer

Device access layer is in the bottom of the middleware architecture. It connected with IOT acquisition devices and provides a direct dialogue with acquisition device. Device access layer is the direct undertaker of Equipment management module in Application of interactive layer .Equipment management module can manage and control the acquisition equipment .Its principle as shown in figure 2.

Device access layer contains multiple virtual devices (light gray dotted line inside, as shown in figure 1), data preprocessing and communication module. Virtual device is the mapping of the physical device in the middle tier system. It is the middle of the agent of equipment management module and the actual physical hardware device. Information world and the physical world is not in the same environment, so if the physical device wants to enter the information world to participate in work, it needs to create a virtual devices belongs to itself to each physical equipment[8].

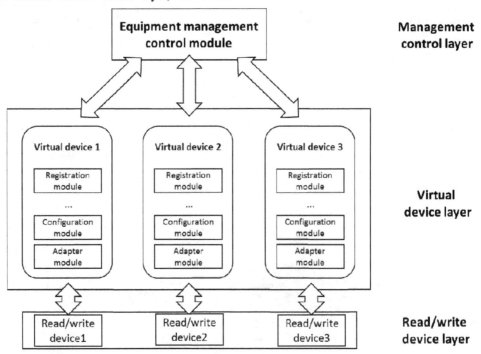

Figure 2. Equipment management principle diagram.

Each virtual devices are included in the child module of the virtual device module under the access layer. If the middleware finds that a new collection device is attempting to access to the system, the system will generate a new virtual device. This virtual equipment is the information agent in the world of the equipment. It interacts with other modules.

Equipment management module sends instruction to virtual device. Virtual device receives and executes instructions .It can also complete different operation like accessing and controlling hardware, speaking and reading labels and data collection, etc. Device access layer including

virtual module - adapter module that linked to IOT acquisition device, configuration module, monitoring module, registered module, communication module and data preprocessing module.

The main function of this layer:

1) To provide standard unified protocol interfaces for each type of equipment in equipment layer such as providing standard unified protocol interfaces based EPC-global reading and writing device for reading and writing equipment.

2) Receiving and preprocessing data that is collected by the

Internet of things devices including data standardization and simple data filtering, etc.

3) Receiving and executing instructions from the equipment management module and managing equipment of the equipment layer.

(2) The event processing layer

Event processing layer is the core part of the middleware system. It also is in the middle layer of middleware system at the same time. It connects device access layer bellow and application interaction layer above.

Event processing layer includes two modules which are event processing module and communication module. There is also a communication module in the device access layer. These two communication modules have the same meaning and function. The lower communication module sends the preprocessed data to upper communication module after encapsulating it for the message. The upper communication module parse the message received. Then it sends the message to event processing module to wait for the subsequent processing.

Communication module ensures that the instructions of equipment management module can be accurate delivery and execution at the same time. It can guarantee the normal work of the read-write equipment [9]. Communication module, as the name implies, have played an important role on communication between lower and upper.

The main features of event processing layer:

1) Parsing encapsulated message of different sources of data which is processed by data preprocessing module in the device access layer;

2) Detecting complex event information based on the business;

3) Meeting the needs of the user or application system, fusing events of a variety of data sources, forming a complex event information that is needed. Event information is stored in the event manager module for extracting by users.

(3) The application of interactive layer

Application interaction layer is an interfaces which middleware system keeps for system or user that can operate and manage. It is also the management center of middleware. It is one of the core component of the middleware. It contains equipment management module, user management module, event subscription and publish module. These three modules allow users and administrators to operate.

Equipment management module manages virtual equipment of equipment access layer in fact. It provides equipment registration management, equipment configuration management, equipment monitoring management and other functions. It manages the access device through ordering the virtual devices to allow multiple devices to work together. System administrators can sign up for accounts for other Application system or developer in user management module. Different users can view or add the business model through permissions management. Users can subscribe events which he needs by using event subscription and publish module.

The main functions of the application of interactive layer:

1) Checking the equipment registration, equipment initialization or the configuration of new equipment in the equipment layer. Ask for monitoring equipment status, etc.

2) Registering the identity of users include personnel, procedures and systems which need to use middleware system.

3) According to the needs, users subscribe for some complex event of warehousing business module. It can also distribute events.

3.2. The Functional Configuration of Middleware

From the perspective of function, the middleware system is divided into three functional modules: IOT acquisition equipment management module, data processing module and the event service module, as shown in figure 1. Three modules do their job and rely on each other, jointly complete the reserve functions of middleware.

(1) IOT collection equipment management module

Collection equipment management module is the most basic module of IOT middleware, and responsible for management of sub module and controlling the intelligent storage aspects variety of IOT heterogeneous devices.

It consists of seven sub modules, which are adapter module, the register module, configuration module, monitoring module, equipment management module, and two communication modules.

1) Adapter modules: collection device types differ from each other, modes of communication interface are various, such as a serial port connection, USB connection, etc. On the other hand, equipment developers will provide the corresponding development kit to decrease the difficulty of access, and due to the difference of the developers, the development kits are often different. The adapter module shoulders to provide a unified standardized protocol interface for the IoT acquisition device, convenient effective access to various acquisition devices.

2) Register module: when there is a new device access to the network, registration module detects the acquisition equipment, submit the information to the equipment management module, including the type of equipment, power equipment, the geographical position, etc., and then apply for registration.

3) Configuration module: responsible for the access to the middleware system of IOT's capture device initial configuration and real-time reconfiguration. When a new device to be connected to the network, after registration module performs a registration, the device enters configuration link, configuration module detects device configuration, then automatically configuring it. If the configuration is incorrect or need to be adjusted, it can be manually modified by the equipment management module.

4) Monitoring module: responsible for obtaining the equipment running status data, processing equipment failure, including equipment failure and network failures.

The equipment of the access system is monitored, and the dynamic monitoring of each specific device is carried out, and transmitted to the equipment management module during work. At the same time the problems of equipment and network, such detail information would be sent to the management module.

5) Equipment management module: responsible for the management and controlling the collection devices, including transmission management and control instructions to the virtual device; processing feedback information of equipment, analysis and decision; Receiving and processing the registration module's application; according to registration information and real-time running status of reading and writing equipment, coordinate multiple thing to read and write equipment working.

6) Communication module, communication module 1, communication module of equipment access layer, is responsible for the receiving equipment management module of the control instructions and reply the execution result; Upload different data sources that the IOT devices read; Communication module 2: in the event processing layer communication module is responsible for sending equipment management module of the management and control instructions for IOT devices read and reply the related news; Receive different data source that communication module 1 uploaded and transmit to the data processing module. Above that, each sub module mutually work together to complete the IOT collection equipment management module function.

(2) The data processing module

Data processing module is the core of middleware, it integrate all the information that comes from RFID, sensors, GPS and mobile terminal and other multi-source, to filtering, complex event detection and multisource information fusion, to realize the integration of the Internet of business information, provides the upper application based on the logistics business event service. Data processing module is composed of two sub modules, data preprocessing module and complex event processing module.

1) Data preprocessing module: responsible for preliminary processing of raw data from sampling equipment, including simple data filtering, data classification and data standardization to ensure the correctness of the data to be uploaded.

The data collected by the equipment layer has the characteristics of large amount of data and redundancy and high error rate. Firstly, the data is not reliable. In practice, it may produce a variety of acquisition error, including, tag conflict, the influence of position error, metal, water etc. Misreading, missing and repetition are RFID common phenomenon for data error. Secondly, redundancy, collected duplicate data will be great amount (sometimes reader-writer, sensor can be collected more than 1000 times a second) [10]. So filtering is very necessary and important function. The purpose of the filter is to eliminate the redundant data, which

eliminate the 'useless' in order to transmit useful information to the application.

Set up several kinds of filters:

A. de-duplication filter, filtering out the redundant data, in order to reduce system load. For example, setting a period of 10m, collect this data from 0 seconds, if equipment still not collect this data until 10 seconds, the program will determine whether the period within 10 m, because it will determine to kick out the collected information or record the information.;

B. equipment filter: equipment filter can send only one type of equipment or a specific attribute of the node information, that is to say, the filter only send the data of a certain range or mode;

C. time filter, filter events according to the time records, for example, a time filter can send only the last 10 minutes of events;

D. smoothing filter: responsible for dealing with errors, including missing and misreading information. According to the actual requirement, these filters can be used jointly.

2) Complex event processing module: It is responsible for synthesizing basic events though preprocessing the data information. These basic events combined with business to detect complex event that based on logistics business and extract these complex events;

According to the needs of the business and users, complex event processing module fuses filtering data of a variety of sources and complex events. Then it forms more complex events information and uploads to the service module.

(3) The event service module

Event service module is the module which can directly interact with the backend application. It is mainly responsible for managing and releasing the complex event information that based on storage business, providing user registration function and subscribing/publishing storage complex event. It is made up of the user management module and event subscription and publish module.

1) User management module:

Responsible for managing registration, user privileges, and user information management of middleware back-end users.

2) Event subscribe/publish module:

Subscription

It is responsible for managing storage business complex events that is required by subscribing of users and submitting the relevant business information. The system transforms business information that the user submits to the corresponding business model.

Submitted

It is responsible for publishing the complex event information which is based on storage business and submitted by data processing module.

4. Summary

Firstly, the article introduces in detail the service-oriented SOA architecture. Secondly, it analyses and designs the middleware structure which is based on SOA architecture and oriented intelligent logistics system. Middleware system structure is divided into three levels which include device access layer, event processing layer and application of interactive layer and three functional modules which include IOT acquisition equipment management module, data processing module and service module.

Acknowledgements

This paper is supported by the Funding Project for Technology Key Project of Municipal Education Commission of Beijing (ID:TSJHG201310037036); Funding Project for Beijing Key Laboratory of intelligent logistics system(NO:BZ0211); Funding Project of Construction of Innovative Teams and Teacher Career Development for Universities and Colleges Under Beijing Municipality (ID:IDHT20130517), and Beijing Municipal Science and Technology Project (ID: Z131100005413004); Funding Project for Beijing philosophy and social science research base specially commissioned project planning (ID:13JDJGD013).

References

[1] http://china.cnr.cn/news/201406/t20140612_515653926.shtml. cnr.cn. Keqiang Li Presiding over meetings of the state council.

[2] Feng Liu. The Internet evolution [M]. Tsinghua university press, 2012. 9.

[3] Yunsong Tan, Jianjun Han. A service-oriented IOT middleware model [J]. Computer science, 2011. 10(38).

[4] Fahong Li. The research and preliminary design of digital city that is based on SOA [J]. Journal of Shanxi normal university, 2008.11(36).

[5] Lichao Liu. Comprehensive monitoring of SOA architecture design and value analysis [J]. Telecom science, 2010(11).

[6] Haisheng Deng. Research and implementation of the RFID middleware based on SOA [J]. Electronic technology applications, 2007(10).

[7] Qing Hu, Yiju Shan, Xiaohu Huang. Based on Internet of things and RFID middleware technology research [J]. Micro computer information, 2009(25).

[8] Jie Li, Using JMX and JMS technology of RFID middleware design based on SOA [J]. Electronic technology applications 2010(4).

[9] Jincan Fang, Port logistics oriented iot technology research and design of RFID middleware [D]. Dalian university of technology, 2013.

[10] Gonzalez H, Han J, Shen X. Cost-conscious cleaning of massive RFID data sets[C].Proc of ICED, 2007: 1268-1272.

26

Model to Quantify Availability at Requirement Phase of Secure Software

Nikhat Parveen[1], Mohammad Rizwan Beg[1], M. H. Khan[2]

[1]Department of Computer Application, Integral University, Lucknow, India
[2]Department of Computer Engineering, Institute of Engineering and Technology, Lucknow, India

Email address:

nikhat0891@gmail.com (N. Parveen), rizwanbeg@gmail.com (M. R. Beg), mhkhan.ietfaculty@yahoo.com (M. H. Khan)

Abstract: A number of security mechanisms are available to protect data such as digital signature, audits log, encryption, refining etc. however they completely not able to stop malevolent attacks. Hackers and attackers continuously try to exploit security which can be easily pushed through loopholes that are available at users end. The core reasons for such problem are mainly generated by terrible software requirements which are implemented without proper analysis of risks and threats. In order to reduce vulnerabilities security requirements standards, policies are tightly bound and used right from the beginning of software development. The major purpose of security standards and policy is to ensure that the data is always available at random in order to support security requirements against identified risks. The focus on this paper is to propose a model to quantify availability (MQA^R) by using multiple regression technique at requirement phase. To rationalize the model statistical data is used to validate assess availability at requirement level and the significance of this study concludes that the calculated data is highly acceptable.

Keywords: Software Security, Requirement Attributes, Security Quantification, Availability Quantification Model

1. Introduction

The world is moving rapidly to be Hi-Tech and it is totally dependent on computer and internet of things (IOT). Most of the computer and internet services facilitates user with online services. Such services lie on the network platform in order to provide facility to end user without placing any restrictions. This is the fact that unsecured requirement will lose the reliability of the system and hence breaches security. The trait of availability with respect to software security may intentionally pose to deny access to services by making it unavailable. Such actions behave to protect sensitive data from security breaches. For example session duration play important role to maintain availability of services, as the session expire the data becomes unavailable. Security experts believed that incorporating security at an early stage of development will reduce flaws, vulnerabilities and unwanted data at requirement time.

Availability behaves as fraction of instance that a produced system is functioning adequately. It is the extent to which the information is accessible and functional. Denial of services makes system's service unavailable for unauthorized users [1, 2]. Availability ensures that services are available for authorized user and it is operational when they are needed. It is suggested that to improve security, security policies and measures must be incorporated during requirement phase to eliminate vulnerabilities. For an outfitted design, all functional requirements must be available to serve its purpose. Availability and reliability are often interrelated to each other [3]. Software reliability measures possibility of error free services that are intended by the software for specified interval under stated conditions. Rap tool is used to appraise reliability and availability of software, which consists of three phases: the first phase defines reliability and availability goals; second phase transforms goals into architectural elements and third phase represent these elements in architectural models and perform evaluation in order to verify that the resultant architecture is satisfying the requirements or not[4].This is true that reliable software has high availability but available software may or may not be reliable.

2. Availabily at Requirement Phase

Setting availability goal is a complex process. For any software system to provide its services, the information must be available whenever it is needed. Such actions confirm that the processing of information must be correct and reliable. This reliable information must be protected by providing minimum privilege services in order to avoid ambiguity so that the available information can be secured. This is the fact that if information is available at high priority, the security reluctantly decreases. However securities of services need adequate protection in the form of physical security which behaves as fundamental security precaution and it is essential for the system to meet the user's availability requirements.

The three basic security requirements confidentiality, integrity and availability namely CIA has been acknowledged. CIA being the cornerstone of security and it totally depends on authentication and authorization [6]. On account of user's authentication and authorization level, system services are provided to authorize user only. For any decisive system if data is unavailable, it will directly affect the functionality of the system. To avoid unavailability at requirement phase, it is mandatory to make a proper adjustment of occurrence for document structure. Secure transmission at requirement time allows trusted authorization or trusted authentication mechanism to process operation. This can be incorporated with completeness of requirement that ensure the traceability and Unambiguity of requirement which could not disclose any information at any given time. These can be evaluated by direct measurement of attributes of requirement which includes ambiguity, completeness, understandability, traceability which all influence the availability as security at requirement time.

3. Building Correlation Between Security Attributes and Requirement Parameters

An estimation of security can be evaluated through quantification which helps to assess the cost and effort made by developers in order to secure software. Accurate and precise results are only generated through quantification. After lots of scrupulous discussion on security quantification concluded that a negligible effort has been done during requirement time. Many procedures and technique are based on either theoretical or best practices that can implements security [7]. The unwanted requirement

violates the security and gives negative impact to its acceptance level. The study shows that whenever the requirement is gathered to design any software, this should be kept in mind that the ambiguity and volatility of the requirement will be minimize in order to increase security. For any information when it is shared, it increases the availability of same information but due to any vague or modified session information gets tampered [8]. Probability of remains accessible for data is always not valuable from security perspective. For example, in online banking system if the data is available for longer period, it is easy to breach the security but due to session expired the data becomes unavailable and thus increases security. Impact of some requirement constructs on security attributes has been shown in table 1. The requirement constructs ambiguity and volatility has negative impacts on security whereas requirement constructs completeness, understandability and traceability have positive impact on security which is shown by downward arrow and upward arrow respectively.

The best time to incorporate security issues is at requirement time. To better understand the relationship between requirement and security a correlation has been established and model is proposed for quantification of security at requirement time. The primary objective is to identify the qualitative metrics for security estimation through requirement perspectives.

Information security plays an important role while developing safe and sound software. Several security metrics are available at system level or design level. Attackers try to identify the weakness of the system and exploit them. It has been observed that the weakness can be found during design time of software development. In order to remove weakness from design time, it is required to gather secure requirement. The core requirement constructs are Unambiguity, completeness, understandability and traceability with respect to SATC's attributes [9], [10], [11]. The metrics are helpful to maximize/control the security perspective with respect to requirement parameters are taken from [12], [13]. To increase maximum potency of protection at requirement time, it is mandatory to remove ambiguity and volatility of the requirement that avoid unnecessary authorization of services. The significance of this study is to quantify security with synchronized set of requirement attributes which is depicted as relation diagram in Fig 1.

Table 1. Impact of requirement constructs on security attribute.

Requirement Constructs /Security Attributes	Access Control	Authenticity	Availability	Confidentiality	Integrity	Non-Repudiation
Ambiguous	↓	↓	↓	↓	↓	↓
Completeness	↑	↑	↑	↑	↑	↑
Understandability	↑	↑	↑	↑	↑	↑
Traceability	↑	↑	↑	↑	↑	↑
Volatility	↓	↓	↓	↓	↓	↓

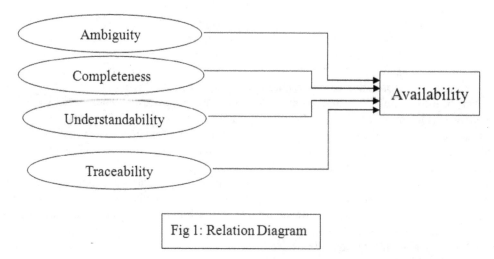

Fig 1: Relation Diagram

Fig. 1. *Relation Diagram.*

4. Model Development to Quantify Availability

The generic quality models have been considered as a basis to develop security quantification model from requirement perspectives [5], [14], [15]. Model to quantify availability at requirement phase (MQAR) the following steps are involved.

- Identification of quality factors that influence availability at requirement phase.
- Identification of requirement characteristics.
- Develop correlation between them.

Based upon the relationship between the security factors and requirement attributes, a relative significance of individual factors shows a major impact on security at requirement time which influence the quality attribute and is proportionally weighed. A multiple linear regression is used to get the coefficients. The regression established a relation between dependent variables and multiple independent variables. Thus the multiple regression equation may get the form as follows:

$$Y = \alpha + \beta 1\ X1 + \beta 2\ X2 + \ldots + \beta n\ Xn \qquad (1)$$

where
- Y is dependent variable,
- The Xs are independent variables related to Y and are expected to explain the variance in Y.
- The βs are the regression coefficients of the particular independent variables. Regression coefficient represent average amount of dependent increase/decrease when the independents are held constants.
- And α is the intercept.

The multiple linear regression models are fitted for the minimal set of availability metric and result is shown in equation (3).

$$Availability = \alpha + \beta 1 * AR + \beta 2 * CR + \beta 3 * UR + \beta 4 * TR \qquad (2)$$

$$Availability = -.273 - .777 * AR + .458 * CR + .253 * UR + .826 * TR \qquad (3)$$

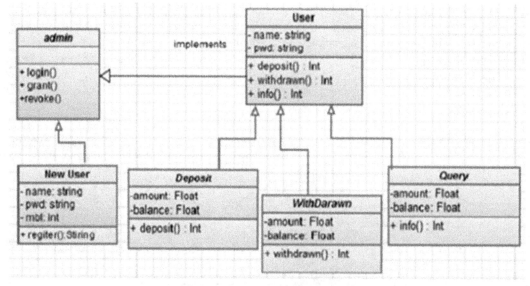

Fig. 2. *Online Banking System.*

Ambiguity Requirement (AR), Completeness Requirement (CR), Understandability Requirement (UR) and Traceable Requirement (TR) incorporate the quality requirement of software. Taking deliberators for the same, multiple regression equation to quantify availability of requirement has been established. A requirement hierarchy of Online Banking System is depicted in Fig: 2. has been presented to quantify availability. The seven versions of requirement hierarchies diagram are being used for metric value depicted in Table1 and data needed for standard availability values is taken from [16].

The model summary of deliberated data is mentioned in Table 2 which imparts the statistical elucidation of used data and signifies the high value of R Square represents that model is highly effective. Table 3 summarizes the outcome of the correlation analysis for quantify availability, and shows that for all the System, all of the requirement constructs are strongly correlated with security as availability.

Table 2. Summary of model.

Model	R	R Square	Standard Error	Significance F Change
1	.922	.850	0.051	0.276

Table 3. Availability computation table.

Requirement Diagram	Standard Availability	AR	CR	UR	TR
RD1	0.894	0.133	0.881	0.867	0.793
RD2	0.921	0.121	0.787	0.85	0.877
RD3	0.961	0.23	0.839	0.782	0.957
RD4	0.83	0.116	0.724	0.711	0.837
RD5	0.786	0.21	0.84	0.653	0.865
RD6	0.811	0.113	0.772	0.673	0.738
RD7	0.753	0.158	0.633	0.879	0.777

5. Validation of Model

The viable experiments are useful to validate proposed model in order to establish its effectiveness for practical use. Therefore, an experimental validation of the proposed model namely Model to quantify availability (MQAR) at requirement phase has been carried out using sample tryouts. The details of validations and data regarding availability formulation is carried out for ten version of requirement hierarchy diagram of online shopping system in Fig.3 and the estimated data is shown in table 4.

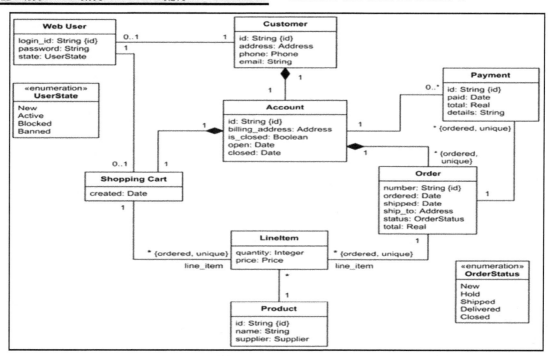

Fig. 3. Online Banking System.

Table 4. Availability estimation.

Requirement Diagram	AR	CR	UR	TR	Standard Availability	Computed Availability
RD1	0.113	0.883	0.667	0.893	0.847	0.950
RD2	0.171	0.777	0.875	0.897	0.879	0.912
RD3	0.127	0.679	0.832	0.877	0.863	0.874
RD4	0.116	0.834	0.731	0.893	0.928	0.941
RD5	0.133	0.754	0.673	0.875	0.836	0.862
RD6	0.18	0.835	0.773	0.878	0.711	0.890
RD7	0.167	0.738	0.677	0.886	0.753	0.838
RD8	0.197	0.897	0.757	0.933	0.801	0.947
RD9	0.133	0.768	0.886	0.837	0.811	0.891
RD10	0.12	0.874	0.837	0.897	0.934	0.987

It is compulsory to check the validity of proposed model for acceptance. A 2-tail sample test has been initiated to test the difference between two population means i.e., standard availability and computed availability values. The t test observation of availability values is shown in table 5.

Table 5. *T test for availability.*

	N	Mean	Std. Div.
Standard Integrity	10	0.836	0.071
Computed Integrity	10	0.909	0.046
t Statistic= 2.72			
P value = 0.014 (Two Tailed)			
Conclusion: Accept Alternate Hypothesis			

Null hypothesis (H0): There is significant difference between standard availability and computed availability.

Alternate hypothesis (HA): There is no significant difference between standard availability and computed availability.

$$H0: \mu1-\mu2 = 0 \text{ verses } HA: \mu1-\mu2 \neq 0$$

where $\mu1$ and $\mu2$ are the sample population means and '0' (zero) is the hypothesized difference between the two sample population means. Mean and Standard Div have been computed for given two samples and shown in Table 4. The hypothesis is trusted using 95% confidence. The p value is 0.014. Hence, null hypothesis is rejected and alternate hypothesis is accepted. Therefore the equation used in requirement parameter for availability computation is highly accepted.

6. Limitation of Study

Every coin has two sides. In research point of view both surfaces hold crucial position. However optimistic appearance offer new dimensions to proposed study while pessimistic portion highlights the deficiencies of work. The approach can be applied only to evaluate availability as security attribute with respect to requirement parameters. The validation of, the proposed models are only validated with a small set of data as industry data is unavailable. The recognition of the model is based on perception. However, this approach has been observed in previous research on vulnerability estimation at design phase.

7. Conclusion

Availability is the most significant security requirements. It becomes crucialin real-time systems. The quality of applications such as e-commerce, online banking highly affects by availability of services. Session duration play important role to maintain availability of services. In this paper a model has been developed to quantify availability (MQA^R) from requirement perspective. It estimates the security as availability with respect to requirement parameters which are weighted according to their influence. A multiple linear regression technique is used to quantify the model. The early quantification specifies the quality of software at the early stage of SDLC. Numerical results shown in the work supportsthe claim of acceptability of the proposed model to assess availability that improves the security at the beginning of the software i.e., at requirement phase. The proposed model has been validated and statistical analysis signifies the acceptance of the model.

References

[1] Pfleeger, Shari Lawrence, and Robert K. Cunningham. "Why Measuring Security Is Hard." copublished by the IEEE computer and reliability societies. (2010): 46-54.

[2] Wayne Jansen, "Directions in Security Metrics Research", National Institute of standards and technology, NISTR 7564, March 2009.

[3] M. Grottke, H. Sun, R. Fricks, and K. Trivedi, "Ten fallacies of availability and reliability analysis," in Service Availability, ser. Lecture Notes in Computer Science, T. Nanya, F. Maruyama, A. Pataricza, and M. Malek, Eds. Springer Berlin Heidelberg, 2008, vol. 5017, PP. 187– 206.

[4] Antti Evesti, Eila Niemela, Katia Henttonen and MakoPalviainen, "A Tool Chain for Quality-driven Software Architecting", 2008, IEEE International Software Product LineConference.

[5] DOI: http://www.cert.org.

[6] I. Flechais, M. Sasse and S M V Hailes, "Bringing Security Home: A Process for developing secure and usable systems", NSPW'03, ACM, August 2003, pp: 18-21.

[7] B. B. Madan, K. G. Popstojanova, K. Vaidyanation and K. S. Trivedi, "A Method for Modeling and Quantifying the Security Attributes of Intrusion Tolerant System", An International Journal of Performance Evaluation, 56, 2004, Elsevier. 167-186.

[8] Nikhat, Parveen, Md. Rizwan Beg, et al. "Software Security Issues: Requirement Perspectives." International Journal of Scientific & Engineering Research ISSN 2229-5518. Volume-5.Issue-7, July 2014, pages: 11-15.

[9] G. H. Walton, T. A. Longstaff, R. C. Linder, Computational Evaluation of Software Security Attributes, IEEE, 1997.

[10] DOI: http://www.sqa.net/softwarequalitymetrics.html.

[11] Parveen, Nikhat, Md. Rizwan Beg, and M. H Khan. "Bridging the Gap between Requirement and Security through Secure Requirement Specification Checklist." International Journal of Advanced Computational Engineering and Networking(IJACEN), ISSN: 2320-2106, Volume-3, Issue-2, Feb.-2015.

[12] Iqbal, Shahid, and M. Naeem Ahmed Khan. "Yet another Set of Requirement Metrics for Software Projects."International Journal of Software Engineering and Its Applications. 6.1 (2012): 19-28.

[13] Bokhari, Mohammad Ubaidullah, and Shams Tabrez Ubaidullah Siddiqui. "Metrics for Requirements Engineering and Automated Requirements Tools."Proceedings of the 5th National Conference; INDIACom-2011.

[14] Ali, Mohammed Javeed. "Metrics for Requirements Engineering." (2006): <www.cs.umu.se/education/examina/Rapporter/JaveedAli.pdf>.

[15] C. Wang and Wulf, "A Framework for Security Measurement," in Proc. National Information Systems Security Conference, pp: 522-533, 7-10 Oct. 1997.

[16] S. Chandra, R. A. Khan, "Implementing Availability State Transition Model to Quantify Risk Factor", Advances in Computer Science, Engineering & Application, AISC, Springer, 2012 -, Pages: 937-952.

27

Music/multimedia technology: Melody synthesis and rhythm creation processes of the hybridized interactive algorithmic composition model

E. J. Garba[*], G. M. Wajiga

Department of Computer Science, Modibbo Adama (Federal) University of Technology P.M.B. 2076 Yola, Adamawa State, Nigeria

Email address:

e.j.garba@mautech.edu.ng (E. J. Garba)

Abstract: Music composition, by machine, requires the solution of a number of difficult problems in the fields of algorithm design, data representation, human interface design, and software engineering in general. These aforementioned problems led to the emergence of the objectives of this research. Consequently, a concept formulation was derived from the existing algorithmic composition models – where their strengths were harnessed and their weaknesses transparently subdued. This brought about the hybridization of the existing models that gave birth to Hybridized Interactive Algorithmic Composition model that leverages on the speed and accuracy of the computer to complement human creativity in music improvisation and composition. This paper presents both the melody synthesis and rhythm creation processes of the Hybridized Interactive Algorithmic Composition Model.

Keywords: Hybridized Interactive Algorithmic Composition Model, Algorithmic Composition, Melody Synthesis, Rhythm Creation

1. Introduction

Music is the skillful arrangement and alternation of sound and silence within a given period of time with appreciable aural perception. When musicians play instruments, sound is produced (as the sound-producing parts of the instruments vibrate/oscillate). These vibrations cause air molecules to displace one another in a systematic continuous flow, which moves away from its source. In the end, our ears perceive these air pressure fluctuations as sounds that are translated by our brains as music [1].

Musically speaking, the sounds produced are musical notes and the silences/pauses between the notes are called rests. The musical notes and rests vary in duration. That is, a note could be played for a long or short time. Thus, in contemporary music, there are six types of notes – whole, half, quarter, eighth, sixteenth and thirty-second. For proper interpretation of notes/rests duration, a piece of music is divided into portions called measures (bars). Each measure is bounded by two bars – within which a fixed number of notes/rests are required [1].

To determine the number of notes/rests in a measure, a time signature (also known as meter) is required. This is usually placed in front of a musical staff. The time signature is a fractional number written in front of any musical piece. The numerator indicates the number of beats in a measure, while the denominator specifies the type of note/rest assigned to one beat. There are so many types of meters, but the common [C] time signature is 4/4 (i.e. four beats in a measure, and each beat is a quarter note) [1]. See Table 1 for details.

Table 1. Musical Notes/Rests Interpretation.

Note Type	Note symbol	Rest symbol	Number of Notes/Rests
Whole			16
Half			8
Quarter			4
Eight			2
Sixteenth			1.

2. Computability of Music

According to [1], music is the alternation of sound and silence. It is therefore obvious that the concept of music conforms to binary theory; where only the values of 0 and 1 are considered. The binary value of "0" indicates certainly that an event will not occur; while "1" indicates certainly the event will occur.

Logically put, when sound is produced (or a note/tone is played) the binary value is 1, otherwise it is 0. That is:
- 1 ➔ sound is produced (or a note/tone is played)
- 0 ➔ silence (no note is played)

Therefore, the binary musical concept perceives music as a stream of 1s and 0s. This therefore, means that musical ideas and concepts are logical – hence computable.

3. Algorithmic Composition

Algorithmic composition is the technique of using algorithms to create music. Music composition is usually a complex and difficult task for the people not having musical knowledge or skill, and composer's expertise plays an important role. Nevertheless, there have been many studies on automatic music composition using computer since the conception of the computer, and some automatic music composition models have been proposed [2].

The formal technique of generating music was adopted again in the 20th century. The *tone-row technique* was introduced by Arnold Schönberg at the beginning of the century and further developed into *serialism* by Anton Webern and his successors [3]. In the serial technique music was factorized into parameters such as pitch, duration, and timbre that were controlled separately. A permutation was chosen from the possible values of each parameter and arranged into a row. The parameter values changed according to the row or its inversions or retrogrades [4].

According to [3], mentions some common techniques of algorithmic composition; which include state machines, rule-based, grammars, stochastic processes, and genetic algorithms. Therefore, Systems for the algorithmic composition of music can be conveniently categorized into three types; rule-based systems, systems which learn by example – knowledge-based and genetic algorithms [5] and [6].

4. Concept Formulation

A complete theory of general creativity, or even musical creativity, remains elusive. While many attempts have been made to study and document the creative process [7],[8],[9],[10] for example, any generality seems difficult to uncover. In many cases people do not know how or why they make creative decisions, and much of the creative process is difficult to repeat in controlled experiments. The question of whether creativity is computable is an issue of even greater controversy. Many researchers have argued against a computable model of creativity because, simply put, the underlying mental processes are not computable. These arguments depend largely on speculation and the personal opinion of the authors.

For instance, it has been observed that almost all forms of music involve repetition [11], either of individual sequences of notes or at some higher levels of structural grouping. Often these repetitions appear at a number of different levels simultaneously. Some compositions repeat patterns that are slightly changed at each repetition, or revolve around some musical 'theme', whereby complex harmonic, timing or key shifts in a basic theme provide a pleasing musical diversity.

It is also commonly known that what allows us to identify an individual piece of music is the *change* in pitch between notes, not the pitch of the notes themselves. We can change the key of a composition (equivalent to multiplying all frequencies by some fixed amount) and still recognise the melody [12].

According to the generative theory of tonal music, music is built from an inventory of notes and a set of rules. The rules assemble notes into a sequence and organize them into hierarchical structures of music cognition. To understand a piece means to assemble these mental structures as we listen to the piece [13].

A hybridized interactive algorithmic composition model was developed from the existing algorithmic composition models in order to minimize the weaknesses experienced when such models are used singlehandedly in music composition. The hybridization of the models (at different stages of composition) capitalized on the advantages of such models. The models for algorithmic composition used included: Mathematical [14], Grammar (Rule-Based) [15], stochastic [16], Knowledge-based [3], and Evolutionary (Genetic Algorithm) [17].

4.1. Rhythm Creation Process

Rhythmic composition is based on both mathematical and grammar models [18]. Therefore, in any contemporary music composition, the most important parameter is the meter – indicated as a time signature on the musical staff.

That is,

$$met = \frac{m}{n} \qquad (1)$$

Where: met stands for meter, m is the numerator that indicates the number of beats in a measure, n is the denominator that specifies the type of note/rest assigned to one beat. This means, therefore that a beat in any rhythm could be represented with streams of binary digits (bits) known as Binary Code (BC). See Table 2 for details:

Table 2. Beat Binary Code.

Note Type	Note symbol	Rest symbol	Beat Binary Code (this is the stream of bits required to represent a beat)		
			Bits	Note Binary Value	Rest Binary Value
Whole			16	1000 0000 0000 0000	0000 0000 0000 0000
Half			8	1000 0000	0000 0000
Quarter			4	1000	0000
Eight			2	10	00
Sixteenth			1	1	0

Therefore,

$$B_{BC} = Random(Abs(2^n - 1)) \tag{2}$$

Where: B stands for Beat, BC stands for Binary Code, Abs stands for absolute value and n is the denominator that specifies the type of note/rest assigned to one beat in a meter.

In contemporary music, the bar/measure forms the basic rhythmic and melodic unit. That means that Rhythm (R) Binary Code, which is made up of a measure, is a function of the given meter. That is:

$$R_{BC} = f(met) \tag{3}$$

$$R_{BC} = \{B_{BC_1}, B_{BC_2}, \dots, B_{BC_m}\} \tag{4}$$

Where: R stands for Rhythm, BC stands for Binary Code and m is the numerator that indicates the number of beats in a measure of a given meter. Note: R_{BC} logically represents a musical rhythmic pattern (RP). Therefore, RP = R_{BC}.

For example, if the meter (of a given piece of music) is 3/4, then it means there will be only three beats (or three Beat Binary Code) and each of the beats is assigned a quarter notes (4 bits); thus, the following mathematical, logical/binary and musical expressions are obtainable in Table 3.

Table 3. Example of Mathematical, logical/binary and musical expressions.

Mathematical expression	Logical/Binary expression	Musical expression
Based on equation (4), the following denary values could be randomly or interactively generated: RP = {10, 8, 14} This equation has only three beat values because m = 3 from the given meter of 3/4.	R_{BC} = {1010, 1000, 1110} This is the binary/logical equivalent of the denary values of the RP. Each Beat Binary Code is allocated 4 bits; n = 4 (a quarter note) from the meter of 3/4.	From Table2, it should be noted that 1 bit represents a sixteenth note. Therefore, the musical expression of this RP is:

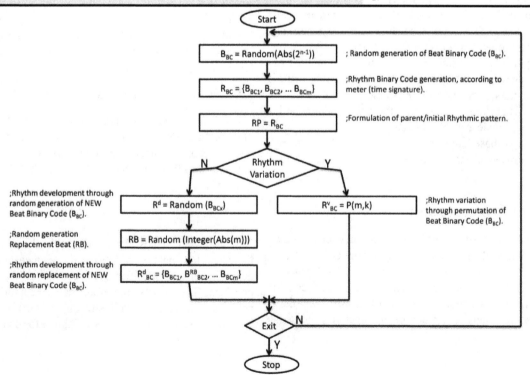

Figure 1. Rhythm Creation Process[19].

The rhythm creation process of the Hybridized Interactive Algorithmic Composition Model is developed from the concept formulation of this research [19]. Here, the beat binary code, which could be generated through the process of randomization, makes up a rhythm binary code (which in essence is a rhythmic pattern based on the given meter/time signature).

Variations of the rhythmic patterns could be generated or created through randomization or permutation of the beat binary code. The result of the rhythm creation process of the Hybridized Interactive Algorithmic Composition Model is a rhythmic pattern devoid of melody.

4.2. Melody Creation Process

According to [20], the key problem is to get explicit musical knowledge, which is both formally represented and computationally useful. With this knowledge, the composition system is built using programming techniques. The composition of music was discussed at two levels. On the level of *microstructure*, relations between notes in horizontal direction (melodic intervals) and in vertical (synchronous) direction (harmony) were discussed. *Macrostructure* deals with the larger structural parts in horizontal direction, for instance, the length of phrases and their thematic and tonal relations. The vertical (synchronous) direction is described by harmony. Voice leading rules (for instance, the *forbidden parallel fifth*)-rule combine the vertical and micro structurally horizontal direction. The processes of classical music composition were divided into several subtasks: Using a top-down-approach, it started with planning the macrostructure of the piece.

4.3. Compositional Parameters and Operational Constraints

Some of the key parameters for music composition include scale/key, meter (time signature), tempo, articulations and dynamics. Beat melody/motif is a melodic sequence that consists of notes in one beat. Beat motif is determined by the composer [21].

$$\text{Beat Motif} = f(\text{beat note in a bar}) \qquad (5)$$

$$\text{Beat Motif} = f(\text{beat note in terms of } 16^{th} \text{ note}) \qquad (6)$$

4.3.1. Operational Note Type
The operational note type is the 16th note. This means that the Beat Motif is made of 16th notes of a beat. The number of 16th notes in the Beat Motif depends on the value of n from the given meter. For instance, if a meter (m/n) is 6/8, it means there are six 8th notes in the bar. Note that n = 8 - meaning each beat is an 8th; and because the Beat Motif is expressed in terms of 16th notes, then the Beat Motif is made up of two 16th notes.

4.3.2. Octave Range
This determines the types of pitches to be used in the musical composition. Here, the pitches were denoted using

the Pitch-Octave convention. In this convention, alphabets are used to denote pitch classes while the number indicates the octave. For instance, C5 means pitch class "C" and octave "5". Therefore, for instance, an octave range of C3 – B5 means that during composition, notes/pitches that fall within this range are eligible for usage.

4.3.3. Operational Domains
It determines the possible pitches that could be assigned to one note in the Beat Motif. Therefore, the operational domains of a note is {P1, P2, ... , Pmax}. Where: P stands for pitch and max is the total number of pitches as specified by the Octave Range. For instance, if the number of notes in the Beat Motif is U, the operational domain is [{P1, P2, ... , Pmax}1, {P1, P2, ... , Pmax}2, ... , {P1, P2, ... , Pmax}U]. Therefore, the total possible Beat Motif from such an operation domain is $(\sum_{i=1}^{max} P)^U$.

4.3.4. PC Segment
The Pitch Class (PC) segment consists of a bar of melodic sequence. Note that the melodic sequence is made up of Beat Motifs (note that the number of Beat Motifs corresponds to the number of beats in a bar). That is:

$$PC_{seg} = \{BM_1, BM_2, ..., BM_m\} \qquad (7)$$

Where: PC_{seg} stands for PC segment, BM stands for Beat Motif and m stands for number of beats in a bar from a given meter.

The PC segment is defined either by the composer or automatically generated by the computer. The user could define all the BMs which make up the PC segment; alternatively, the user could define the initial BM while the rest of the BMs are automatically generated by randomization or permutation of the notes of the initial BM.

For example, if given a 4/4 meter, a beat motif of four 16th notes of c, e, g and a; then BM = (c, e, g, a). This means that the pitch class values of the BM = (1, 5, 8, 10). However, through randomization and permutation, there are 23 more possible beat motifs. From the possible 24 beat motifs, just four BMs were required (according to the meter – 4/4) to form the PC segment. This gives rise to 255,024 possible PC segments. One of PC segments could be this:

$$PC_{seg} = \{(c,e,g,a),(a,g,e,c),(c,c,c,c),(e,g,c,a)\} \qquad (8)$$

5. Prime Form

The Prime Form is created when rhythm is now added to the PC segment. Note that the PC segment contains melodic sequence dependent on the value of beat in the given meter. Therefore, Prime Form = PC Segment + Rhythm.

For instance, given this PC segment:

$$PC_{seg} = \{(c,e,g,a),(a,g,e,c),(c,c,c,c),(e,g,c,a)\} \qquad (9)$$

While the rhythm pattern is:

$$R_{BC} = \{(1010),(1110),(1000),(1101)\} \qquad (10)$$

In order to get a prime form from the PC segment and rhythm pattern, the only notes picked were those where the rhythm binary code value is 1. See Table 4.

Table 4. Prime Form Creation.

Note	1	2	3	4	5	6	7	8	9	10	11	12	13	14	15	16
PC_{seg}	c	e	g	a	a	g	e	c	c	c	c	c	e	g	c	a
R_{BC}	1	0	1	0	1	1	1	0	1	0	0	0	1	1	0	1
Prime Form	c		g		a	g	e		c				e	g		a

6. Note Duration Parser

The note duration parser is used for refining the prime form where the "_" symbol was appended to a note preceding it or the "_" symbol is used as rest. Note duration is determined through a stochastic process of probability and randomization. The end results of this stage were prime forms with different combinations of note duration.

From prime form: Prime Form: {(c, _, g, _),(a, g, e, _), (c, _, _, _),(e, g, _, a)}, the following results are possible:

Note that with just one PC segment, several prime forms could be created from different rhythm variations. That is, one PC segment could be applied to several rhythm patterns; likewise, one rhythm pattern could be applied to several PC segments. This is the flexibility of Hybridized Interactive Algorithmic Composition (HIAC) model.

7. Composition Rules Parser and Optimizer

At this point, the Composition Rules Parser analyzes the Prime Form based on the basic prevalent contemporary music composition rules; after which, the Prime Form was further refined by the Optimizer. The optimization process could be done either manually by the composer or automatically. The final result of this stage is known as Optimized Prime Form. See the following example of an Optimized Prime Form:

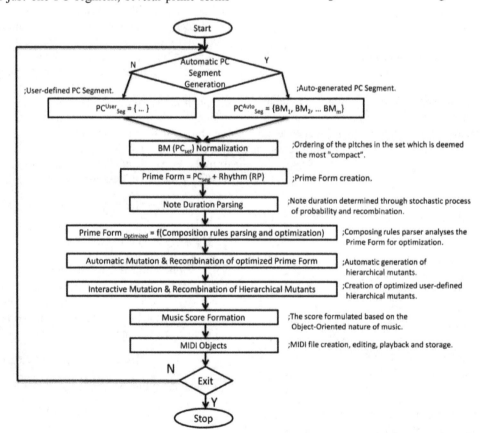

Figure 2. Melody Creation Process[19].

8. Conclusion

The above formulated melody synthesis and rhythm creation processes of the Hybridized Interactive Algorithmic Composition Model have their place in music composition; thereby, offsetting the complex task of music creation from the human composer to the machine via algorithms. This ensures speed and accuracy with minimal and interactive interference by the human composer.

References

[1] Garba, E. J. (2003). Computer Music – Rhythm Programming, Processing and Mastering. Trafford Publishing, Canada.

[2] Unehara, M. and T. Onisawa. (2009). Construction of Music Composition System with Interactive Genetic Algorithm. University of Tsukuba, 1-1-1 Tennodai, Tsukuba, Ibaraki, 305-8573, JAPAN. http://www.idemployee.id.tue.nl/g.w.m.rauterberg/conferences/CD_doNotOpen/ADC/final_paper/549.pdf.

[3] Järveläinen, H. (2000). *Algorithmic Musical Composition.* Helsinki University of Technology, Telecommunications software and multimedia laboratory. Retrieved December 5, 2007, from www.tml.tkk.fi/Studies/Tik-111.080/2000/papers/hanna/alco.pdf.

[4] Grout, D. J. (1996). History of Western Music. W.W. Norton & Company, 5th edition.

[5] Todd, P. M. and G. M. Werner. (1999). Frankensteinian Methods for Evolutionary Music Composition. In Griffith and Todd, P. M. (Eds.) *Musical networks: Parallel perception and performance*, 313-339.

[6] Espi, D., P. J. Ponce de Leon, C. Perez-Sancho, D. Rizo, J. M. Inesta, F. Moreno-Seco, and A. Pertusa. (2009). A Cooperative Approach to Style-Oriented Music Composition. Departamento de Lenguajes y Sistemas Informaticos University of Alicante, Spain. http://193.145.231.49/repositori/grfia/pubs/186/wijcai07.pdf.

[7] Barron, F. (1969). Creative Person and Creative Process. Holt, Rinehart and Winston, Inc.

[8] Crutchfield, R.S. (1973). The Creative Process. In *Creativity: Theory and Research.* College and University Press, Bloomberg, M., 54 – 74.

[9] Schillinger, J. (1948). The Mathematical Basis of the Arts. The Philosophical Library, New York.

[10] Johnson–Laird, P.N. (1993). Human and Machine Thinking. Lawerance Eribaum Associates.

[11] Leach, J. and Fitch, J. (1995). Nature, Music, and Algorithmic Composition. *Computer Music Journal 19(2)*, 23 – 33.

[12] McCormack, J. (2009). Grammar Based Music Composition. Computer Science Department Monash University, Clayton Victoria 3168. http://www.csse.monash.edu.au/~jonmc/research/Papers/L-systemsMusic.pdf.

[13] de Mantaras, R. L. and J. L. Arcos. (2002). AI and Music: From Composition to Expressive Performance. American Association for Artificial Intelligence.

[14] Gilkerson, J., Li, W. and Owen, D. (2005). *An Introduction to Random Number Generators and Monte Carlo Methods.* Retrieved June 1, 2007, from http://www.mgnet.org/~douglas/Classes/cs521/rng-mc/RandomMonteCarlo2005.ppt.

[15] Towsey, M., Brown, A., Wright, S. and Diederich, J. (2009). *Towards Melodic Extension Using Genetic Algorithms.* Queensland University of Technology Kelvin Grove, QLD 4059, Australia. Retrieved September 23, 2009, fromhttp://eprints.qut.edu.au/169/1/towsey.pdf.

[16] Microsoft Encarta Encyclopedia. (2009). *Stochastic.* Microsoft Encarta 2009 [DVD]. Redmond, WA, USA: Microsoft Corporation.

[17] Holland, J.H. (1975). *Adaptation in Natural and Artificial Systems.* USA: Ann Arbor, University of Michigan Press (Second edition: MIT Press, 1992).

[18] Garba, E. J. and Wajiga, G. M. (2011). A Review of Multimedia and Music Technology: Mathematical Foundations of Rhythm Generations in Algorithmic Composition, *Bagale Journal of Pure and Applied Sciences,* Volume 8, Number 1, December 2011, pp. 64-74. http://www.mautech.edu.ng/

[19] Garba, E. J. (2012). *Multimedia Technology: A Software Framework for Interactive Music Composition.* (PhD Thesis in Music/Multimedia Technology, School of Pure and Applied Sciences Federal University of Technology, Yola, Nigeria).

[20] Lothe, M. (2007). *Knowledge-based Composition of Classical Minuets by a Computer.* Universitat Stuttgart; Institut fur Informatik Breitwiesenstr. 20-22 D-70565 Stuttgart, Germany. Retrieved August 10, 2008, from www.informatik.uni-stuttgart.de/ifi/is/Forschung/Papiere/mathis/aisb2000-loethe-pn.ps.

[21] Garba, E. J., Wajiga, G. M. and Oye, N. D. (2011). Multimedia and Music Technology: Mathematical Foundations of Melody Synthesis in Algorithmic Composition, *International Journal of Computer Vision & Applications,* Volume 1, Number 1, April 2011, pp. 9-14. http://www.3kbioxml.com/3k/index.php/IJCVA

28

Using BRs Filtering Method for Transform Pre-CIM to CIM in MDA Approach

Najiba Addamssiri, Azzeddine Dahbi, Mohammed Mouhir, Abdelouahed Kriouile, Taoufiq Gadi

Lavete Laboratory, Hassan 1 University, Settat, Morocco

Email address:

addam.naji@gmail.com (N. Addamssiri), azdine.im@gmail.com (A. Dahbi), mouhir38@gmail.com (M. Mouhir),
kriouile1970@gmail.com (A. Kriouile), g.taoufiq@yahoo.fr (T. Gadi)

Abstract: In order to facilitate communication between business experts and analysts, we adopt the pre-CIM as the most abstract level in the MDA process, integrating the SBVR (Semantics of Business Vocabulary and Rules) to express the rules in this level. Incomplete communication among these stakeholders will produce anomalies in the BRs (redundancy, conflict, circularity). This will lead to serious errors in the system and will heavily increase the final cost. We propose to incorporate a crucial step to filter and correct these BRs. Going through this step will verify their consistency and coherence before turning them into BPMN located in the CIM level. This is a great advantage in terms of saving time and reducing maintenance costs.

Keywords: MDA, CIM, PIM, Model Transformation, BPMN, Business Rules

1. Introduction

The MDA (Model-Driven Architecture) [1] is an initiative of the OMG released in 2000. It is a proposal to both an architecture and a development approach. The basic idea of MDA is to separate functional specifications of a system from its implementation details on a given platform. For this, the MDA classify the models in the development process into three levels. The first level CIM defines the business process model and aims to get the key activities of the company. It is designed to enable the link between the business analyst who works on the requirements and the IT architect who offers technical solutions [2]. The second level PIM (Platform Independent Model) shows a view of the system independently of the details of the technology. In addition, the third level (PSM Platform Specific Model) contains information for the realization of a technology on a specific platform. The MDA approach allows applications to interoperate by linking their models and promotes adaptability to changing platforms and techniques. The MDA implementation is entirely based on models and their transformations.

John K [3] has proposed to add pre-CIM as the first level of analysis of the problem to simplify the production of domain models during the development of MDA. Thus avoids the complexity of the immediate study of CIM formalization and

PIM notations modeling. In this article, we adopt the idea of John K by adopting the pre-CIM as the most abstract level in the MDA, the fact which helps to express and filter anomalies of business rules to avoid any unexpected assignment at CIM that will spread to PIM and PSM levels.

The anomalies identification of the business rules is increasingly a matter of great concern for the development of the information systems (IS) because it affects their final costs, particularly where this identification occurs at a later stage. In order to test the coherence and consistency of the business rules we propose to move the SBVR [4] (vocabulary and semantics of business rules) to the pre-CIM level and add to it a crucial step for filtering and correcting the found structural anomalies.

The rest of this article is organized as follows: section 2 introduces relevant literature review. The Section 3 presents the proposed approach. In section 4, an example given to illustrate the applicability of our approach. Finally, section 5, concludes the paper and informs the reader about the future prospects of our ongoing research.

2. Background and Related Work

2.1. The Architecture of Pre-CIM

The architecture of the pre-CIM should be simple and

understandable by both business experts and analysts. The latter have various languages which allow the establishment of complex constructions. Among these languages we mention, first and foremost, flowcharts that have 6 basic structures and 4 extended ones whereas BPMN [6] had 11 basic structures and 39 extended ones.

Wahl and Sindre [8] analyzed BPMN based on the Semiotic Quality Framework and concluded that the former is far from being understood by both non-technical domain experts and IT professionals. In fact, there are 23 different pre-defined elements in the BPMN to represent different types of events. Most of them have their origin in the IT domain and not the business domain and they are therefore not intuitive for the business user.

Dima [5] tried to model the pre-CIM by presenting a notation based on the notions of rules, activities, objects, data, and bloop for expressing the unidentified concepts. These concepts are hard to understand by business experts with no IT knowledge. In addition, these concepts are very limited and they do not allow creating a complete CIM level.

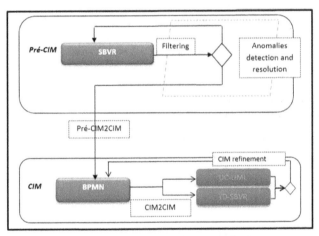

Figure 1. Our proposed architecture.

2.2. Architecture of CIM

In our previous work [8], we have constructed the architecture of the CIM level that introduces their static, dynamic, and functional perspectives. We have represented the models of business process by BPMN, and we have proposed to transform them horizontally to detailed use case models with the textual description formalized by SBVR. In [9] we have presented the refinement of the CIM level using a horizontal transformation from use case diagram to BPMN.

Olfa and Jack [10] and Steen Bas and al [9] present an automatic transformation from SBVR to BPMN without supporting the automatic filtering and correction of the business rules. Knowing that any automation based on incoherent business rules leads to serious errors in the system and generates at the end a different product that differs from the customer expectations, which affects the development time and the final cost.

Taking advantage of the utility of pre-CIM we can

overcome these problems through the displacement of the SBVR at this level and the addition of a step for filtering the business rules before transforming them to BPMN located in the CIM level.

3. Overview of Our Proposed Approach

We are introducing our approach in three fundamental steps, as illustrated in the figure 1. First, we present the architecture of pre-CIM level represented by SBVR that describes the business rules based on natural language. Secondly, we expose the SBVR filtering step by detecting and resolving its structural anomalies as well as redundancy and conflict. Finally, we automatically transform the SBVR to BPMN located in the CIM level.

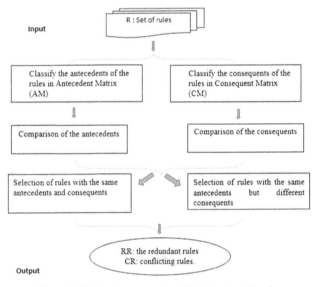

Figure 2. BRs Redundancy and conflict detection algorithm.

3.1. Model Representing the Pre-CIM of our Method: SBVR

We have chosen the SBVR for modeling the architecture of pre-CIM. This choice of displacement of SBVR in pre-CIM level responds to two fundamental aspects. Primo, the chosen model in this level is able to describe the contextual problem using natural sentences understood by business experts and analysts. In addition, it is usable and implementable by the system respecting CIM specifications. Secondo, before transforming the BRs into CIM level, the chosen model permits the integration of the step of filtering and correction of BR's structural anomalies.

3.2. Filtering and Correction of Business Rules

We have made a comparative study of a set of methods used for the treatment of structural anomalies of business rules. Among these methods; Zhang [12] presents a novel rule model known as SOECAP (Subject, Object, Event, Condition, Action, Post-condition) treating dynamically the BR's conflict resolution using Vague set Theory [13]. Denilson [14] presents a method for verifying the consistency of business rules using alloy model. It identifies and specifies the BRs to build up a conceptual model, describing the business concepts and their relations. Then it transforms the rules into an Alloy Model that verifies their consistency and coherence.

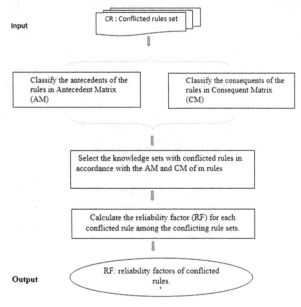

Figure 3. *URKCTA algorithm for resolving conflicted rules.*

Richard [15] describes a conflict resolution theory using propositional logic in order to exclude the inference engine for systems during the development process. It uses verification criteria and solution strategies and finally derives four classes of rules and their rule ordering strategies. Rule based systems using FRS (First Rule Satisfied) rules contain four classes of rules.

Method URCKTA [16] uses a decision group, with an algorithm that has a confidence factor. In the algorithm, a "reliability factor" refers to the reliability level of the conflicting or redundant rules. The rule with a higher reliability factor will be chosen.

From a comparative study we have deduced that URKCTA method is the only one studied method. It automatically resolves redundancy and conflicts among Business Rules. Unfortunately, this method doesn't propose a step of anomalies detection. Therefore, in this work we propose firstly, an algorithm that detects redundancy and conflict of the business rules as shown in figure 2, then we call for URKCTA method to resolve these anomalies as shown in figure 3.

After the detection and resolution of the structural anomalies in business rules, we present in the next section the transformation rules between the SBVR and the BPMN.

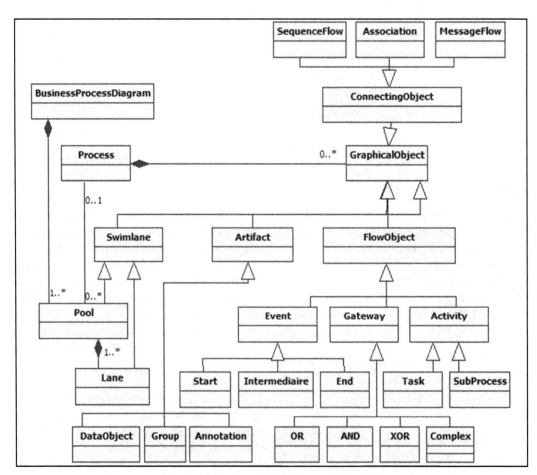

Figure 4. *Main fragment of the meta-model BPMN.*

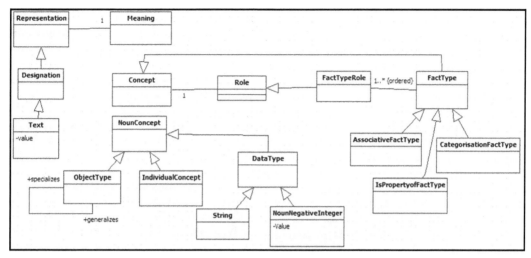

Figure 5. *Main fragment of the meta-model SBVR.*

Table 1. *BPMN2UC Transformation Rules.*

Rule	Source element	Target element	Example
1	action in Fact type with transitive verb	Activity	the activity 'inserts card' from the fact type 'client inserts card'
2	Subject of sentence having a transitive active verb	Swimlane	the swimlane 'client' from the fact type 'client inserts card'
3	the subject with transitive active verb in the same sentence	Activity within a swimlane	the activity 'inserts card' in the swimlane 'client'
4	two successive actions with one subject	sequence Flow	'the machine displays main-screen' and 'the machine requests password'
5	Two Successive actions with two subjects.	message Flow	'the machine requests PIN' and 'user enters PIN'
6	action in Fact type with condition	exclusive Gateway	It is obligatory that the client renters PIN If the bank determines invalid PIN
7	action in Fact type with condition and parallel transitions	Parallel Gateway	It is obligatory that the machine retains the card, and the client contacts the bank, if the client enters the PIN after three tries
8	multiple transactions followed by one action	Multiple Gateway	it is obligatory that the user inserts the card and inters the PIN in order to the machine opens her account

3.3. SBVR and BPMN Mapping Rules

In order to establish the transformation rules between the SBVR and the BPMN we need a SBVR meta-model and BPMN meta-model. These meta-models are briefly discussed later.

3.3.1. BPMN Meta-Model

Figure 4 present the BPMN meta-model provided by the Eclipse BPMN modeler [17].

3.3.2. SBVR Meta-Model

The figure 5 presents an excerpt of simplified meta-model of SBVR [11] that has been used for the representation of rules.

3.3.3. Transformation Rules

Table 1 present the transformation rules between SBVR and BPMN. SBVR elements present the source meta-model elements and BPMN elements presents target meta-model elements.

The transformation will be constructed with QVT language [18] on EMF eclipse framework that will be able to extract the swimlanes, activities, getways, sequences flow and messages flow from the corrected SBVR.

The obtained result is an improved BPMN model avoiding any errors that may occur due to conflicted or redundant rules.

To show the interest of the filtering step which we propose, we present, in the next section, a case study containing a number of conflicting and redundant rules.

Machine *displays* main-screen
Client *inserts* Card
Client *enters* PIN
Bank *verifies* PIN
PIN *is* incorrect
Machine *retains* card
Client *contacts* Bank
PIN *is* correct
Machine *prompts for* amount
Client *enters* withdraw
Bank *checks* balance
Bank *debits* account
Machine *prints* receipt
Machine *renders* notes
Machine *ejects* card
Client *accepts* notes
Client *accepts* card

Figure 6. *A sample SBVR business vocabulary.*

4. Case Study

To evaluate our approach, we propose to use this ATM system case study which enjoys a significant data flow.
- The first step is the modeling of SBVR:

Figures 6 and 7 illustrate the business vocabulary and business rules extracted from the customer specifications that are generated for an ATM machine showing the interaction with the customer.
- The second step concerns filtering and correction of business rules:

After the Classification of antecedents and consequents of all rules presented in Table 2, we generate both AM and CM matrices and we compare them to generate redundant and conflicted rules. Table 3 present redundant and conflicted rules selected.

It is obligatory that each machine verifies PIN if client enters PIN
It is obligatory that the client enters PIN if bank verify that the PIN is invalid
It is obligatory that the machine ejects the card, if the PIN is invalid
It is obligatory that each client receives exactly one card if machine ejects at least one card
It is obligatory that machine prompts for amount if the client enters a correct PIN
It is obligatory that the bank checks balance if client enters withdrawal
It is obligatory that the machine ejects card and prints receipt if 20> requested amount> 400 dollars.
It is obligatory that the machine ejects card and prints receipt if 10> requested amount> 500 dollars.
It is obligatory that the machine ejects card and prints receipt if 20> requested amount>= 200 dollars.
It is obligatory that the bank debits account if the requested amount less or equal to account balance.
It is obligatory that the bank debits account if the requested amount less or equal to account balance.
It is obligatory that machine renders notes, ejects card and prints receipt if the bank debits account
It is obligatory that client accepts notes if the machine renders notes
It is obligatory that client accepts card if machine ejects card
It is obligatory that client accepts card if machine ejects card

Figure 7. Sample SBVR business rules.

Table 2. antecedents and consequent rules.

Number of rule	Antecedent	Consequent
R1	Client enters PIN	Machine verifies PIN
R2	Bank verifythat the PIN is invalid	client enters PIN
R3	PIN is invalid	Machine ejects the card
R4	Machine ejects at least one card	Client receives exactly one card
R5	Machine prompts for amount	Client enters a correct PIN
R6	Bank checks balance	Client enters withdrawal
R7	400 >requested amount> 20 dollars.	machine ejects card and prints receipt
R8	500 dollars >requested amount> 10 dollars.	machine ejects card and prints receipt
R9	200 dollars >=requested amount> 10 dollars	machine ejects card and prints receipt
R10	requested amount less or equal to account balance.	Bank debits account
R11	requested amount less or equal to account balance.	Bank debits account
R12	bank debits account	Machine renders notes, ejects card and prints receipt
R13	Machine renders notes	Client accepts notes
R14	Machine ejects card	Client accepts card
R15	Machine ejects card	Client accepts card

Table 3. redundant rules and conflicting rules.

Redundant rules	R10, R11
	R14, R15
Conflictual rules	R7, R8 et R9

We remove repetitive rules from the discovered redundant ones, then we go to competition of the reliability factor of each conflict rule detected as presented in Table 4, at last we choose the rule having the highest reliability factor:

Table 4. conflicting rules reliability factors.

Number of rule	reliability factor
R7	0.63
R8	0.66
R9	0.34

- The third step is to implement the mapping between BPMN and SBVR:

After running mapping rules proposed in Table 2 to generate automatically the new BPMN model, we have obtained the Swimlane client (with the activities: inserts card, enters PIN, enters withdraw, contacts bank, accepts notes, and accepts card), and the swimlane machine (with their activities: the swimlane bank (with the activities: verifies PIN, checks balance, and debits/deposit account). The figure

9 illustrate the generated BPMN model.

5. Conclusion

This article proposes an approach in the context of the architecture model driven by modeling a pre-CIM level and transforms it to CIM level. We have presented an architecture for pre-CIM using SBVR and adding an important step for filtering business rules before transforming them into BPMN located at CIM. This step leads us to achieve a very

important result by generating a correct CIM without any human intervention.

This proposal completes our previous work [8], [19], [20] and [9] that subscribe under the global approach that aims to automate the whole development process.

Future improvements are strongly suggested such as the generation of a method that detects and resolves other anomalies of business rules like overlapping, circularity and the incompleteness.

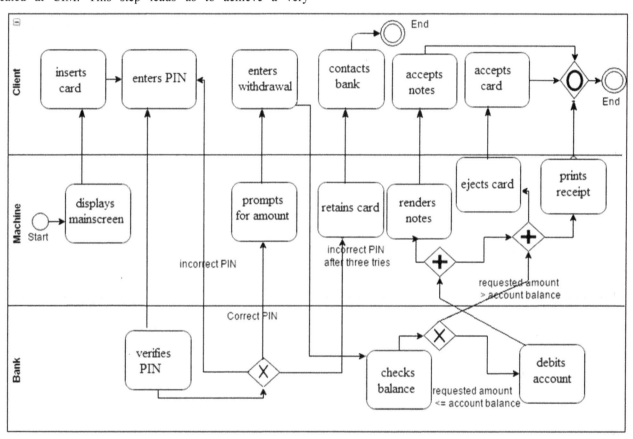

Figure 8. BPMN diagram from above SBVR vocabulary and rules.

References

[1] M. J et M. J, MDA Guide Version 1.0.1, , Object Management Group (OMG), 2003.

[2] B. A W, I. S et J. S, A rational approach to modeldriven, IBM SYSTEMS JOURNAL, 2006.

[3] D. Harel, «Statecharts: A Visual Formalism for Complex Systems,» Science of Computer Programming, vol. 8, n° %13, pp. 231 - 274, 1987.

[4] S. Imran, M. G. Bajwa et B. B. Lee, «SBVR Business Rules Generation from Natural Language Specification,» Artificial Intelligence for Business Agility, pp. 541-545, 2011.

[5] OMG, "BPMN 2.0 by Example Version 1.0 (non-normative)," http://www.omg.org/spec/BPMN/2.0/examples/PDF, June 2010.

[6] T. Wahl et G. Sindre, «An analytical evaluation of BPMN using a semiotic quality framework.,» the 10th International Workshop Exploring Modelliong Methods in Systems Analysis and Design (EMMSAD '05).

[7] P. Dima, S. Christian, P. Keith et J. Sheridan, Enriching the Model-Driven Architecture with Weakly Structured Information, 2012.

[8] K. Abdel ouhed, A. Najiba, B. Younes et G. Taoufiq, «Obtaining Behavioral Model of PIM from the CIM,» chez Multimedia Computing and Systems (ICMCS), 2014 International Conference , Marrakech, 2015.

[9] A. Najiba, K. Abdelouhaed, B. Youssef et T. Gadi, «Generating the PIM Behavioral Model from the CIM using QVT,» Journal of Computer Science and Information Technology, 2015.

[10] C. Olfa et A. Jacky, «Automated transformation of business rules specification to business process model,» SEKE2014, pp. 684-687, 2014.

[11] S. Bas, P. Luís Ferreira et I. Maria-Eugenia, «Automatic generation of optimal business processes from business rules,» chez Enterprise Distributed Object Computing Conference Workshops (EDOCW), Vitoria, 2010.

[12] Z. Qingchuan, Z. Guangping, X. Chaoen et Y. Yang, «A rule conflict resolution method based on Vague set,» Soft Computing , vol. 18, pp. 549-555, 2013.

[13] L. An et N. Wilfred, «Vague Sets or Intuitionistic Fuzzy Sets for Handling Vague Data: Which One Is Better?,» Lecture Notes in Computer Science, vol. 3716 , pp. 401-416, 2005.

[14] G. Denilson dos Santos, S. Eber Assis et J. A. Antônio, «A Method for Verifying the Consistency of Business Rules Using Alloy,» chez International Conference on Software Engineering & Knowledge Engineering, Vancouver, Canada, 2014.

[15] H. Richard C, «The no inference engine theory — Performing conflict resolution during development,» Decision Support Systems, p. 435–444, 2006.

[16] C. MIN-YUAN et H. CHIN-JUNG, «A Novel Approach for Treating Uncertain Rule-based Knowledge Conflicts,» JOURNAL OF INFORMATION SCIENCE AND ENGINEERING, vol. 25, pp. 649-663, 2008.

[17] Eclipse, BPMN Modeler, 2009.

[18] O. M. Group, Meta Object Facility (MOF) 2.0 Query/View/Transformation, V1.1, 2011.

[19] A. A. N. G. T. &. B. Y. Kriouile, «Getting the Static Model of PIM from the CIM,» chez 3rd Colloquium IEEE on Information Science and Technology (CiSt'14), Tetuan, 2014.

[20] A. K. S. B. T. G. Najiba Addamssiri1, «MDA Approach: Refinement and Validation of CIM Level Using SBVR,» Mediterranean Conference on Information & Communication Technologies'2015, 2015.

Oil and Gas Pipeline Design Management System: A Case Study for Domain-Specific Modeling

Japheth Bunakiye Richard[1], Asagba Oghenekaro Prince[2]

[1]Department of Mathematics/Computer Science, Faculty of Science, Niger Delta University, Yenagoa, Nigeria
[2]Department of Computer Science, Faculty of Physical Science and Information Technology, University of Port Harcourt, Port Harcourt, Nigeria

Email address:
rb.japheth@ndu.edu.ng (J. B. Richard), asagba.prince@uniport.edu.ng (A. O. Prince)

Abstract: The intent of this paper is to define a common case study for the domain-specific modeling research community. The domain of the case study is oil and gas pipeline design management systems, i.e., systems that help in identifying, handling, and controlling a pipeline design task by coordinating the communication between all component models and dimensions involved in handling the design, by allocating and managing resources, and by providing access to relevant design-related information to domain experts. This document contains general informal requirements for a pipeline design management systems (PDMSs), a feature model for the PDMS product line, and a domain model for the PDMS, as well as an informal physical pipeline model of the PDMS. Domain specific modeling researchers who want to demonstrate the power of their technique can hence apply the approach in other related areas at the most appropriate level of abstraction in the domain of pipeline engineering.

Keywords: Oil and Gas Pipeline Engineering, Domain-Specific Modeling, Feature Models, Design Models, Computer Aided Design (CAD)

1. Introduction

The need for cost-effective and efficient design tools and methodologies that could aid better, and provide faster and productive solutions to pipeline designs has grown significantly over time. A pipeline design can range from interactive aggregation of graphics primitives to the formation of a graphics model through assemblies and subassemblies of the primitives in a typical CAD system [1]. Applying the principles of solid and parametric modeling, these graphics models can be built up to possible display in various ways and also to determine some material properties, they can even be assigned parametric dimensions and geometric constraints to define features, and to create relationships between these features in order to create what is referred to as intelligent models [12]. Though these intelligent models can be functional to determine the analysis of the application of the properties of the members of the oil and gas pipeline domain of engineering activities such as withstand external constraints, flow dynamics, applied loads, temperature and pressure, the process is still classified as a repetitive and time wasting task.

The reason for the repetition is that objects are explicitly described in conventional design modeling systems (i.e. Computer Aided (CAD) Systems). When one aspect of the model is changed, often several changes have to be made to satisfy design intent or the implicit rules of the design. This is because the software [1] does not keep track of the rules and the designer must decide where and when they are broken. The challenge is the issue of interaction between models, interactions in the way of concepts devoid of possible parametric constraints within a CAD system [10]. Interactions that can produce other complete models with noticeable properties relative to a given set of concerns in relevant domains that captures accurately and concisely all of its interpretation and design intent for specific problems and solutions.

Domain specific modeling is predicated on seeing the pipeline design (i.e. the graphics model from a CAD) as the entity during development, it is the model that reflects the prescriptive technical characteristics prevalent in the domain. It also represents the concepts of the domain within which language formalism is created to enhance model interaction and processing to produce an executable program or other models [10]. The aim is to abstract away technical details of computing from the domain engineer, allowing them to create pipeline designs or specifications without having to be an expert programmer or user of CAD systems. To make sure that the domain-specific modeling approach is somehow applicable to this case study, we present a collection of models from AutoCAD that describe the components of a pipeline design at different levels of abstraction [12].

2. Related Work

Domain-Specific Modeling raises the level of abstraction beyond programming by specifying the solution directly using domain concepts. So generating some final products from high-level specification abstractions is a worthwhile software engineering venture for productivity. In this same line of thought Kienzle et al. [3], defined a common case study for the aspect-oriented modeling (AOM) research community. In their work, the domain of the case study is crisis management systems (CMS), i.e., systems that help in identifying and handling a crisis situation by orchestrating a communication and allocating managing resources between all parties involved in handling the crisis. Their goal was to making sure that all AOM approaches and techniques are somehow applicable to this case study, by presenting a collection of models that describe the CMS at different levels of abstraction. Afredo et al. [14] in their case study defined the requirements of a Software Product Line (SPL) aimed at managing car crash crises. Basic features along with desired variations were proposed such that it results in a small SPL definition. The primary focus of their proposed variations was to allow for static and dynamic variations (i.e., dynamic change between variants at runtime). All the information concerning possible variations and their possible implementations were introduced, which serves to illustrate the individual advantages and disadvantages of aspect-oriented modeling (AOM), feature-oriented models (FOM), and object-oriented modeling (OOM). This work adopted the same approach to defining a case study for the domain specific modeling (DSM) research community. The domain of our case study is pipeline systems design management and is closely tied to the DSM manifesto, which is, raise the abstractions; such that a language metamodel has to represent concepts from the domain of consideration, i.e. the domain of oil and gas pipeline engineering.

3. Methodology

We are basically looking at requirements in a pipeline systems modeling system. Our approach is hinged on user requirements documentation for a pipeline systems modeling system based on the theory and practice of domain specific modeling. In line with Domain specific modeling guidelines, we have to as a first step visit an industry for a case study. BG Technical Nigeria limited was visited for over a period of three months and the user requirements as real requirements analysis

document was created.. BG Technical Limited (BGT) [11] is a pipeline service company located in Nigeria with significant activity in Africa. The key requirements for the system work flow are as follows [9]:

1 Stakeholders design intent characterized as the view points of the input parameters should be part of the design concept. The term design intent refers to identified interests and disciplines of all the stakeholders of this system as it relates to pipeline design and highlights physical attributes that must be considered in completing the modelling process. Physical attributes are those parameters that govern the size, layout, and dimensional limits or proportions of the pipeline components. The components here refer to the graphics models produced from primitives commonly found in CAD systems.

2 To ensure that the graphics models represents the pipeline domain model with sound underlying pipeline engineering principles, which can be linked to produce a total life cycle approach to pipeline systems design and operation.

3 To be embedded in the domain model a semantic model subset with a focus on the user's perspectives, and consisting of the classes of the concepts and their relationships. As knowledge changes, the semantic model can change too, to ensure that physical components continue to do what the users want them to do in order to preserve and to produce clear design specifications for pipeline physical assets such as pipes, valves, active equipment (pumps, compressors, etc.,), instruments and supports.

4 Functional commonalities of the application domain should be identified in the modelling language structure. These common and differing functions can be abstracted and represented so that specific design scenarios are evolved as an adaptation or refinement of the model.

5 A domain analysis module should be incorporated with a feature model representing the physical components to support communication between the requirements analysis and the design phases respectively.

4. Contribution

Pipeline Design is the process of creating detailed plans and drawing of the nature of the pipeline with a view to solving problems that might occur in the construction and operation of the pipeline these problems may be hydraulic, structural or geotechnical. Pipelines are the most common means of transporting oil or gas [11]. A pipeline is like any other flow line. The main differences are that pipelines are long and continuously welded; they are most often either buried or otherwise inaccessible due to their location over the majority of their length. These differences mean that small sections of pipeline are not easily removed for maintenance and consequently great care is taken to prevent problems arising in the first place [10]. Also pipelines are extremely expensive to lay, and as such great care must be taken to put the design from inception in the right perspectives and on time. Generally, when designing a pipeline, the engineer considers the physical and chemical properties of the fluid, to be pumped through the pipeline; the maximum volume of fluid that will be pumped through the pipeline at any time, the nature of the environment through which the pipeline is going to traverse; whether the pipeline is on land or offshore and the whether the climate is warm or cold and the required delivery pressure [4]. More specifically the engineer considers Pipe diameter required (The larger the diameter of the pipeline, the more fluid can be moved through it), Pipe length (The greater the length of a segment of pipeline, the greater the total pressure drop), Specific gravity and density Compressibility, Operating and ambient temperatures, Viscosity and Vapour Pressure etc. In the design of oil and gas pipelines, pressure drop, flow capacity and pumping or compression horsepower required are key calculations [4]. In most pipeline calculations, assumptions must be made initially. For instance, a line size may be assumed in order to determine maximum operating pressure and the pressure drop in a given length of pipe for a given flow volume. If the resulting pressure drop, when added to the known delivery pressure exceeds the allowable working pressure, a larger pipe size must usually be chosen [9].

4.1. Materials for Adaptability

The pipeline design management system should contain the following functionalities for adaptability with conventional DSM platform:

a. A rule processing module responsible for coordinating the communication between graphics models specific to transmission pipelines and a layer of reusable software interface crafted to handle modeling in a timely manner [11].
b. The user could make some input through guided notations from an interface, and the system can then match these inputs with a library of domain concepts to produce desired designs.
c. Creating models that can be processed to produce artefacts.
d. Wrap up and archive designs to produce target codes

4.2. Materials for Usability

The pipeline design management system shall exhibit the following non-functional properties for usability:

a. Screen Organization
  • The sequence of the screen items should not be confusing.
  • The system shall not contain characters in the screen that are hard to read.
  • The system shall provide support for highlighting that simplifies text.
  • Organization of information should not be confusing.
b. Terminology and System Information
  • Use of terms throughout the system should be consistent.
  • Terminology used in the system should always relate

to task.
  • Prompts for input should be clear.
  • The system shall be able to inform about its progress.
  • The system shall provide error messages that are helpful.
  • Position of messages on screen shall be consistent.
c. Learning
  • Learning to operate the system shall be easy.
  • The system shall provide support for remembering names and use of commands.
  • Performing tasks shall always be straightforward.
  • Supplemental reference materials shall be clear.
  • Help messages on the screen shall be helpful.
  • Exploring new features by trial and error shall be user friendly.
d. System Capabilities
  • System speed shall be fast
  • The system shall be reliable enough to provide interaction between modules.
  • The system shall be stable.
  • The system shall provide support for easy correction of mistakes.
e. Adaptability
  • The system shall provide alternate strategies for dealing with design intent.
  • The system shall showcase all familiar notations.
  • The system shall be able to maintain effective design artefacts.
f. Accessibility
  • The system shall support all input requesting for resource at a time.
  • The system shall support coordination, and information access.
  • The system shall support management of all design intent at a time.
  • The system shall support management of designs at all times.
g. Real time
  • The control of artefact orientation shall be updated.
  • The system shall be able to retrieve any stored information promptly.

4.3. Representing Domain Knowledge

The models presented in this paper focus particularly on oil and gas pipeline designs. Based on domain-specific modeling; the PDMS includes all the functionalities of general domain-specific modeling languages, to this end, the models must represent things in the pipeline engineering domain so that the determining factors in the pipeline design management system can be accommodating in order to come up with an optimal solution [11]. Critical in the determining factors are the stakeholders; stakeholders are the domain experts and related users of the system whose design intent is characterised as the viewpoints of the input parameters [1]. There are competing design requirements among stakeholders; each one has their own set of constraints, objectives and responsibilities. Whereas stakeholders' objectives describe the bit of problem(s) addressed by the typical modelling tool, the responsibilities describe associated design intents [4]. The stakeholders who are the actors are defined along their lines of interest on design bases such as the physical attributes, loading and service conditions, and environmental and materials-related factors [6]. Physical attributes are those parameters that govern the size, layout, and dimensional limits or proportions of the pipeline.

1. Stakeholders in the aspects of Loading and Service Conditions- Stakeholders in this category are typically interested in working on pipeline designs with parameters such as forces, pressure changes, temperature changes, thermal gradients, or any other parameters that affect the state of stress of the piping system [3]. Their main objectives are:

1 to ensure that loading conditions are both internally and externally clearly specified,
2 to clearly describe service conditions as combinations of loads,
3 to state accurate estimation of dimensions of resources needed,

To achieve these objectives, their responsibilities are:

1 to determine what, and how many parameters to be encoded,
2 to propose a strategy for handling the pipeline design process,
3 to specify appropriate pipeline design codes and standards,
4 to provide the designer with guidance in setting appropriate design stress limits.
5 to state clear, executable instructions to appropriate staff.

2. Environmental Factors- Stakeholders concerned with environmental factors in a pipeline are interested in pipeline design products with features which can ultimately lead to a breach of the pressure boundary or a gross structural failure [3]. Their main objectives are:

1 to determine appropriate pipe bed during design,
2 to define adequacy of performance of the pipeline system,
3 to list sufficient environmental hazards.

To achieve these objectives, their responsibilities are:

1 to give concise localized information on the environment,
2 to assist in materials selection,
3 to ensure maintenance of the pressure integrity of a piping system, within predefined criteria limits.

3. Use of Codes and Standards in Pipeline Design- Stakeholders in this category are most widely interested in making sure that a pipeline design adheres to required standards. Their main objectives are:

1 to verify that piping codes provide specific design criteria such as permissible materials of construction, allowable working stresses, and load sets that must be considered in design,
2 to certify that piping codes that relates to pipeline design such as American Society of Mechanical Engineers [4 (ASME B31.1, ASME B31.3)] are followed.

To achieve these objectives, their responsibilities are:

1 to give accurate and detailed records on standards and codes,
2 to source for recent sources of publications on piping standards and codes,
3 to give designers clear view on the difference between standards and codes.

4. Piping Joints- Stakeholders in this category are interested in major impact on the initial installed cost, the long-range operating and maintenance cost, and the overall performance of the piping system. Their main objectives are:

1 to state the physical design attributes of the joints,
2 to specify the relationship criteria between joints,
3 to identify the components in a joint,
4 to define the type of units (e.g. metric).

To achieve these objectives, their responsibilities are:

1 to determine the joint location,
2 to verify the pipe section,
3 to determine the type of fittings,
4 to put in place factors necessary for joint selection and design.

5. Relative Anchor Movements- Stakeholders in this category usually valued the inclusion of support for a pipeline system to function properly.

Their main objectives are:

1 to state the physical design attributes of the supports,
2 to specify the relationship criteria between joints and supports,
3 to identify the components in a support,
4 to define the type of units for pipe size (e.g. metric).
5 to define the type of units for fluid flow design and pressure-integrity design (e.g. metric).

To achieve these objectives, their responsibilities are:

1 to determine the support positions,
2 to verify the pipe size and support sections for fittings,
3 to determine the type of supports,
4 to put in place factors necessary for support selection and design.

5. Model Selection for Pipeline Physical Models

The DSM approach requires models representing things about a domain. Our domain here is the pipeline engineering that concerns with transmission of fluids. To this end, we are adopting CAD models to represent pipeline physical components in the domain. The pipeline physical components are referred to as the design models for the pipeline design management system and are given in this section [1]. Such components include pipes, flanges, fittings/joints, bolting, gaskets, valves, and the pressure components. Also included are pipe support components. The pipeline domain concepts are clearly structured from the attributes of these components, which invariably forms the library framework and vocabulary that maps the concepts to appropriate abstraction levels within the modeling system metamodel. In this context, the vocabulary necessary for the subsequent system specification can be captured from the components as a suit of AutoCAD objects [12]. The design models, therefore, are AutoCAD objects that depict the typical pipeline fundamentals and materials, which form the instance of the pipeline design management system. A cross section of some of the design models are shown in table 1.

Table 1. Typical Pipeline Design Models.

Component	Design Model
Pipe Cross Section	
Bolt and Nut	
Flanges	
Tank	
Supports	
Valve	
Reducer Fitting	
Elbow Fitting	
Tee Fitting	
Grooved Joint	
Butt Joint	
Meters/Gauges	

5.1. Feature Extractions

Any domain specific modeling system has a common set of responsibilities and functionalities, and can be applicable to a broad range of domains [2]. However in the pipeline engineering domain the common set of responsibilities and functionalities are based primarily on the physical components that form the building blocks of a pipeline. It is, therefore, natural [8] to build a framework or software product line of pipeline design management systems, which

can be specialized to create systems for a particular kind of design viewpoint and a particular context. A feature diagram (feature model) listing many possible features of a pipeline design management system is given in figure 1 [3]. The features represent the characteristically distinctive aspect of the different pipeline physical components for definition, organization and display of design data. The feature model is a tree structure, with features forming nodes of the tree. The root node represents the complete pipeline build concept. The features are hierarchically arranged with relationships between a parent feature and its child features categorized into AND, mandatory and optional nodes with the arcs and groupings of features representing feature variability and commonalities [2]. The variability indicates precisely what evidence is needed to specify an instance of a feature that could fit into a particular pipeline design event [5]. The commonalities in this respect define the set of common operations and primitives of the system.

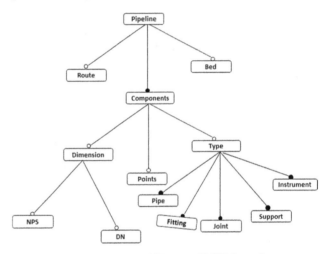

Figure 1. Feature Model Parent - Child Relationship.

Selection of some features requires the selection of other features. Examples of such dependencies are characterised in a feature relationship grammar as follows:

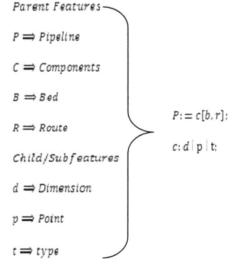

Figure 2. Parent - Child Relationship Grammar.

The feature diagram defines the pipeline design standard reference attributes and relationships of the product family. The product family defines the pipeline components p, f, j, i, s, and an associated tree grammar as shown in figure 2 above. From the grammar b is an optional feature; so optional child features of b, may or may not be included in the configuration of the design system. The other parent feature such as component is a compound mandatory feature that consists of optional features d, p and t, which means that D, P, and T must be selected optionally to be included in the configuration if and only if p, f, j, i, and s is included in the configuration [8].

5.2. The Metamodel Aspect

The domain model offers insight into the problem domain, in our case, the pipeline design management system [7]. Taking the form of expressions as refinements; sub setting the semantic space of the C# base language, the internal part of it is built on the DSL processor engine that compiles the DSL Builder files at the core of Microsoft DSL tool [13]. The domain model illustrated in figure 3 provides a description of the concepts of the problem domain relevant to the PDMS.

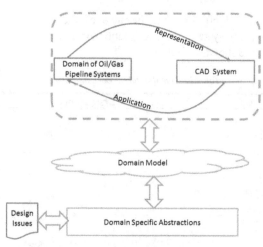

Figure 3. *The Domain Model.*

Although any domain concept could be added to the domain model, we decided to include here only concepts that must define information that must be recorded for the purpose of fulfilling the system's responsibilities over time. In other words, the domain model presented here only contains concepts that are used to describe the necessary information to fulfil system goals [6]. Figure 4 is the metamodel aspect representing the concepts as classes, attributes, generalization/specialization hierarchies and associations inherent in the domain of the PDMS [13].

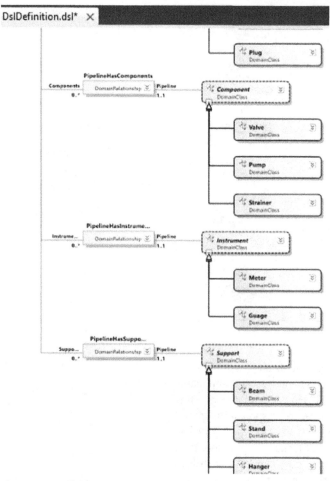

Figure 4. *Metamodel.*

6. Informal Physical Designs

Physical components in a pipeline project includes pipe, flanges, fittings and joints, bolting, gaskets, valves, and the pressure containing portions of other piping components [8]. It also includes pipe hangers and supports and other items necessary to prevent over pressurization and overstressing of the pressure-containing components [12]. It is evident that pipe is one element or a part of piping. Therefore, pipe sections when joined with fittings, valves, and other mechanical equipment and properly supported by hangers and supports results into a pipeline system as shown in figure 5.

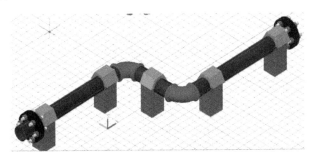

Figure 5. A Typical Pipeline System.

7. Conclusion

The domain specific modeling (DSM) approaches and techniques are meant to be used during different phases of software development. As a result, the DSM approaches work with different kinds of models and modeling notations. To make sure that the DSM approaches and techniques are applicable to a case study, we present a collection of models that describe the management of the design of a typical oil and gas pipeline system at different levels of abstraction. The models include a feature model representing the software product line, an informal physical pipeline model, and a domain model. The domain model, which offers insight into the problem domain, takes the form of expressions as refinements describing the concepts of the problem domain relevant to the pipeline design management system.

References

[1] Autodesk Inc. (2013) AutoCAD Release 2013 Programmers Reference Manual.

[2] Feature-Oriented Domain Analysis (FODA http://www.sei.cmu.edu/reports/90tr021.pdf.

[3] Kienzle J"org, Nicolas Guelfi, and Sadaf Mustafiz Crisis Management Systems: A Case Study for Aspect-Oriented Modeling Transactions on AOSD VII, LNCS 6210, pp. 1–22, 2010. Springer-Verlag Berlin Heidelberg.

[4] Nayyar, Mohinder L. Piping handbook / [edited by] Mohinder L. Nayyar.—7th ed. p. cm. ISBN 0-07-047106-1 McGraw-Hill 2000.

[5] Zekai Demirezen, Marjan Mernik, Verification of DSMLs Using Graph Transformation: A Case Study with Alloy, MoDeVVa'09, Denver, CO, United States, 2009 ACM 978-1-60558-876-6/09/10.

[6] Assessing Composition in Modeling Approaches Gunter Mussbacher1, Omar Alam2, CMA`12, September 30 2012, Innsbruck, Austria Copyright © 2012 ACM 978-1-4503-1843-3/12/09 ...$15.00.

[7] D. Méndez Fernández, D. C. Petriu, N. Rouquette, Ø. Haugen (Eds.): A Meta Model for Artefact-Orientation: Fundamentals and Lessons Learned in Requirements Engineering; MODELS 2010, Part II, LNCS 6395, pp. 183–197, 2010 Springer-Verlag Berlin Heidelberg 2010.

[8] Markus Voelter, Eelco Visser: Product Line Engineering using Domain-Specific Languages Independent, acm.org 2011 15th International Software Product Line Conference 978-0-7695-4487-8/11 2011 IEEE DOI 10.1109/SPLC.2011.25.

[9] Bashar Nuseibeh, Steve Easterbrook: Requirements Engineering: A Roadmap... Department of Computer Science, Imperial College.

[10] Engineering & Piping Design Guide Manual No. E5000, October 1, 2007 National Oil well Varco Company, San Antonio, Texas, http://www.starfiberglass.com.

[11] B. G. Technical LTD - B. G. Technical Oil & Gas industry Port Harcourt, Nigeria. www.bgtechnical.com/Annual Reports 2009 to 2012.

[12] Alessandro NADDEO, Cad Active Models: An Innovative Method in Assembly Environment, Journal of Industrial Design and Engineering Graphics Volume 5 Issue No. 1 – 2010.

[13] Steve Cook, Gareth Jones, and Stuart Kent, (2007) Domain-Specific Development with Visual Studio DSL Tools, Pearson Education, Inc, USA.

[14] Afredo Capozucca, Betty H. C, Cheng, Geri Georg (2013) Requirements definition document for a software product line of car crash management system.

Permissions

All chapters in this book were first published in AJSEA, by Science Publishing Group; hereby published with permission under the Creative Commons Attribution License or equivalent. Every chapter published in this book has been scrutinized by our experts. Their significance has been extensively debated. The topics covered herein carry significant findings which will fuel the growth of the discipline. They may even be implemented as practical applications or may be referred to as a beginning point for another development.

The contributors of this book come from diverse backgrounds, making this book a truly international effort. This book will bring forth new frontiers with its revolutionizing research information and detailed analysis of the nascent developments around the world.

We would like to thank all the contributing authors for lending their expertise to make the book truly unique. They have played a crucial role in the development of this book. Without their invaluable contributions this book wouldn't have been possible. They have made vital efforts to compile up to date information on the varied aspects of this subject to make this book a valuable addition to the collection of many professionals and students.

This book was conceptualized with the vision of imparting up-to-date information and advanced data in this field. To ensure the same, a matchless editorial board was set up. Every individual on the board went through rigorous rounds of assessment to prove their worth. After which they invested a large part of their time researching and compiling the most relevant data for our readers.

The editorial board has been involved in producing this book since its inception. They have spent rigorous hours researching and exploring the diverse topics which have resulted in the successful publishing of this book. They have passed on their knowledge of decades through this book. To expedite this challenging task, the publisher supported the team at every step. A small team of assistant editors was also appointed to further simplify the editing procedure and attain best results for the readers.

Apart from the editorial board, the designing team has also invested a significant amount of their time in understanding the subject and creating the most relevant covers. They scrutinized every image to scout for the most suitable representation of the subject and create an appropriate cover for the book.

The publishing team has been an ardent support to the editorial, designing and production team. Their endless efforts to recruit the best for this project, has resulted in the accomplishment of this book. They are a veteran in the field of academics and their pool of knowledge is as vast as their experience in printing. Their expertise and guidance has proved useful at every step. Their uncompromising quality standards have made this book an exceptional effort. Their encouragement from time to time has been an inspiration for everyone.

The publisher and the editorial board hope that this book will prove to be a valuable piece of knowledge for researchers, students, practitioners and scholars across the globe.

List of Contributors

Adegboye Adegboyega
Dept. of Maths & Statistics, Computer & Information System, Achievers University, Owo Nigeria

Akpan Julius Aniefiok
Federal Ministry of works, Abuja, Nigeria

Zhengxi Wei, Pan Zhao and Liren Zhang
School of Computer Science, Sichuan University of Science & Engineering, Zigong Sichuan 643000, PR China

Yang Hongli
Science College, Shandong University of Science and Technology, Qingdao, Shandong, P. R. China

Hu Yunhong
Applied Mathematics Department, Yuncheng University, Yuncheng, P. R. China

Ting Xiang, Dazhi Pan and Haijie Pei
College of Mathematic and Information, China West Normal University, Nanchong, China

Ahadiyan J.
Hydraulic Structure Water Science Engineering Faculty of Shahid Chamran University (SCU), Ahwaz, Iran

Haji Ali Gol S.
Hydraulic Structure in Sharab Consulting Engineers, Ahwaz, Iran

Xiao Yu Chen, Bo Liu, Zhe Feng Zhang and Xin Xia
Department of Information Centre, East Hospital, Tongji University, School of Medicine, Shanghai, China

Sunday Anuoluwa Idowu, Olawale Jacob Omotosho and Stephen Olusola Maitanmi
Department of Computer Science, Babcock University, Ilisan Remo, Ogun State Nigeria

Olusegun Ayodeji Ojesanmi
Department of Computer Science, Federal University of Agriculture, Abeokuta, Ogun State, Nigeria

Asade Mojeed Adeniyi and Akinola Solomon Olalekan
Department of Computer Science, University of Ibadan, Ibadan, Nigeria

Qamil Kllogjeri
University of Gjovik, MSc Student of Information Security, Gjovik, Norway

Pellumb Kllogjeri
University of Gjovik, MSc Student of Information Security, Gjovik, Norway
University "Aleksander Xhuvani ", Department of Mathematics and Informatics, Elbasan, Albania

Herbert Peter Wanga and Khamisi Kalegele
School of Computational and Communication Sciences and Engineering (CoCSE), Nelson Mandela African Institution of Science and Technology (NM-AIST), Arusha, Tanzania

Nasir Ghani
College of Engineering, Department of Electrical Engineering, University of South Florida, Florida, USA

Dalila Souilem Boumiza and Amani Ben Azzouz
Applied Computer Science Department, National Engineering School of Sousse, Sousse, Tunisia

Salma Boumiza
Computer Science Department, Technical University of Sofia, Sofia, Bulgaria

Bolanle F. Oladejo and Dimple T. Ogunbiyi
Department of Computer Science, University of Ibadan, Ibadan, Nigeria

Jie Zhu, Yiming Wei and Binbin Fu
School of Information, Beijing Wuzi University, Beijing, China

Yusmadi Yah Jusoh and Noraini Che Pa
Dept. of Software Engineering and Information Systems, Faculty of Computer Science and Information Technology, Universiti Putra Malaysia (UPM), Serdang, Selangor, Malaysia

Khadijah Chamili
Centre of Information Technology, USIM, Nilai, Negeri Sembilan, Malaysia

Jamaiah H. Yahaya
School of Computer Science, Faculty of Information Science and Technology, National University of Malaysia (UKM), Bangi, Selangor, Malaysia

Herbert Peter Wanga and Khamisi Kalegele
School of Computational and Communication Sciences and Engineering (CoCSE), Nelson Mandela African Institution of Science and Technology (NM-AIST), Arusha, Tanzania

Wasif Abdel Aziz Saluos
Faculty of Engineering Technology, Zarqa University, zarqa Jordan

Mohammad Abdelkarim Alia
This research is Supported by Zarqa University, zarqa-Jordan

Wisdom Kwami Takramah
Department of Epidemiology and Biostatistics, School of Public Health, University of Health and Allied Sciences, Ho, Ghana

Wisdom Kwasi Atiwoto
Department of Biostatistics, School of Public Health, University of Ghana, Accra, Ghana

Pawan Singh and Mulualem Wordofa Regassa
School of Informatics, IOT, Hawassa University, Awassa, Ethiopia

Japheth Bunakiye Richard
Department. of Mathematics/Computer Science, Faculty of Science, Niger Delta University, Yenagoa, Nigeria

Asagba Oghenekaro Prince
Department of Computer Science, Faculty of Physical Science and Information Technology, University of Port Harcourt, Port Harcourt, Nigeria

Mohamed Elhady Keshk, Mohamed Ibrahim, Noran Tobar, Hend Nabil and Mohamed Elemam
Testing and Devleopment of Satellites Systems Group, Egyptian Space Program, NARSS, Cairo, Egypt

Abdelouahed Kriouile, Najiba Addamssiri and Taoufiq Gadi
LAVETE Laboratory, Hassan 1 University, Settat, Morocco

Chieh Ming Wu
Dept. of Computer Science, Taiwan Water Corporation, Taichung City, Taiwan

Yin Fu Huang
School of Computer Science & Information Engineering, National Yunlin University of Science and Technology, Douliou, Yunlin, Taiwan

John Lee
Dept. of Sales, Formula Chemicals Corporation, New Taipei City, Shulin District, Taiwan

Mostafa Boutahri, Samir Zeriouh, Said El Yamani, Abdenbi Bouzid and Ahmed Roukhe
Optronic and Information Treatment Team, Atomic, Mechanical, Photonic and Energy Laboratory, Faculty of Science, Moulay Ismail University, Zitoune, Meknès, Morocco

Jie Zhu, Ruoling Zhang
School of Information, Beijing Wuzi University, Beijing, China

Nikhat Parveen and Mohammad Rizwan Beg
Department of Computer Application, Integral University, Lucknow, India

M. H. Khan
Department of Computer Engineering, Institute of Engineering and Technology, Lucknow, India

E. J. Garba and G. M. Wajiga
Department of Computer Science, Modibbo Adama (Federal) University of Technology P.M.B. 2076 Yola, Adamawa State, Nigeria

Najiba Addamssiri, Azzeddine Dahbi, Mohammed Mouhir, Abdelouahed Kriouile and Taoufiq Gadi
Lavete Laboratory, Hassan 1 University, Settat, Morocco

Japheth Bunakiye Richard
Department of Mathematics/Computer Science, Faculty of Science, Niger Delta University, Yenagoa, Nigeria

Asagba Oghenekaro Prince
Department of Computer Science, Faculty of Physical Science and Information Technology, University of Port Harcourt, Port Harcourt, Nigeria

Index

Printed in the USA
CPSIA information can be obtained
at www.ICGtesting.com
JSHW052022301024
72690JS00004B/136